THE SOUTH CAROLINA ONE-DAY TRIP BOOK

To my good friends and fellow explorers,
especially gustatorially:
Diane and Don Dezzutti
and Joan and Ralph Klug

THE SOUTH CAROLINA ONE-DAY TRIP BOOK

JANE OCKERSHAUSEN

SHORT
JOURNEYS
TO HISTORY,
CHARM
AND
ADVENTURE
IN THE
PALMETTO
STATE

EPM Publications, Inc.
McLean, Virginia

Library of Congress Cataloging-in-Publication Data

Ockershausen, Jane.
    The South Carolina one-day trip book : short journeys to history, charm,
    and adventure in the Palmetto State / Jane Ockershausen.
        p.   cm.
    Includes index.
    ISBN 1-889324-08-6
    1. South Carolina —Tours.   I. Title.
    F267.3.026   1998
    917.5704 ' 43—dc21   98-5269
                                                           CIP
Copyright © 1998 Jane Ockershausen
All Rights Reserved
EPM Publications, Inc., 1003 Turkey Run Road
    McLean, VA 22101
Printed in the United States of America

Cover and book design by Tom Huestis
Page layout by Scott Edie, E Graphics
Cover Photographs:
    Eastatoee Falls, courtesy of Discover Upcountry Carolina Association
    Rice Mill & Rice Mill Pond, courtesy of Middleton Place
    Beach umbrellas, courtesy of Leslie Advertising
    East Battery homes, courtesy of Charleston Area Convention
        & Visitors Bureau

Contents

THE SOUTH CAROLINA ONE-DAY TRIP BOOK

===

GRAND STRAND/MYRTLE BEACH AREA

HISTORIC CHARLESTON

LOWCOUNTRY & RESORT ISLANDS

SANTEE COOPER COUNTRY

PEE DEE COUNTRY

CAPITAL CITY & LAKE MURRAY COUNTRY

THOROUGHBRED COUNTRY

OLD 96 DISTRICT

OLDE ENGLISH DISTRICT

DISCOVER UPCOUNTRY CAROLINA

Discover South Carolina!

In the early seventies when I began writing the *One-Day Trip Books*, most families only traveled during their annual two-week vacation. In the intervening years changing vacation habits have put a new emphasis on day-tripping. Lifelong residents, newcomers and visitors alike will discover daytrips they never expected to find in or near their own backyards. The selections in *The South Carolina One-Day Trip Book* reveal little-known facts and stories often omitted in guidebooks and overlooked on brief visits.

In more than two decades of traveling to hundreds of historic homes, museums and other sites, I find that at each spot visitors learn or see something new. Day-tripping is an enjoyable way to learn. I encourage you to visit spots you toured years ago; even if the sites remain the same, your experience of them changes because you see them from a different perspective.

Day trips take only a few hours, so you can pursue new challenges, revive old hobbies, or just concentrate on and expand your current interests. Trips highlight history, horticulture, viticulture, agriculture, architecture and a host of other academic disciplines. When you pick a destination, read about the other options in the area. It is often possible to combine several nearby attractions for a diverse day's fun. You can easily plan a weekend or week-long vacation in any of the state's ten regions.

South Carolina boasts an impressive series of firsts, all of which can be appreciated on day trips throughout the state. The first European settlement in North America was in 1526 at Winyah Bay as you will discover when you take a tour of historic Georgetown. The scene of one of the first decisive American victories in the American Revolution was at Fort Moultrie. The first shots of the Civil War were fired at Fort Sumter. One of the country's first semi-submersible torpedo boats was the *Little David*, and you can see a replica and learn the story in the Santee Cooper region. Here too you can see the location of the country's first dug channel canal, the Old Santee Canal. Another transportation first is the Charleston-Hamburg Railway, the country's first commercial railway. Charleston is also the location of America's first and

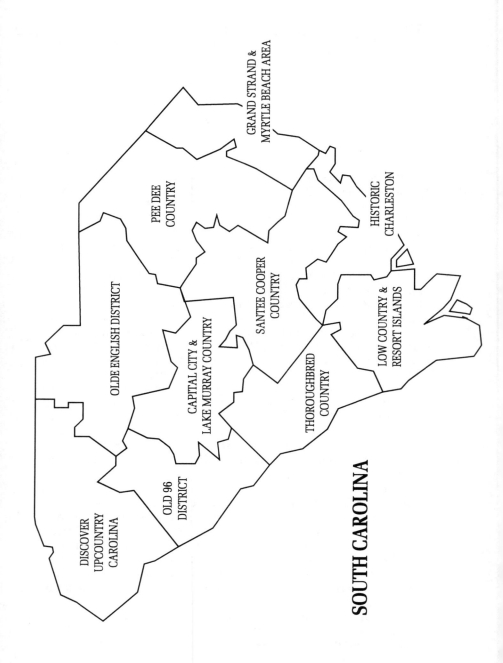

DISCOVER UPCOUNTRY CAROLINA

OLD 96 DISTRICT

OLDE ENGLISH DISTRICT

CAPITAL CITY & LAKE MURRAY COUNTRY

PEE DEE COUNTRY

GRAND STRAND & MYRTLE BEACH AREA

SANTEE COOPER COUNTRY

THOROUGHBRED COUNTRY

HISTORIC CHARLESTON

LOW COUNTRY & RESORT ISLANDS

SOUTH CAROLINA

oldest museum, the Charleston Museum.

During the two years I traveled around South Carolina I found a myriad of fascinating stories at Atalaya, the Burt Stark Mansion, Penn Center, the Provost Dungeon and Old Santee Canal State Historic Site to name just a few. There are splendid scenic areas such as the Jones Gap, Caesars Head and Table Rock in the northwest mountains, and Kiawah, Hilton Head and Hunting islands on the coast. There are gardens of unparalleled beauty such as Middleton Place, Magnolia Plantation, Swan Lake Iris Garden, Edisto Memorial Garden, Cypress Garden and the South Carolina Botanical Garden. The state also offers diverse recreational opportunities at sites such as Adventure Carolina, Edisto River Canoe and Kayak Trail and Bermuda High Soaring School.

Where to go and what to see are important decisions, but you must also decide when to go. The calendar of events in each region alerts you to fairs, festivals, birthday celebrations, blooming cycles, holiday festivities, sports events, concerts, competitions and much more. For some travelers these special activities are the main attraction. Other travelers prefer to visit at less crowded times. Be sure to read the entire selection before you set out; you don't want to arrive to find the site closed. It is always advisable to call ahead to check fees and possible changes in hours.

Short excursions spaced weekly or monthly throughout the year can offer an escape from the winter doldrums, a jump on spring, or a whole series of summer holidays as well as a chance to enjoy an amazing array of autumn delights. One-day trips provide enrichment for the whole family and create shared experiences that children will long remember. As South Carolina's Travel Guide urges, "It's your life. Fill it Up."

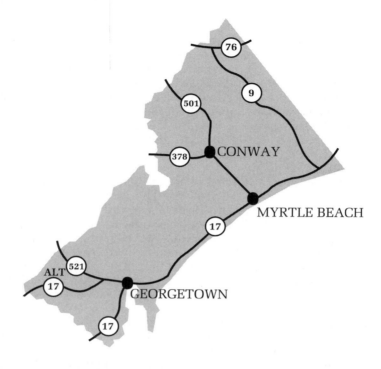

Grand Strand / Myrtle Beach Area

Grand Strand
══ Myrtle Beach Area ══

It all started here—in 1526 Europeans established the first settlement in North America on Winyah Bay near what is now
Georgetown. To put that in perspective, North Carolina's Lost
Colony was established in 1584 and Virginia's Jamestown
Colony in 1607. Nothing remains of that early settlement, but the
legacy of the past is certainly part of the Georgetown Historic
District's charm. You will discover that, before cotton, rice
brought great wealth to this region. The story of rice cultivation
is not as widely known as that of King Cotton. To broaden your
background, stop at the Rice Museum, or visit plantations where
rice was once grown—Hampton Plantation, Mansfield Plantation
and Hopsewee. The latter also has the distinction of being the
home of Thomas Lynch, Jr., one of South Carolina's signers of the
Declaration of Independence.

The sprawling acreage of two other rice plantations are now mag-
nets for visitors. Brookgreen Gardens is located on the site of four
plantations acquired by Anne and Archer Huntington in 1930.
They transformed their property into the country's most outstanding sculpture garden. Their home, Atalaya, part of Huntington
Beach State Park, provides a fascinating look at their lifestyle and
particularly of Anne's, a premier American sculptress.

The park's beach is just one of the public beaches along the 60-
mile Grand Strand that extends from Little River on the Atlantic
Ocean near the North Carolina state line to Georgetown. The
stretch was dubbed the Grand Strand on December 3, 1949 by a
local columnist, Claude Dunnagan, who chose it as the title of
his weekly column about noteworthy local happenings.

Grand Strand is used interchangeably with "the Myrtle Beach
area." The region is also called Nashville, or Branson, By the
Sea. The expansive listing of theatrical choices leaves no doubt
why that nickname is catching on, since complexes like
Broadway at the Beach, Barefoot Landing and Fantasy Harbour
offer a wide range of entertainment. Theme restaurants are
booming in Myrtle Beach. You can drop by the Hard Rock Cafe,

Planet Hollywood, House of Blues, NASCAR Cafe, All Star Cafe and the Easyriders Cafe.

Golf is another enormous draw for the area. There are more than 100 courses and the count keeps climbing. Golf packages keep visitors flocking to Myrtle Beach. It has become one of the most popular golf destinations in the world. With the addition of golf and musical entertainment, what was once a summer beach resort is now a year round getaway.

Barefoot Landing and Fantasy Harbour

Boffo Waterfront Attraction

Barefoot Landing is a festival center offering shopping, entertainment, dining and sightseeing. On one side of the complex is a freshwater lake, a habitat for a wide array of waterfowl and other marshland wildlife; bordering the other side is the Intracoastal Waterway. There is a Cape Cod village look to many of the more than 100 specialty shops, including a number of factory direct stores such as London Fog, Van Heusen, Capezio, Bass Shoes, Geoffrey Beene and others.

Whether its lunch or dinner, there are more than a dozen waterfront dining options. Popular with locals is Dick's Last Resort, where your meal is served with "attitude" (waiters enjoy engaging in a dialogue with the customers) and you have a choice of 74 beers. The Crab House is renowned for their all-you-can eat seafood, salad and raw bar.

Youngsters visiting Barefoot Landing enjoy the carousel with its 41 hand-painted animals. Also popular is the simulator that provides a virtual reality experience. From the intracoastal landing you can climb aboard the *Barefoot Princess II* for a riverboat cruise (see Hershell-Spillman Carousel selection).

The **Alabama Theatre** is the home theatre of this popular singing group who entertain here at selected times. Other headliners play the theatre, which also mounts an Opryland production. From mid-November through December you can enjoy their holiday show, "Christmas in Dixie." The show blends country, gospel, rock, pop, comedy and dance.

For another musical experience stop at the **House of Blues**, a themed restaurant and concert venue. Like the company's establishments in New Orleans, West Hollywood and other domestic locations, this rustic-looking farmhouse and barn, with a Charleston influenced courtyard, incorporates original African-

American folk or "Outsider" art in its decor. Ceiling panels feature original bas-relief portraits of blues greats. The menu features Southern Delta-inspired dishes and Creole/Cajun specialities. There is music at the House of Blues nightly, including concerts in the music hall and performers on the outside deck beside an old-fashioned southern-style barbecue pit. The selections range from blues to gospel, jazz, R&B, hip hop, reggae, zydeco and alternative. A merchandise shop within the House of Blues sells a wide variety of logo items, as well as original folk art, unique guitars, music, books and other blues-related merchandise.

From the House of Blues deck, you may spot some of the residents of **Alligator Adventure**, a 15-acre wetlands experience. In the swamps and marshes you will see approximately 800 alligators and crocodiles. The specimens range from youngsters to formidable old gators. The collection even includes the only known rare albino alligators with pink eyes. The serpentarium houses venomous snakes including enormous pythons, boas and anacondas. There are also colorful parrots and other exotic birds, lizards, Galapagos turtles, dwarf West African crocodiles and Komodo dragons. Alligator Adventure is open daily; the hours vary depending on the season. Be sure to pick up a schedule of the day's live animal shows.

Down Highway 17 Bypass on the other side of Route 501, there is another amazing array of entertainment opportunities at **Fantasy Harbour**. This is strictly a theater complex, although across the street is the sprawling Waccamaw Pottery Outlet Park. One of the theaters houses **Snoopy's Magic on Ice**, a family favorite which features the cartoon character and award-winning skaters from Olympic and World Championship competitions. The **Gatlin Brothers Theater** plays host to this award-winning group each spring and fall. At other times the theater showcases headliner revues, big band shows and other performances. Country is also a big part of the program at the **All American Music Theatre**. For something quite different head for **Medieval Times** and enjoy a meal while you root for your jousting team. The colorful pageantry of the tournament games makes for a unique evening.

There are two additional theater experiences that should not be missed. **The Dixie Stampede**, a Dollywood Production, offers wholesome family fun. Few can resist the spectacle of wagon races, stunt riding and Southern belles. This is a dinner theater that serves a four-course meal while the show unfolds. The theater is located at the north junction of Route 17 and 17 Bypass.

Finally, one of the most enduring and popular theaters in Myrtle Beach is Calvin Gilmore's **Carolina Opry**. This was the beach's first Nashville-style show. Here you'll find the talent to mount a show that ranges from big band and musical comedy to country and bluegrass. The facility even has its own recording studio. You'll find this theater in Surfside Beach.

Directions: From I-95 take Exit 193, Route 501 south. Between Conway and Myrtle Beach on Route 501 you will see Fantasy Harbour on your right, just before Route 17 Bypass. If you turn north on Route 17 Bypass (toward North Myrtle Beach) you'll pass Broadway at the Beach (see selection), Dixie Stampede, Carolina Opry and Barefoot Landing.

Broadway at the Beach

The Nashville/Branson By the Sea

Broadway at the Beach is an attraction, not an oversized shopping center, although shopping at the more than 80 specialty shops is indeed one of its lures. In 1996, the South Carolina Governor's Conference on Travel and Tourism selected this 350-acre entertainment complex as 'South Carolina's Most Outstanding Attraction."

In addition to the shops, it has live theater, nightclubs, restaurants and Ripley's Sea Aquarium (see selection), pedal boats on the 23-acre lake and the Dragon's Lair, a Las Vegas-style miniature golf course that features a live volcano and a fire breathing dragon that pops out on the hour.

The complex's most distinctive attraction is the Carolinas' only **Hard Rock Cafe**, and that chain's only pyramid-shaped cafe. A pyramid shape was chosen to suggest that rock music, like the pyramids in the Nile Valley, is timeless and has the power to transcend not only time but cultures and borders. The exterior of the 70-foot pyramid looks like it has been transported from Egypt, since it has matching 1,800-pound sphinx-like statues at the base of the steps. The point is lit at night and on the hour the pyramid changes colors to the beat of rock music. It was designed exclusively for Hard Rock Cafe and the Myrtle Beach restaurant is the first to have it.

The interior has hieroglyphics that echo sentiments from Beatles songs and Hard Rock philosophy like "Take Time to be Kind," "All Equals One" and the company's logo "Deliver the Word" (Save The Planet). No matter where you are sitting, be sure to wander around inside as there is much to see, including a Egyptian sarcophagus, or time capsule. After a century passes, it's hard to imagine what visitors will conclude about the memorabilia from South Carolina's musical group Hootie and the Blowfish or the brick from Liverpool's Cavern Club where the Beatles first performed. Cases around the restaurant display clothes and musical instruments from a wide array of musical legends including Elvis Presley, Bob Dylan, Jimi Hendrix, Jerry Garcia, Diana Ross, Buddy Holly, James Brown and Marilyn Monroe. Even President Clinton's saxophone occupies a place of honor. Be sure to stop at the merchandise counter even if you do not stay for a meal. Hard Rock guitar pins and logo products are collector items.

The Hard Rock Cafe is at the end of Celebrity Square (but not part of it). This nightclub district has one cover charge that lets visitors into a wide variety of clubs featuring disco, live blues, shag, country western and Top-40. Broadway at the Beach also has 15 well-known restaurants. You can enjoy ribs at Tony Roma's, stop at the country's second Gilley's Texas Cafe, peruse the photo collages while enjoying a meal at Tripps, watch beer being brewed at Liberty Steakhouse and Brewery, sample a wide array of seafood at The Crab House or watch your meal being prepared by hibachi chefs at Yamato Steak House of Japan.

There is a 16-screen movie complex as well as the John Q. Hammons **IMAX Discovery Theater** with a 60- by 80-foot screen—that's five times the size of the average screen. You'll feel like you're in the middle of the action. To really be part of live entertainment, plan an evening at **The Palace** where the shows feature top name entertainers like Kenny Roger, Lou Rawls and Wayne Newton. They also offer a series of popular Broadway musicals.

Two popular theme restaurants are located across the highway from Broadway at the Beach: Planet Hollywood and NASCAR Cafe. The world's most successful concept restaurateur, Robert Earl, joined with Keith Barish, film producer, to open the first Planet Hollywood in New York in 1991. Since then they've opened in major cities across the country and the globe. Actually the globe figures prominently in the design of many of these establishments as you will see when you enter the large planet-shaped entryway that is 60 feet in circumference.

Planet Hollywood has three themed dining rooms: the Adventure room has memorabilia from action/adventure movies, the Sci-Fi rooms feature a collection that reflects that genre and the Sky has a colorful Hollywood diorama where you can identify the stars. Cases in all these rooms have costumes and artifacts from the movies. Sylvester Stallone, one of the major stock holders along with Bruce Willis, Demi Moore, Whoopi Goldberg and Arnold Schwarzenegger, contributed a complete costume and motorcycle from *Judge Dredd*. Other memorable items include: the black leather kid boots Audrey Hepburn wore in *My Fair Lady*, Ginger's full-length beaded dress from *Gilligan's Island*, Val Kilmer's bat suit from *Batman Forever*, Dorothy's dress from *The Wizard of Oz*, Kevin Costner's costume and jet ski from *Waterworld* and a variety of flying craft from *Independence Day*. Video monitors throughout Planet Hollywood show previews and montages featuring some of the greatest scenes from all-time movie classics and popular hits. You can stop by for a meal or a drink in the pool bar on the mezzanine, which has an upside down swimming pool overhead and a "bubble wall" backdrop. Within the restaurant, at 2915 Hollywood Drive, are three merchandise shops with Planet Hollywood clothes and accessories. Planet Hollywood is open daily from 11:00 A.M. until 2:00 A.M.

On the corner of 21st Avenue North and Route 17 Bypass is **NASCAR Cafe**, another theme restaurant with enough energy to power one of the many race cars exhibited in the circular display area that rings the dining area. There are interactive activities for young visitors, a merchandise area and huge video screens that project races and NASCAR personalities.

Directions: To reach Broadway at the Beach from I-95 take Exit 193, Route 501 south. Make a right on Route 17 Bypass and continue to 29th Avenue, North.

Brookgreen Gardens

Country's Finest Public Sculpture Garden

There is a felicitous marriage of art and nature at **Brookgreen Gardens**. Lush foliage and formal plantings provide a backdrop for massive sculptures and delicate works of art. A great many gardens use sculpture as random focal points, but Brookgreen has 580 pieces done by more than 250 sculptors. The garden areas are arranged to showcase the art and there is a pleasing, planned transition from one landscaped area to the next.

It was Anna Hyatt Huntington and her husband, Archer, who created this stunning visual wonderland. After acquiring, in 1930, four colonial rice plantations—Laurel Hill, Springfield, The Oaks and Brookgreen—they began creating the nation's first public sculpture garden—and it's still a work in progress. Anna and Archer built Atalaya (see selection) on the oceanfront of their property and established the garden on approximately 300 of their 9,100-acre holding (the only larger private property holding was the King Ranch). Anna worked on her own sculpture at her studio and placed her work, and that of other renowned artists, on the plantation grounds. The Huntingtons retained the avenue of live oaks, planted around 1750, that led to one of the former plantation houses which burned in 1901, and incorporated the Spanish-moss draped oaks into the garden design. The newly renovated original plantation kitchen remains.

Anna Huntington laid out the garden in the shape of a butterfly with outspread wings. All the paths wind around a central

20

area where the original Brookgreen plantation house once stood. In addition to the colorful azaleas that are at their peak in April, there is also a dogwood garden walkway. Adding to the artistic ambience of the garden are verses carved into plaques on the walls and the base of sculptures. You have to enjoy a garden that not only reaches lyrical heights in works by Walt Whitman, Emily Dickinson, William Cullen Bryant, Rudyard Kipling, Ralph Waldo Emerson and both Huntingtons, but includes such whimsical humor as this:

"I used to love my Garden.
But now my love is dead:
I found a Bachelor's Button
In Black-eyed Susan's Bed."

The sculptors represented here include outstanding artists like Frederic Remington, Daniel Chester French, Carl Milles, Gaston Lachaise and Gutzon Borglum. Anna Hyatt Huntington's *Fighting Stallions*, standing at the garden's entrance, is one of the largest sculptures ever cast in aluminum. And the largest sculpture in the collection, Laura Gardin Fraser's *Pegasus*, was carved on site from a 125-ton granite rock. Some of the delightful works are incorporated into pools like Carl Milles's *Fountain of the Muses* and Anna H. Huntington's *Diana of the Chase*.

The sculpture gardens would in themselves warrant an extended visit but there is far more to see at Brookgreen Gardens. In the Rainey Pavilion that includes the welcome center, terrace cafe and Keepsakes shop, there is the redesigned Jennewein and Noble Galleries. The walls of glass and mirrors create a sense of blending the indoors and the outside. The result is a stunning exhibit area.

Adjoining the garden are Brookgreen's wildlife park with its cypress bird sanctuary and raptor aviary. Walkways take visitors into these protected environments to see a wide array of animals and birds native to the southeast. As you walk the wooded paths you may spot grey and red foxes, deer, otters, alligators and other indigenous species. A winding boardwalk through the cypress aviary takes you to see herons, ibis, egrets and other waterfowl. While in the raptor aviary you can see hawks, owls and other birds of prey.

New ways to explore the native plants and animals are becoming available as Brookgreen develops a project called **The Lowcountry at Brookgreen Gardens**. This will ultimately open up hundreds of additional acres to visitors. Already parts of this new avenue of exploration are available. You can arrange at the Keepsakes shop to take a 50-minute creek excursion that takes you on a tour of the tidal freshwater creeks and abandoned rice fields along the Waccamaw River. A guide aboard the 48-foot

Many gardens have pieces of sculpture as focal points, but Brookgreen Gardens exceeds expectations with more than 550 pieces created by 240 artists. Manicured gardens and a wildlife sanctuary add to the diversity of this appealing natural attraction.

pontoon boat provides background on the lucrative rice culture that supported this area from the mid-18th century until the Civil War (see Rice Museum selection). There is also a program of EcoAdventures that includes guided horseback trail rides, bicycle treks, kayak trips and river excursions into the marshland. All are led by naturalists and historians. A Rice Field Trail links the three environmental exhibits areas. It will eventually be connected with a proposed cultural and natural history facility that is on the drawing boards.

Brookgreen Gardens is open daily from 9:30 A.M. until 4:45 P.M. and special evening hours during the summer months. The evening hours provide an opportunity to enjoy the gardens at sunset or take a sunset pontoon excursion. Twinkling lights add a new dimension to the sculptures and the setting. Admission is charged to Brookgreen Gardens. The garden has special garden tours, history tours and wildlife park programs.

Directions: From I-95 take Exit 193, Route 501 south. Turn right on Route 17 Bypass. Brookgreen Gardens is on Route 17 south between Pawleys Island and Murrells Inlet.

Georgetown Historic District

Winning Winyah Bay

In the early 1520s, just three decades after Columbus discovered America, the Spanish explored the area that is now Parris Island (see selection) and established the Santa Elena settlement, the northernmost known bastion of Spanish Florida. Historians believe that the Spanish may have established an outpost on Winyah Bay even earlier. Winyah was the name of a Native American tribe in the area and means "people of the bend." Little is known about this Spanish enclave, although it is thought that it might have been the first European settlement, excepting Mexico, on the North American mainland.

In the early 1700s, the first permanent English settlers trickled into the area seeking trade with the Native Americans. With the English crown in control of this region, large land grants were made to planters. The Georgetown area proved ideal for the cultivation of indigo and rice. Slave labor was imported to work the immense fields (see Rice Museum selection).

The town of **Georgetown** was established in 1729, making it the third oldest in the state, after Charleston and Beaufort. Three years later, after much acrimonious discussion, it became an official port, making it unnecessary for all shipping to be done through Charleston. Georgetown had a navigable ocean inlet and port so a customs official was appointed by the crown authorities. Before the American Revolution, indigo was the main crop;

after the war production virtually ceased and rice became the significant crop. The local variety "Carolina Gold" was prized around the world and virtually half of all the rice consumed in the United States was grown in the Georgetown area.

The Civil War, the abolition of slavery and a series of violent storms signaled the end of the plantation age. Gradually lumber became the number one export from the Georgetown port; by 1914 the town had the largest lumber producing plant on the east coast. The lumber boom lasted until the Depression. In 1936, a paper mill was built in town and by 1942 the International Paper Company was one of the largest paper mills in the world. Today, in addition to the paper mill, there are other industries and a thriving commercial fishing operation.

The houses in Georgetown's historic district date from colonial days and span a wide range of architectural styles. Within a 16-block radius there are 60 homes on the National Historic Register. A number of churches are also on the register including the Prince George Winyah Episcopal Church, which first held services in 1747. Although suffering damages during the American Revolution and the Civil War, it has still maintained continuous services. This is one of a few original church buildings in South Carolina dating to the colonial era. The adjacent churchyard has burial markers dating to 1767. For more than half a century the church has been holding the Georgetown Plantation Tours in mid-April. This annual event provides an opportunity to tour a number of the gracious private homes in the historic district as well as plantations in the Georgetown area.

One of the enjoyable ways to explore the historic district and learn about the individuals who built and lived in Georgetown's interesting homes is to take an **Ashley Cooper Carriage Tour**. The pace of the horse-drawn wagon is an ideal way to appreciate the charm of this waterfront community. You'll even get down to the water at the Independent Seafood warehouse, where locals and visitors can buy fresh fish daily from incoming boats. You can purchase carriage tour tickets at the carriage in front of the visitors center. The 55-minute tours begin running at 10:00 A.M. Monday through Saturday, year round, weather permitting. If you want a boat tour, stop at the Georgetown Landing Marina. The *Jolly Rover* takes two cruises Monday through Saturday from May through October. You'll pass lovely plantation houses, see abandoned rice fields with the remnants of their trunk docks and spot a variety of plant and wildlife. These narrated tours include pirates' tales and folk lore; call (800) 705-9063 for details. A third option is a tram tour offered by Swamp Fox Tours II, which departs from the visitors center, weather permitting, year round Monday through Saturday from 10:00 A.M. to 4:00 P.M.

Georgetown boasts two noted restaurants, both overlooking the Harborwalk and harbor area. The **Rice Paddy Restaurant** at 819 Front Street is known for its fresh seafood, lamb, veal and Lowcountry specials. It is open for lunch and dinner Monday through Saturday; call (803) 546-2021 for reservations. At 719 Front Street, you can enjoy southern cuisine at **The Pink Magnolia**; call (803) 527-6506 for reservations.

If you call ahead, you can arrange a visit to the **Bellefield Nature Center and Hobcaw Barony**, which is 1.5 miles north of Georgetown. The center has aquariums and terrariums with both common and unusual specimens. You'll also learn about Hobcaw's rich natural history and its well-known research programs. A saltwater touch tank allows close encounters with indigenous wild life. There are exhibits and videos in the nature center. Call (803) 546-4623 to obtain a schedule of the center's special programs and guided tours.

Directions: From I-26 take I-526 around north Charleston and then head north on Route 17 for 60 miles to Georgetown. Once you are in town Route 17 becomes Fraser Street. Turn right on Front Street and the Georgetown Visitors Center will be on your right in the Old Post Office Building, just past the Kaminski House Museum (see selection).

Hampton Plantation State Park

These Walls Do Talk

So often when standing within a historic house, people reflect on the stories the walls could tell. This is particularly true when, as in the case of **Hampton Plantation State Park**, visitors have included George Washington, the Marquis de Lafayette and Francis Marion. Although the walls have no stories to tell about the mansion's illustrious guests, they do tell the story of the house's structural history. This is significant because Hampton Plantation is considered one of the finest examples of Colonial architecture.

No furniture fills the rooms of this once-prosperous rice plantation, owned over the years by some of South Carolina's most prominent families—the Horrys, Pinckneys and Rutledges. The last owner, from 1937 until his death in 1973, was the state's first poet laureate, Archibald Hamilton Rutledge.

It was Rutledge who restored his ancestral home. He wrote in *Home by the River*, "When I first came back, it was sagging in places and it had not been painted in a generation. Now everything has been done to restore it without changing it and it gleams under its four coats of white paint. It is not unusual for visitors to say that in its simple dignity it is the most impressive home they have ever seen. The Adamesque-style portico with its lovely columns, decorated entablature between the columns and raking cornice was the first of its kind in the southeast and perhaps in the entire country. The portico, modeled on the English Hampton House on the River Thames, was added in 1791 in time for a visit by President George Washington. The mansion was built somewhere between 1730 and 1750 and was originally a six-room farmhouse. By 1778, the house had doubled in size with the addition of two wings and an elegant ballroom, transforming the house into a stately mansion. Builder Daniel Horry made his fortune cultivating rice, using one-third of his acreage for rice production.

The decision was made not to furnish the house because over the years the rooms served different purposes and were not clearly designated as to their function. Today you will see cutaway sections of walls and ceilings, exposed timber framing, and finely wrought hinges and hardware. Hanging on the walls are tools used in 18th century construction, such as the board axe, froe, adz, and mallet. Drawings indicate how the house was constructed. The house retains its original fireplaces and mantels. The ornate ceiling molding in the ballroom was carved by slaves. When you go upstairs, you will see the arch that supports the ceiling in the ballroom.

In 1971, when Archibald Rutledge was 90 years old, he sold his home to the state of South Carolina so the public would always have access to this National Historic Landmark. It was Archibald who planted the flowers, camellias and azaleas that brighten the grounds. The 322-acre park along the Santee River also has trails and a boardwalk through the marshy terrain to Wambaw Creek, providing an opportunity to see the wildlife of the Lowcountry. The park has a picnic area and campgrounds.

Hampton Plantation State Park is open Thursday through Monday from 9:00 A.M. to 6:00 P.M. The mansion is open Thursday through Monday from 1:00 to 4:00 P.M. There is an admission charge.

Directions: From I-26 take I-526 around North Charleston and take the Georgetown exit onto Route 17 north. Fifteen miles south of Georgetown, you will see the sign for Hampton Plantation State Park on your left.

Hershell-Spillman Carousel and the Children's Museum of South Carolina

Fun for the Young—and Young at Heart

Children and beaches just seem to go together, and at Myrtle Beach there's plenty to interest children of all ages. The beach, of course, is seen by many children as an endless sandbox. Water for washing off is just steps away. There are also amusement parks, more than 40 innovatively-designed miniature golf courses and a children's museum.

For nearly fifty years, families have been flocking to **The Myrtle Beach Pavilion**. This once rustic gathering spot for vacationers is now the hub of a bustling downtown area. There are more than 30 exciting rides including coasters, a log flume and whitewater rapids. The very young and the very timid enjoy the 1912 **Hershell-Spillman Carousel**. The 48 wooden animals on this classic carousel are all hand-carved; the bi-level arrangement features 27 horses as well as zebras, pigs, ostriches, frogs, roosters, cats and twin golden labradors, among others. Great workmanship is evident on these individualized pieces, some of which are valued at twenty-five thousand dollars. The original Wurlitzer organ provides the distinctive music. Before being moved here in 1950, the carousel was at Anniston Beach, Alabama. Above the park's arcade and restaurant is The Attic, an under-21 nightclub.

A few blocks south of the Pavilion park at 3rd Avenue is **The Family Kingdom Amusement Park**. Here too you'll find an arcade, go-karts, and the state's largest ferris wheel. The Swamp Fox Roller Coaster, with a 62-foot free fall drop, is the largest roller coaster in South Carolina. The park has a wide variety of skilled games including a horse derby race. There is also a special Kiddieland.

Myrtle Waves is a water park where many choose to spend the day. There is a single admission for all the water rides. The park, at 10th Avenue N. and Route 17 Bypass, has shops and food outlets.

The ideal spot to visit on a rainy day, or any day, is **The Children's Museum of South Carolina**. Young children, aged one to 12 (accompanied by an adult), find a wide array of interactive activities that stimulate, educate and entertain. An oversized soft sculpture doll, Stuffie, doesn't wear his heart on his sleeve. But he does open his heart and other internal organs to teach youngsters how their bodies work. There's also a magic school bus, a mock ER, an aquarium, a painting gallery, computers and a series of wetlands murals that provides the backdrop for some beachcombing. There is a nominal admission to this museum that is open Tuesday through Saturday from 10:00 A.M.

to 4:00 P.M. During the summer months there are programs designed for various age groups. The museum is across Oak Street from the Myrtle Beach Convention Center next to Myrtle Square Mall in the Office Depot Building. It is in the southwest corner of the Myrtle Beach Square Mall (just 16 blocks from the Pavilion on Highway 17 Business).

Of course, the beach is the area's main draw. A 60-mile-long stretch of beach communities that runs from Little River to Georgetown is called the Grand Strand. There is public access to the beach all along this corridor as well as in two outstanding state parks: Huntington Beach (see selection) and **Myrtle Beach State Park**. It opened on July 1, 1936, the state's first park. (Cheraw State Park was the first to have land set aside as a park, but Myrtle Beach opened first.) Myrtle Beach State Park also had the first fishing pier and campground along the Grand Strand. There are now 350 camping sites, some available by reservation and others on a first come/first serve basis. The park also has five cabins and two apartments as well as picnic areas. Park hours are 6:00 A.M. to 10:00 P.M.

Visitors of all ages enjoy the chance to get out on the water. **Great American Riverboat Company** offers riverboat cruises with sightseeing, dining and dancing. The *Barefoot Princess II* sails from Barefoot Landing (see selection) while the *Barefoot Princess I* departs from **Waccatee Zoological Farm**, a family-run animal park begun as a private collection of over 100 exotic and domestic animals. It is open daily from 10:00 A.M. to 5:00 P.M. Admission is charged.

Directions: From I-95 take Exit 193, Route 501 south through Dillon and Latta to Myrtle Beach. Make a left on Route 17 Business and head to the downtown area. Visitors may obtain maps and brochures at four sites: the North Myrtle Beach Office at 213 Highway 17 North, the South Strand Office at 3401 South Highway 17 Business, the Official Grand Strand Welcome Center at 2090 Highway 501 E. (at Horry-Georgetown Technical College) and the Myrtle Beach Office at 1200 North Oak Street.

Hopsewee Plantation

Home of a Signer of the Declaration of Independence

Thomas Lynch, Sr. and Thomas Jr. were the only father and son to serve in the Continental Congress. Both were to have signed the Declaration of Independence, but Thomas Sr. suffered a stroke and the space where his name was to have been remains empty. His son did sign this unique document.

Thomas Lynch, Sr. was a wealthy rice planter. His home, **Hopsewee Plantation**, was built almost 40 years before the

28

American Revolution on the North Santee River just outside Georgetown (see Historic Georgetown District selection). By 1733, Lynch had over 13,000 acres and 350 slaves. His namesake was born at Hopsewee on August 5, 1749. Young Thomas attended Georgetown's Indigo Society School, but in 1764 he went abroad to study at Eton and Cambridge. He read law in London, but decided against practicing it when he returned to South Carolina. He married and settled at Peach Tree Plantation, on the South Santee River, four miles south of Hopsewee.

Lynch Sr. served in the Continental Congress from 1774 to 1776. His son became a captain in the First South Carolina Regiment of Continentals, but Lynch Jr.'s military service ended when he fell victim to bilious fever on a recruiting trip into North Carolina. The sickly 27-year-old Thomas Jr. was elected to the Continental Congress after his father suffered a stroke. Lynch Jr. was the second youngest man to sign the Declaration (the youngest was fellow South Carolinian Edward Rutledge).

While returning from Philadelphia, Thomas Lynch Sr. suffered another stroke and died. Lynch Jr. died only three years later when the ship on which he and his wife were sailing to Europe, in hopes he would regain his health, was lost at sea.

Hopsewee Plantation is little changed since the Lynches era because it has been owned by only four families and has been preserved over the years. It is a typical 18th-century Georgian-style Lowcountry house with two rooms on each side of a wide center hall on the first and second floor and a wide porch across the front on both floors. It has a full brick cellar as well as attic rooms. The brick foundation and black cypress wood have endured through the centuries, as have the almost one-and-a-half-inch thick heart pine floors. Each room still has the original hand-carved molding. The name, Hopsewee, is taken from the emperor of the Cherokee Nation and the local Sewee tribe.

Tours of this National Historic Landmark are given by owner/residents James and Helen Maynard. They point out lovely antiques that fill the rooms. The furniture is an eclectic mix of periods that span over a century of stylistic change. The present kitchen was the original serving room, while all the cooking was done in the two cypress outbuildings that still stand. You can wander into these kitchen outbuildings which now contain a few items recovered from archaeological digs on the grounds as well as a collection of old tools.

The house and grounds are open March through October, Tuesday through Friday, from 10:00 A.M. to 4:00 P.M. Tours are given on the hour and half-hour; there is a charge. At other times Hopsewee is open by chance or by appointment; call (803) 564-7891. Throughout the year, the grounds are open daily.

Directions: From I-26 take I-526 around North Charleston and

Huntington Beach State Park is just one of the many popular spots for fishermen along the Grand Strand. At this park fishermen try their luck along the jetty and at the park's beach. The park office even loans fishing gear to visitors.

head north on Route 17 for 48 miles. Hopsewee Plantation is on the left 12 miles south of Georgetown.

Huntington Beach State Park and Atalaya

Hidden Paradise

You could easily spend an entire day or weekend at **Huntington Beach State Park**. It has a wide array of appealing features from its three-mile Atlantic coast beach, to the marshland boardwalk and the uniquely appealing home of renowned American sculptor Anna Hyatt Huntington.

In January 1930, Archer Huntington, son of transportation magnate Collis P. Huntington, and Anna, his wife, purchased Brookgreen (see Brookgreen Gardens selection) and three adjoining plantations for their winter getaway. They wanted a seasonal retreat, and Anna needed a mild winter climate as she had tuberculosis. They also sought a place to display Anna's sculpture. Archer, an authority on Spanish history, based his designs for his beach home, **Atalaya**, on the Moorish architecture of the Spanish Mediterranean coast.

There were no written plans for the house that evolved from 1931 to 1933. Local workers built the square fortress-like one-story building. On the inside it has an open courtyard. Since Mrs. Huntington did not like frame houses, this house was brick covered by mortar. The house has 30 rooms around three sides. Across the front portion that faced the ocean was a sunroom, library, dining room and bedrooms. The southern wing had Archer's study, his secretary's office and Anna's studio with a 25-foot skylight. The studio opened onto an enclosed courtyard where she worked on her massive sculptures. She liked to work with live subjects and so the estate included horse stables, a dog kennel and even a bear pen. Both Huntingtons liked to ride, although Mr. Huntington was so large—he was six feet six inches and weighed 350 pounds—that one of their riding horses collapsed under him.

With a house this unusual, even the operating details are fascinating. To protect from the hurricane force winds, the windows had hand-wrought iron grillwork (which also protected against possible kidnaping) and shutters. To improve access there were no stairs, only ramps leading from the courtyards to entry doors. The house was heated by coal room heaters and wood fireplaces. Small carts were used to haul the wood. An artesian well supplied water to a concrete cistern; it was then pumped into a 3,000-gallon water tank made of cypress. The tank was within a 40-foot-square tower (the name Atalaya is Spanish for "watch tower") placed prominently within the inner court. The tower's height gave the water enough pressure to permit it to flow through the house. Be sure to note Mr. Huntington's shower—it had seven shower heads providing somewhat the same effect as a car wash. To soften the austerity of the inner walls creeping vines were planted; the courtyard has numerous Sabal palmettoes, the state tree, and Phoenix palm.

The Huntingtons last stayed at Atalaya the winter of 1946-47 (during World War II it had been used as a military facility). After Archer's death in 1955, the furnishings were sent to their New York home and Anna's studio equipment was moved across the street to her new studio at Brookgreen Gardens. In 1960, the Huntington's 2,500-acre tract, including Atalaya, was leased to the state. Anna Hyatt Huntington died in 1973.

Sixty percent of the park is wetlands and salt marsh. A handicapped-accessible plank walkway extends into the marsh. This provides an ideal vantage point for crabbing as well as an observation deck for spotting wildlife. This is one of the best birding spots on the East Coast, more than 280 species have been sighted at the park. Whistling swans and bald eagles are frequently spotted. Whenever you drive through the park you will see clumps of people watching the alligators. Another appeal of Huntington Beach, is the beach. Its wide sandy expanse makes this one of the best public beaches along the Grand Strand. There are convenient bathhouse facilities. Fishermen flock to the park to fish in the surf and along the jetty. The catch includes flounder, spottail bass, croakers and whiting. If you forget your tackle, you can stop at the park office and they will loan you a rod and reel.

Another impressive feature of this state park is the Coastal Exploration programs and activities offered by the park each day. There are activities at 10:00 A.M., 2:00 and 4:00 P.M. and, on some days, at 6:00 P.M. Programs include: coastal birding, coastal fishing, castnetting, beach combing, ghost stories and talks about alligators, sea turtles, snakes, creatures of the sea and secrets of the salt marsh. There are also guided tours of Atalaya.

Huntington Beach State Park is open sunrise to sunset daily. The park has camping and picnicking areas.

Directions: From I-95 take Exit 193, Route 501 southeast to Myrtle Beach. Then head south on Route 17 for 18 miles to Huntington Beach State Park on your left.

Kaminski House Museum

Homey Historic Property

The **Kaminski House** may well be the most impressive in Georgetown; it certainly has the most magnificent view. The estate's gently sloping lawn extends to the banks of the Sampit River. Three of the city's highest elected officials called this property home, while the builder, Paul Trapier, was called the "King of Georgetown."

Paul Trapier opened a small store in Georgetown around 1740. He soon had another store in Charleston, established partnerships with other successful businessmen and started a shipping company. In 1743, he married Magdalene Elizabeth Horry and they had two children: Elizabeth and his namesake, Paul Trapier.

At the beginning of the American Revolution, Paul Trapier, Sr. supported the Patriot cause. He organized residents of Charleston to supply relief to the Port of Boston. He also lent South Carolina money and supplied the military with provisions. But when Charleston fell to the British in 1780, Trapier went over to the British side. No action was taken against him at the end of the war and he was elected to the state legislature.

In May 1769, four days before Paul Trapier married for the second time, he gave his spinster daughter Elizabeth two tracts of land in Georgetown and 32 slaves. It is likely but not certain that the house, later known as the Kaminski House, stood on one of those tracts. Elizabeth's father was concerned for her future since she did not have a husband, but shortly after she became a woman of independent means, she married the sheriff of Georgetown, Edward Martin. When her brother Paul died, Elizabeth raised his three sons and his daughter Magdalene Elizabeth Trapier. It was to the latter that she deeded her Georgetown house.

Magdalene Elizabeth Trapier married John Keith, an influential plantation owner and politician. He was elected the first Intendant of the City of Georgetown in 1806 (a position that was later called mayor). In 1855, the house passed from the Trapier/Keith families and was owned by a series of successful businessmen, including George R. Congdon, the second Intendant of Georgetown to reside there. The third was Harold Kaminski, who bought the house in 1931 and served as the city mayor from 1931 to 1935.

In the late 1700s when the house was built, it followed the popular Charleston single house design, with two rooms off the hallway on the first and second floors and wide porches, or piazzas, around two sides. By 1947, there was an extensive addition that included an indoor kitchen, butler's pantry, library, guest bedrooms, bathrooms and a sun porch. The house has the com-

Mansfield Plantation is one of the few plantations with visible reminders of its pre-Civil War slave population. The six antebellum slave cabins and slave chapel provide an in-depth look at life on a rice plantation in the 1840s.

fortable appearance of a home, even though it is furnished with lovely antiques, many collected by Harold's mother, Rose Kaminski, in the 1880s.

An exceptional piece is the unique 1725 Queen Anne ladies' side chair with carved shoe feet. London's Victoria and Albert Museum is interested in this chair because it is one of only two such booted pieces the museum has documented; the other is a small tea table in a private collection in England. Note the low door leading to the butler's pantry, constructed so only the help would enter. The dining room is considered the most beautiful in the house, and indicates the social standing of the Kaminskis. The Regency banquet table seats 24 and the chairs are in the Duncan Phyfe style. On the table is a Victorian epergne.

It is in the library that you really get a sense of Harold and Julia Kaminski. The more than 1,000 volumes reveal the scope of their interests from Shakespeare to romance novels. Harold was a Naval Reserve Officer and was the District Duty Officer for Pearl Harbor. He was on duty when the Japanese attack occurred. There are numerous books on naval history and five antique sailing ship models. All but one of the paintings in the room are seascapes. This is obviously where the Kaminskis relaxed as there is a small 1950s RCA television and an early FM model radio.

If you want to relax, sit for a time on the front porch in a rocking chair and contemplate a bygone era. House tours are given daily on the hour from 10:00 A.M. to 4:00 P.M. Sunday hours are 1:00 to 4:00 P.M. There is a gift shop in the visitors center where you pay the nominal admission charge.

Directions: From I-26 take I-526 around North Charleston and then head north on Route 17 for 60 miles to Georgetown. Once you are in town Route 17 becomes Fraser Street. Turn right on Front Street and the Kaminski House is on the right at 1003 Front Street.

Mansfield Plantation

History, Horticulture and Hospitality

Authentic antebellum ambience imbues **Mansfield Plantation**, which has been proclaimed, "the most architecturally intact plantation in Georgetown County." The landscape of this 900-acre plantation seems frozen in time. The plantation retains several features lost at other pre-Civil War properties. As you drive down the long, dirt entrance road, which is flanked by live oaks, you will see some of the plantation's 1840s slave cabins and the chapel where the slaves worshiped. At its peak, nearly 100 slaves lived in this community and cultivated rice on 215 acres of the plantation. Dr. Francis Parker kept a journal that provides details on the slaves in the village, when they were born and when they died. His wife, Mary Lance, was part of the family that owned Mansfield.

A unique reminder of the rice plantation's heyday is the **Winnowing House**, which is the only surviving example in the county (see Rice Museum selection). The Mansfield slaves produced 7,000 bushels of rice annually. It was in the winnowing house that the rice chaff was separated from the kernels.

It is very unusual to have this complete a picture of slave life. Six antebellum slave homes have survived. They were two family structures with approximately five members per family. Each was built by slave carpenters with materials produced on the property. The interiors of the cabins were whitewashed to make them brighter. Window openings could be shuttered to keep out the elements, but a low fire had to be kept burning in the fireplace even in hot weather to keep mosquitoes away. Parker's slaves had gardens around their cabins where they grew vegetables and kept livestock to help feed their families.

Having a chapel on the plantation kept the slaves from leaving the property to attend service. Many plantation owners felt that religion was good for morale, as it encouraged the slaves to be concerned about their behavior, so they would deserve a better afterlife. Visitors today are often curious about why the slave cabins lined the main road into the plantation, instead of being in a more unobtrusive location. The location provided a way for the plantation owner to reveal his wealth and the extent of his slave holdings—it was essentially a form of showing off, as slaves were indicators of status.

After the Civil War, Parker reputedly died of a broken heart unable to adjust to the changes. His sons managed Mansfield for a time before selling it in 1912 to Charles W. Tuttle, a New York businessman who used it as a winter home and hunting club. In 1930, the plantation was purchased by Colonel Robert L. Montgomery of Pennsylvania for his seasonal haven. The Montgomerys brought a zestful lifestyle to this antebellum plantation. They added a stable for their horses, a landing strip and hangar for their plane, a dock for their yacht and guest houses for their friends. They converted the plantation school house and kitchen house into guest houses, as well as adding decorative touches and 1930s amenities to the main house.

In 1970, Montgomery's daughter sold the property to Wilbur Smith, the father of current owner Sally Smith Cahalan and her husband, Jim. Sally was executive director of Wheatland, the Lancaster, Pennsylvania home of President James Buchanan. Several years after inheriting Mansfield Plantation, the Cahalans moved to their southern plantation and began operating it as an historic site open to the public for guided tours (by appointment) and as a bed and breakfast country inn.

Mansfield Plantation offers a selection of historic guided tours; some include lunch or a formal tea. Bed and breakfast guests enjoy attractively furnished guest rooms and a full country breakfast. For information call (803) 546-6961 or (800) 355-3223. In season, members of Mansfield's Duck Club can take advantage of the plantation's duck blinds situated around the hundred acres of ponds planted in millet and rice.

Directions: From I-26 take I-526 around North Charleston and head north on Route 17 into Georgetown. When Route 17 intersects with Route 701, take Route 701 north to the intersection of Route 51. Mansfield Plantation's entrance is 400 yards past the intersection of routes 701 and 51 on Route 701. The dirt entrance road is 1½ miles long.

The Rice Museum

Garden of Gold

Cotton may have been king in much of South Carolina, but through the 1800s the area around Georgetown was dominated by rice cultivation. Although rice continued to be grown after the Civil War, like cotton, its golden era was prior to the Civil War. During the 1840s, the plantations around Georgetown produced nearly half of the rice grown in the United States. In 1850, Georgetown exported more rice than any seaport in the world. It is appropriate that **The Rice Museum** is prominently located in the town's Old Market Building, topped with a distinctive clock tower.

A short video is shown in The Rice Museum Extension, formerly Kaminski Hardware, circa 1842. You will learn that two factors contributed to the successful cultivation of rice in this area. First, there are six rivers and during high tide they overflow their banks flooding the low lying fields. Secondly, the plantations were able to utilize the labor of their large slave populations. In 1810, nearly ninety percent of the district's population of a little more than 20,000 were African slaves. It was the rice farming experience of slaves from Senegal and Gambia that provided the expertise needed to produce rice crops. The sweetgrass baskets still sold in the Lowcountry region and the Charleston area were made to separate chaff from small kernels of rice. Like all other agricultural pursuits, the loss of slave labor due to the Civil War severely diminished the area' s productivity. But the most important reason for the demise of the fabulous rice culture was the advent of mechanized farm tools. This new technology became available to farmers in the 1880s. Combines, tractors, seeders and harvesters did not function properly in

Georgetown due to the soft, boggy soil. The machines spawned the prairie rice culture. Texas and Arkansas also began growing rice and by 1900, the western states produced about 90 percent of the nation's crop due to mechanization. The Georgetown area was also ravaged by a series of ten violent storms between 1893 and 1911. After 1911, rice cultivation in the area started to collapse; by the 1930s it had ceased.

The video is free, but there is a nominal charge if you want to climb the old market's stairs and see museum exhibits. As you enter you'll see a large map of the area that pinpoints the location of rice cultivation and the names of property owners in 1825. The area had 150 rice plantations and 46,000 acres planted in rice. Georgetown County was the wealthiest district in the state, and South Carolina the second wealthiest state in America. (The first was Massachusetts.)

The museum has dioramas that show how rice was cultivated through a series of dikes and trunk docks. On exhibit are tools of the trade and photographs of rice winnowing houses (one of the few still standing is at Mansfield Plantation; see selection), loading flats and rice cultivation.

The museum is open 9:30 A.M. to 4:30 P.M. Monday through Saturday. It is closed Sunday and major holidays. There are changing exhibits in Prevost Gallery where the video is shown. Above the gallery, museum staff and volunteers have rebuilt the Brown's Ferry Vessel using the salvaged hull. This vessel's hull was found on the bottom of the Black River at Brown's Ferry in Georgetown County by Hampton Shuping, a dive instructor. Shuping, recognizing the historical significance of his find, waived his claim and the ship was raised on August 28, 1976. It is believed that the flat-bottomed river freighter sank during the 1730s.

Lafayette Park provides a floriferous greenspace around the museum which backs up to the Sampit River. Behind the museum is the quarter-mile-long Harborwalk along the river. Planters filled with flowers and benches make this a charming spot to relax and enjoy river traffic.

Directions: From I-26 take I-526 around North Charleston and head north on Route 17 for 60 miles to Georgetown. Once you are in town Route 17 become Fraser Street. Turn right on Front Street and the museum will be on your right. If you are traveling from the north on I-95 take Route 521 west through Andrews into Georgetown. The Rice Museum is at the intersection of Front and Screven Streets. From Myrtle Beach, take Route 17 south approximately 30 miles to Georgetown. Turn left on Screven Street and follow to Front Street. The two streets meet in front of the museum.

Ripley's Sea Aquarium

That's A-Moray!

Once upon a time only scuba and skin divers could experience the rapture of being surrounded by brilliant tropical fish. Innovative technology has made it possible to bring that experience to a wider audience as you will discover at **Ripley's Sea Aquarium**. A moving pathway, the world's longest moving walkway, through a 310-foot acrylic tunnel takes you into an aquatic world. You are surrounded by colorful, exotic and dangerous sea life in the 600,000-gallon Dangerous Reef. Floating over and around you are a variety of huge sharks, moray eels, venomous lionfish and thousands of beautifully patterned, brightly-hued reef fish.

This is only one of the many state-of-the-art interactive exhibits in the five-story, two-level aquarium. This multi-sensory aquarium is designed as an entertainment facility—that's not to say you won't learn things during your visit. In Ray Bay, you learn what it feels like to touch and interact with graceful winged rays. You won't, however, be able to interact to the same degree as the diver you'll watch in the Rainbow Rock exhibit that features reef fish from the Indian Ocean, Hawaii and Australia. An underwater communication system encourages conversation between visitors and diver.

Even in the rainforest habitat, the Rio Amazon exhibit of freshwater species, you won't get wet. The Living Gallery displays aquatic specimens—living corals, octopus, weedy seadragons, sea horses, pipefish and jelly fish—like art works. Special lighting and classical music in the background heighten the gallery illusion.

In a number of the exhibits, divers feed and swim with the fish every hour. In the Sea-For-Yourself Discovery Center, interactive exhibits provide a fun way to learn about the aquatic world. There is a multi-level restaurant overlooking the Dangerous Reef exhibit. A classroom gives aquarium staff a chance to conduct seminars for school groups and the general public. Supporting the aquarium is Ripley's Sea Aquarium Research & Receiving Facility where the aquatic life acclimatizes to their new environment. This wet lab is not open to the public.

Ripley's Sea Aquarium is open daily during the summer months from 9:00 A.M. to 10:00 P.M. Hours vary at other times during the year. Admission is charged.

Directions: From I-95 take Exit 193, Route 501 south through Dillon and Latta to Myrtle Beach. Make a left on Route 17 Bypass. Ripley's Sea Aquarium is at Broadway At The Beach (see selection) on Route 17 Bypass between 21st Avenue N. and 29th Avenue N.

Grand Strand/Myrtle Beach Area Regional Tourism Contacts (Area Code 803)

MYRTLE BEACH AREA CHAMBER OF COMMERCE & WELCOME CENTER
1200 North Oak Street, P.O. Box 2115
Myrtle Beach, SC 29578-2115
626-7444, fax: 626-0009
www.myrtlebeachlive.com

MYRTLE BEACH HOSPITALITY ASSOCIATION RESERVATION
P.O. Box 1303
Myrtle Beach, SC 29578-1303
626-7477, or outside SC (800) 866-9785, fax: 448-8143

CONWAY AREA CHAMBER OF COMMERCE
P.O. Box 831, 203 Main Street
Conway, SC 29526
248-2273

GEORGETOWN COUNTY CHAMBER OF COMMERCE & WELCOME CENTER
Corner of Front and Broad Streets, P.O. Box 1776
Georgetown, SC 29442
546-8436, (800) 777-7705

LITTLE RIVER CHAMBER OF COMMERCE
P.O. Box 400
Little River, SC 29566
249-6604

LORIS CHAMBER OF COMMERCE
P.O. Box 356
Loris, SC 29569
756-6030

Grand Strand/Myrtle Beach Area Calendar of Events (Area Code 803)

Mid-January
  Myrtle Beach Wildlife Expo. Animal exhibits, interactive displays and educational seminars are part of this event. Myrtle Beach, 237-3899.
Early March
  Canadian-American Days Festival. Yearly celebration of Canadians on spring break with sporting events, concerts and historical tours. Myrtle Beach, 626-7444.
Mid-March
  Andrews Gospel Music and Storytelling Festival. Rural communities celebrate cultural and ethnic understanding. Andrews, 264-3471
Late March
  Waccamaw Arts and Crafts Art Show. Annual guild show with more than 100 artists. Myrtle Beach, 497-3897.
Mid-April
  Georgetown Plantation Tours. For more than half a century, this his-

toric port city has showcased its plantations and town houses during this annual event. Georgetown, 527-2603.

Chicora Indian Day Celebration. Native American celebration of local Chicora legacy with arts and crafts, dancing and food. Georgetown, 264-2331.

Late April

Myrtle Gras. Cajun cuisine and New Orleans blues and jazz highlight this event. Myrtle Beach, 448-8578.

Early May

Frantic Atlantic Spring Classic. Fishermen vie for biggest king mackerel; the festival includes children's tournaments, food and entertainment. North Myrtle Beach, 280-4262.

Mid-May

Good Ole' Days Festival. Chubby Checker returns to play in his home town, plus a car show, fun run, food and more entertainment. Andrews, 221-5100.

Mid-May (and mid-June and mid-July)

Art in the Park. Juried arts and crafts from more than 100 artists in Chapin Park. Myrtle Beach, 249-4937.

Early June

Sun Fun Festival. Beach celebration with fireworks, a beauty contest, sporting events and a two-day art show. Myrtle Beach, 626-7444.

Late June

Harborwalk Festival. Celebration of the heritage of a coastal town. Georgetown, 546-1511.

Early August

Carolina Craftsmen's Summer Classic. Huge arts and crafts show at the Convention Center. Myrtle Beach, 274-5550.

Early September

Bayfest. Display of wooden boats, coastal heritage traditions, food and entertainment. Georgetown, 546-2481.

Late September

Atalaya Arts and Crafts Festival. Juried art show in historic castle-like home of sculptor Anna Hyatt Huntington. Murrells Inlet, 734-0517.

Frantic Atlantic Fall Classic. Fishermen vie for biggest king mackerel; the festival includes children's tournaments, food and entertainment. North Myrtle Beach, 280-462.

Early October

Oktoberfest. Dance to "oom-pah" music, enjoy German food and crafts at this harvest festival. Myrtle Beach, 448-8578.

St. Andrew's Taste of the Beach. The Grand Strand's popular restaurants provide taste treats; musical entertainment is included. Myrtle Beach, 448-5930.

Mid-October

Chicora Indian Tribe Pow Wow. Dancing, music and crafts celebrate the traditions of this indigenous Native tribe. Georgetown, 264-3231.

Late October

Ghost Hunt. Self-guided tour of "Ghost Capital of the World" with carnival rides and contests. Georgetown, 546-8441.

Early November – Mid-February

Treasures by the Sea. Grand Strand is decorated with nautical themed lights. Myrtle Beach, 626-7444.

Mid-November

Dickens Christmas Show & Festival. Victorian-era crafts show. Myrtle Beach, 448-9483.

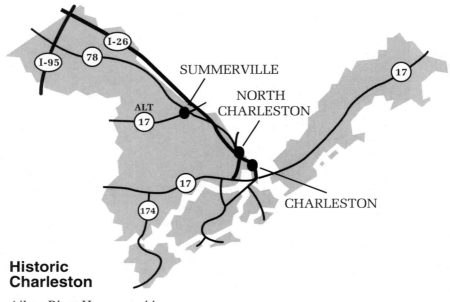

Historic Charleston

═══Historic Charleston ═══

C harlestonians like to quote an aging and wealthy resident who, when asked why she seldom traveled, replied, "My dear, why should I travel when I'm already here?" Even first-time visitors soon understand her complacence since Charleston offers such a felicitous blend of architectural treasures, pivotal historic sites, sumptuous plantation gardens and some of the finest restaurants in the country.

While strolling the tree-lined streets, it may seem as if you've stepped back to the 18th century when Charleston was the seat of British rule and a cultural capital of British America. But the city is a living community, not a restored museum. Church bells peal, the smell of the sea wafts through the air and gayly colored flowers peek out through intricate wrought-iron fences and gates. Charleston is truly a feast for the senses.

The city's history extends back to the 1600s; the walls of British America's only walled city date to between 1680 and 1718 and remnants can still be seen in the Provost Dungeon beneath the Old Exchange Building. The only public building in the Carolinas that dates back to the era of the Lord Proprietors is the Powder Magazine. Fort Moultrie is the third fort to protect Charleston's harbor. The first was built at the onset of the American Revolution and was the scene of an early decisive American victory. The complete history of this beguiling city is revealed at America's oldest museum, the Charleston Museum. You can explore houses of noted Charlestonians, and discover the city on walking tours, carriage rides and boat cruises. A fascinating cruise takes you to Fort Sumter, where the Civil War began. More modern maritime history is presented at Patriots Point, the world's largest naval and maritime museum which includes the aircraft carrier *Yorktown*, a submarine, nuclear merchant ship and a destroyer.

Outside the city, along the Ashley River are splendid plantations with elaborate gardens. Middleton Place, Magnolia Plantation and Gardens and Drayton Hall reveal the stories of their fascinating and historically significant owners within the context of their gracious homes and lavish gardens.

For many, Charleston is the heart of the Lowcountry and the region includes lush island resorts and public beaches. The 10,000-acre Kiawah Island has ten miles of broad beach with abundant wildlife as well as a deluxe resort with award-winning golf courses. The Isle of Palms is also noted for its spectacular waterside golf courses.

Recreational options are matched by cultural choices. The Gibbes Museum of Art showcases regional artists, while the galleries on the narrow streets in the historic district offer a wide array of talents both local and international. In May the world famous Spoleto Festival USA features more than 100 performances of opera, chamber music, symphonic and choral work, jazz, theater, classical ballet, modern dance and a full spectrum of the visual arts. According to The Washington Post it is "the number one festival of the arts." Charleston's very existence is a festival of the arts.

Aiken-Rhett House

Step Into 1858

The **Aiken-Rhett House** is a remarkably intact "urban plantation." This opulent mansion, with support buildings, still has furnishings and decorative items in the exact spot for which they were purchased, much like a time capsule. This allows visitors a glimpse of the pre-Civil War lifestyle of the Aikens, who were among South Carolina's wealthiest citizens.

The African-American National Heritage Museum, a cooperative venture that encompasses a number of Charleston sites, includes the Aiken-Rhett House because the intact two-story slave quarters, the slaves' basement working area and other support buildings provide a unique look at the urban African-American experience in the Antebellum South. This is the only property in Charleston and one of the few in the south where the support buildings have survived unaltered. William Aiken, Jr. was, for a time, the largest slave holder in the state, owning 878 slaves, most of them on his Edisto plantation.

The house, originally a Federal-style mansion, was built in 1818 by John Robinson. William Aiken, Jr. acquired it shortly after his father's death in 1831. The elder Aiken had purchased the house in 1826 (though some reports indicate he was given the house in payment of debts). Aiken and his wife Harriet L. Lowndes soon transformed the house into a Greek Revival style mansion, with heavy molding featuring Greek designs. They also added an east wing with a dining room and ballroom. At this time the imposing cast iron railing was added to the interior entrance steps. The house was remodeled again in 1858 and the Aikens added chandeliers they acquired in Paris as well as new carpets, wall coverings and paintings, sculpture and other bibelots from European travels. A large formal portrait of Mrs. Aiken, which originally hung in the art gallery, now dominates the east drawing room.

During the Civil War, Jefferson Davis, president of the Confederate States, was a guest of Aiken, who had served in South Carolina politics as governor, U.S. congressman and state legislator. Also during the war years, the house served as headquarters for Confederate General P.G.T. Beauregard. The house remained in the family until 1975 when the nearly 100-year-old Francis Hinson Dill Rhett, widow of one of Governor and Mrs. Aiken's five grandchildren, gave the property to the Charleston Museum. The museum opened the house for a time to the public in the 1980s. In 1995, the Historic Charleston Foundation purchased the 23-room mansion and its outbuildings. Two of Governor William Aiken's carriages still stand in the Gothic Revival carriage house, which even has Gothic details in the horses' stalls. The grounds also retain the old animal sheds.

When you tour the estate, the only furnishings you will see are those that are original to the house or belonged to the governor's family. For example, Mrs. Aiken's sleigh bed remains in her bedroom, while Governor Aiken's room has his 1850 Empire style bed. This sparsely appointed look allows you to savor and appreciate each piece in the context of rooms that have remained virtually unchanged for 100 years. The aging wood and fading paint in some areas provides an authentic living classroom for architectural scholars and interested history buffs. The house has been stabilized, not restored in the sense that it has been repainted and refurbished.

Visitors enter through the basement, where old photographs of the house and its residents hang on the wall and antique furniture is exhibited. There is also a museum shop on this level. The self-guided tours are augmented by an audiotape. The Aiken-Rhett House, on the National Register of Historic Places, is open Monday through Saturday from 10:00 A.M. to 5:00 P.M. and Sunday 2:00 to 5:00 P.M. It is closed Thanksgiving, Christmas Eve and Christmas Day. Admission is charged.

Directions: From I-26 take Meeting Street into Charleston and turn left on Mary Street. Make a left on Elizabeth Street. The Aiken-Rhett House is at 48 Elizabeth Street on the corner of Judith Street.

Discover Charleston's African-American heritage at the Avery Research Center, housed in the former Avery Normal Institute. This school was established in 1865 to educate African Americans.

Avery Research Center for African-American History and Culture, The Philip Simmons Garden and Slave Mart Museum

Charleston's Window on the African-American Experience

Forty percent of all Africans that came into the American colonies arrived in the port of Charleston. The city is enriched by its African-American heritage as you will discover when you visit the **Avery Research Center for African-American History and Culture**, which preserves and documents the culture and history of African Americans in Charleston and the South Carolina Lowcountry. Here you will find primary documents and manuscripts that present an accurate account of social, political and economic events. Records document the lives of public figures but equally important are the lives of the "grass-roots" people. The center's archives has books, periodicals, videotapes, microform, photographs and slides.

The research center takes its name and is housed in the former Avery Normal Institute, established in 1865 to educate African Americans. The faculty was from the American Missionary Society until 1916 when the first black faculty began teaching. Until 1920, teachers trained at Avery were not permitted to teach in Charleston, they could only work on the Sea Islands. In 1920, Thomas Ezekiel Miller petitioned the city to allow African-American teachers to teach the city's African-American students. Within the center there is a permanent memorial exhibit that re-creates a social studies classroom. You'll see the teacher's platform and desk, student desks, a woodburning stove, books and other reminders of 19th-century education. Photographs on the wall capture memories of the Avery School, which closed in 1954 when desegregation opened public schools to all of Charleston's children.

Another exhibit concentrates on Sea Island artifacts—handwoven fish and shrimp nets, sweetgrass baskets and other items—that reveal a close cultural link with the Mano River Union Region of West Africa, the countries of Guinea, Liberia and Sierra Leone. This link is reflected to this day in the Gullah dialect and crafts of the Sea Islands. The Krio language of Sierra Leone is very close to Gullah.

The downstairs gallery is used for changing exhibits. Upstairs is the site specific circular cosmogram (essentially an intricate design on the gallery's floor) created as a project of the 1991

Spoleto Festival. The work by Houston Conwill was part of "Places with a Past: New Site Specific Art." The cosmogram invites visitor involvement; you can take off your shoes, listen to the music and move from Sierra Leone to South Carolina.

The Avery Research Center is open NOON to 5:00 P.M. Monday through Saturday. It is closed on Thanksgiving and during the College of Charleston's Christmas break. Admission is by donation.

The Avery Center recognizes African Americans who have made architectural and aesthetical contributions to Charleston. Enslaved blacks and free persons of color worked in over 60 artisan occupations producing a rich body of work that helped make Charleston the beautiful city it is today. This legacy is continuing. One individual who made a significant contribution is master blacksmith Philip Simmons. His decorative wrought iron gates and window grills enhance homes in Charleston and the Lowcountry.

In 1925, at the age of 13, Philip Simmons was apprenticed with a master craftsman, Peter Simmons (no relation), with whom he went into partnership for several years before becoming self-employed. A number of Simmons' decorative gates are exhibited in museums. The South Carolina State Museum has an exhibit on his work (see selection) and one of his gates is at the Smithsonian Institution. Simmons was awarded the highest honor given to folk artists, the American Folklife Award and he is a member of the South Carolina Hall of Fame.

Charleston honors the man and his work at **The Philip Simmons Garden**, 91 Anson Street. This commemorative landscaped garden on the grounds of St. John's Reformed Episcopal Church displays some of Simmons ironworks. Simmons is called "Keeper of the Gate" and this garden tribute features a decorative gate especially made for the site that incorporates a heart and a cross into the design. Simmons makes his own design for each of his gates and doesn't use molds. He also designed a gate for the Charleston Visitors Center. Distinctive gates done by Simmons can be seen at the Christopher Gadsden house on East Bay Street where he entwined a rattlesnake in the design, at the Rhett house on St. Michael's Alley with its artistically profiled egret and at the First Baptist Church. Simmons has created over 200 gates, window grilles, balconies and fences.

Another more bitter part of the African-American story unfolds at the **Slave Mart Museum**, 6 Chalmers Street in the heart of Charleston's historic district. Once Ryan's Mart stood on this site. In 1856, Thomas Ryan acquired a four story building (originally a fire engine house) where African Americans were held after coming into the port of Charleston and before being auctioned off. The last auction was held here in 1863. Exhibits detail the African-American experience in Charleston

48

from their earliest arrival in 1670 through the Civil Rights movement. Many visitors do not realize before their visit to this museum that the first branch of the National Association for the Advancement of Colored People was established in Charleston in 1917 by Edwin Harleston. The Slave Mart Museum is open 10:00 A.M. to 5:00 P.M. Monday through Saturday and 2:00 to 5:00 on Sunday. Admission is charged.

There are a number of guided tours that provide a wealth of information on the African-American experience in Charleston. Sandra Campbell's **TOURrific Tours** offer private, personalized tours of the historic district that detail African-American history. This Charleston native knows a wealth of stories about the people who once lived in the lovely old homes along the cobbled street. It is enlightening to discover the varied contributions of Charleston's many free people of color. You'll learn that for most of the 19th century African inhabitants outnumbered their white counterparts in Charleston. By 1850, approximately 82% of free African-American males were skilled craftsmen. The wealth of details and colorful anecdotes will enliven your tour and improve your understanding of the city. For details on the tours call (803) 853-2500 or 722-7407.

Al Miller's **Sites and Insights Tours** also provide an African-American perspective of Charleston. You'll hear about the slave market, the hanging tree and the Denmark Vessey slave uprising. Call (803) 762-0051 for information and rates. Another option is **Alphonso Brown's Gullah Tours**, which intersperses Gullah dialect and culture into the "Chaa'stun" experience. You'll see Catfish Row where *Porgy and Bess* was set and hiding spots along the Underground Railroad. Alphonso Brown has a 30-page booklet, *A Guide to Gullah Charleston*, that is available throughout Charleston, but for information on his two-hour tours, call (803) 763-7551.

It should also be mentioned that the famed dance named for this city originated with African Americans. Young African-American children in the 1920s, danced the distinctive steps on the streets of Charleston. Locals who migrated north took the steps with them. In 1923, Eubie Blake and Noble Sissle, authors of *Shuffle Along,* the first African-American musical to play on Broadway, wrote a tune that introduced the Charleston to theater audiences in October 1923 at the New Amsterdam Theatre.

Directions: From I-26 take King Street exit to Calhoun Street. Take a right on Calhoun Street and a left on Gadson Street. Then make another left on Bull Steet. The Avery Research Center is at 125 Bull Street in Charleston. For the Philip Simmons Garden, take Ashley Avenue one block past Bull Street to Wentworth Street and turn left. Proceed down Wentworth Street to Anson Street and turn left. The garden is at 91 Anson Street. For the Slave

Mart Museum, take Rutledge Avenue to Broad Street and turn left. Continue on Broad Street, then make a left on Church Street and a right on Chalmers. The museum is at 6 Chalmers Street.

Boone Hall Plantation

America's Most Photographed Plantation

Spanish and French explorers preceded the English in South Carolina. But in the 1670s, the financially strapped King Charles II gave to eight Lords Proprietors land he dubbed Carolina, a tract that stretched from Virginia to Spanish Florida. One of those who sailed in 1671 with the First Fleet of settlers from England was Major John Boone. He was granted 17,000 acres in the Lowcountry. Boone began the development of Boone Hall Plantation around 1681.

Boone Hall Plantation stayed in the family for 125 years. Major Boone's son Thomas planted the first avenue of live oaks in 1743. The plantation's one-quarter mile avenue of enormous Spanish moss-draped live oaks is one of the most impressive plantation entrances in the south. The avenue is included on the National Register of Historic Places.

The slave street dates back to the cotton era. Boone Hall is one of the few plantations in the southeast that still has its original slave street. There are nine original brick cabins, also on the National Register of Historic Places, that date back to 1743. The house servants and skilled craftsmen lived along this street. Today when you visit you will see basket weavers making sweet-grass baskets, like those made decades ago.

The house that stands today was rebuilt in 1935 by owner Thomas Stone. Wherever possible the original materials were used. In 1954, the estate was purchased by the McRae family who opened it to the public two years later. The top two floors are private but visitors can tour the downstairs. The rooms are filled with the McRaes' antique collection. Be sure to notice the free flying, or cantilever, staircase in the entrance hall; the only support is at the top and bottom. You'll also see a grandmother clock, that is smaller than the more traditional grandfather style. The Hepplewhite dining room table, circa 1780s, seats 22 guests. The corner cabinet has English porcelain that was dipped in 24K gold. If, on your first visit the house looks familiar, it may be because you recognize it from the television series, *North and South*. A great deal of the location shooting for the mini-series was done at Boone Hall.

Before leaving, note the circular brick smokehouse that dates back to the 1740s and the original two-story gin house where cotton seeds were removed and the cotton made ready for shipping to England. The grounds also have lush plantings that peak in the spring when the camellias and azaleas bloom. Included in the parterre gardens is a rare collection of antique flowers and, in particular, antique roses. The Noisette roses, which had their beginning in Charleston, are among the spectacular array of the almost-forgotten flowers of the past.

Boone Hall Plantation is open Labor Day through March on Monday through Saturday 9:00 A.M. to 5:00 P.M. and Sunday 1:00 to 4:00 P.M. From April through Labor Day hours are 8:30 A.M. to 6:30 P.M. and Sunday 1:00 to 5:00 P.M. The house is closed on Thanksgiving and Christmas Day. Admission is charged. On the second floor of the cotton gin house you can enjoy breakfast or lunch at the Plantation Kitchen Restaurant. There is also a well-stocked gift shop on the ground floor of the gin house.

Directions: From I-26 at Charleston take Route 17 north for six miles and you will see the entrance to Boone Hall Plantation on the left.

Calhoun Mansion

Private Splendor

Visitors today enjoy the architectural beauty of Calhoun Mansion because of the vision of two men: builder George Walton Williams and restorer Gedney Howe. Williams, touted in the 1860s as "Carolina's wealthiest citizen" built this impressive five-story, 25-room mansion after the Civil War. In fact, he purchased the land at 16 Meeting Street with $40,000 in Confederate money.

Williams's shrewd business sense not only served his own interests, but served the city of Charleston. As a successful merchant, first in Augusta, Georgia, and then in Charleston, Williams was highly respected. His financial acumen secured his appointment as Chairman of the Ways and Means Committee of the Charleston City Council. When the Civil War came, Williams stayed in business until 1863, then became one of the south's most successful blockade runners.

It was Williams who, at the request of the city, invited General A. G. Bennet to bring his Union troops into Charleston to restore order. Williams also persuaded the Confederate commander, who was under orders to burn all supplies, to leave warehouses of food that Williams could distribute to city residents. This food fed Charleston's population of 20,000 for four months.

It is not surprising that when the cornerstone was laid in 1876, Williams was in attendance with his second wife and four children (all from his second marriage; his first seven children and wife died of yellow fever). Also on hand for the occasion were city dignitaries and news reporters. One reporter said of the construction, "It is, perhaps, the most important work of the kind ever undertaken in Charleston and will be a credit to the city founder, and an ornament to the city." It was (and still is) the city's largest private residence and the grounds spread across four city lots. When Williams's daughter Martha married Patrick Calhoun, grandson of South Carolina's revered U.S. Senator and twice Vice-President John C. Calhoun, 25,000 invitations were sent. In describing the event the local paper claimed the house, "looked like a fairy palace in which the Queen of the Fairies was holding revel." After the wedding, the house gradually became known as the Calhoun Mansion.

The house passed out of the family in the 1930s and was on the brink of being condemned in the 1970s. Gedney Howe, a young Charleston attorney, decided to save this Victorian mansion with its ornate plasterwork and 75-foot domed ceiling. Howe purchased the property in 1976 for $220,000. It took another $4.5 million and 17 years to complete the restoration work. The mansion once again glitters and gleams. The rooms are filled with exquisite antiques, lavish curtains and intricately patterned rugs. In the gentlemen's library you will see one of the original sets of Minton tile depicting scenes from various Shakespearean plays. In the dining room, the original Williams's table has been repurchased from a Charleston antique shop. The table seats 26 and has an elaborate silver service. The music room is breathtaking with its original 45-foot skylight.

When you tour the house you will see three symbols repeated in many designs: the draped rope design indicated Williams's status as a wealthy merchant; the dogwood symbolized the four points of the Holy Cross; and the clover was indicative of the Holy Trinity.

The Calhoun Mansion is still owned by Howe. The first and second floors are open for tours, lasting approximately 45 minutes, Wednesday through Sunday from 10:00 A.M. to 4:00 P.M. except during January. The admission is slightly higher than other Charleston historic homes.

Directions: From I-26 take Meeting Street south into Charleston. The Calhoun Mansion is at 16 Meeting Street.

Cape Romain National Wildlife Refuge

A Bully Spot

Getting to **Bull's Island**, part of **Cape Romain National Wildlife Refuge**, is part of the fun. You'll see waterfowl and other wildlife as soon as you board the ferry at Moore's Landing in Awendaw. During your 30-minute ferry ride through scenic saltwater creeks you're apt to spot osprey, bald eagles, great blue herons and pelicans. Dolphin often swim alongside the boat, leaping and cavorting to the delight of passengers. If you are lucky you may even spot a sea turtle in the tidal creeks close to the island. There are rich shorebird feeding grounds along the island's coast that are covered with mud and thick oyster beds.

You'll want to bring binoculars to get a close look at the wide variety of wildlife from the boat and on Bull's Island, part of the 64,000-acre wildlife refuge. Over 260 species of birds have been sighted at the refuge including a wide range of shorebirds and ducks. There is a two-mile interpretative trail, a part of the National Recreational Trails System, that takes you deep within the island. In all there are 17 miles of hiking trails around the fresh-water impoundments and through scrub brush and sprawling live oak stands. In the interior, you are apt to see deer, turkeys, squirrels, raccoons and alligators. The island has a population of between 800 and 1,000 alligators, some quite sizeable.

Red wolves roam Bull Island, which is one of four breeding sites used to supplement the re-introduction efforts in North Carolina and Tennessee. This was the first spot chosen by the Red Wolf Recovery Program to free captive red wolves and breed a species that has become extinct in the wild. In Awendaw, stop at the Sewee Visitor & Environmental Education Center on Highway 17. An outdoor exhibit area contains red wolves. The center is open at no charge Tuesday through Sunday from 9:00 A.M. to 5:00 P.M.

The island is totally uninhabited. The only sign of man's encroachment is an old summer house; otherwise it is untouched. The pristine seven-mile beach is a treasure trove for shellers.

When you visit the island you should carry food and drinking water as there is nothing available on the island. In all but the winter months, you will want to liberally apply insect repellent. A camera and binoculars are advantageous. There is a visitor comfort station with restrooms and nearby are picnic tables.

Directions: From I-26 east heading onto Charleston, take I-526 east around Charleston and exit on Route 17 north. Take Route 17 approximately 10½ miles. Turn right at the sign for Moore ' s Landing and keep following the signs to Moore's Landing, where you will board the Coastal Expeditions ferry. From March through November on Tuesday, Friday and Saturday the ferry departs at 9:00 A.M. and 12:30 P.M., and returns at NOON and 4:00 P.M. From December through February, the ferry runs on Saturdays only departing at 9:00 A.M. and returning at 4:00 P.M. For additional information on rates and schedules call Coastal Expeditions at (803) 881-4582.

Getting to Bull Island, part of Cape Romain National Wildlife Refuge, is part of the adventure because it is only accessible by boat. Once visitors arrive they can take one of the intriguing paths. They are sure to spot indigenous wildlife.

Charles Pinckney National Historic Site

Founding Father's Farm

The Pinckney name is one heard frequently as you travel around South Carolina. Charles Pinckney, born to Colonel Charles Pinckney and his wife Frances Brewton on October 25, 1757, was a Lowcountry leader and one of the principal authors of the United States Constitution.

The **Charles Pinckney National Historic Site** encompasses 28 acres of the 715 acres in Christ Church Parish (now called Mount Pleasant) that Colonel Charles Pinckney purchased in 1754. The property, called **Snee Farm**, was owned by the Pinckney family until 1871 when Charles Pinckney sold it to settle debts. A survey plat dated 1818 shows cultivated fields (primarily rice), gardens, slave quarters (in 1878, there were 40 slaves at Snee Farm), swamps, ponds and woodlands. Archeologists have uncovered the foundation of what was probably the Pinckney era main building plus the kitchen, a smoke house and a building that may have been a slave quarter. There is also evidence of a slave village with more slave cabins in another area of the property. Plans call for these foundations to be marked so visitors will be able to visualize the historic setting.

In 1791, President Washington visited South Carolina as part of his tour of southern states. Governor Charles Pinckney invited the President to stop at "a little farm of mine in Christ Church...where your fare will be entirely that of a farm." The President stopped here for breakfast on May 2, 1791 and ate under the trees in the garden. He left early, anxious to reach the ferry and cross into Charleston, where he was received by Pinckney and others.

The house you see today, an excellent example of a Lowcountry coastal cottage, was built in 1828, after Charles Pinckney sold the property and four years after he died. The pine and cypress, one and one-half story house is built on a raised foundation. It has a full-width porch and a gable roof with dormers. The house was modernized in 1936 when two wings were added to the back of the house (that was also the year the kitchen was moved inside). This building houses exhibits about Charles Pinckney, his life and political contributions, the emergence of the United States from colonies to country, and the influence and impact of slavery. Exhibit cases contain some of the 150,000 artifacts unearthed by staff archeologists such as horseshoes, harness buckles, jar fragments and patent medicine bottles. Other exhibits include some of Pinckney's books. Charles Pinckney had a 20,000-volume library in his downtown Charleston home. All but 81 books were lost when fire destroyed the house in 1861. Most of the remaining books are preserved in the collection of the Thomas Cooper Library at the University of South Carolina.

Charles Pinckney NHS is open at no charge 9:00 A.M. to 5:00 P.M. daily except Christmas. The park closes at 6:00 P.M. between Memorial Day and Labor Day. To fully appreciate this National Park site, take time to watch the 18-minute video about Charles Pinckney and his farm. There is also a 15-minute video about the Constitution, how it was written and how it applies today.

If you head back to Charleston after your visit why not stop for lunch or dinner at the **Pinckney Cafe and Espresso**. It's delightful to sit on the porch of this casual dining establishment just two blocks north of the historic market at Motley Land and Pinckney streets. The cafe, which features specialty coffees, is open Tuesday through Saturday.

Directions: From I-26 heading into Charleston, take I-526 east to the first exit in Mount Pleasant, Long Point Road. Turn left and follow Long Point Road for 2½ miles to the park entrance on the right. From Charleston take Route 17 north six miles from the Cooper River bridges. Turn left on Long Point Road. The park entrance is ½ mile ahead on the left.

The Charleston Museum

America's First Museum

The Charleston Museum, America's first museum, was founded in 1773. Among the group of original curators was Thomas Heyward, a signer of the Declaration of Independence. Dubose Heyward, a direct descendant of Thomas and the author of the book from which the opera *Porgy and Bess* was derived, wrote a short play on the founding of the museum. In 1920 when it was performed, Dubose Heyward and Josephine Pinckney played the role of their ancestors. The Heyward-Washington House (see selection), acquired by the museum in 1928, was the first house museum to open in Charleston. The Charleston Museum preserves and interprets the social and natural history of Charleston and the Lowcountry region of the state.

The museum has received awards for its outstanding exhibits, although perhaps not for the ones in an 1826 museum sign that advertised attractions such as: "The Head of a New Zealand Chief, An Egyptian Mummy (A Child), The Duck Bill'd Platypus from New Holland, The Bones of an Ostrich as large as those of a Horse, Shoes of the Chinese Ladies, and 800 Birds, 70 Beasts, and 200 Fishes."

The museum has a collection of 12,207 bird eggs, some dating from the 19th century. The shells were used in a study of the effects of DDT. There are exhibits on Native Americans, trade and commerce, the plantation system, African-American contributions and the Civil War. To gain a personal perspective of Charlestonians there are clothes, furniture, photographs, ceramics, tools and pewter as well as toys and games. The museum's Charleston silver exhibit has internationally recognized work by local silversmiths from the colonial times through the late 19th century. Young visitors enjoy the *Discover Me Room*.

A unique item in the museum's collection, a replica of the Civil War-era Confederate submarine *Hunley*, sits outside the entrance. Clive Cussler, noted author and leader/founder of the nonprofit National Underwater and Marine Agency, found the iron shell of the submarine in May 1995 in about 20 feet of water four miles off Charleston's harbor. The *Hunley* sank on February 17, 1864 after nine Confederate sailors headed it toward a picket line of Union ships blockading Charleston's harbor. The sub rammed 100 pounds of black powder into the Union frigate *USS Housatonic*. The Union ship sank and it is speculated that the explosion may have popped some rivets causing the *Hunley* to leak and sink. Eventually, the *Hunley* will be raised, preserved and exhibited.

The Charleston Museum, directly across the street from the Charleston Visitor Center, is open daily Monday through Saturday from 9:00 A.M. to 5:00 P.M. and Sunday 1:00 to 5:00 P.M.

The museum is also a significant research facility. Admission is charged. In the downstairs foyer there is a gift shop with unique items that speak of Charleston and the region.

Across Meeting Street in buildings once occupied by the South Carolina Railway Freight Depot is the **Charleston Visitor Center**. Dating back to 1865, these are the oldest collection of railway structures in the nation; they are listed on the National Register of Historic Places. These buildings served the line where the *Best Friend of Charleston* began the world's first scheduled rail passenger line.

The visitor center has a wealth of information on attractions, tours, hotels and restaurants. Visitors can leave their cars at the center and take shuttles into the city's historic district. This is also the departure point for carriage, van and bus tours of the city. In the center there is a 144-square foot scale model of the city, under a 12-foot section of clear, acrylic floor, that will help you get your bearings. A welcome wall presents a two-minute slide and film snapshot of Charleston. There is also a 24-minute multi-image slide show, *Forever Charleston*, which features over 1,800 slides shown by 27 computerized slide projectors. You'll hear residents talking about their city. Admission is charged for this program, shown every 30 minutes from 9:00 A.M. to 5:00 P.M. daily.

This is a good place to get information on Charleston's many

North America's only commercial tea plantation is outside Charleston on tiny Wadmalaw Island. At the Charleston Tea Plantation visitors can see tea fields, learn how tea is processed and sample the tasty result.

outstanding restaurants. The city is rapidly gaining a reputation as one of the best dining towns in the country. **Carolina's** at 10 Exchange Street in the heart of the historic district offers Lowcountry cuisine with an Asian influence (803-724-3800). **Louis's Charleston Grill** in the Omni is popular with locals and travelers. Louis Osteen has garnered numerous awards for his culinary expertise. Adding to the relaxed ambience is live jazz (803-577-4522). Another local favorite is **Slightly North of Broad**, 192 East Bay Street, where regional cuisine is given a distinctive touch by the restaurant's talented chef (803-723-3424).

Directions: From I-26 take Route 17 north one block, then make a right on Meeting Street. The Charleston Museum is at 360 Meeting Street.

Charleston Tea Plantation

Classic Brew

On tiny Wadmalaw Island, 25 miles south of downtown Charleston, you'll discover **Charleston Tea Plantation**, the continent's only commercially-grown tea plantation. While this is the only such facility, others have attempted to grow tea in the United States. These attempts have almost all been in South Carolina because of the propitious climate with its high temperatures and high humidity. In 1799, Andre Micheaux introduced tea plants and seeds to this country on the grounds of what is now Middleton Place. It wasn't until 1848 that the commercial production of tea was attempted by Dr. Junius Smith at his Golden Grove Plantation in Greenville. He succeeded in propagating tea plants, but his operation was abandoned after his death in 1853. In 1874, Dr. Alexis Forster began growing tea commercially in Georgetown but, again, his death in 1879 ended the operation.

It was Dr. Charles Shepard's Pinehurst Tea Plantation, begun in 1888 in Summerville (northwest of Charleston), that really proved tea could be a successful commercial crop. In 1904, Pinehurst's oolong tea won first prize at the World's Fair in St. Louis. Shephard's farm flourished until his death in 1915. In 1903, Major Roswell Trimble, a former student of Dr. Shepard, with his partner Augustus C. Tyler, planted thousands of plants from Pinehurst at their American Tea Growing Company near Rantowles. After a dispute between Trimble and Tyler's son, the company dissolved and Trimble returned to work at Pinehurst.

In 1963, Thomas J. Lipton, Inc. created a research station on Wadmalaw Island, and transplanted Dr. Shepard's remaining plants from the wild and overgrown grounds of the former Pinehurst operation. Lipton's experimental work demonstrated that a high quality tea could be grown. The Lipton team, with then-manager Mack Fleming, also solved a problem that had plagued past operations, the high cost of labor. They designed a mechanical harvester that could replace 500 workers picking tea by hand.

In 1987, Mack Fleming with his partner William Barclay Hall, a third-generation English-trained tea taster, purchased the Lipton research center and began the Charleston Tea Plantation. They reintroduced Camellia sinesis plants to the country and began marketing **American Classic Teas**, which is now the official Hospitality Beverage of South Carolina.

Visitors are welcome to tour on the first Saturday of the month during the harvest season, May through October. Free tours of America's only tea plantation start at 10:00 A.M. and continue on the half-hour, with the last tour at 1:30 P.M. Call (800)443-5987 or (803)559-0383 on the day you plan to tour because conditions sometimes preclude offering tours. The plantation is open to the public only at these scheduled times. There are no rain dates for the tours. Although this is a walking tour and visitors can go out into the tea fields, the 127-acre plantation can accommodate wheelchairs.

After a short video introduction to your 45-minute tour, co-owner Mack Fleming offers some background on tea history and horticulture. You will also get a chance to see the tea harvester that really made this operation possible as well as the tea fields, where the tea plants resemble flat-topped hedges growing in neat rows. Next, the plantation's other owner, William Hall, professional tea taster, discusses tea processing and tasting. You will discover that tea is one beverage that doesn't improve with age, it's better fresh. You will also learn that tea should be stored in your freezer to maintain its freshness. It is the freshness that gives American Classic Tea a real advantage since it can be in stores within weeks of harvesting, and it takes nine to 12 months for tea from India, Brazil, Sri Lanka and other foreign plantations to get to stores in America. It is astonishing to learn that 200 million pounds of tea is imported each year. At the tour's conclusion you will get a chance to sample American Classic Tea, as well as a variety of the tea jellies. There is a gift shop which sells tea and related products. They also do a brisk mail order business and you can obtain a catalog by calling (800)443-5987.

After your visit to the tea plantation, continue down Route 700 another mile to **Rockville**, a small community that was featured in the 1991 movie *Paradise* with Melanie Griffith and Don Johnson. The road ends at the waterfront where a regatta is held each year in early August. Take a drive along Rockville's dirt roads and enjoy the picturesque houses and church.

On your way back to the Charleton area on Maybank Highway, cross over onto Johns Island and make a detour at the sign for **Angel Oak**, on Angel Oak Road. This incredible 65-feet-high live oak tree is reputed to be over 1,400 years old. Its massive tree limbs rest on the ground; the lighest limb has a circumference of 11.25 feet and a length of 89 feet. The land on which Angel Oak stands is now a City of Charleston park and provides a wonderful picnic venue. This property was originally part of a grant made to Abraham Waight in 1717. After being in the family for generations, it acquired its name when Martha Waight married Justis Angel in 1810.

If you want to stop at a charming little lunch spot on Johns Island, head for the **St. Johns Island Cafe**, 3140 Maybank Highway. They serve breakfast, lunch, supper and Sunday brunch.

Directions: From I-26 make a right on Route 17 and continue to either Main Road, Route 20, or Route 171. You can take either of these routes to Route 700, Maybank Highway that will take you over Jenkins Bridge from Johns Island onto Wadmalaw Island. From the bridge it is ten miles down Route 700 to the entrance for the Charleston Tea Plantation on the left. The plantation is at 6617 Maybank Highway.

Churches of Charleston

Often Called the "Holy City"

The settlers who came to the Carolinas were guaranteed the greatest latitude of religious freedom in all the 13 colonies. In 1704, Charles Town (named to honor King Charles II of England) was a small community where English, French, Quaker, Anabaptist and independent churches worshiped peacefully. Despite wars, hurricanes, fires and an earthquake in 1886 many of Charleston's earliest churches survived. But counting the spires that lend a picturesque appeal to the city's skyline does not adequately reveal the number of churches in the city—Charleston boasts over 180 houses of worship.

The oldest church building in Charleston is **St. Michael's Episcopal Church**, built between 1752 and 1761. It is one of the few city churches in the country to retain its original design. Sitting in this historic edifice, visitors are linked with such illustrious worshipers as George Washington, who attended service here during his 1791 southern tour and Robert E. Lee who, in 1861, worshiped here in the same pew—pew 43. This was the pew set aside for the Royal Governor's use (since South Carolina was still under British rule at the time the church opened for services) and as such was more decorative and more comfortable. Each pew chair has its own small reading desk.

During Washington's visit he climbed to the top of the distinctive 186-foot multi-tiered steeple for a view of the city. St. Michael's steeple clock and eight bells were made in England in 1764. During the American Revolution the British confiscated them and sent them back to England as a war prize. Returned to the church, they were dismantled again during the Civil War and sent to Columbia for safe keeping only to be damaged by fire. This necessitated another return to England for recasting at the original foundry. In total, the bells crossed the Atlantic five times. Buried in St. Michael's churchyard are noted Constitution signers and political leaders: Charles Cotesworth Pinckney and John Rutledge. The church is at the corner of Meeting and Broad streets.

Meeting Street was named for **The Circular Congregation Church**'s independent Meeting House. The congregation was organized in 1681 as The Independent Church of Charles Towne. In 1806, noted South Carolina architect, Robert Mills, designed a unique Circular Church, which was destroyed by fire in 1861, rebuilt and destroyed again by the 1886 earthquake. The fourth reconstruction which still stands used the bricks from the previous structure. The Circular Church is noted for establishing the state's first Sunday School. Internments in the church's graveyard date back to 1696, making it the oldest graveyard in the city. Tours of the church, at 150 Meeting Street, are given when church volunteers are available—currently Fridays from 10:00 A.M. to 3:00 P.M.

The birthplace of American Reform Judaism was at **Congregation Beth Elohim**, the second oldest synagogue in the country and the oldest in continuous use. The congregation, Kahal Kadosh Beth Elohim, was organized in 1749, although Jewish settlers had arrived in the area as early as 1670, attracted by the colony's civil and religious freedom. Their first synagogue, a Georgian-style edifice built in 1794, was destroyed by fire. The second, an outstanding example of Greek Revival architecture, was built in 1840. This was the first Jewish synagogue to have an organ. It was also among the first to have a Jewish Sunday school, a Jewish charitable organization and a Hebrew orphan society. It is open to the public Monday through Friday from 10:00 A.M. to NOON at 90 Hasell Street.

Another group to benefit from Charleston's religious tolerance was the Free African Society, established in 1791 and actually included both slave and free African Americans. This group eventually became known as the Bethel Circuit. Morris Brown was responsible for organizing the Negro Methodist independent organization, and the group built **Emanuel African Methodist Episcopal Church** in 1818. It was in this church that Denmark

Vessey allegedly began planning a slave uprising that he anticipated would include 5,000 plantation slaves who would join him. Some thought he intended to burn the city and kill white slave owners. When the plan became known the authorities closed down the church. Vessey was arrested and hung, although he never admitted planning the uprising. The congregation was reorganized in 1865 and the present church at 110 Calhoun Street was built in 1891. Emanuel is the oldest AME church in the south and, with its 2,500 seat capacity, the largest African-American church in the city.

Charleston also has the oldest Baptist church in the south. **First Baptist Church** at 48 Meeting Street was founded in 1682. This is another of Robert Mills designs, completed in 1822. Visitors are welcome to attend Sunday worship services.

Twelve Caledonian families established the **First (Scots) Presbyterian Church** in 1731, rejecting the idea of becoming part of the Anglican Church. The church you see today was built in 1814 and has the seal of the Church of Scotland in the window above the entrance. The congregation has never replaced the bells they donated to the cause of the Confederacy in 1863. This church is at 53 Meeting Street.

French Huguenots began worshiping on the site of **The French Protestant (Huguenot) Church** in 1687. The church that stands today at 136 Church Street is the group's fourth edifice, designed by Edward B. White and built between 1844-1845. The church has an 1845 Henry Erben pipe organ that is still used. Services are on Sunday at 10:30 A.M. In the spring the church has a French Liturgy service.

In 1798, **The Old Bethel Methodist Church,** at 222 Calhoun Street, was dedicated as the congregation had become too large for the Blue Meeting House on Cumberland Street. When Bethel Methodist Church built a new edifice, they used it for class meetings for African-American church members; in 1880 it was given to the African-American congregation.

Old St. Andrews Parish Church, outside the historic city on Ashley River Road, is the oldest surviving church in the Carolinas. The church was built in 1706 and much of the interior is original. (Remember that St. Michael's holds the title of the oldest church in the city.)

Another church that has roots going back to colonial days is **St. John's Lutheran Church**, which is the mother church for South Carolina Lutherans. The first recorded service was May 26, 1734. In 1742 Henry Melchior Muhlenburg, the "father of Lutheranism in America," established a congregation here. A church was built on this site in 1759 and the present structure in 1817. The church is on the corner of Clifford and Archdale streets.

St. Mary's Roman Catholic Church is the oldest Catholic

church in the state and the Mother Church of the Dioceses of South Carolina, North Carolina and Georgia. Established in 1789, the first church was destroyed by fire; the present church at 89 Hasell Street was completed in 1839. It was badly damaged during the Civil War and services were held in private homes until the church was renovated in 1901.

German-speaking Lutherans established **St. Matthew's Lutheran Church**, the second of its denomination in the city. The Gothic structure with its 297-foot steeple was built in 1872 and rebuilt after a major fire in 1965. The church at 405 King Street is noted for its outstanding stained glass windows depicting Biblical themes.

The first Anglican church was built on the site of **St. Philip's Episcopal Church** in 1680, and was the Mother Church of the Province. As early as 1697, the name "St. Philip's" was added. In 1723, a church was built closer to the docks, but after it was destroyed in a fire in 1835, the present building was erected. The towering steeple made the church a target for Union fire during the Civil War and the church was hit more than a dozen times. The war prompted the donation of the church bells, which were melted down and used for cannon balls. New bells were installed and dedicated on July 4, 1976. St. Philip's is called the lighthouse church because lights in the steeple guided ships into Charleston's harbor. The U.S. government maintained this light into the 20th century. St. Philip's churchyard is the resting place for a number of distinguished public figures: John C. Calhoun, Secretary of War and Vice-President; Edward Rutledge, signer of the Declaration of Independence; Charles Pinckney, signer of the Constitution; and Dubose Heyward, author of *Porgy* from which the operetta *Porgy and Bess* was derived (see Catfish Row selection). St. Philip's Episcopal Church is at 146 Church Street.

The Unitarian Church, an adjunct of the Circular Church, was established as the Second Independent or Congregational church. In 1817 the Unitarian and Trinitarian members separated. The Unitarian congregationalists began building their church at this location at 8 Archdale Street. Begun in 1772, church construction was interrupted by the American Revolution and it was not finished until 1787. Using plans drawn up for the Chapel of Henry VII in Westminster Abbey, the church was remodeled in 1852. It is the only church in the United States to have a fan tracery ceiling.

The Presbyterian Church of the United States designates **The Second Presbyterian Church** as Historical Site Number One, as it is the oldest edifice of this faith in Charleston's historic district. The Classical Revival church was built in 1809 and both races worshiped here, with African Americans seated in the galleries. The original communion service is still used. The church was damaged by a series of hurricanes and the 1886 earthquake.

Many of the legends and lore associated with Charleston's lovely churches are detailed on the carriage and bus tours. Notice the elaborately designed wrought iron gates on the fences that enclose many of the churchyards. A significant number are the work of Philip Simmons (see the Philip Simmons Garden selection). For a walking tour map of the city stop at the Charleston Visitor Center (see Charleston Museum selection).

The Citadel

The Military College of South Carolina

It's a stirring sight to see a **Dress Parade** at **The Citadel**. During this spectacle the South Carolina Corps of Cadets march in even ranks around the parade field. Following a tradition that extends back to Alexander the Great and introduced in this country by Baron von Steuben at Valley Forge, the troops parade for review. In the European tradition, United States drill procedures and movements follow tactical maneuvers used on the battlefield. In combat situations, brigades form in order of battle, but at ceremonial parades ranking represents length of duty and outstanding performance.

The Citadel Corps marches to the music of the regimental band with its fife, bugle, drum and bagpipe. The cadet's sharply creased white pants and gold-buttoned gray jackets are trim and martial. At the center of the formation, selected cadets carry the colors: the United States flag, the South Carolina flag and the South Carolina Corps of Cadet colors. The cadet colors has nine battle streamers earned by the Corps during the Civil War. Once the battalions are in place, the reviewing commanders troop the line and inspect the Corps.

During the inspection ceremony, those watching from the Summerall Field bleachers will hear about the first troop review when the Citadel opened on March 20, 1843. Twenty cadets reported to the new college at the State arsenal, located within a section of the 1780 ramparts built to protect Charleston from a British invasion (today the area is Marion Square). The 20 members of the first South Carolina Corps of Cadets replaced the state militia guard. At the opening ceremony, the Washington Light Infantry acted as the "Old Guard" of the Citadel buildings. Later, in 1922, the college's 300 cadets moved from Marion Square to its present location on the Ashley River. Although the Corps has grown to approximately 2,000 cadets, the mission of the Citadel remains the same as it was when there were only 20 students: to turn out "citizen soldiers" who will excel in their civilian professions and serve their country as officers in the

The Corps of Cadets marches to the cadence of the regimental band's bugle, drum and bagpipes during the Citadel's Dress Parades held on most Fridays during the school year.

armed forces.

The Citadel Dress Parade ends with Pass-in-Review, which originated in medieval days when departing crusaders marched before the King who would pay his respect as the assembled throngs cheered. As the colors pass in front of the viewing stands, the onlookers rise and pay their respect. The troops then march from the field ending the ceremony. Dress parades are held almost every Friday during the college term at 3:45 P.M. The parades are cancelled for bad weather and during school holidays.

While on the Citadel campus stop at **The Citadel Museum**, 171 Moultrie Street, where photographs and memorabilia trace the history of this military college from its founding in 1842 to the present day. The museum is the first building on the right inside the main gates. It is open at no charge Sunday through Friday from 2:00 to 5:00 P.M. and Saturday from NOON to 5:00 P.M.

When college is in session, visitors are also welcome to visit Summerall Chapel, on the Avenue of Remembrance across from Summerall Field and the Munnerlyn Snack Bar. There is also a gift shop, located in Mark Clark Hall; the hours and days of operation vary. The campus is open to visitors 8:00 A.M. to 6:00 P.M. daily.

Directions: From I-26 take Rutledge Avenue exit. Follow Rutledge Avenue to Moultrie Street. Turn right on Moultrie Street, which will bring you to the front gates of The Citadel.

Drayton Hall

South's Oldest Georgian Palladian House

Only one plantation house along the Ashley River outside Charleston survived burning during the Civil War, and that is **Drayton Hall**. Seven generations of Draytons owned this property, keeping its colonial construction virtually unaltered. It is the oldest surviving example of Georgian Palladian architecture in the south. To this day the house, now a National Historic Landmark, has no running water, electric lights or central heating. The significance of Drayton Hall is that it is preserved, not restored.

Drayton Hall is unfurnished, but this adds to your appreciation of the details of the plasterwork ceiling, decorative wood paneling, wall friezes and finely carved fireplaces. There is no record of the architect, or master builder, used by John Drayton in 1738 when he began building his home, which adjoined his father's plantation (now Magnolia Plantation, see selection). The house, which took four years for the European and African-

American craftsmen to build, adopted design styles popular in England after 1715. Balance and symmetry were essential elements in the design and you will see sham doors with nothing but a brick wall behind them. For the first time a two-story portico was added to a house in the colonies. The grandiose plans and expensive building materials, such as English limestone and West Indian mahogany, prompted one 18th-century neighbor to call the house "Mr. Drayton's palace."

From the river side, which has a double staircase with a wrought iron railing, visitors entered the 27-foot-high, mahogany paneled stair hall. An intricately carved double staircase led to the great halls on the first and second floors. The Draytons, one of the wealthiest families in South Carolina, frequently held candle-lit receptions and entertainments in these halls. Some interior sections still retain their original coat of paint; others were repainted in 1880.

To put this house in perspective, remember it was built in the Carolina countryside at a very early date. In 1738, when construction began, George Washington was only six years old and Thomas Jefferson was not even born. The house was not originally a working plantation, but rather a gentleman's country residence. It was supported by a system of other Drayton-owned working plantations located in the area. The property was originally laid out with a formal garden and small fields of rice and table crops. Later generations added cotton fields. The house remained in the Drayton family until 1974 when it was sold to the National Trust.

There are two trails on the grounds; it takes roughly 45 minutes to explore the Marsh Walk and 30 minutes for the Garden Walk. On the marsh trail you will see indications of the calcium phosphate that was mined at Drayton Hall after the Civil War. Narrow gauge railroads traveled along the dikes (formerly used in the rice cultivation) to haul phosphate rock, which was carried across the Ashley River to be processed as fertilizer. You will see southern live oaks that survived Hurricane Hugo that hit here on September 21, 1989. The reflection pond was created at the turn of the 20th century and the dirt taken out formed the Victorian garden mound that dominates the lawn.

The garden trail begins in front of the gift shop and passes in front of the privy one of the few surviving outbuildings. A ditch, called a "ha ha" in the 18th century, survives from the estate's colonial garden. A fence was built in the deep trench to keep out large animals but still provide an unobstructed view of the garden from the house. A greenhouse (which no longer stands) was built in 1747 to grow exotic plants. Charles Drayton wrote on July 11, 1791, "Sowed in the garden 118 olive stones sent in earth from France by Mr. [Thomas] Jefferson."

It took about four hours to reach Charleston by river from Drayton Hall. To ensure that the view across the Ashley River remains unchanged the National Trust acquired enough land to preserve and protect Drayton Hall's natural vista.

Tours of Drayton Hall are offered daily on the hour March through October from 10:00 A.M. to 4:00 P.M. The remainder of the year, hours are 10:00 A.M. to 3:00 P.M. It is closed on Thanksgiving, Christmas and New Year's Day. Admission is charged.

Directions: From I-26 take I-526 southwest to Route 61. Head north on Route 61, Ashley River Road, and Drayton Hall will be on your right. It is nine miles northwest of Charleston.

The Edmondston-Alston House, the Battery and White Point Gardens

Spectacular View, Exquisite Appointments Make for Dream House

Touring historic houses is addictive, but few strike such a responsive chord that visitors would immediately move in. One that evokes this response is **The Edmondston-Alston House**. Among its many selling points is its location on Charleston's **High Battery**. It is one of a row of mansions fronting Cooper River and the harbor.

Scottish merchant Charles Edmondston, a native of the Shetland Islands who came to America at age 17, built his elegant Federal-style home in 1825. He was at the height of his success in Charleston. His was one of the first water-front homes, away from the noise and confusion of the city's bustling stores, warehouses and wharves. His piazza not only overlooked a scenic harbor view, it also afforded the opportunity to monitor the arrival and departure of ships carrying his merchandise.

Edmondston was one of many businessmen to suffer economic reversals in "The Panic of 1837." His losses were so great, he was forced to sell his stylish home to Charles Alston, a wealthy Lowcountry rice planter (the Alston family was one of the wealthiest in the state). Under Alston's direction the house achieved a Greek Revival look with the addition of a third floor piazza supported by Corinthian columns, and a second floor iron balcony on the east facade. A family coat of arms was added on the parapet at the front of the house. An Alston cousin still owns the house; it has been in his family for more than eight decades. Under the auspices of the Middleton Place (see selection) Foundation, the first two floors are open to the public.

Visitors see the Alston family furnishings and bibelots filling the rooms as they have for over a century and a half. Family portraits, paintings, silver and books give a lived in look—albeit of a luxurious life style. A faded oriental carpet covers part of the wooden floor in the East Drawing Room, while the ormolu and glass chandelier hanging from the ornate plasterwork medallion is one of a pair made in 1850 by the Cornelius Company of Philadelphia.

You can see Fort Sumter from the upper piazza. On April 12, 1861, Alston and others watched rockets being fired at the fort when Major Anderson refused to surrender. Robert E. Lee later took refuge at the Alston house when a hotel he was staying in was threatened by fire. In March 1865, during the Civil War, the house was occupied by Union Major General Rufus Saxton.

The Edmondston-Alston House is open Tuesday through Saturday from 10:00 A.M. to 4:30 P.M. On Sunday and Monday tours are given from 1:30 to 4:30 P.M. Admission is charged.

At Oyster Point there is a park called **White Point Garden**. Native Americans heaped oyster shells at the point, serving the same purpose as a lighthouse. The bright white color of the shells was visible from boats and marked the shoreline. The original plan for the city did not extend as far down as the point. The precursor to what is today High Battery was built in 1755 and consisted of an earthwork protection for the city that extended from Granville Bastion, where East Bay Street ended at that time, to Broughton Battery, which is today White Point Garden. The battery was constructed of mud and sand, held together by long bundles of sticks, called fascines. To further bond this mixture, it was planted with grass. Wooden platforms were placed along the top to hold guns to protect the harbor. Just south of what is now Atlantic Street, a middle bastion was built and renamed in 1757 for Governor William Lyttelton. During the American Revolution the Lyttelton Bastion became Fort Darrell. Also in 1757, there was easy passage along the fortifications on what ultimately became East Battery. The street received its name during the War of 1812 when cannons were placed along this line of fortification to protect Charleston. After a destructive hurricane in 1854, the seawall of the High Battery was increased to its present height and solidity.

Directions: From I-26 take Route 17 north (Mt. Pleasant) exit. Follow to East Bay Street exit. Follow East Bay Street past Broad Street. East Bay becomes East Battery. The Edmondston-Alston House is at 21 East Battery.

Fort Moultrie

Two Centuries of Coastal Defense

Coastal defenses from 1776 through 1947 can be traced at **Fort Moultrie**. This, the first fort on Sullivans Island was still being constructed when it was attacked by nine British warships commanded by Admiral Sir Peter Parker on June 28, 1776. The palmetto-log fort's 31 smooth-bore cannons fired for 12 hours before the British retired from the fray, despite their advantage of nearly 300 mounted guns. The porous sandy fill between the logs and the spongy palmetto construction had absorbed the cannon shells fired by the British. This was one of the first decisive victories for the American forces in the American Revolution. In celebration of its escape from British occupation, the fort was named for its defender, William Moultrie. Four years later, the British captured Charleston and held it until the end of the war.

In the next decade the fort was neglected and little remained when war broke out between England and France in the 1790s. Concerned that the fledgling country might be drawn into the conflict, Congress embarked on the establishment of the country's first coordinated system of coastal fortifications. As part of a series of new forts, a second Fort Moultrie was completed in 1798. This five-sided earth and timber fort was wiped out by a hurricane in 1804. In 1807, Congress, recognizing that the first series of forts were badly neglected and in need of repair, appropriated funds for a second system. As part of this effort, a third Fort Moultrie, constructed of brick, was completed in 1809.

All the forts built on Sullivans Island were ideally situated to protect Charleston's harbor, because any ship sailing into the harbor had to sail close to the island to avoid the shoals and sandbars. Ships were not positioned correctly to fire on the fort until after they turned into the harbor, giving the fort guns a chance to take the first shots. The addition of Fort Sumter (see selection) in 1829 provided cross fire and helped keep ships from the harbor.

In December 1837, Osceola, a Native-American leader of the Seminole people, along with 237 of his followers were imprisoned at Fort Moultrie. Osceola led the Seminole resistance to the Federal government's attempts to remove the Seminoles to Oklahoma from their reservation in central Florida, where they had been moved from Alabama after their defeat in the Creek War of 1813-1814. Osceola, who was captured while negotiating under a white flag of truce, died from malaria complications on January 30, 1838. He was buried at Fort Moultrie and his grave is marked by a gravestone protected by an iron railing (the original gravestone is in the fort's visitor center).

Only minor changes were made in Fort Moultrie between 1809 and 1860; the parapet was slightly altered and 32-pounder cannon were added. In addition to Fort Moultrie and Fort Sumter, Fort Johnson and Castle Pinckney ringed Charleston's harbor. These four fortifications were designed to support each other and protect the city, but circumstances of war dictated otherwise.

When South Carolina seceded from the Union in December 1860, the day after Christmas, Federal troops abandoned Fort Moultrie for the newer and stronger Fort Sumter. Less than four months after the Federal garrison moved to Sumter, the Confederates shelled the fort into submission, and catapulted the nation into the Civil War. Three years into the war, Northern ironclads and shore batteries began a more than 20-month bombardment of Sumter and Moultrie, that never broke through the forts' defenses. By the time the Confederates abandoned the city in 1865, Fort Sumter was crumbling and the walls of Fort Moultrie were covered by an immense pile of sand that had protected its walls from Northern cannon balls. (The Patapsco monument near the entrance to the fort marks the graves of five of the 62 seamen who drowned on January 15, 1865, when the *USS Patapsco* struck a Confederate torpedo and went down between Fort Sumter and Fort Moultrie.)

During the Civil War, a rifled cannon was developed that wrecked havoc on brick-walled fortifications. After the war, Fort Moultrie was modernized to take advantage of the new technology. Concrete magazines and bombproofs were added and immense new cannons installed. By 1885, the coastal defenses had again fallen into neglect so President Grover Cleveland asked Secretary of War William C. Endicott to examine the situation and suggest improvements. Endicott's board suggested the rearmament of 26 sites along the coast and three on the Great Lakes. The Endicott System included the addition of breachloading steel cannon on "disappearing carriages, mortar batteries and underwater electronic minefields protected by rapid fire guns."

In Charleston, the implementation of the Endicott System began in March 1896 with the construction of Mortar Battery Capron and the following year Battery Jasper, a 10-inch disappearing gun emplacement located just east of Fort Moultrie (and now part of the National Park Service's interpretation of the fort). Six additional batteries were built on Sullivans Island and one 12-inch battery was built on Fort Sumter. Battery Jasper, which cost $235,000 was never in battle and was taken out of service in 1943. Its 65,000-pound steel guns were scrapped for the war effort.

At the onset of World War II, new thought was given to the Atlantic coastline. In June 1941 sixteen HECP/HDCPS (Harbor Entrance Control Posts/Harbor Defense Command Posts) were established. One of the HECPs was at Fort Moultrie in its World War I signal building. Using signal flags, blinker lights and searchlights the duty officers communicated with commercial and Navy ships entering and leaving Charleston Harbor. During the war, the harbor was closed at least twice due to the threat of German mines and the coast was patrolled in search of U-Boats.

As the war progressed the HDCP centers had to be either bombproof, splinterproof, and/or gasproof. The Fort Moultrie structure did not conform to these requirements and a new building housing up to 40 Army and Navy personnel was built by March 1944. The HECP at Fort Moultrie has been restored to its WWII appearance and is part of the self-guided tour.

There is an introductory video you will want to view at the visitors center before beginning your self-guided tour. The center also has doll-size figures in uniforms appropriate to the combat that took place at Fort Moultrie. The fort is open year round from 9:00 A.M. to 5:00 P.M. It is closed on Christmas Day. A nominal admission fee is charged.

Directions: From I-26, take Route 17 North (business) to Mt. Pleasant and turn right on Route 703. At Sullivans Island, turn right on Middle Street. The fort is 1.5 miles from the intersection.

Fort Sumter National Monument

Where the Civil War Began

There are names that resonate from our past—Lexington and Concord, Valley Forge, Yorktown, Gettysburg, Appomattox and **Fort Sumter**. As every school book tells us, the Civil War started when Confederate troops fired on the Federal garrison at Fort Sumter.

The background of this incident goes back to December 20, 1860, when South Carolina seceded from the Union in response to Republican Abraham Lincoln's presidential victory. Within six weeks, five other states in the deep South had also seceded. In February 1861, South Carolina, Mississippi, Florida, Alabama, Georgia and Louisiana formed the Confederate States of America. By March, Texas was added to the new nation and most of the Federal forts within the Confederate states' borders were seized. Fort Sumter was one of the few holdouts.

There were four Federal forts in the Charleston harbor: Sumter, Moultrie, Johnson and Castle Pinckney. But Major Robert Anderson, who commanded the larger company at Fort Moultrie (see selection), concluded that only Sumter was defensible. On December 26, he moved all the Federal troops, approximately 85 men, to Fort Sumter. The following day, South Carolina troops took charge of the three empty forts. South Carolina formally asked the United States government to move its troops from Fort Sumter but President James Buchanan (Lincoln had not as yet been inaugurated) refused.

Buchanan attempted to reprovision the fort in January but South Carolina forces resisted the attempt. By March, Brigadier General P.G.T. Beauregard was in command of Charleston's

73

Confederate troops and efforts were redoubled to fortify the harbor. Fort Sumter stood as a symbol of the growing division between North and South. Lincoln, after his inauguration, was determined to supply the garrison with food and other essentials and the Confederate government resolved to resist.

The stage was set for the first shot of the war, and it was fired from Fort Johnson on James Island at 4:30 A.M. on April 12th. It was the start of a cannonade that lasted throughout the entire day and night. On the morning of the 13th, shots fired from Fort Moultrie set the officers' quarters at Sumter on fire. By 2:00 P.M., after 34 hours, Major Anderson agreed to surrender the fort that evening. No one lost their life during the war's first conflict.

Once the Confederates got control of Fort Sumter, they had complete access to Charleston's harbor. Into this Southern stronghold came needed war supplies that were kept from other Atlantic ports by blockading Union ships. Fort Sumter, armed by the Confederates with 95 guns, repulsed Federal attempts to regain control. One attack was launched on April 7, 1863 by nine ironclads who bombarded the fort for 2½ hours with no real impact, except five Union ships were severely disabled from returning Confederate fire.

The first shots of the Civil War were fired at Fort Sumter on April 12, 1861. After enduring more than 30 hours of bombardment, Major Anderson surrendered the fort. No one lost their life during the war's first conflict.

For 22 months, Fort Sumter was fired on from land and sea. Although the fort sustained heavy damage and the five-foot-thick walls were reduced to ruins, the garrison refused to surrender. Approximately 46,000 shells were fired at the fort, which translates into 7 million pounds of metal. The Confederates lost 52 men with 267 wounded. But the garrison never surrendered, and only the approach of General William T. Sherman's troops forced the Confederates to evacuate the fort on February 17, 1865.

When it came time to assess the damage at the end of the Civil War, little remained of Fort Sumter. A small portion of the left flank, left face and right face remained intact but the rest was simply a rubble of sand, earth and debris sloping down to the water's edge. The army repaired the fort, even reclaiming 11 of the original first tier gun rooms, which were armed with 100-pounder Parrott guns. But the fort was not garrisoned and from 1876 to 1897, it served as a lighthouse station. As the country stood poised to enter the Spanish-American War in 1898, the army constructed Battery Huger at the fort.

During World War I, a small garrison was stationed at Battery Huger, but in the two decades following the war the fort remained unstaffed. Tourists visited the historic site during this period until World War II prompted its reactivation. Anti-aircraft guns were added and the fort became part of the coastal defense system. In 1948, Fort Sumter became a national monument.

This must-see historic site offers the added bonus of a boat ride, as it is located in Charleston Harbor and is accessible only by water. Concession-operated boats leave from the City Marina on Lockwood Drive and from Patriots Point (see selection). There is a fee charged for the boat trip. Once visitors arrive at the fort, park service rangers are available to answer questions.

There are 11 points of interest including the sally port, casemates and the ruins of the enlisted men and officers quarters. In the fort's museum are exhibits and memorabilia, including the fort's battle flag from the Civil War and later conflicts.

Fort Sumter is open daily from 10:00 A.M. to 5:30 P.M. from April through Labor Day; at other times there are abbreviated hours. It is closed on December 25th. Call for specific non-summer hours, at (803) 883-3123. To obtain a boat schedule, call (803) 722-1691.

Directions: From I-26 in Charleston take Route 17 south. Turn left on Lockwood Drive and park at the City Marina. Tour boats also leave from Patriots Point.

The classical appearance of the imposing dome at Gibbes Museum of Art is part of the Beaux Arts design. American paintings, prints and drawings from the 18th century to the present are exhibited. Ten delightfully detailed miniature rooms are among visitors' favorites.

Gibbes Museum of Art
and Charleston Galleries

It's A Small World

On April 12, 1905 the *Charleston Evening Post* reported on the opening of the Gibbes Memorial Art Gallery: "The scene in the hall was striking. The assemblage of many beautiful women handsomely gowned, engaged in admiring criticism, with their gentlemen friends or among themselves, of the pictures before them, seeing a point of beauty here or a bit of charming color there and going from this or that group of pictures in search of their favorite, made up a picture in itself of great attractiveness." Today, coverage of the opening of what is now the **Gibbes Museum of Art** in the center of Charleston's historic district could, excepting the formal dress, be equally true.

A bequest by Charleston merchant James S. Gibbes financed the museum's construction and underwrote the Carolina Art Association. The building was designed by architect Frank Milburn in a Beaux Arts style, a classical look that includes an imposing dome, pediments and Doric columns. Inside, the collection covers American paintings, prints and drawings from the 18th century to the present. You will see portraits of notable South Carolinians: Benjamin West's study of Thomas Middleton, Thomas Sully's capturing of Charles Izard Manigault and Rembrant Peale's portrait of John C. Calhoun. Charleston and other Lowcountry scenes are captured in many of the landscape paintings. This depiction of regional heritage is captured by noted artists such as Alice Ravenel Huger Smith, Anna Heyward Taylor, Elizabeth O'Neill Verner and Alfred Hutty. The Charleston Renaissance Gallery features the work of artists responsible for the cultural renaissance of the city in the 1920s and 1930s. There is a visual link between the depictions of delicate flowers common to the Charleston area and some of the wood-block prints in the Japanese print collection.

For many repeat visitors, the **Elizabeth Wallace Miniature Rooms** are a favorite. These ten exquisitely detailed rooms replicate historic houses that museum visitors may have seen. Others re-create historical French style. All the details represent traditions of American and French architecture, decorative arts and design. There is a drawing room from Wilton, a James River Plantation outside Richmond; a parlor from Savannah's Owens-Thomas House in Georgia; a drawing room from Charleston's Nathanial Russell House and others. The rooms, given to the museum by collector Elizabeth Wallace Ellis of Hilton Head Island, contain a wealth of tiny items such as real pewter plates, ceramic Canton ware, embroidered rugs and seat covers as well as carved chairs and tables. Through the windows you glimpse painted scenes reflecting the landscape you would see if you toured each of these homes.

Another exhibit features one of the oldest and finest collections of miniature portraits in the world. The earliest work dates back to 1750. There are small masterpieces painted by James Peal and renowned Charleston artist, Charles Fraser. Items in this exhibit are rotated.

The Gibbes Museum of Art is open 10:00 A.M. to 5:00 P.M. Tuesday through Saturday and 1:00 to 5:00 P.M. on Sunday and Monday. Admission is charged. The museum has a gift shop visitors shouldn't miss; it's stocked with a wide array of handcrafted items, artistic reproductions and unusual items. Throughout the year the Gibbes mounts special exhibits and presents lectures, seminars, concerts and films.

While visiting Charleston you can pick up a booklet that provides information on **Charleston Galleries**. There are 28 galleries in the downtown area. The brochure has ads and a map that provide additional information on the range of their collections.

Not far from the Gibbes Museum of Art is **Cafe Brio** at 129 Meeting Street, noted for its creative sandwiches of housemade herb bread. Salads are enhanced by dressings with a wide array of herbs. The restaurant is open for lunch Monday through Saturday and dinner on Tuesday through Saturday.

Directions: Take I-26 to the Meeting Street Exit. Turn right on Meeting Street. The Gibbes Museum of Art is at 135 Meeting Street.

Heyward-Washington House and The Thomas Elfe House

Home of Declaration of Independence Signer

Thomas Heyward, Jr. was the eldest son of one of South Carolina's wealthiest rice planters, Colonel Daniel Heyward. In 1770, the Colonel purchased property within the boundaries of the old walled city of Charleston. He demolished the two-story building on the lot and, in 1772, began work on a grand brick double house with an architectural style and interior detail reflecting his prosperity and prominence.

By 1773, Thomas Heyward, Jr., who had returned from reading law at the Middle Temple of the Inns of Court in London, was spending his time at his father's Charleston house with his new bride, Elizabeth Mathews Heyward. Young Thomas Heyward was a defender of Americans' rights against England and, in 1776, was a member of the Second Continental Congress. He was one of South Carolina's four signers of the Declaration of Independence along with Arthur Middleton (see Middleton Place selection), Edward Rutledge and Thomas Lynch, Jr. (see Hopsewee Plantation selection). Heyward remained in the Continental Congress until 1778 and also signed the Articles of Confederation. Back in Charleston, Heyward served as a circuit court judge. He fought and was wounded during Brigadier General William Moultrie's resistance to the British attack on Port Royal Island in 1779.

The following year, the British plundered Heyward's plantation and carried off all his slaves. When Charleston surrendered, Heyward was one of the 29 Revolutionary leaders that were arrested by the British and exiled to St. Augustine, where he remained until 1781. After the war, Heyward continued the efforts he had begun as a member of the founding committee for The Charleston Museum. He also represented the city in the state legislature. When he retired in 1789, he returned to White Hall, his plantation home near Beaufort. He died there at age 62 in 1809.

The **Heyward-Washington House** became linked with George Washington in 1791, when Thomas Heyward, Jr. leased it to the President during his ten-day visit to Charleston. At the time, Heyward was living at his plantation and the house was occupied by his aunt, Mrs. Rebecca Jameson, who ran a girls boarding school. Washington hosted a tea for the ladies of Charleston in the Heyward House drawing room. He said that Charlestonians were, "wealthy-Gay-& hospitable."

The wealth and hospitality of the Heywards can still be felt as the house is filled with a valuable collection of 18th-century Charleston-made furniture. There were 250 cabinetmakers plying their craft in Charleston between 1720 and 1825. Many of these cabinetmakers were trained in London and others availed themselves of style books such as Chippendale's *The Gentleman and Cabinet-Maker's Director*. One of the pieces, the Holmes bookcase is considered by many experts to be the finest piece of American-made furniture known because of its exquisite workmanship. Another prominent carpenter was Thomas Elfe, who produced 1500 pieces in his workshop between 1768 and 1775, according to a surviving account book (now in the Charleston Library Society archives). Elfe's work can be seen in the Heyward-Washington House and includes the fretwork above the drawing room's mantle and a chest-on-chest. Elfe did not sign his work, but he did include a trademark design in the shape of a numeral eight with four diamonds in the center of the eight. The house has been recently restored with documented colors of the period.

This is the oldest house in Charleston open to the public and visitors' appreciation of the past is enhanced by the house's surviving dependencies including the original kitchen building and carriage house. Before the house tour, take time to stroll through the gracious garden and peek in the kitchen at the period utensils and table crockery. A fire was kept burning in the kitchen constantly and it was common for hot coals to tumble out into the room. Kitchen injuries were second only to childbirth as the leading cause of death for women in the 18th century. There is also a laundry area; exhibit signs explain how household chores were done. There is a cellar below the kitchen and servants' quarters above.

The house is open Monday through Saturday from 10:00 A.M. to 5:00 P.M. and Sunday 1:00 to 5:00 P.M. The last tour begins at 4:30 P.M. Admission is charged.

After your tour of this grand establishment, it is interesting to visit **The Thomas Elfe House**, a modest frame house on Queen Street, circa 1760. This street abounded with cabinetmakers and was the home of Thomas Elfe. You can see some of his carpentry touches in the original four finely paneled rooms; each has fireplace walls of cypress paneling. China cabinets and closets are placed in the chimney alcoves. The rooms also have carved cornice moldings. Elfe had two partners and eight slaves who worked in his shop.

The current owners of the Elfe house have filled the rooms with their collection of antique furniture (but none are by Thomas Elfe) and give tours of the dining room and sitting room, as well as the kitchen, which was not part of the original design. Tours are given Monday through Friday at 10:00 and 11:00 A.M. and at NOON. Admission is charged.

Directions: From I-26 take the Meeting Street exit. Turn left on Cumberland Street, right on Church Street, and right on Queen Street. The Heyward-Washington House is at 87 Church Street. The Thomas Elfe House is at 54 Queen Street.

Historic Magnolia Plantation and Its Gardens and Audubon Swamp Garden

Oldest Surviving Garden in the Western Hemisphere

In *Charles Kuralt's America*, the noted late commentator reminds readers that, in 1900, the Baedeker Guide for America named three must-see attractions: the Grand Canyon, Niagara Falls and Magnolia Gardens. Kuralt added that he would put **Magnolia Plantation** first.

Since the mid-1600s, nine generations of Draytons have lived at Magnolia Plantation. The family's roots go back to the

Norman Conquest of England and the family name comes from the Saxon stronghold in Northampton given to Aubrey de Vere by William the Conqueror for his valorous service in the Battle of Hastings. The family assumed the name Drayton in the early 13th century. Family notables include Walter de Drayton, who embarked on the 1190 Crusade to the Holy Land and Michael Drayton, noted English poet and a friend of William Shakespeare, who is buried in London's Westminister Abbey.

Thomas Drayton and his son Thomas Jr. sailed from England to Barbados in the mid-1600s, but by the 1670s they, and other British colonials, were seeking new and less-populated British regions of the Caribbean, Virginia and Massachusetts. A few chose the newly-settled Carolina colony. The Draytons settled in the Charleston area around 1676. Thomas Drayton, Jr. married the daughter of another Barbadian transplant, Stephen Fox, owner of a large tract on the Ashley River. Thomas and Ann Drayton inherited the property that became Magnolia Plantation and built what may have been the colony's first residence of note shortly afterward.

Thomas Drayton, Jr. was buried in the Magnolia Family Tomb, which was used by the family until 1917. Drayton F. Hastie, uncle of the present owner J. Drayton Hastie, was the last to be buried there. Visitors can see the marks of Union bayonets and rifle balls made on the tomb by Federal troops during the Civil War when they burned the second plantation house in 1865. A large crack in the tomb was caused by the 1886 earthquake, which wrecked havoc on Charleston.

The first two houses built at Magnolia did not survive, but the gardens laid out by Ann Fox Drayton did. She called her garden *Flowerdale*, and the original formal portion remains virtually unchanged. By 1717, when her husband died, Ann's garden covered ten acres.

It was one of their sons, John Drayton who, failing to inherit the family home in 1738, bought adjoining acreage and built Drayton Hall (see selection). He subsequently acquired Magnolia Plantation from his nephew, William Drayton, who moved to Florida to assume the position of Royal Chief Justice.

The first house, built in the 1680s, burned in 1811. It was replaced in 1812 by a three-storied second house of brick and cypress. The ground floor of that house survived the fire set by Union troops and is the foundation of the third house, which stands today.

During the Civil War, Magnolia Plantation was owned by Reverend John Grimke Drayton, who suffered great economic losses during the war. In order to rebuild and hold onto Magnolia Plantation, he sold his Sea Island plantation and his Charleston home, then disassembled his Summerville pre-

Revolutionary cottage, floated it down the Ashley River and mounted it on the surviving brick foundation at Magnolia. Subsequently, the present living and dining rooms were added as was a water tower. Since then, only exterior changes have been made, largely by widening the porch, adding the necessary support columns and removing Victorian elements to restore the house to its original Greek Revival appearance. The house is furnished, as you will see on a house tour, with an outstanding collection of Early American furniture. Guided tours are given every half hour.

While the house has retained its formal appearance, the expanded garden was, in the 1840s, converted to an informal landscape design as was the English mode of that day. It is now viewed as one of the world's foremost informal gardens. While Ann Fox Drayton planned the first small formal garden (which still survives), the Civil War owner, John Grimke Drayton, who served as rector of nearby Saint Andrews Church, created the extensive additions. For almost 50 years, the Reverend worked on the plantation gardens, trying, in his words, "to create an earthly paradise..." To achieve this objective, he introduced the first azaleas to America and was among the first to plant Camellia Japonica outdoors. The massive plantings of these early spring blooming bushes makes this a virtual wonderland in April. His great grandson, John Drayton Hastie, extended his planting to achieve year round color, and added many noteworthy and tasteful horticultural attractions, including the creation of a 60-acre Audubon Swamp Garden with miles of nature and wildlife trails.

The gardens opened to the public in 1870, making this the country's oldest man-made tourist attraction. For a time the gardens were open only during the spring, but new plantings have made the gardens a year round delight. Recent additions include an 18th-century herb garden, a 16th-century horticultural maze, a Barbados tropical garden, a Biblical garden and a gallery of wildlife and nature art. The expansive gardens are only part of the estate; the remaining 500 acres remain a wildlife sanctuary with biking and walking trails and canoeing. An observation tower provides an excellent vantage point from which to spot abundant wildlife. A nature train leaves for a 45-minute, four-mile tour of the sanctuary every hour. A naturalist/historian provides details on the estate and its flora and fauna. Young visitors also enjoy the petting zoo and the miniature horses.

Also on the estate grounds, where the plantation's fresh water reservoir for its ricefields was once located, is the **Audubon Swamp Garden**. Boardwalks and dikes lead through this 60-acre habitat with its concentrated population of Lowcountry wildlife.

Its cypress and tupelo swamp is home to great blue herons, wood ducks, snowy egrets, anhingas, turtles and alligators. There have been 224 species of birds sighted within this blackwater swamp. John James Audubon visited the plantation to paint its wildlife inhabitants in the 1840s. Here, too, colorful native plants cast their pastel-hued reflection in the water.

Historic Magnolia Plantation and Its Gardens is open daily year round from 8:00 A.M. until dusk. Admission is charged for Magnolia Plantation. There is an additional charge for the Audubon Swamp Garden and for the house and the nature train tours. You will need most of the day to fully appreciate everything there is to see. However, if you are not able to enjoy all of its experiences in one day, you may return the following day at no charge. Pets on leashes are permitted. After exploring, many visitors agree with Charles Kuralt who proclaimed Magnolia Plantation "my greatest Charleston pleasure."

Directions: From I-26, take Exit 99A to Summerville on Route 17A. Pass through the town and turn left off Route 17A onto Route 165 south, which merges into Route 61. Turn left on Route 61 for seven miles. Magnolia Plantation will be on the left. From downtown Charleston, take Route 17 south to Route 61, Ashley River Road, for ten miles.

Joseph Manigault House

Featured on America's Castles

In 1803, when Joseph Manigault's brother Gabriel designed the elegant Adam-style mansion on the corner lot of Meeting and John streets, Charleston had rebounded from the post-Revolutionary War economic depression. City merchants were again shipping huge cargoes of rice and cotton to the northeast and Europe. Charleston was expanding into newly established neighborhoods. One was created by Manigault's uncle, John Wragg, who established a suburb called Wraggborough on 79 acres. Manigault inherited half of his lot within this suburb and purchased the other half from his sister Anne.

Joseph and Gabriel, sons of Peter Manigault, inherited about 40,000 acres and 500 slaves when their grandfather Gabriel died. Joseph's first wife was Maria Henrietta Middleton, daughter of Declaration of Independence signer Arthur Middleton (see Middleton Place selection). Nearly a decade after her death in 1791, Joseph married Charlotte Drayton, with whom he had eight children, seven boys, and a girl who was "spoiled rotten and run ragged."

He had only been married to Charlotte for two years when his brother, an amateur architect, designed his home (Gabriel is also credited with designing the Charleston branch of the Bank of the United States which is now City Hall, as well as three other city buildings). The Manigault house was the second house built in Wraggborough—and certainly the most elegant. Like Robert Adam, Gabriel incorporated neoclassical elements in his design such as the curving central staircase. The house has high ceilings, generous windows and a two-story porch.

Joseph died in 1843, but the house remained in the Manigault family until 1852 when Joseph's son Gabriel sold it. In 1920, the Society for the Preservation of Old Dwellings, one of the city's first preservation groups, bought the rundown property. They gave teas and lunches and sold off part of the grounds in order to begin restoration efforts. The house was operated as a tenement until 1933 when Henrietta Politzer (the Princess Pignatelli) paid $3,001 in back taxes and donated the house to The Charleston Museum, which opened it to the public in 1949. In 1974, it was recognized as a National Historic Landmark.

The house is furnished with an outstanding collection of American, English and French furniture from the early 19th century, approximately 1790 through 1810. The rooms are painted in the original colors, such as the dining room's gray painted woodwork and aqua walls. Seventy percent of the decorative trim is original. The original Adam-style ceiling frieze features a Greek design. In the hallway is a gentleman's secretary desk that belonged to Joseph Manigault. There is also a platter with the Manigault coat of arms, which reads: "It is better to anticipate than to avenge." A portrait of Joseph, done in the Gilbert Stuart style, hangs in the library.

The Joseph Manigault House at 350 Meeting Street is open Monday through Saturday from 10:00 A.M. to 5:00 P.M. and Sunday 1:00 to 5:00 P.M. Admission is charged. Though the house at one time had dependencies, now only the gate temple survives.

Directions: From I-26 take Route 17 north one block. Make a right on Meeting Street. The Joseph Manigault house is across the street from The Charleston Museum.

Kiawah Island

Semitropical Barrier Island

Few fascinating American cities have a lush beach island just minutes from its hub, but Charleston is so blessed. **Kiawah Island** is 21 miles from the historic city but worlds apart. Named for the Native-American tribe that lived on the island in the 1600s, it still retains its centuries-old maritime forest of tall pines, palmettos, magnolias and live oaks. Within this lush vegetation, visitors are apt to spot abundant wildlife. Kiawah is home to 170 species of birds, 30 varieties of reptiles and amphibians, and 18 different mammals, including white tail deer, raccoon, fox and dolphin. The island has abundant waterways—marshes, lagoons, the Kiawah River and the Atlantic Ocean. More than 18 miles of trails make the island accessible to hikers, joggers and bikers.

The ten miles of secluded beach is one of the island's most appealing features. The Atlantic shoreline has been kept unspoiled. Beachcombers find abundant sea shells on this beach that stretches so far that mile markers are needed along the dunes. Maintaining the natural state ensures that wildlife can continue their customary practices. Sea turtles nest on the island. Coming ashore at night during breeding season, they lay their eggs between mid-May and mid-August; they hatch from mid-July through October. Each turtle lays up to 150 eggs.

The island was purchased in 1974 by a resort developer for $18.2 million from C.C. Royal, who had purchased the land just 23 years earlier for $125,000 from the Vanderhorst family. The Vanderhorsts had maintained it in the family for more than 200 years. Local legend claims that the ghost of Arnoldous Vanderhorst, IV, killed in a hunting accident, can be seen on the island. The earliest island owner was George Raynor who, in 1699, was given the island acreage by the colonial Lords Proprietors. William Penn, Quaker founder of Pennsylvania, wrote in a letter on February 28, 1700: "Carolina is known to be harboring suspected pirates connected with Captain Kidd. They are settled as planters, etc., one, Raynor, their captain, lives in Carolina."

The only resort on the island is **Kiawah Island Resort**, an award-winning property with four renowned golf courses—designed by Jack Nicklaus, Tom Fazio, Gary Player and Pete Dye. Kiawah is the only resort in the country to have three courses included on *Golf Digest*'s list of "America's Top 75 Resort Courses." Dye's Ocean Course was the scene of the 1991 Ryder Cup Matches and the 1997 World Cup of Golf. All 18 holes have dramatic views of the Atlantic, but golfers have to look to their play, not the scenery. *Golf Digest* picked it as "America's Toughest Resort Course." Jack Nicklaus's Turtle Point Course has three holes stretching along the sand dunes that separate the course from the rolling surf. The 1990 PGA Cup Matches were played here. Four large, natural lakes and fingers of marsh form the backdrop to Fazio's Osprey Point Course. The newest layout is Player's Cougar Point along the tidal marsh.

Tennis Magazine considers Kiawah the "3rd Greatest U.S. Tennis Resort" in the country. The first of the resort's two facilities, the West Beach Racquet Club has 14 Har-Tru clay courts, two lighted hard courts and a backboard. The East Racquet Club

Middleton Place was the home of Henry Middleton, President of the First Continental Congress and his son Arthur, a signer of the Declaration of Independence. This is one of the country's oldest formal landscaped gardens with vast and splendid scenic plantings of azaleas and camellias.

has nine Har-Tru clay courts, three hard courts and two lighted courts. Kiawah's tennis program includes free clinics, round robins for all ages and skills, and free pro doubles exhibitions. There are continuing instructional programs and drill sessions.

Within the resort is a 21-acre park, 31 miles of paved bike trails and a wide variety of nature programs for children and adults. Interpretive excursions include canoeing, biking and bird walks. A camp for children has a wide range of activities and the resort has a pool complex with an adults-only pool, family pool, lap lane and a children's wading pool.

Eight restaurants and lounges offer a variety of cuisine in scenic settings. Among the most popular are Jasmine Porch which overlooks the Atlantic and has a Sunday champagne buffet brunch, the Indigo House's Italian and Mediterranean cuisine, the Ocean Course Restaurant and The Osprey Point Clubhouse which overlooks golf courses. Situated by the oceanfront pool is the Sundancer Bar & Grill. The resort has a Monday night Lowcountry Oyster Roast & Barbecue at Mingo Point and a Family Cookout at Night Heron Park on Tuesdays.

There are also a wide range of accommodations; to obtain more information or make reservations call (800) 654-2924.

Directions: From I-26 at Charleston, take Route 17 south. Turn left on Route 171 and right on Route 700. Make a left turn on Main Road and follow the signs to Kiawah Island Resort.

Middleton Place

There is no Middle Ground, This is a Top Spot!

Middleton Place has a history dating back to America's earliest days. In 1741, when Henry Middleton married Mary Williams, he acquired this plantation on the Ashley River. He built two flanking dependencies to the original house and spent ten years landscaping and terracing the grounds.

Middleton was a financially successful planter who owned several plantations and hundreds of slaves. Henry Middleton was elected a delegate to the First Continental Congress in Philadelphia and ultimately became its president. Poor health led to his son Arthur taking his place at the Second Continental Congress. Arthur was more radical than his father. He advocated tarring and feathering those loyal to the British crown and the confiscation of property belonging to those who fled the colonies. Arthur also raised money for armed resistance and led a night raid to seize military arms stored in Charleston before they fell into British hands. Arthur Middleton was a signer of the Declaration of Independence. He served in the militia and, along with fellow signers Thomas Heyward (see Heyward-Washington

House selection) and Edward Rutledge (who was married to Arthur's sister Henrietta), was captured by the British and imprisoned at St. Augustine. Upon his release from his Florida imprisonment, Arthur served the remainder of his term in the Continental Congress, then returned to Middleton Place, which had been badly damaged by the British.

Henry's grandson and namesake continued to live at Middleton Place. He, too, was politically active, serving as state governor and the U.S. Minister to Russia from 1820 to 1830. His son, William Middleton, strongly supported the Southern cause and was a signer of the Ordinance of Secession. Just as in the earlier conflict, the estate was harshly dealt with when the Union forces of the 56th New York Volunteers arrived at Middleton Place in February 1865. After helping themselves to the plantation's bounty, they burned the main house and the north flanker to the ground. The south flanker was also damaged but not as severely. This loss was compounded by an earthquake in 1886 that leveled the fragile ruins of the main house and north flanker. The repaired and renovated south flanker became the family home. It had previously been the plantation office and a guest house for visiting gentlemen, who had to spend the night if they came by water because the Ashley was a tidal river.

In 1916, a member of the Middleton family, J.J. Pringle Smith and his wife, began to restore the south flanker and decorate it to reflect the illustrious family history. Portraits of the first four generations grace the walls. The rooms contain treasures collected by Henry Middleton, II while he served in St. Petersburg, including a portrait of Tsar Nicholas I and an oil painting *The Picture Gallery at the Winter Palace*. Another interesting piece from Henry's stay in Russia is a fete book that was given to his daughter Maria. The book is 52.5 feet long and illustrates the funeral procession of Tsar Alexander I. Ninety percent of the furnishings belonged to the Middleton family as do the silver and art objects. Both a winter and summer bedroom reveal the seasonality of life on an antebellum rice plantation.

Another aspect of life at Middleton Place is revealed in the outdoor museum of the **Plantation Stableyards** where a blacksmith, potter, carpenter or weaver demonstrate the work of the plantation's extended community. Agricultural displays and farm animals complete the picture.

The Smiths also undertook the formidable task of restoring and enhancing the **Gardens of Middleton Place**. This garden, begun in 1741, was the earliest landscaped garden in America. The garden restoration received the Garden Club of America's highest award "in commemoration of 200 years of enduring beauty." When Henry Middleton envisioned his garden, he conceived it on a grand scale employing the ideas of Andre le Nôtre, who designed Versailles. Incorporated into the design is a long central path and greensward providing an unobstructed view across the Ashley River into the woods on the opposite shore.

The gardens extend from the river to the house since most 18th-century guests arrived from Charleston by boat. This manicured look is more suggestive of an English country manor house than a southern plantation. Looking down the rippling terraces to the river, you can see the lovely butterfly wing lakes with a grassy bridge forming the body. To the left, but not obstructing the clear lines of the terraces, is the formal garden.

The formal garden also uses water effectively, as the western garden border is a reflection pool. True to 18th-century custom, swans grace the pool, adding a further picturesque note to the scene. Near the pool is a camellia allee, with bushes so thick that they become flower-strewn tunnels during the early spring blooming season. The first bushes were planted under the supervision of the third generation Henry Middleton. Also dating back to the gardens' early days are the giant crape myrtles directly in front of the pool. The formal garden includes a sunken octagonal garden, the geometric sundial garden and the secret garden where the Middleton family played games.

In the mid-19th century an informal azalea pool garden was added. Narrow paths wind through azalea banks. The low hills surrounding the rice-mill pond are also planted with azaleas and the springtime vista is striking. Another relatively new area is the cypress lake which forms a barrier between the garden and the marshy terrain beyond. The lake has numerous southern bald cypress with spiky cone-like protrusions called knees.

The symbol of Middleton Place is the *Wood Nymph* statue, the only garden statue to survive Civil War destruction. It was buried in 1865 before Union troops arrived. The grounds also contain the family tomb where some members of the family are buried.

Middleton Place, a National Historic Landmark, is open daily 9:00 A.M. to 5:00 P.M. Admission is charged for a self-guided tour of the gardens and stableyards. There is an additional charge for a guided tour of the house. You should allow two hours to see the entire estate. There is a restaurant and a museum shop with an extensive collection of hand-crafted items..

Directions: From I-26 take I-526 west to the Ashley River Road exit, Route 61. Follow Route 61 north to Middleton Place. The plantation will be on your right.

Nathaniel-Russell House

One of America's Most Important Neoclassical Houses

In 1808, Nathaniel and Sarah Russell had an elegant townhouse built on Charleston's Meeting Street. In 1857, Henry Deas Lesesne, a cousin of the second owner claimed it was, "...beyond all comparison, the finest establishment in Charleston."

Russell, an agent for Northern merchants, arrived in Charleston in 1765. His burgeoning career as a merchant became even more prosperous when in 1788, at age 50, he married Sarah Hopton, the daughter of the immensely wealthy Charleston merchant William Hopton. The couple actively involved themselves in the city's philanthropic and cultural activities. Mrs. Russell provided financial assistance to establish St. Stephen's Church at 67 Anson Street, one of the first churches for the poor. Nathaniel Russell, founded and was the first president of Charleston's New England Society, a still-thriving fraternal and philanthropic organization.

The Russells' Federal "Adam-style" townhouse which, by legend, cost approximately $80,000 to build, has an ornately embellished interior with a striking free-flying mahogany staircase that spirals from floor to floor, geometrically shaped rooms, elaborate plasterwork ornamentation and enormous mirrored panels flanking the drawing room door. Visitors entered through an impressive doorway with oval glass panels in a rose medallion design. Above the door is an attractive fanlight. The glass allows more light in the entranceway than the traditional wood paneled door. The house is now filled with period antiques, all dating to before 1820, the year that Nathaniel Russell died. Works of art evoke the life style of this prosperous couple.

House tours also reveal details about the 18 African Americans who worked in this urban setting. Russell, like many transplanted New England merchants, was active in the slave trade, importing several cargoes after the revolution. The slave quarters were over the stable behind the house.

The Russells had two daughters, Alicia and Sarah. Both girls were enormously accomplished and dedicated to philanthropic causes in the city. They were educated in Medford, Massachusetts at Mrs. Newton's School, operated by the sister of artist Gilbert Stuart. Reports of the era refer to the Russell girls as "great belles" and both married. There is a miniature of the oldest daughter, Alicia, who married Arthur Middleton in 1809, that reveals a charming lady with sparkling eyes.

The Nathaniel Russell House is open Monday through Saturday 10:00 A.M. to 5:00 P.M.; on Sunday it doesn't open until 2:00 P.M. It is closed on Thanksgiving, Christmas Eve and Christmas Day. Admission is charged.

Directions: From I-26 take Meeting Street into Charleston; the Nathaniel Russell House is at 51 Meeting Street.

Patriots Point Naval and Maritime Museum

Immense Aircraft Carrier Showcases Naval History

Patriots Point Naval and Maritime Museum reveals the enormity of the country's naval power and tradition through an extensive array of tour options. There are seven self-guided tours aboard the *Yorktown* plus tours of a submarine, destroyer and Coast Guard cutter. You can begin in the morning, get your hand stamped, tour awhile, leave for lunch, then return for the afternoon. Boats for historic Fort Sumter (see selection) also leave from Patriots Point, so this is another way to extend your day.

It is absolutely fascinating to be aboard an aircraft carrier. As immense as they appear from a distance—it's actually 888 feet long—they are even more overwhelming once you step inside. Also slightly overwhelming are all the tour options. Probably the most popular and the one to choose if you are on a tight schedule is the **flight deck and bridge tour**. Like all the options, this involves climbing up and down ladders with low overheads. On the galley deck, you will have a chance to see the pilots' ready room, then go up to the flight deck—a carrier's seagoing airport. Here, and on the hangar deck, are some of the more than 25 vintage planes that make up the museum's collection including prop-driven fighters, bombers and torpedo planes. The B-25 Mitchell dates back to World War II and is similar to the one flown by Lieutenant Colonel James H. Doolittle in his famous "60 Seconds Over Tokyo" raid. The *SBD Dauntless* was the Navy's most successful dive bomber, credited with sinking all four Japanese aircraft carriers at Midway. (The first *Yorktown* was sunk in 1942 by the Japanese at the Battle of Midway.) Also exhibited is a TBM Avenger, a highly successful WWII torpedo plane, the F6F Hellcat carrier-based fighter which had a 19-to-1 kill ratio; and the F4U Corsair fighter/interceptor which had an 11-to-1 kill ratio. Moving to more recent times, you'll see the UH-34D Seahorse, a Cold War carrier anti-submarine helicopter, and the A7 Corsair, a light attack aircraft used during Vietnam and the Persian Gulf conflict. Movie buffs will recognize the F-14 Tomcat from *Top Gun*.

Standing on the flight deck, you can imagine the combat planes roaring off into the sky and returning to the deck to be hooked by the cable bringing their mission to an abrupt halt. The tour then leads you up to the *Yorktown*'s bridge, giving you a command perspective. Here you'll see the captain's quarters, the chart room and the pilot house. Standing on the signal bridge, you'll have a splendid view of Charleston's harbor.

Another tour option is the **living and working space tour** that

Patriots Point has four ships for visitors to explore but the most impressive and most popular is the aircraft carrier Yorktown, which is the length of three football fields. Numerous tour options aboard this craft give visitors a glimpse of what life was like for the 3,000 crewmen.

includes enlisted men berthing (the *Yorktown* had approximately 3,500 men on board) and the crew's washroom, galley, mess and sick bay. You'll see the mess and galley for the chief petty officers as well. An aircraft carrier was a floating mini-city as you'll see from peeking into the shops, medical centers and repair facilities. As you make your way through the ship, you will also see exhibits (this is true on all the tour options). On this tour they include women in the military, maritime legends, WWII escort carriers, details about the Imperial Japanese Navy and a tribute to the aircraft carrier *USS Franklin*.

The **engine room tour** takes you down four decks. Old sea hands can often be found down at this level comparing notes. A fourth tour highlights the **Korean War Room, Saratoga Room and Enterprise Room**. The *Enterprise* was the most decorated ship of World War II. This tour also includes the air officers' and executive officers' state rooms. In all there were 380 officers aboard the *Yorktown*. You'll also see the ship's laundry and the tailor's shop. There are exhibits on other carriers, African Americans in the military, naval battles during World War II and the Korean conflict. Tour five is the **bomb fusing and rocket assembly area**, plus the *Yorktown* wardroom. Young children enjoy this as it also includes the ship's brig. Other points of interest include the officers' galley, an officer's stateroom and the ship's print shop.

Highlights of the sixth option are the **captain and flag officers' in-port quarters**. Although these accommodations are certainly better than those for enlisted men in terms of space and privacy, they are not much of an improvement in terms of comfort and decor. The final option is the **Charleston Naval Shipyard Exhibit** where you will learn the history of the shipyard.

All tours depart from the hangar deck where part of the aircraft collection is exhibited. You'll get more out of your tour of the *Yorktown* if you begin your visit by watching the 1944 Academy-Award-winning documentary, *The Fighting Lady*. From 1943 to 1945, the *Yorktown* earned 11 battle stars and the movie contains some exciting WWII 'dogfighting' aerial footage. The movie about this aircraft carrier is shown daily at 10:00 A.M., NOON, 2:00 and 4:00 P.M. The movie was made more than two decades before a later chapter in the carrier's history: in 1968 it was used to recover the astronauts from Apollo 8 after ocean splash-down. The ship was retired in 1970 and brought to Patriots Point in 1975.

Before leaving the hangar deck, be sure to stop at the **Congressional Medal of Honor Museum** where all 3,400 recipients of the award are commemorated. Many of the names are instantly recognizable such as Alvin York, Audie Murphy and

James Doolittle. Elsewhere on the hangar deck, combat enlisted men and aircrew who lost their life in World War II and subsequent conflicts through the Persian Gulf are memorialized on bronze plaques. This is the only museum that offers a tangible reminder of all who sacrificed their lives fighting for their country.

There is still much more to see before leaving Patriots Point. Moored along the dock with the 40,000-ton *Yorktown* are three other fascinating vessels. A movie could be made about the destroyer *Laffey*. During a one-hour attack off Okinawa on April 16, 1945, the *Laffey* survived five Japanese suicide planes that dove onto its decks, and three bombs. The Japanese lost 11 planes to the ship's gunners, while almost a third of the *Laffey*'s 336-man crew were killed or wounded. The *Laffey* was commissioned in February 1944, and played a role in the D-Day landings at Normandy before being transferred to the Pacific fleet. When you walk through "the ship that would not die," you can reflect on the tumultuous engagements in which it fought. On board you will find the **World War II Destroyer Memorial Exhibit** and the **Destroyer Escort Sailors Association Museum**.

Near the end of World War II, the diesel submarine *Clamagore* (named for a fish as so many submarines were) was commissioned. It prowled the Atlantic for three decades and was involved in the Cuban missile crisis in 1962 before coming to its final berth at Patriots Point. Some visitors may even find a short visit aboard the *Clamagore* claustrophobic, as they duck their heads to avoid the overhead and move through the narrow passageways. It is hard to imagine 72 men and eight officers sharing the cramped quarters on this 325-foot vessel. No book or movie adequately conveys the entombed feeling you'll get as you explore the submarine. You'll leave with new respect for those who sailed in such restrictive conditions.

The third vessel in the Patriots Point fleet is the Coast Guard cutter *Ingham*. Distinguished service during World War II, including the sinking of U-626, was followed by three tours of duty in Vietnam. The *Ingham* earned a Presidential Unit Citation for its Vietnam duty.

The complex also includes a replica of a Vietnam river support base with an observation tower, ammo bunker, two Huey helicopters, jeeps and support huts filled with artifacts. There is a 31-foot patrol boat moored near the exhibit. The Navy's role in supporting the ground troops is highlighted in this new true-scale exhibit.

Patriots Point also has a flight simulator where, for a nominal fee, visitors can experience five minutes of the Navy's air war over Iraq during the Persian Gulf War. It feels as if you are looking through the windshield of an F/A-18 Hornet fighter as it flies off the flightdeck on the aircraft carrier *Carl Vinson*. You'll feel the plane as it banks at a 90-degree turn, fights a MIG and gets hit by a missile. It then makes an emergency landing back on the carrier. The program was written by aviators who served in Desert Storm and it packs a real wallop.

Patriots Point Naval and Maritime Museum, one of only four multi-ship naval museums in the country, is open daily from 9:00 A.M. to 5:00 P.M. during the winter and fall and until 6:00 P.M. in the spring and summer. Admission is charged; call (803) 884-2727 for current rates. Good places to eat in the Mt. Pleasant area include The Wreck, Slightly North of the Creek, Shem Creek Bar & Grill and Captain Guilds Cafe.

Directions: From I-26 take Route 17 north to Mount Pleasant. You will see the sign for Patriots Point on your right at Patriots Point Road.

Powder Magazine, Old Exchange Building and Provost Dungeon

Pirates, Patriots and Presidents

There is only one public building still standing in the Carolinas that dates back to the time when Lord Proprietors owned and ruled the colony. The **Powder Magazine** was built in the late 1600s as part of Charles Towne's defenses. Walls were built around the city and forts protected the harbor. Spanish naval ships from St. Augustine made frequent forays against the city. To arm Charles Towne's militia, this powder magazine was built under the direction of Sir Nathaniel Johnson, a former colonel in the British army and ex-Governor of the Leeward Islands. Johnson was knowledgeable on British, continental European and Caribbean military fortifications. This powder magazine was replaced by a new facility prior to the American Revolution in 1748.

After 1820, the Powder Magazine and its downtown lot on Cumberland Street reverted to descendants of the families who had owned the land before 1703, the Izard and Manigaults. Over the years, the structure was used as a printing house, storage building and livery stable. In 1899, the Colonial Dames acquired and restored the historic structure. A restoration completed in 1997 takes it back to its mid-19th century appearance. The Historic Charleston Foundation has opened it to the public, Monday through Saturday from 10:00 A.M. to 5:00 P.M. and Sunday from 2:00 to 5:00 P.M.

The oldest portion of the Old Exchange Building is found in

the **Provost Dungeon**, where beneath this venerable old building's floor you will see part of the fortified wall built around Charles Towne between 1680 and 1718 (between 1715 and 1783 the town name dropped the "e"). This was the only British-walled city in North America, necessitated because of frequent attacks not only by the Spanish but by pirates, Native Americans and even wild animals. At one point, the pirate Blackbeard and his men blockaded Charleston's harbor and seized Samuel Wragg, a member of the Governor's Council, and his son for a ransom of medical supplies.

Projecting from the seawall, excavation uncovered the Half-Moon Battery, a semicircular fortification. Behind the fortification stood the Provost Dungeon. It was in this dungeon that Stede Bonnet and his pirate crew were incarcerated after their capture by Colonial William Rhett. The pirates were hung at White Point Gardens (see Aiken-Rhett House selection).

In 1767, in preparation for construction of the Exchange Building, the top of the seawall was lowered and the Court of Guard that stood several feet from the Provost Dungeon was demolished. What you see today is a representation of the dungeon that was once located here. Its construction is interesting as the vaulted ceiling employs the groin arch principle of architecture. Two simple arches cross at right angles, then the arches join the semi-supporting column. The center of the arch is one brick thick. Over these arches is six to eight inches of sand upon which builders laid the stones for the Exchange's first floor.

Fascinating to young visitors are the mannequins that represent specific American patriots imprisoned in the Provost during the British occupation of Charles Town from 1780 to 1782. Three signers of the Declaration of Independence were held in this dungeon: Arthur Middleton, Edward Rutledge and Thomas Heyward, Jr. These and other leading patriots were held in cramped confinement along with common criminals. From his confinement, Captain Richard Ellis with the First Regiment of South Carolina, wrote to the British Commandant of Charles Towne complaining about the horrific conditions and the number of criminals tightly confined. Christopher Gadsden, a member of Charles Town's patriotic organization, the Sons of Liberty, was also imprisoned here. Gadsden designed the snake flag with the inscription "Don't Tread on Me." Jonathan Sarrazin, a patriot spy, was imprisoned along with his sisters. In order to be released, patriots had to sign an oath of loyalty to the King.

The Powder Magazine was not the only place munitions were held; a corner of the dungeon had 10,000 pounds of gunpowder. You will see a replica of the secret room that General William Moultrie created when he realized the British were going to take Charles Town. He bricked the northeast corner of the dungeon, creating a secret room where he hid gunpowder. During their two-and-a-half year occupation, the British never discovered the room.

After the seawall and the existing buildings were leveled, construction began in 1767 on a large Palladian-style exchange and customs house to regulate Charles Town's thriving shipping industry. The **Exchange Building** was completed in 1771 with the first floor being an open arcade trading floor and the second floor, city and customs offices. Also on the second story was the Great Hall, an elegant assembly room. The lower level cellars were storage areas.

Originally the front and back were reversed, and the front overlooked the water, although now the harbor is two blocks removed. The Exchange soon became the social, political and economic hub of the city. Every merchant ship coming into port—and sometimes there were as many as 300 ships at this busy 18th-century port—had to send a representative to pay duties at the Customs House. Rice and indigo were the city's major exports.

Today when you visit there are two rooms on the first floor you should see. The Rebecca Motte Room is the meeting room for the building's owners, the Daughters of the American Revolution. When the local chapter began meeting here in 1921, they each contributed their own chairs. Be sure to notice the mirrors from the palace of Queen Wilhelmina of the Netherlands. Across the floor is the South Carolina State Society NSDAR Room (National Society of Daughters of the American Revolution), which displays artifacts and paintings from the state's colonial era.

After the Revolution, on August 13, 1783 the city became incorporated as Charleston and this building housed City Hall. In 1818, the Federal government purchased the building and used it as a post office until 1896. It was during this period that the first floor rooms were created in the former open arcade space. When the Federal government decided to sell the building in 1912, there was some talk of using the location for a gas station. It was at this point that the DAR became involved; their efforts resulted in the building being preserved as a historic site.

The Great Hall encompasses most of the second floor. Citizens met here in 1773 to protest the Tea Act; this led to the Exchange being called "The Independence Hall of South Carolina." The citizens of Boston dumped tea into the harbor; Charles Town residents seized tea and stored it in the Exchange Building's cellar. The tea was eventually sold to pay for patriot supplies. In 1774, delegates to the Continental Congress were elected during a meeting in the Great Hall. It was from the Exchange's steps that South Carolina declared its independence from England on March 28, 1776.

On May 23, 1788, South Carolinians met in the Great Hall and voted 149 to 73 to ratify the United States Constitution. During President George Washington's week-long visit to Charleston in 1791, two banquets, a concert and a ball were held in his honor in the Great Hall. Using William Rigby Naylor's original 1767 blueprints, the Great Hall was restored in 1981 to its original appearance.

The Old Exchange Building and Provost Dungeon is open daily from 9:00 A.M. to 5:00 P.M. There is an admission charge. It is closed on major holidays.

Directions: From I-26 take Route 17 north and make a right turn on East Bay Street. For the Powder Magazine turn right on Cumberland Street; the magazine is at 79 Cumberland Street. The Old Exchange Building is at 122 East Bay Street.

Historic Charleston Regional Tourism Contacts
(Area Code 803, September 1998 changes to 843)

CHARLESTON AREA CONVENTION AND VISITORS BUREAU
81 Mary Street, P.O. Box 975
Charleston, SC 29402
853-8000, (800) 868-8118,
fax: 853-0444. Website: http://www.charlestoncvb.com

MT. PLEASANT/ISLE OF PALMS VISITOR CENTER
Highway 17N & McGrath Darby Blvd.
Mt. Pleasant, SC 29464

NORTH CHARLESTON VISITOR CENTER
307 Firestone Road
N. Charleston, SC 29418

CHARLESTON VISITOR RECEPTION & TRANSPORTATION CENTER
375 Meeting Street
P.O. Box 975
Charleston, SC 29402

EDISTO CHAMBER OF COMMERCE
P.O. Box 206
Edisto Beach, SC 29438
869-3867

GREATER SUMMERVILLE/DORCHESTER COUNTY CHAMBER OF
COMMERCE
P.O. Drawer 670
106 E. Doty Avenue
Summerville, SC 29484
873-2931

Historic Charleston Calendar of Events
(Area Code 803, September 1998 changes to 843)

Mid-January
Lowcountry Oyster Festival. Steamed oysters, shucking contest, live music and children's events highlight this annual happening. Charleston, 577-4030.

Late January/Early February
Camellia Walks. Guided walks reveal the beautiful flowering camellias at Middleton Garden. Charleston, 556-6020.

Mid-February
Southeastern Wildlife Exposition. Wildlife art on display at locations throughout city. Charleston, 723-1748.

Late March/Mid-April
Festival of Houses and Gardens. The homes of one of America's historic port city are open to the public during an annual event that has taken place for more than a half a century. Charleston, 723-1623.

Early April
Flowertown Festival. A parade, arts and crafts, regional cuisine and a tennis tournament showcase the community. Summerville, 871-9622.

Mid-April
Lowcountry Cajun Festival. Cajun, Creole and Lowcountry food and music highlight this event at James Island County Park. Charleston, 762-2172

Annual Spring Candlelight Concert. For centuries piano concerts have been given in Drayton Hall's Great Hall. Charleston, 766-0188.

Sheep-to-Shawl Demonstrations. A spring ritual will be demonstrated by members of the Spinners Guild at Middleton Place. Charleston, 556-6020.

Late May/Early June
Spoleto Festival, U.S.A.. America's counterpart to the international festival in Italy showcases renowned performers in drama, dance, music and art. Charleston, 722-2764.

Piccolo Spoleto. As a companion to the Spoleto events, regional artists from the Southeast take part in showcasing their talent. Charleston, 724-7305.

Late August
Labor Day Laser Light Show. The end of summer is celebrated at James Island County Park with a laser light show choreographed to music. Charleston, 762-2172.

Mid-September
Scottish Games and Highland Gathering. The clans gather and participate in medieval games, bagpipe performances and dancing. Charleston, 554-5871.

Late September
Rhythms Along the Ashley River. Middleton Place hosts an afternoon of dance, music and song highlighting the traditions of African-Americans from Antebellum days to the present. Charleston, 556-6020.

Charleston Bluegrass Jubilee. Gospel, old-time country and bluegrass music are part of a celebration that includes children's games and plenty of food. Charleston, 762-2171.

Late September/Early October
Moja Arts Festival. African and Caribbean influence on Charleston is

celebrated through dance, music, visual arts and lectures. Charleston, 724-7305.

Late September/Late October

Fall Candlelight Tour of Homes and Gardens. The historic homes and gracious private gardens of Charleston are open to the public during an annual event that has taken place for more than 20 years. Charleston, 722-4630.

Mid-October

Golden Age Tour. Self-guided tour of Edisto Island's historic properties. Edisto Island, 869-1954.

Taste of Charleston. A substantial number of Charleston's fine restaurants offer a taste of their signature cuisine. Charleston, 577-4030.

Children's Day Festival. A day for kids to enjoy themselves with puppet show, pony rides, face painting, games, food, entertainment and a parade of characters. Mt. Pleasant, 884-2528

Early November

The Great Charleston Chili Cook-Off. Enter your favorite chili recipe, sample a variety of chili dishes and enjoy live country music. Charleston, 762-2172.

Plantation Days. At Middleton Place you can watch 18th and 19th-century crafts such as cider and syrup making, candle dipping wool dyeing, spinning and weaving and basketmaking demonstrated as the sights and sounds of harvest time are brought to life. Charleston, 556-6020.

Battle of Secessionville Reenactment. Boone Hall Plantation is the site of a Confederate and Union army encampment, military drills, horse brigade drills and a church service. Mt. Pleasant, 799-8000.

Early November/Early January

Holiday Festival of Lights. James Island County Park sparkles with more than 300,000 lights to celebrate the holidays. Charleston, 762-2172.

Early December

Christmas Boat Parade. More than 50 boats traditionally take part in this nautical holiday celebration in Charleston Harbor that concludes with a fireworks display. Charleston, 762-2172.

Christmas Made in the South. More than 300 artists and craftsman display their wares in this juried show. Charleston, 847-9480.

Holiday Parade. Floats and bands from local schools and civic groups highlight this event. Mt. Pleasant, 884-2528.

Holiday House Tour. Private homes are decorated for the holidays and open to the public. Charleston, 722-2706.

Mid-December

Annual Spirituals Concert. African-American spirituals sung by the Senior Lights of Johns Island at this yearly event. Charleston, 766-0188.

Christmas in Mazyck Wraggborough. A musical tour of historic homes and churches. Charleston, 723-3135.

Family Yuletide. Middleton Place showcases the plantation's holiday preparations with wreathmaking, a live nativity and caroling. Charleston, 556-6020.

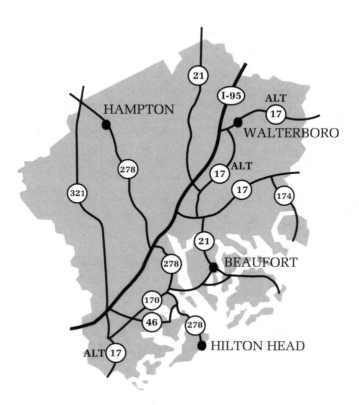

Lowcountry & Resort Areas

Lowcountry
══ & Resort Islands ══

Black water and ocean tides sweep the shores of the Lowcountry and its Resort Islands. It is not uncommon for visitors to come for a vacation and look for a home. There is much that is deeply satisfying about the region, from the friendly residents to the scenic beauty. Hunting, fishing, canoeing, kayaking, swimming, hiking and biking draw those seeking outdoor recreation. Wildlife abounds at Savannah National Wildlife Refuge, the ACE Basin's Wildlife Management Areas (the acronym is derived from the Ashepoo, Combahee and Edisto rivers) and the region's five state parks. The Gullah tradition derived from the rich contributions of African Americans and the Marine Corps' time-honored traditions at Parris Island appeal to those interested in history. Local color is found in the museums of Walterboro, Colleton and Hampton. Although you may unlock the past, you'll find it impossible to unlock the old bank safe in the Hampton Museum—no one has succeeded in the past 50 years.

Visitors to the Lowcountry need to be aware of certain regional peculiarities that could, if overlooked, interfere with a successful outing. First of all, it is unwise to pull off onto the sandy berm along the side of some Sea Island roads. In many cases, the berm is not hard-packed and vehicles may sink up to their hubcaps. Secondly, some of the rivers of the ACE Basin and the placid water at Lake Warren State Park have alligators, so it is wise to heed the "no swimming" signs in areas so marked. Thirdly, while enjoying the beaches and water be sure to use a strong sun screen, even for those who are frequently in the sun. Finally, be alert to tidal changes. Many boaters and even beachgoers along these resort islands are caught unaware by the dramatic fluctuation between high and low tides, which can be a difference of up to nine feet.

You can take a little of the region home with you if you stop at the South Carolina Artisans Center in Walterboro. The state's finest artists and artisans are showcased in this fascinating center. You'll also find skilled artisans selling their sweetgrass baskets when you visit St. Helena's. Writers and movie makers have also flocked to the Lowcountry and even first-time visitors are apt to recognize locations used in such popular films as *Forrest Gump*, *The Big Chill*, *Prince of Tides* and others.

ACE Basin and
Old Sheldon Church Ruins

Atlantic Coast's Significant Wetland Ecosystem

In 1990, the **ACE Basin National Wildlife Refuge** was established to protect wildlife and their habitats along the Ashepoo, Combahee and South Edisto river basin (the name is an acronym formed by the river's names). This cooperative effort of government and private conservation agencies has established two refuges: one along the Edisto River and the other on the Combahee River. Total acreage is 11,019, but it will likely reach 18,000; the Basin itself consists of 350,000 acres.

This river side acreage has not always been undeveloped. From the early 1700s to mid-1800s, large plantations grew Carolina Gold, considered the best rice in the world. As related in *The Historical Atlas of the Rice Plantations of the ACE Basin*, "They harnessed the moon and turned the marshes into fields of gold." For more than a century the wetlands yielded wealth; then came an era when sportsmen purchased the plantations as hunting retreats. None of this activity, however, adversely affected the diverse habitats of the wetlands region.

The refuge headquarters in the Edisto section is in an 1828 former rice plantation house, which is on the National Register of Historic Places. It is one of only three surviving antebellum mansions in the ACE Basin. The refuge manages habitats for a wide variety of wildlife including endangered species such as the American alligator, bald eagle, wood stork, loggerhead sea turtle, shortnosed sturgeon, pitcher plant and others. The refuge is used by wintering waterfowl as well as migratory and resident birds, mammals, reptiles, amphibians and plants. The former rice fields are now impoundments providing food needed by the various wildlife species. Over 40% of the refuge is tidal marsh with small islands called hummocks. Tidal marshes provide a rich variety of food. When the tide recedes you might glimpse a raccoon, otter or mink and you will certainly see a wide variety of water birds including herons, egrets, ibises and sandpipers.

The refuges are open to the public sunup to sundown year round. You can access the area by car or by boat. Fishing is a popular recreational pursuit and there is a limited hunting season. Many choose to take shots with a camera as wildlife photography is a big draw at the refuges.

The two sections of the refuge are just part of the public lands within the ACE Basin. You can also enjoy the wetlands environment at Bear Island, Donnelley and Victoria Bluff Wildlife Management Areas. **Bear Island WMA** is a 12-acre habitat for waterfowl with 4,419 acres of impounded marshland. It is located between the Asheppo and South Edisto rivers, two miles east of Green Pond off Route 17. From mid-January through October the habitat is open to the public for bird watching and photography. The remainder of the year, only the paved roads are open. In September and October one of the prettiest drives in the Lowcountry is along Bennett's Point Road through Bear Island WMA—the foliage is striking and the road ends at the public boat

The crumbling walls of the 1753 Sheldon Church are an evocative sight. The church was burned by the British in 1779 and again by Sherman's army in 1865. The church was named for the ancestral home of the Bull family whose graves still rest beside the ruins.

landing. If you are walking along the impoundments or dike roads, be alert for snakes and sunning alligators. In the warmer months be sure to liberally apply mosquito repellent. Hunting is permitted within the habitat at designated times with the appropriate license. Fishing is permitted from April through October and the blue crab is a popular and tasty catch. For additional information call (803) 844-8957. The habitat is open 8:00 A.M. to 5:00 P.M. Monday through Saturday, and is closed on Sunday.

Also near Green Pond on another former rice plantation is **Donnelley WMA** near the junction of Route 17 and Route 303. On 8,048 acres you will find a variety of habitats: forested wetland, tidal marsh, managed rice-field impoundments and an upland forest area. Visitors are requested to check in at the office. The hours and activities are the same as at Bear Island. The third habitat is **Victoria Bluff Heritage Preserve WMA** near Bluffton on Route 278. Of the habitat's 1,255 acres, roughly 800 acres are managed for deer and small game hunting. There are some striking views of the Colleton River from the bluff.

As you drive the Lowcountry between these hauntingly beautiful habitats, there is one man-made site that is equally haunting—the **Old Sheldon Church Ruins**. The crumbling walls and columns of this 1753 church seem to be part of the natural environment. It is a favorite spot for photographers. The church was burned twice, once by the British in 1779, and then the rebuilt church suffered the same fate at the hands of Sherman's men in 1865. The church was named for the ancestral home of the Bull family who emigrated from Warwickshire, England. Bull family grave sites still rest beside the ruins. William Bull was the lieutenant governor of South Carolina from 1737 to 1744. Memorial services are held each year at the ruins on the second Sunday after Easter.

Directions: From I-95 take Exit 33, Route 17 north to Route 35 and head toward Yemassee for the Combahee Unit of the ACE Basin refuge. For the Edisto Unit, continue on Route 17 north. Just past Adam's Run on Route 174, turn right on Route 55 and left on Route 346 to head into the refuge. The Old Sheldon Church Ruins are 1½ miles off Route 17 on Route 21 near Gardens Corner.

Beaufort

Beautiful Beaufort by the Bay

You pronounce **Beaufort** like beautiful—BYEW-fert. Just be sure you don't say Bow-fert which is how you pronounce the similarly named waterside town in North Carolina. Historic Beaufort Foundation, which has its office in the John Mark Verdier House (see selection), has a small booklet outlining two driving tours of the town. One covers Beaufort's sites in the main town area and the other the point area. It's amazing to learn that Port Royal Sound was named in 1520 before William Shakespeare was born and before the Spanish Armada sailed. Less than 30 years after Columbus discovered the New World, Spanish explorer Captain Francisco Gordillo sailed close enough to the sound to note and name it on his maps. Nine years later the Spanish established a settlement they called Santa Elena (see Parris Island selection).

The first Englishman to arrive was William Hilton in 1663. By the early 1700s planters and traders were established at Port Royal, the thriving seaport at Port Royal Sound's natural harbor. The settlement that became Beaufort got its start in 1710 when English planters from Barbados arrived with their servants. Also settling here were religious dissenters, Huguenots who were followers of Jean Ribaut and traders.

Houses in Beaufort were built of tabby (a mixture of oyster shells, clay and lime) and clapboard. With prosperity the houses grew larger, with the peak building period between 1820 and 1860. What emerged was the Beaufort style, which blended elements of Georgian, Greek Revival and semi-tropical Spanish. The free-standing houses were built on raised foundations and were positioned to take advantage of the southwesterly breeze. Most Beaufort homes have a two-story piazza. On some, it extends part way around the sides of the house; on others, as is the case with the John Mark Verdier House, the portico is positioned above the front entrance. Stylistic touches include low-pitched roofs and Palladian windows. By the early 1800s, there were scores of elaborate summer homes built by plantation owners who couldn't take the heat of their Lowcountry, Sea Island acreage. For a time Beaufort was called "the Newport of the South." Beaufort's homes survived the Civil War because the town was occupied by Union troops from 1861 until the end of the war and the officers commandeered the houses as their headquarters.

Today much of Beaufort is part of a National Historic Landmark District best seen on foot. You can pick up an historic district tour map at the Chamber of Commerce Visitor Center in Waterfront Park at 1006 Bay Street. It's important to keep in mind that most of the houses marked on the maps are privately owned and are not open for tours. Photographers should respect the property boundaries when angling for the perfect shot.

One house that always appeals to camera buffs is **The Castle**, an Italian Renaissance estate built in 1859, and also known as the Joseph Johnson House. A former director of the National Trust calls it "One of the great houses of the South Carolina coast." He goes on to extoll the "extraordinary grandeur of the almost medieval house...its air of somber mystery, set in great oaks at the water's edge." The branches of one massive live oak seem to reach into the very heart of the house.

It's not just amateur photographers who have flocked to the azalea-bedecked, pillared antebellum mansions; Hollywood has also traveled to Beaufort. The Edgar Fripp House, called **Tidalholm**, was used in *The Great Santini* and *The Big Chill*. Tidalholm, built in 1856 in an Italianate style, was by the time of the Civil War owned by Edgar's brother James. He arrived back from the war in time to see his house sold at auction for back taxes. Local lore claims it was purchased by a Frenchman sympathetic to the Southern cause, who gave James Fripp the deed and sailed back to France. The house served as a guest house from the 1930s to the 1970s, but it is again a private residence. The Lewis Reeve Sams House, now the **Bay Street Inn**, was used in *Prince of Tides* (whose author Pat Conroy lives on one of the Sea Islands in the Lowcountry) and in *Forrest Gump*. The Bay Street Inn at 601 Bay Street, (803) 522-0050, accommodates guests in a much more gracious manner than did the Union hospital that operated out of this house during the Civil War.

Other homes of note are the 1717 Thomas Hepworth House, Beaufort's oldest house; Riverview, the Elizabeth Hext House built in 1720 and the town's second oldest; and the Thomas Rhett House, circa 1820 with two-story wrap around piazzas— it's now the **Rhett House Inn**. This picturesque inn, 1009 Craven Street, (803) 524-9030, is on the Point facing the water. Also overlooking the bay is the Keyserling Home, built in 1917 and used as a home for teachers. It's now the **Two-Suns Inn** with "tea and toddy" in the evening, 1705 Bay Street, (803) 522-1122. Located on the Beaufort River is the 1810 **Cuthbert House**, now an inn, where you can see Union soldier's names carved into the marble mantle. General Sherman stayed here as the guest of the Union military governor, 1203 Bay Street, (803) 521-1315.

While it's easy to stroll the historic district equipped with a tour map and perhaps a handy reference book, it's much more fun to be privy to the local yarns about early residents and historic happenings. These are available on a variety of tours of Beaufort. **"The Spirit of Old Beaufort"** tour provides a wealth of anecdotes as you take an escorted two-hour walk around either the town's Westside or Eastside district. Hosts in period dress provide details on local history, architecture, horticulture and Lowcountry culture. Tours depart from the Traveler's Oasis, at 210 Scott's Street behind the John Mark Verdier House Museum. Westside tours leave at 10:00 A.M. and 2:30 P.M. and Eastside tours at 11:15 and 3:45 P.M. from Tuesday through Saturday, weather permitting. From January until mid-February, only afternoon tours are offered.

What could be more appropriate than seeing this historic old

The 1852 Lewes Reeve Sams House at 601 Bay Street, now the Bay Street Inn, is one of the many splendid homes in Beaufort's National Historic Landmark District. The house was used in the films Prince of Tides *and* Forrest Gump.

PHOTO BY J. W. WESCOTT

town by horse-drawn carriage? **Carriage Tours of Beaufort** provide architectural details, legends and lore during 45-minute tours that leave from the visitors center parking lot on Bay Street. The first tour is at 9:00 A.M. and they continue into the evening hours on a daily basis; call (803) 521-1651 for more details. One final option is to see Beaufort from the water. **The Islander** offers a cruise on weekends, and daily during summer months. Tickets can be purchased at the visitors center.

For casual dining in Beaufort you can't beat The Bank Grill & Bar, 926 Bay Street, (803) 522-8831 and Plums, 904½ Bay Street, (803) 525-1946. For an evening meal try Emily's Restaurant and Tapas Bar, 906 Port Republic Street, (803) 522-1866, the Beaufort Inn, 809 Port Republic Street, (803) 521-9000 or the Rhett House Inn, 1009 Craven Street, (803) 524-9030. You can also drive over to St. Helena Island and stop at the Gullah House, 761 Sea Island Parkway, (803) 838-2402, (see Gullah 'n' Geechie Mahn Tours).

You can visit Beaufort by water since the downtown marina has mooring space for visiting craft almost directly in front of the visitors center. The Waterfront Park is a great place for cast-netting for shrimp in the spring and fall. The park is also the scene of evening concerts and special events throughout the year. Among the popular events is the Gullah Fest in May, the Water Festival held the third week in July and the Shrimp Fest at the end of October.

If you enjoy fiction, Lois Battle's novel, *Bed and Breakfast*, is about an establishment in Beaufort and makes a nice companion volume for your visit.

Directions: From I-95 take Exit 33 and follow Route 21 to Beaufort.

Beaufort Arsenal
and the John Mark Verdier House

If These Walls Could Talk

An overview of Beaufort's colorful past can be seen at the **Beaufort Museum,** located in the historic **Beaufort Arsenal,** and at the headquarters of the Historic Beaufort Foundation on the first floor of the **John Mark Verdier House**.

Beaufort was founded in 1711 but it wasn't until 1795, three years after a national militia act created new military units in South Carolina, that the state allocated funds for the building of the Beaufort Arsenal, a powder magazine and laboratory where shot and explosives were produced. Finished in 1798, it was completely rebuilt in 1852 in a Gothic-style military fashion with pointed windows, fortress-like walls and a massive pointed arch gateway. When Port Royal's Fort Walker fell in 1861, Union troops occupied Beaufort and used the arsenal to store quartermaster and artillery supplies.

The Beaufort Arsenal was headquarters for the Beaufort Volunteer Artillery, a unit established in April 1775—making it the fifth oldest military unit in the country. The unit, now part of Troop B 202 Cavalry, is also noted because it has taken part in every major conflict the country has fought since the Revolution. From 1862 to 1875, the arsenal served as the garrison for the Beaufort Light Infantry, an African-American unit. Among its ranks was Robert Smalls, a former slave who became a United States congressman.

During the 1930s, the Works Progress Administration undertook a third expansion of the arsenal, adding a wing designed to serve as a museum area. The Beaufort Museum opened in 1939 with a focus on local history, local personalities and the region's natural features. One large room encompasses the bulk of the collection from archaeological materials to household items and military memorabilia. There are artifacts from Santa Elena, the Spanish settlement founded in 1566, which served for nearly a decade as the capital of "La Florida," (see Parris Island selection).

One local hero commemorated at the museum is General Stephen Elliot. First a lieutenant and then captain of the Beaufort Volunteer Artillery, he went on to serve as commander of Fort Sumter in 1863. Wounded in the Civil War, he eventually died of his wounds and is buried in St. Helena's Church cemetery (see selection). Brigadier General Elliot's portrait, which hangs in the museum, was painted by fellow Beaufort Volunteer Artillery member Reeve Stuart.

The Beaufort Museum is open Monday through Saturday from 10:00 A.M. to 5:00 P.M. It is closed on Wednesday and Sunday. A nominal admission is charged.

In 1790, 26-year-old John Mark Verdier built a two-story frame Federal-style house in Beaufort. The house sits on a raised tabby foundation with pillared porches on the first and second floors. Over the entrance is a semi-elliptical fanlight embellished with carved garlands. The interior reveals the same symmetry. On the right of the entrance hall is the reception parlor and on the left is the dining room; both have attractive Adam-style mantels. Period furnishings from the 1800s fill the rooms. One of the few family pieces is the dining room silver service that belonged to John Mark Verdier.

When the house was built, Verdier was just starting what became a highly profitable career as a merchant. He had a well-stocked general store. Later, his son lived in the house, except during the Civil War, and descendants remained until the 1900s.

In addition to being noted for its architectural details, the house is famous for its brush with history. On March 18, 1825, the Marquis de Lafayette, during his tour of the new country he had helped to win its freedom, was scheduled to stop in Beaufort. Throngs of grateful citizens were at Beaufort's wharves to greet the hero, only to learn that he was delayed at Edisto Island. He arrived in the middle of the night, but an advance messenger brought word of his new schedule and the crowd gathered again to welcome him. Lafayette disembarked and addressed the crowd from the balcony of the John Mark Verdier House. During the Civil War, Union forces were head-quartered in the house. Over the years the house served a wide range of uses: fish market, icehouse, law office, telephone company office and barbershop. It was condemned in 1942 but was saved by the concerted effort of a citizens' committee. In 1968 it was acquired by the Historic Beaufort Foundation which restored and refurnished the house.

The John Mark Verdier House is open Tuesday through Saturday from 11:00 A.M. to 4:00 P.M. Admission is charged. A well-stocked gift shop can be found on the first floor (there is no charge if you just want to visit the museum shop).

Directions: From I-95 take Exit 42, Route 303 to Gardens Corner. Continue south on Route 21 which becomes Boundary Street in downtown Beaufort. Turn right on Carteret Street and right again on Craven Street. The Beaufort Arsenal is at 713 Craven Street. For the John Mark Verdier House, continue down Carteret Street two more blocks past Craven to Bay Street and turn right. The Verdier House is at 801 Bay Street.

Edisto River Canoe and Kayak Trail and Colleton State Park

Black Water

The Edisto River is the longest free-flowing black water stream in the world. The term "black water," is not as familiar as "white water." It refers to the water's slow flow, without rapids. The water takes on a dark cast as tannin acid leaches out of the leaves in the swampy terrain. It looks rather like the strong ice tea enjoyed throughout the south. Despite the dark hue, the water quality of the Edisto River is highly rated for cleanliness.

The **Edisto River Canoe and Kayak Trail** is an award-winning 56-mile-long trail established in 1987. Many visitors are unfamiliar with a canoe trail; it is a water route that has all the obstacles removed (this is an ongoing activity) to provide safe passage along the trail. There are both public and private access points

112

to the trail. The river is like a road with markers, access points, and even overnight sites, although they are merely primitive camping areas. Much of the river bank is private property that must be respected. The establishment of this trail reduced the conflicts from the many different groups who used the river: fishermen, speed boaters and canoe and kayak enthusiasts. The long-range goal is to have the entire river become a trail.

Canoe and kayak trips are suitable for all ages, from pre-teens to senior citizens. Floating along the river in this leisurely fashion gives you time to enjoy the passing scenery and spot the wide variety of wildlife prevalent in the Lowcountry. Along the shore you're apt to see deer, foxes, river otter and alligators. Birds frequently seen include great blue herons, kingfishers, egrets and a wide variety of ducks. Wildflowers bloom along the river bank which is often overhung with majestic giant live oaks draped with Spanish moss. If you have a fishing license you can combine a canoe trip with a little fishing. One fish caught in this river is the red-breast sun fish. The Edisto is a wild river and you may also spot alligators and snakes, so you should be cautious and avoid swimming in the river.

Five boat landings offer access to the trails; two are in Colleton and Givhans Ferry State Parks. At Colleton you can access the trail from either side of the river. The other public spots are Stokes Bridge and Mas Old Field. At all these spots you will find clearly marked float plan deposit boxes, where you file a notice of how many are in your party, plus when and where you are traveling. While it is not legally required that you fill out a form, it is highly recommended. Signs also designate the water accessible camp sites. There are three privately operated access points where a fee is charged: at Whetstone Crossroads, Simmonds Landing at Springtown and Wire Road Bridge.

For up-to-date information on the depth of the water and the air and water temperature call (803) 538-3659. South Carolina Electric and Gas makes this information available daily. If the river level is above 7.5 feet it is unsafe for canoeists. If you would like information about renting a canoe or kayak call the Walterboro-Colleton Chamber of Commerce at (803) 549-9595. One of the excellent suppliers is Carolina Heritage Outfitters, (800) 563-5053, which offers guided river trips, rentals, tent sites, cabins, treehouses and nature trails.

Colleton State Park is only five minutes from I-95 and within its woodsy 35 acres you are transported to another world—of primeval wilderness. The Edisto River flows through this park making it a popular spot with canoeists, fishermen and campers. There are 25 camp sites as well as a picnic and playground area. The park is open April through October daily from 9:00 A.M. to 9:00 P.M. At other times the park closes at 6:00 P.M. In early June

The award-winning 56-mile Edisto River Canoe and Kayak Trail gives visitors a chance to explore the world's longest free-flowing black water stream. Among the five access points are launching areas in Colleton and Givhans Ferry State Parks.

SOUTH CAROLINA DEPARTMENT OF PARKS, RECREATION AND TOURISM

the park is the site of the **Edisto Riverfest** which features guided canoe and kayak lessons and trips, outdoor workshops, outdoor equipment exhibits, food and entertainment. Some of the trips end at Givhans Ferry State Park in the Historic Charleston region which also offers cabins and camping. For information on this annual event call (803) 734-0156.

Hikers may opt for Westvaco's **Edisto Nature Trail**, a one-mile trail that meanders through typical Carolina Lowcountry terrain. Edisto is part of the ACE Basin (see selection), which includes the Ashepoo, Combahee and Edisto River Basin. This is one of the largest undeveloped estuaries on the east coast and offers travelers a unique opportunity to enjoy an unspoiled natural area.

The Edisto Nature Trail has natural and historical points of interest marked along the trail. The trail takes you past the Old Charleston Road, a major transportation link in colonial times, used by George Washington and much of the southern populace. Predating that was the King's Highway that in the 1700s linked Charleston and Walterboro on the way to Augusta, Georgia. The trail takes you past abandoned fields once used for rice cultivation and spots where phosphate mining was carried out. There are remnants of canals and railroad beds. You can do the mile-long trail or take a shorter half-mile section. Wear comfortable walking shoes because the boardwalk is slick when wet; you should also apply sun screen and insect repellent. To obtain a brochure outlining the various points of interest along the trails write: Westvaco Corporation, Southern Region, Public Affairs Department, P.O. Box 1950, Summerville, SC 29484.

Directions: From I-95 take Exit 68, Route 15 east for four miles to Colleton State Park.

Gullah 'n' Geechie Mahn Tours

Vite Ya to de Sea Islandts ob Bufat, Sous Carolina

"Ef oona ent kno weh oona da gwine, oona should kno weh oona." Kitty Green quotes this Gullah proverb to visitors who take her **Gullah 'n' Geechie Mahn Tours** of St. Helena Island. It means: "If you don't know where you're going, you should know where you come from." The Gullah heritage is unique to South Carolina's Lowcountry and is the history and heritage of many African Americans. Geechie comes from the African word Kisi, which means country or countrified. Gullah represents a cultural tradition that includes language, folk stories, food, music and crafts such as sweetgrass baskets.

South Carolina was one of the south's largest slave holding states. Eighty percent of West African slaves came to the Sea

Islands through the port of Charleston, 70 miles north. The isolation of the islands and the minimal white supervision enabled the slaves to retain a great deal of their African traditions. Gullah is thought to be a variation on Angola, the country from which many of the slaves were taken in the 1700s and 1800s. But slaves were also taken from other African nations that spoke different languages and dialects. Slaves brought to the Sea Islands came primarily from the west coast, or "rice coast," because they were skilled at farming in similar conditions to those found in the islands. When they came together in the Sea Islands they needed to learn to communicate with each other and with the plantation overseers. The Gullah dialect is the result of the merging of these languages.

It is the Gullah culture you will discover on Kitty Green's fascinating tours. St. Helena is the largest of the Sea Islands and at one time had 55 plantations worked by approximately 10,000 slaves. When the Union army occupied nearby Beaufort in 1862, the slaves were liberated (see Penn Center selection) and St. Helena became the property of the former slaves. Farming and shrimping enabled the former slaves to maintain a self-sufficient life style removed from that of the mainland. The first bridge connecting the island with Beaufort was not built until 1927. This continued isolation helped residents retain the Gullah traditions, although for many years speaking the Gullah dialect was discouraged, even by the teachers at Penn Center, one of the country's first schools for freed southern slaves. It is only recently that the importance of retaining this rich cultural heritage has been fully realized.

Gullah guide Kitty Green married a St. Helena native and moved to the island from Ohio more than 20 years ago. She became fascinated by the history and heritage of the islands. Kitty thoroughly researched all the material she presents on her tours to make sure that the African American experience is accurately presented. Gullah proverbs and folktales enhance her van tours of St. Helena's.

One of the first stops on the two-hour tour is the campus of Penn Center where the saga of this historic educational experiment is recounted. Here you will see a brick chapel built by slave labor. You will discover that Christianity was imparted to the slaves quite early. But here too, African traditions merged with Christian ceremony. Because so few whites could endure the summer heat and health conditions, the slaves were frequently under black supervision. So they incorporated their African religious ideas within the framework of Christianity. Before being baptized, a slave would go out into the countryside and spend the night. The spiritual leader would interpret their dreams to determine whether they were worthy of becoming a

Christian. This became a rite of passage similar to those practiced on the African continent. The slaves initially worshiped in a Praise House and their leader was an African, who was selected by the slaves. This leader would handle grievances among the slaves. There are five Praise Houses left on the island and you will see examples on your tour. You'll also see the tabby ruins of the Episcopal Chapel of Ease, which was built by slave labor in 1740. As you talk about religion you will learn that many of the early spirituals were message songs. For example, "Swing Low Sweet Chariot" was about the underground railroad, the route used by escaping slaves to reach freedom in the north.

You can combine your tour with lunch or dinner at the **Gullah House Restaurant**, also owned by the Green family. Sherrill McRae, Kitty's daughter, and her husband Mark studied culinary arts and, after working at several prestigious establishments, came to St. Helena to take over the kitchen in the family restaurant. It has gained national attention and critical acclaim. The restaurant features Gullah cooking and is noted for its gumbo, shrimp and grits, Frogmore stew, Jollof rice and Lowcountry boil. On weekends the restaurant features live jazz and blues music. Regional art hangs on the restaurant walls and is featured next door at the Red Piano, a general store that has been converted to a folk art gallery.

Gullah 'n' Geechie Mahn Tours depart daily from the Gullah House Restaurant at 10:00 A.M., 1:45 and 3:45 P.M. and from the Beaufort Chamber of Commerce, at the Waterfront Park Visitors Center at 9:45 A.M., 1:30 and 3:30 P.M. Call for reservations at (803) 838-7516, 838-3758 or 838-7560. It's fun to visit during one of the annual festivals; the Gullah Festival is held in the spring and features stories, language, arts, music, dance and food. In early November Penn Center Heritage Days Festival, a three-day event, focuses on Sea Island history and culture.

Directions: From I-95 take Exit 42, Route 303 to Gardens Corner. Continue south on Route 21 past Beaufort. The Gullah House Restaurant is four miles east of Beaufort off Route 21.

Hampton and Lake Warren State Park

Small Town Lure

Hampton, the town and the county, are named for Wade Hampton, General of the Confederacy and governor of South Carolina (see Hampton-Preston Mansion selection). The town was built around the courthouse, erected in 1878-1879, and is now on the National Historical Register. Be sure and note the cork tree on the Courthouse Square. This tree is found in Spain and Portugal and it is surprising to find one in this area. It was planted in 1933 by Miss Izora Miley, a local county extension home economist, and her students.

The history of the area is meticulously presented at the

Friendly and proud Hampton residents delight in sharing their past and present with visitors at the Hampton Museum. The museum, town and county are named for Wade Hampton, general of the Confederacy and governor of South Carolina.

Hampton Museum and Visitors Center, housed in an 1892 bank. Visitors to the museum can explore the inside of the bank vault and try their skill at opening the safe. The combination has been lost, and no one has stumbled across the correct numbers in the last 50 years.

You'll learn about the region's first inhabitants—the Native Americans. Between 3,000 and 2,500 B.C., in the southern part of South Carolina and the southeast tip of Georgia, the indigenous population first made pottery. In 1685, there were 10,000 Native Americans in the state and 1,400 white settlers. By 1715, the numbers were matched at 5,000. By 1790, only 300 Native Americans remained while the white population had grown to approximately 140,200. The tribes in the Hampton area were collectively called the Casabos, related to the Creeks in Georgia and Alabama. The most significant individual tribal group was the Yemassee. The museum's Native American exhibit has examples of pottery and other artifacts found in the county. The museum also has a model of a Creek village.

Hampton's first multi-storied building was built by Miles McSweeney for the county's first newspaper, *The Hampton County Guardian*. McSweeney, the 57th governor of South Carolina and vice president of the bank once located in this building, bought a printing press and began publishing in 1879. The museum has a printing press with patents dating from 1885 and 1887. The communication exhibit also includes a Dictaphone, radio, 1960 telephone, as well as written messages in Cherokee and examples of hieroglyphics.

The museum is supported by enthusiastic volunteers who are especially proud of their town. It has photographs of Hampton County churches displayed on the museum wall. Another wall traces events at the annual Hampton County Watermelon Festival, the state's oldest continuous festival. The event has been held in June for over 50 years (with the exception of three years during World War II and the Korean War). Photographs of past pageant queens and other events fill another wall. Just before going upstairs to see the additional exhibits, take note of the medical exhibit on the back wall.

Upstairs, the first display is memorabilia from the *USS Hampton*, a nuclear-powered fast-attack submarine that was christened in Hampton, Virginia in August 1991. The commanding officer's uniforms are displayed in the military room. Uniforms from all of the wars this country has been involved in are exhibited, as are military medals and other artifacts. Other upstairs exhibits include children's toys, clothing and accessories, household appliances, bottles and glass, and photographs of all Hampton's mayors.

The Hampton Museum and Visitors Center is open at no

charge Thursday and Saturday from 2:00 to 5:00 P.M. There is a modest gift shop where local craftsmen and artisans exhibit their work on a rotating basis.

Just a few blocks away is the **Hampton County Museum**, housed in the former Hampton County jail, and operated jointly by Hampton County and Hampton County Historical Society. One exhibit room resembles a country store circa 1878 with bolts of cloth, button shoes, a hat rack, sundries and medical nostrums. There is also a natural history room with shells, wood samples and mounted specimens. Another room has a selection of children's toys. This is a hands-on collection and small children delight in playing with the dolls, puppets, books and other old-fashioned toys. The museum is noted for its Civil War memorabilia as well as other military exhibits. An album made by a member of Battery D, formed in Hampton County, has photographs made after Germany surrendered, including pictures of Hitler's bunker and concentration camps. There is also extensive genealogical references available for those doing family histories. Hours for this museum are Thursday 10:00 A.M. to NOON and 4:00 to 7:00 P.M. and Sunday 3:00 to 5:00 P.M. There is no admission charge.

Five miles southwest of Hampton, you will find the relatively new 422-acre **Lake Warren State Park**. This park, which offers fishing and boating, was established in 1990. Only trolling motors are allowed on the 200-acre lake and there is absolutely no swimming. The lake has numerous alligators, one is at least 16 feet long. Overlooking the lake are picnic facilities and a children's playground area. The park is open daily April through September from 9:00 A.M. to 9:00 P.M. It closes at 6:00 P.M. the rest of the year.

Directions: From I-95 take Exit 38, Route 68 west to Hampton. (Route 68 merges with Route 278 between Cummings and Varnville, therefore signs will also indicate Route 278.) The Hampton Museum and Visitors Center is at 99 Elm Street, East, the same road you enter the town. The Hampton County Museum is at 702 First Street, West, which is the first street to the left after passing the Courthouse Square. For Lake Warren State Park, take Route 601 south out of Hampton. (This route is the same street on which the county museum is located.)

Hilton Head Island

Island in the Sun

At 12 miles long and 5 miles wide, only Long Island is a bigger Atlantic coast island than **Hilton Head Island**. This foot-shaped barrier island encompasses 42 miles of semi-tropical Lowcountry terrain. There are 12 miles of sandy ocean beach, plus acres of sea marsh and a vast network of lagoons and creeks lined with moss-draped oaks, pines and palmettos.

Unlike most Atlantic coast resort islands, you cannot drive the island's streets and see the ocean. But there are four public access points to the miles of hard-packed sandy beach: Coligny Circle (adjacent to Holiday Inn Oceanfront), Alder Lane (off South Forest Beach Drive), Folly Field Road and Dreissen's Beach Park (Bradley Beach Road).

When you cross the bridge onto the island on Route 278, you will see the **Hilton Head Welcome Center and Museum of Hilton Head** on the right. Stop here for brochures, details on scheduled tours and information on the island's natural and cultural history. Some visitors mistakenly believe the name Hilton refers to the hotel mogul and the chain he established. But Hilton Head got its name from an English sea captain, William Hilton, who landed on its shore in 1663. He claimed the land in the name of England and a group of British planters from Barbados who were soon growing indigo on the island. They had also wanted to grow sugar, but it was not successful here.

French Huguenots had briefly settled here in the 1560s, calling it "Ile de la Riviere Grande"—Island of the Broad River. The French soon moved to what is now Beaufort. When the British arrived, they stayed on Hilton Head and by 1860 there were 24 plantations on the island, most growing cotton. At the onset of the Civil War, plantation owners and overseers fled the island and Federal troops took control. The land, abandoned by the planters, was sold to the former slaves and to land speculators for about a dollar an acre. For many years descendants of former slaves maintained small farms and supplemented their diet by hunting and fishing. Like nearby St. Helena, the Gullah tradition endured (see Gullah 'n' Geechie Mahn Tour selection).

In the 1940s, the lumber industry harvested the island's loblolly pines. It wasn't until 1956 that Charles Fraser, whose family owned property on the island, saw the tourism potential of Hilton Head. The addition of a bridge earlier that year made it possible for visitors to access his Sea Pines Plantation resort, a prototype of the modern resort that blends with the environment. This was the first of many planned communities, or plantations, on the island complete with lagoons and lakes, golf

121

courses and tennis courts. You can access the plantations if you have business there or are visiting the restaurants or hotels. Sea Pines charges a gate fee per car for visitor access.

The Museum on Hilton Head Island offers a wide range of activities as part of a program called Coastal Discovery. There are historical tours including the tabby ruins of Stoney Baynard Plantation and the archeological dig on Sea Pines. A Fort Mitchell Tour includes its Civil War battery. Another tour covers Civil War forts of Port Royal. There is also the option of an Old House Plantation Tour (but keep in mind there are no plantations from the antebellum era still standing; only the grounds remain). In addition, you can take a tour of Mitchellville and Fort Howell, the country's first Freedman's community and an African-American Civil War fort. There are different tours that focus on natural history such as the evening loggerhead turtle tour, the forest preserve tour, beach tours, marine study trawler cruises, and a tour of the **Pinckney Island National Wildlife Refuge**. Call ahead to obtain a schedule for tours and to make advance reservations at (803) 689-6767.

The Pinckney Island National Wildlife Refuge encompasses 4,053 acres. It's the largest of the refuge islands at 3.8 miles long and 1.75 miles wide. The refuge is at the junction of four inshore waterways. There are 14 miles of nature trails for hiking and biking that will give you a chance to observe the wildlife up close. (Be sure to bring a camera.) Popular hikes include the 1.2 mile round-trip hike to Ibis Pond, the 2.9 mile round trip to Osprey Pond and, for those who have all day, the 7.9 miles round trip to White Point. There is a public boat ramp and fishing pier at Last End Point, on the southern tip of the island. Visitors are welcome at the refuge daily from sunup to sundown. Some trails are closed at certain times to protect nesting and breeding wildlife.

During the peak tourist season you may get around the island more rapidly by bike than by automobile. There are 10.6 miles of public pathways for cyclists and pedestrians. There is a brochure called *Island's Pathways* that has details on the major routes. These pathways definitely lead to Shelter Cove Harbour and Harbour Town, two of the most popular meeting spots on the island. At Shelter Cove you can dine harbor side and enjoy a variety of cuisines from Italian and Mexican to Lowcountry fare. There are rows of shops. From April until August there are free concerts on Tuesday through Saturday evenings. On Tuesday from June through August the night sky explodes with fireworks. During the day it's fun to observe the sleek yachts. If you want to get out on the water, Dolphin Watch Nature Cruises leave from Dock C at Shelter Cove Harbour; call (803) 785-4558 for details.

From sunup to sundown, you can enjoy the action at Harbour Town, one of the best-known marinas on the eastern seaboard.

There's a tradition here that matches Key West, because the sunsets are as equally colorful. You can enjoy the vista from one of the waterside restaurants—Cafe Europa or The Quarterdeck—or from the top of the lighthouse. If you want to get out on the water a variety of charter options are available including sailboats, catamarans and powerboats. There are sightseeing cruises, environmental tours and sport fishing. Shopping and entertainment are also big draws at Harbour Town. (Hilton Head actually has nine public marinas.)

If you want to get away from the action, head for the natural preserves. On the island you can take the walking paths at Sea Pines Forest Preserve or the New Hall Audubon Preserve. Just off the island between the bridges is Pinckney Island Wildlife Preserve. You can also take a ferry excursion to **Daufuskie Island**. Locals claim the name is Gullah for "the first key" as the islands were originally called keys. But "Daufuskie" was a Yemassee word that meant "place of blood." The tip of the island was the scene of early battles between the Native Americans and the British. The beach at the end of the island was called "Bloody Point" because it was so often stained with the blood of warriers killed by cannon fire from British ships. You can rent golf carts or use island transportation to explore. A morning and afternoon ferry leaves from the Broad Creek Marina; call (803) 681-7925 for details.

For more information on the wildlife, nightlife and other recreational options contact the Hilton Head Island Visitors & Convention Bureau at (803) 785-3673.

Directions: From I-95 take Exit 8, Route 278 to Hilton Head Island; once across the bridge stop at the welcome center. Pinckney Island is on the right off Route 278 before you cross onto Hilton Head Island.

Hunting Island State Park

Hunting for a Good Time?

It isn't only the Sierra Club and the Nature Conservancy that recognize the unique ecology of this barrier Sea Island; Hollywood has also eagerly sought to capture its scenic appeal. This is one state park where visitors sometimes go star gazing without looking at the sky. Movies shot on location at the park's lagoon include the Vietnam sequences in Tom Hank's *Forrest Gump* and Demi Moore's *G.I. Jane*. For young visitors there is even a star on staff: Ranger Mike from the popular children's cable show *Gullah Gullah Island* is, in fact, staff ranger Mike Walker. Young children are delighted to learn about the abundant wildlife at this park from so recognizable a character.

The 1875 Hunting Island Lighthouse was built after Confederates destroyed an earlier beacon during the Civil War. Hunting Island State Park has been featured in several movies including Forrest Gump *and* G.I. Jane.

As you walk from the parking lot to the visitors center (the best place to get oriented), you will see some of the park's alligators sunning and swimming in the pond in front of the center. The center has exhibits on the diverse habitats within the three-mile-long and one-mile-wide park. There is a 5,000-acre sandy beach, a maritime forest and saltwater marsh. Once a popular hunting spot, visitors now try to capture the wildlife on film. White-tailed deer and raccoon can be spotted in the slash pine-palmetto forest. This is one of the best places in the state to see South Carolina's state tree, the cabbage palm or palmetto, growing wild. Bird watchers give this park good marks since more than 125 species of birds have been reported. Herons, gulls, terns and egrets are seen in abundance.

A boardwalk extends into the salt marsh, an example of one of the world's most productive habitats. A substantial percent of marine life is either directly or indirectly dependent on salt marshes. Some species, such as the fiddler crab, spawn in the marsh. Others, like the shrimp, seek the protection of the marsh to reach maturity. Some species spend their entire life in the marsh. One example is the clapper rail, or "marsh hen."

There is a four-mile moderately difficult hiking trail that provides access to diverse habitats within the park. A short one-mile trail leads to the 1875 **Hunting Island Lighthouse**. This is not the first lighthouse on the island. In 1859, a brick lighthouse offered a beacon to captains piloting along South Carolina's coast. Current research indicates the 1859 lighthouse was destroyed by Confederates during the Civil War. Its replacement was built one-fourth of a mile from the shoreline. The new facility was one of the world's first portable lighthouses, built of cast iron plate. The new complex also had a three-story light-keeper's dwelling, a fire-proof oil-house and several storage buildings. The decision to make it portable was a wise one. By 1889, erosion caused the lighthouse—along with the keeper's house, oil house and storage structure—to be moved 1¼ mile in land. The last two buildings still stand. The keeper's house was destroyed in 1936 by fire. It was at that time being used as barracks by the Civilian Conservation Corps. The lighthouse was operational until June 16, 1933. Visitors can climb 180 steps to the top for a splendid panoramic view of the Atlantic coast.

Sports enthusiasts find multiple opportunities at Hunting Island State Park. There are boardwalks to the beach at both North and South beaches. There are protected ocean swimming areas at both beaches. Fishermen can choose from three destinations: the ocean surf, lagoon waters at the park's southern tip where the catch includes whiting, spot, trout, bass and drum or Paradise Fishing Pier at the southern tip of the park. The 1,120-foot pier extends into Fripp Inlet. A tackle shop at the pier entrance sells bait and other supplies. The park also has pic-nicking and camping facilities, plus fifteen cabins situated on or close to the ocean. The cabins are booked fast, so call (803) 838-2011 on the first working Monday of January for dates during the next calendar year.

Through the year, park naturalists lead programs and nature hikes. You can usually join the hikes if they are taking place dur-ing your visit, but special programs may require advance regis-tration. If you know when you plan to visit, call ahead at (803) 838-2011 and get a schedule of events. The park is open daily from March through November, 6:00 A.M. to 9:00 P.M. and daily December through February until 6:00 P.M. An entrance fee is charged during the summer season.

Directions: From I-95 take Exit 42, Route 303 south to Gardens Corner. Continue south on Route 21 to Beaufort. Hunting Island State Park is 16 miles east of Beaufort on U.S. 21.

Parris Island

We Make Marines

There are only two spots in the country where enlisted Marines undergo basic training: San Diego on the west coast and **Parris Island** for those east of the Mississippi. Almost 18,000 recruits are trained each year at this coastal island, where roughly half of all male recruits receive basic training and all the female recruits (about 2,000 annually) are trained.

The grueling and challenging 12-week basic training course begins when the recruit crosses the causeway to Parris Island. This is the only way on or off the island, although a few unhap-py recruits have tried to swim the Broad or Beaufort River to reach South Carolina's southeast corner. The recruits arrive at night, but they don't go to bed. Instead they begin the process of shifting their thinking from civilian to military. They go through a lengthy processing, are assigned their gear and quar-ters, and then commence their training.

The training is arduous and recruits need a strong desire to succeed. Training includes close order drill, basic warrior train-ing, water survival, marksmanship, Marine Corps history and tradition as well as other subjects. Marines say that Parris Island is "where the difference begins." The link between Marines and the island dates back to the Civil War when the Union Naval forces established a base on the island and Marines first set foot on the island. On June 26, 1891 the island was formally dedicat-ed as U.S. Naval Station, Port Royal. In 1909, a Marine officers' school opened on the island, but closed in 1911. In November 1915, during World War I, enlisted male training began and

46,602 Marines were trained on Parris Island. Approximately 205,000 recruits trained here for World War II. It wasn't until 1949 that enlisted female recruits began training at Parris Island.

You don't have to be a Marine recruit, or have a military connection, to visit the Marine Corps Recruit Depot Parris Island. The sentry will direct you to the Paul Howard Douglas Visitors Center where you can pick up "The Parris Island Driving Tour Book," which includes a map and descriptive material about the 17 designated points of interest. The center is named for Paul H. Douglas, who at age 50 was the oldest recruit to complete training. At his graduation in 1942 he was selected as his platoon's outstanding Marine. He earned two Purple Hearts in the Pacific during World War II and attained the rank of Lieutenant Colonel. He later became a U.S. senator from Illinois. The center has a small exhibit of Douglas memorabilia.

When you leave the center you can take the self-guided driving tour. Remember that the mandatory seat belt law is enforced at this depot. Another option is to call (803) 525-3650 and reserve a seat on the daily narrated bus tour that leaves at 1:00 P.M. Saturday through Wednesday. Approximately 100,000 people visit this Marine training facility annually.

On Boulevard de France near the columned entrance to the commanding general's headquarters area is the World War I "Iron Mike" statue. Designed by Robert Ingersoll Aitken and dedicated in 1924 in memory of the Marines who died during World War I, this was officially known as the "Monument to U.S. Marines" but it soon acquired the nickname "Iron Mike," although the reason is unknown.

Next, you will drive through the depot's two-acre historic district called "Mainside," which dates back to 1880–1890. In 1891, the Navy began building machine shops and a dry dock for its naval base on the island. At the head of the dry dock is a Victorian-style octagonal gazebo. Though its age is unknown, photographs show Sunday band concerts that date back to the early days of the depot. One of the most historic structures is Quarters One, the two-story Victorian home of Parris Island's commanding generals since 1883. The first occupant was Ensign William Braunerstruther, USN who was in charge of building the naval station from 1883 to 1888. The first commander was Lieutenant Charles H. Lyman, USN. The dry dock, gazebo and commander's home are listed on the National Register of Historic Places. While in this section of the depot you will also see the Parris Island boat landing. Prior to the completion of the causeway in 1929, the only way on and off the depot was by boat. The tides around the island are dangerous with a variance of 11 feet from high to low.

Recruits are not the only ones trained on Parris Island. Drill instructors are also trained here and the driving tour takes you past the Drill Instructor School which was established in 1951. They, too, undergo a vigorous 11½ week training course. After you pass the marina you will cross "DI Bridge" named for the drill instructors. You will see salt marshes on both sides of the road; the Marines share the island with alligators, deer, otters, raccoons and waterfowl.

It's the earliest inhabitants that provide one of the most fascinating stops on the driving tour. Just off the golf course parking lot you'll find the **Ribaut Monument** and the excavations of the Santa Elena settlement. This is the northernmost known bastion of Spanish Florida. The harbor was first explored in 1520, less than three decades after Columbus discovered the New World. When the Spanish explorer Pedro de Queyo saw the harbor he named the headland the Punte de Santa Elena and claimed the land for Spain.

France challenged Spain's foothold on the Atlantic Coast and Jean Ribaut led a French squadron to the New World. He was looking for a site where French Huguenots, Protestants, could settle and from which the French could attack Spanish treasure ships. He arrived off Parris Island in 1562 and established Charlesfort, named after King Charles IX. He hoped this settlement would be a permanent colony. When Ribaut returned to France for supplies, the 28 settlers he left at the settlement suffered a devastating fire, then mutinied and killed their harsh commander. After building a ship, they sailed back to France.

The Spanish sent a warship to destroy Charlesfort, but when they arrived they found the cabins not destroyed by fire were abandoned. This experience convinced the Spanish they needed settlements along the east coast. An armada under Pedro Menendez was formed, but before it sailed, they discovered that the French under Ribaut's command had established a well-fortified settlement called Fort Caroline near present day Jacksonville. To counter this new situation, Menendez sailed farther south and established a military base at St. Augustine and then marched overland to attack Fort Caroline. While he was marching to attack the French, Ribaut sailed south to attack St. Augustine. Both were hampered by a hurricane, but Menendez used the storm to surprise and destroy Fort Caroline. Ribaut's fleet was wrecked and he and his men captured and executed. After this victory, Menendez sailed north and established the city of Santa Elena on Parris Island in 1566.

Approximately 500 Spaniards lived at Santa Elena under the protection of Fort San Felipe. Santa Elena served as the capital of the Spanish province of Florida from 1568 to 1576 when Indian attacks forced a brief evacuation. The Spanish returned in 1577 and built a larger city, Fort San Marcos, that survived until

1587 when English raids forced a permanent move to St. Augustine. English settlers established plantations on the island; by 1820 there were six plantations all growing sea island cotton. This era ended when the Union troops occupied Beaufort. Plantations were broken up into small farms and turned over to former slaves.

As you walk around the area where this settlement once stood you will see concrete blocks that mark the outline of the Spanish Fort San Marcos. For many years it was thought that this was the location of Ribaut's Charlesfort and a monument to the French leader and the Huguenots stands on what is in fact the Spanish fort. You can see artifacts uncovered by archaeological digs at the Parris Island Museum.

Continuing on your driving tour you will pass the rifle range and **Leatherneck Square** which contains the confidence course. If you're lucky you may be able to watch the recruits negotiate the 11 obstacles. The exercise usually takes place on Thursdays from 8:00 to 11:00 A.M. and 1:30 to 4:00 P.M. and Saturday from 7:30 to 10:00 A.M. and 1:00 to 2:30 P.M. Also on Monday and Tuesday mornings there are Pugil stick (a martial training aid roughly five-to six-feet-long with a padded end that is used in combat training) fights at Leatherneck Square.

Be sure to stop at the **Parris Island Recruit Chapel** which has 11 stained glass windows in memory of specific Marine divisions and state Marine Corps Leagues. A window in the Blessed Sacrament Chapel Room was dedicated in memory of Sam Lipton, who worked as the depot cobbler for 62 years.

If you visit on a Friday, you will most likely see a Graduation Parade on the **Depot Parade Field**. There are approximately 46 graduations annually, so you can call ahead and check to see if there will be a ceremony when you plan to visit. The first event is an 8:00 A.M. Morning Colors Ceremony on the steps of the commanding general's building. The graduation ceremony on the Peatross Parade Deck begins at 9:15 A.M. and features the Parris Island Band, pass-in-review and achievement awards. There are bleachers where you are welcome to watch this ceremony. You should arrive a little early.

The parade field is named for Major General Oscar F. Peatross, Operations Officer for the 28th Marines during the Iwo Jima campaign and commanding general of Marine Corps Recruit Depot Parris Island from 1968 to 1971. In front of the parade field is the original prototype for the Iwo Jima Monument, erected at Arlington Cemetery, commemorating the heroic flag raising by the Marines on Mount Suribachi in 1945.

The final stop on your tour is the **Parris Island Museum**, established in 1975, in the War Memorial Building. There are four themes: Parris Island history, local military history, 20th-century Marine Corps history and recruit training. You'll enter into a rotunda with a replica of the Iwo Jima Memorial in the center. Around the wall are cases filled with uniforms, weapons and personal items from various periods of Parris Island's history. Also downstairs is a room that takes you through the recruit training process with narrative boards, exhibits and photographs. Here you'll learn that the term "leatherneck" was derived from the leather collars the Marines once wore to maintain good posture and protect their necks from sword attack. Opposite this room is the local military history room where you will find details about the Spanish and French occupation of the region. On the second floor is a weapons room as well as an exhibit that covers all the wars and conflicts in which Marines have participated.

Visitors are welcome at Marine Corps Recruit Depot Parris Island weekdays from 8:00 A.M. until 5:00 P.M. and weekends 11:00 A.M. to 4:00 P.M. The visitors center is open daily during those hours except on major holidays. The Parris Island Museum is open at no charge from 10:00 A.M. to 4:30 P.M. Monday through Sunday. On Thursday it stays open until 7:00 P.M. and on Friday it opens at 8:00 A.M. It is closed on major holidays. There is a small gift shop in the museum that is open NOON to 5:00 P.M. on Thursday and 10:00 A.M. to 1:00 P.M. on Friday.

Directions: From I-95 take Exit 42, Route 303 to Gardens Corner. Continue south on Route 21 past the Marine Corps Air Station to the intersection with Route 802, turn right and continue for six or seven miles until you see the sign indicating the causeway over to Parris Island and the main gate.

Penn Center

History Happened Here

There are many doctoral candidates in American History who do not know the story of **Penn Center**. It's a fascinating and ongoing saga. Penn Center was one of the first schools for freed southern slaves. Originally called Penn School, it was founded on the Oaks Plantation in 1862 by Laura Towne and Ellen Murray, missionaries from Philadelphia, Pennsylvania. The school taught young children and adults. Before the year was out, Charlotte Forten, an African-American teacher from Massachusetts, joined the two missionaries. Penn Center ranks among the nation's most significant African-American educational and cultural institutions and it is certainly one of the oldest.

Federal troops had occupied this part of South Carolina since late 1861. Their strong presence in the area forced the evacuation of all Confederate forces as well as the South Carolina and

Georgia Sea Islands' plantation owners. A few departing plantation owners took some of their slaves, but most did not. This meant roughly 10,000 slaves were left behind on the Sea Islands. The slaves were essentially freed by default two years before the Emancipation Proclamation in 1863.

The movement to educate the freed African-American, at a time when laws against educating slaves were still on the book, was called the Port Royal Experiment. Penn School was based on the Port Royal Experiment, although it was not part of the program. The federal government wanted the freed slaves to remain on the plantations and harvest the highly profitable long staple cotton. Oaks Plantation was one of these plantations. The government paid the former slaves for their work but was also interested in the educational experiment because it was important that the freed people become self-sufficient.

Penn School proved successful and it prospered through the turn of the century. Through the 1900s, it served as a normal school, a teacher training ground for students from various colleges, an agricultural teaching facility that also offered industrial education. This continued until 1948 when South Carolina began providing public education to African Americans on the Sea Islands. The last class graduated in 1953.

Penn School did not close when South Carolina assumed responsibility for educating all the children in the state. The school became Penn Community Services with the goal of developing individual and community self-reliance. During the 1950s and 1960s, it was one of two biracial conference centers in the south. Dr. Martin Luther King, Jr. and the Southern Christian Leadership Conference staff, which included Jessie Jackson and Andrew Young and others, met for strategy planning meetings between 1963 and 1967 at Penn Center.

Recognizing its historic significance, the 50-acre Penn Center was named a National Historic Landmark District in 1974. The campus contains 19 buildings built by students working under the direction of their instructors. A self-guided information sheet provides details on the construction and former use of 15 of these buildings. It can be picked up at the Butler Building, which also houses the **York W. Bailey Museum**. The museum exhibits fulfill part of Penn Center's mission of preserving the Sea Islands' history and culture. African roots can be seen in many of the crafts created on the sea islands and preserved in the museum.

Each year, during the second weekend in November, Penn Center Heritage Days Celebration is held which brings to life the rich cultural mix of the Sea Islands. The Gullah culture is unique and it influences the food, music, religion and crafts of the Sea Islands (see Gullah-N-Geechie Mahn Tours selection). The

Heritage celebration includes a parade, symposium, community sing, crafts and a traditional oyster roast.

The York W. Bailey Museum at Penn Center is open Tuesday through Friday from 11:00 A.M. to 4:00 P.M. The administration office is open Monday through Friday 9:00 A.M. to 5:00 P.M.

Directions: From I-95 take Exit 42, Route 303 to Gardens Corner. Continue south on Route 21 past Beaufort onto St. Helena Island. From Route 21 turn right on Martin Luther King Drive. This will take you through Penn Center Historic District.

St. Helena's Episcopal Church and Beaufort National Cemetery

Hallowed Ground

In 1710–1711, South Carolina's Lord Proprietors had the town of Beaufort laid out; the following year St. Helena's Parish of the Anglican Church was established. The church, built by this parish in 1724, is one of the oldest in continuous use in the country. The parish's first minister was the Reverend William Guy. His congregation was decimated three years after he arrived by the Yemassee Indians who massacred all but 300 settlers. The survivors managed to escape in a British ship. The settlers returned when the local Native American tribes were subdued.

A great deal of the brick used to build the original portion of **St. Helena's Episcopal Church** arrived in the new world as ship's ballast. The church was enlarged in 1770 and 1817. A silver communion service that is still used on special occasions was given to the church in 1734 by Captain John Bull in memory of his wife who was slain during an Indian massacre.

Beaufort was occupied by Union troops during the Civil War and they used St. Helena's as a hospital. Slab grave stones served as operating tables. Confederate generals Richard H. Anderson and Stephen Elliot are buried in the churchyard. After the Civil War, the *U.S.S. New Hampshire* was stationed in Beaufort and sailors from that ship handcrafted the church altar.

University of South Carolina Professor of History Lawrence Rowland says that St. Helena's Episcopal churchyard is "one of the most historic graveyards in America." One of the first to be interred in this churchyard was Colonel John Barnwell, called " Tuscarora Jack." Barnwell gained the nickname fighting the Tuscarora Indians. He died the same year the church was built, 1724. Although there is a marker in the churchyard, his grave is under the apse of the enlarged church. There are four other graves beneath the church.

The churchyard is the final resting place for two British officers who were killed in a battle off Port Royal on February 3, 1779 during the American Revolution. When Captain Jack Barnwell buried them, he reputedly said, "We have shown the British we not only can best them in battle but that we can also give them a Christian burial."

One interesting story is told about the burial of a Dr. Perry. When he was interred in his brick mausoleum, by previous agreement, his friends put a loaf of bread, a jug of water and a pickax into his tomb with his body just in case he was buried alive, an occurrence he had heard about in the course of his medical career.

When Michael O'Donovan, Principal of Beaufort College, died on May 17, 1821 his tombstone inscription was written by a non-Irish loving individual. It read: "A native of Ireland, *but* for the last 20 years a respectable inhabitant of this State." Robert Woodward Barnwell, grandson of Colonel John " Tuscarora Jack" Barnwell and public servant, is buried here. Barnwell served as a member of the South Carolina and federal legislature and was a candidate for president of the Confederacy. He died on November 24, 1882.

Visitors are welcome daily at St. Helena's Episcopal Church at 505 Church Street. Services are held here on Sunday morning at 8:00, 9:15 and 11:15 A.M. During the summer services are at 8:00 and 10:00 A.M. There is also a service Wednesday at 5:00 P.M. and Thursday at 11:00 A.M.

Another historical burial ground is **Beaufort National Cemetery**, one of the first U.S. National Cemeteries. Its establishment was personally authorized by President Lincoln in a letter dated February 10, 1863. To augment Lincoln's directive, the commanding general of Federal occupation purchased a 29-acre tract, called Polly's Grove, for $75.00 at a tax sale on March 11, 1863. Union dead from Florida, Georgia and South Carolina were reinterred here. In all, there were 7,500 Civil War soldiers buried in this national cemetery, including 4,019 unknown Union soldiers and 117 Confederate soldiers. On May 29, 1989, the remains of 19 Union soldiers of the all Black Massachusetts 55th Infantry, depicted in the movie *Glory*, were reinterred with full military honors after having been found on Folly Island, South Carolina two years earlier.

There are also 6,500 veterans of the Spanish American War, World War I, World War II, Korea, Vietnam, Persian Gulf and peacetime veterans. A German submarine crew member from a U-boat sunk May 9, 1942 off Cape Lookout, North Carolina is buried here. A military hero from the conflict in Vietnam, PFC Ralph H. Johnson is buried in this cemetery. He was posthumously awarded the Congressional Medal of Honor for his heroics while serving as a marine reconnaissance scout in 1968 near

Quan Due Valley.

As you enter the cemetery there is a white box which contains a map of the cemetery. If the office is open you can obtain a map and an explanation of the emblems of belief, such as a cross and Star of David, for government monuments. The cemetery is open daily and Memorial Day services are held annually.

Directions: From I-95 take Exit 42, Rout 303 to Gardens Corner. Continue south on Route 21 to Beaufort. Business Route 21 becomes Carteret Street in downtown Beaufort as you cross Woods Memorial Bridge. For St. Helena's Episcopal Church, turn left on Duke Street and left again on Church Street. St. Helena's is at 505 Church Street. For Beaufort National Cemetery stay on Carteret Street to Boundary Street and turn left. The cemetery is at 1601 Boundary Street.

Savannah National Wildlife Refuge

Don't Harass the Alligators

Signs in the **Savannah National Wildlife Refuge** declare: "It is a violation of federal and state law to feed or harass the alligators." Since the alligators in this refuge reach a considerable size it would seem unnecessary to warn visitors about harassing them. Sometimes they seem so supine though, it's easy to forget that these can be dangerous animals. Alligators are able to travel as fast as race horses for short distances, so it is wise not to get too close when stopping for photographs along the **Laurel Hill Wildlife Drive**. Visitors on the drive frequently see 50 or more alligators ranging in size from one to twelve feet, and there is an unconfirmed sighting of a 14-foot gator. When it is cool the alligators often bask in the sun along the banks of the diversion canal, while on hot summer days all that usually can be seen are their eyes and noses protruding above the water.

This scenic four-mile drive, open from sunrise to sunset, takes you through a sizeable portion of the 26,349-acre refuge. Over 13,000 acres are bottomland and hardwoods with remnants of great cypress and tupelo swamps. Another 6,000 acres were formerly rice plantations along the Savannah River. As you enter the refuge you can pick up a self-guided brochure that will provide details about this refuge for migratory waterfowl and wading birds.

One of the first areas you will come to on the drive is the location of one of the 13 rice plantations, Laurel Hill Plantation. The majestic live oaks that once shaded the front of the plantation house still stand. The plantation was begun in 1813 and utilized 150 slaves whose quarters stood on the site of the refuge's maintenance complex. The only tangible reminder of this plantation is a brick floor from a steam-powered mill that stood within 100 yards of the main house. This was the second mill; the first operated on tidal power from the Little Back River. Later, during the drive you will see a millstone salvaged from this mill. It marks a trail leading to a small cemetery. The tombstone of a slave much regarded by his master once stood here along with the graves of several other plantation residents. Sadly, the slave tombstone was vandalized and it is now stored at the refuge headquarters in Savannah.

As you drive along the dikes you will see ten rice field trunks. These are vital tools to control water flow between the Little Back River and the impoundments within the refuge. The trunks are wooden culverts with flap gates that can control the amount of water that enters and is drained from the managed impoundments (the former rice fields). Trunks like these were first used in the 1700s on the rice plantations along freshwater tidal rivers from Georgetown, South Carolina to Brunswick, Georgia. Another method of controlling water within the refuge is the freshwater diversion canal which borders the drive as you approach on Route 170 at the refuge's northern end.

In addition to the drive, there are 25 miles of dikes open to the public for hiking and biking. Insects such as sand gnats and mosquitoes can be a problem, so before you leave your car be sure to liberally apply repellent. Bird watching is one of the park's main opportunities. Over 260 species of birds have been recorded at the refuge, including the endangered peregrine falcon and the southern bald eagle. No matter when you visit, you are likely to see egrets, herons and ibis. These wading birds like to get their food in pools with no more than six inches of water. You are also likely to see several species of "diving" ducks like the ring-necked and canvasback. Adding to the color at the refuge are water lilies blooming in many pools along the way.

Activities permitted in the park include hiking, biking, picnicking and fishing. The latter is one of the most popular activities in the refuge. Freshwater fishing in the canals yields bream, largemouth bass and crappie. Canals and pools are open to fishermen, with a South Carolina license, from March 15 to October 25. The tidal creeks are open from February 1 to October 25.

The Savannah National Wildlife Refuge is one of seven Savannah Coastal Refuges, a chain that extends from Pinckney Island National Wildlife Refuge near Hilton Head to Wolf Island National Wildlife Refuge near Darien, Georgia.

Directions: From I-95 take Exit 5 at Hardeeville and travel south on U.S. 17/S.C. 170 for 13 miles to Savannah National Wildlife Refuge entrance, Laurel Hill Wildlife Drive.

Walterboro, Colleton Museum and South Carolina Artisans Center

Arts, Architecture and Artifacts

Summer was unbearable for Lowcountry rice planters and most sought a seasonal retreat. Paul and Jacob Walter were seeking just such a getaway when they arrived in the high, sandy, pineland area that is now named in their honor. Their first summer, 1783, they lived in hastily built shelters, while their servants stayed in tents. The following year they built the first house in what they called Hickory Valley. Others followed, and by 1817, the city of **Walterboro** became the county seat. This necessitated a courthouse and by 1822 there was a striking building erected in the Greek Revival style. The exterior walls are 28 inches thick and the front entrance is set off by two curving stairways leading to the second floor portico. The first nullification meeting in the state was held in this courthouse in 1828. Robert Barnwell Rhett, the author of the nullification statute, called for the immediate secession of the state legislation.

Another of Walterboro's striking historic buildings which, like the courthouse, is on the National Register of Historic Places (NRHP), is the Old Colleton County Jail built in 1855. This Neo-Gothic landmark at 239 N. Jeffries Boulevard, the town's third jail, looks like a fortified castle with crenelated parapet and lancet windows. This jail held prisoners until 1937. Now it serves as **The Colleton Museum**. Artifacts date back to prehistoric times and extend through the pre-Revolutionary period, when much of what is now Colleton County was farmland and rice was a significant crop. Exhibits then cover the Civil War period and on to more recent times. Museum hours are Tuesday through Friday 10:00 A.M. to 1:00 P.M. and 2:00 to 5:00 P.M. Plans call for Saturday openings.

Also on the NRHP is the **Walterboro Library Society Building**, or "Little Library," built in the Federal style in 1820. It is now the headquarters of the Colleton County Historical and Preservation Society. There are several walking tours of Walterboro including a two-mile historic route and a natural trail along the water at Ireland Creek Park.

There are a number of interesting churches in Walterboro, although local legend claims that a tornado in 1879 leveled all the churches but left all the bars standing. One that was destroyed, then rebuilt in 1882, was St. Jude's Episcopal Church on Wichman Street. It is done in the Carpenter Gothic style popular during the Victorian era. Across the street is St. Peter's AME Church, a Gothic Revival Church built around 1900 with a gable roof and tower. This congregation was established after the Emancipation Proclamation by former slaves. On Hampton Street you'll see the First Baptist Church and Bethel Methodist; both are noted for their stained glass windows.

You'll also want to drive or walk along the tree-lined streets so that you can see the gracious private residences in Walterboro. One historic old home is the Jones-McDaniel-Hiott House, 418 Wichman Street, built between 1834 and 1838. It was the home of Elizabeth Ann Horry Dent, the widow of John Herbert Dent, who commanded the *U.S.S. Constitution* during the Battle of Tripoli in 1804. The 1844 Revival Period Klein House, 104 Valley Street, has a portico with four giant Tuscan columns. The 1824 Glover-McLeod House is called "The Mounds" because one of the owners, a Mr. Warley, buried horses on either side of the entrance avenue. The grounds of this estate at 109 Savage Street still contain an antebellum slave cabin, stable and carriage house. Hampton Street is noted for its array of historic homes dating from 1824 through the 1920s.

One old house at 334 Wichman Street has been converted to the **South Carolina Artisans Center**. The rooms are filled with a colorful array of handcrafted items from all across the state. Pottery, woodwork, jewelry, batik, wall hangings, weavings, furniture, art works and a tantalizing assortment of unique pieces fill the center. It is open Monday through Saturday from 10:00 A.M. to 7:00 P.M. and Sunday 1:00 to 6:00 P.M.

Just five minutes off the interstate at Exit 57 is **Mount Carmel Herb Farm** where you can purchase hundreds of varieties of herbs. The farm offers tours of their display gardens and schedules a series of lectures on herbs. A gift shop sells herbal products and books. For more information call (803) 538-3505.

Directions: From I-95, Walterboro is just two miles from the exit. If you are heading north take Exit 57, Route 63; if you are driving south take Exit 53, Route 64 into town. Both routes merge with Jefferies Boulevard. For Mount Carmel Herb Farm head west on Mt. Carmel Highway (off Route 64) for 3½ miles and the farm will be on your left.

Lowcountry & Resort Islands Regional Tourism Contacts (Area Code 803)

LOWCOUNTRY & RESORT ISLANDS TOURISM COMMISSION
P.O. Box 366
Hampton, SC 29924
943-9180, (800) 528-6870

EDISTO CHAMBER OF COMMERCE
P.O. Box 206
Edisto Beach, SC 29438
869-3867

GREATER BEAUFORT CHAMBER OF COMMERCE
P.O. Box 910
Beaufort, SC 29901
524-3163

HAMPTON COUNTY CHAMBER OF COMMERCE
P.O. Box 122, Courthouse Annex
Hampton, SC 29924
943-3784

HARDEEVILLE CHAMBER OF COMMERCE
P.O. Box 307
Hardeeville, SC 29927
784-3606

HILTON HEAD ISLAND CHAMBER OF COMMERCE
P.O. Box 5674
Hilton Head Island, SC 29938
785-3673, fax: 785-7110

JASPER COUNTY CHAMBER OF COMMERCE
P.O. Box 1267
Ridgeland, SC 29936
726-8126

WALTERBORO-COLLETON CHAMBER OF COMMERCE
P.O. Box 426
Walterboro, SC 29488
549-9595, 549-9596

Lowcountry & Resort Islands Calendar of Events (Area Code 803)

Early March
Handmade Crafts and Folk Art demonstrated by practitioners at the SC Artisans Center. Walterboro, 549-0011 (Demonstrations on an ongoing basis throughout year.)
Mid-March
St. Helena's Episcopal Church Spring Tours. The annual opportunity (it's been going on for over 40 years) to tour some of Beaufort's

gracious private homes. Beaufort, 524-6334.

Early April

Hilton Head Island Family Circle Magazine Cup. For more than 25 years the best women's tennis players have competed at Sea Pines. Hilton Head, 363-3500.

MCI Classic. PGA tour members compete at Harbour Town Golf Links in this $1.3 million tournament. Hilton Head, 671-2448.

Late April

Colleton County Rice Festival. A rice cooking contest and the "world's largest pot of rice" are highlights of this event. Walterboro, 757-3855.

Late May

Gullah Festival. Storytelling, dance, music, food all celebrate the African-American Gullah culture. Beaufort, 525-0628.

Early June

Edisto Riverfest. Guided trips on the Edisto River, canoe workshops, outdoor equipment exhibits and plenty of food are event highlights. Walterboro, 549-5591.

Late June

Hampton County Watermelon Festival. Started in 1939 this is South Carolina's oldest continuous festival. Week-long event featuring arts & crafts and a parade, enlivened by a seed spitting and watermelon eating contest. Hampton, 943-3784.

Mid-July

Beaufort County Water Festival. Week long event with music, arts and crafts, air and water show, parade and the Blessing of the Fleet. Beaufort, 524-0600.

Late September

Catfish Festival. Arts and crafts, rides, games, a dance, catfish dinners, live entertainment and speedboat races combine to make this a fun event. Hardeeville, 784-6776.

Fall Family Fun Festival. Rides, games, crafts and food highlight this event. Hilton Head Island, 681-7273.

Shrimp Festival. Marine exhibits, shrimp boats, music, family fun and unique cuisine highlight this event. Beaufort, 524-3163.

ACE Basin Triathlon. Athletes compete in three-pronged event: running, canoeing and bicycling. Walterboro, 549-5591.

Early October

Hilton Head Island Corel Champions. Men's tennis tournament. Hilton Head Island, 363-3500.

Gopher Hill Festival. A parade, flea market, games, food booths, outdoor concert and a dance make up this event. Ridgeland, 726-8126.

Mid-October

Fall Tour of Homes. A peek at the private homes of this coastal community. Beaufort, 524-6334.

Golden Age Tour. Self-guided tour of Edisto Island's historic homes. Edisto Island, 869-1954.

St. Luke's Tour of Homes. Self-guided tour of Hilton Head's historic homes. Hilton Head Island, 785-4099.

Mid-November

Heritage Days. The second weekend is Penn Center's annual celebration of African-American cultural lore, local arts and crafts and regional food. St. Helena Island, 838-2235.

December

Christmas at the Verdier House. Tour of historic 1790 home decorated for the holidays. Beaufort, 524-6334.

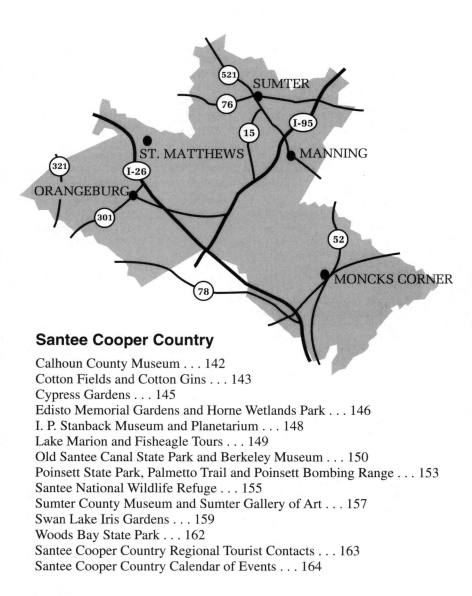

Santee Cooper Country

= Santee Cooper Country =

The Santee and Cooper rivers flow through this south central region. The rivers and linking canal form a 171,000-acre basin offering some of the finest sport fishing and recreation in the state—*and* the country. Hydroelectric projects on the rivers created two lakes—Marion and Moultrie—connected by the Diversion Canal. These lakes were never cleared of trees so hillocks of cypress trees and water plants provide a haven for birds and other wildlife. Excursions with Fisheagle Tours reveal this enormously rich natural environment. Smaller bodies of water have been transformed into vibrant gardens, as you'll see at Cypress Gardens and Swan Lake Iris Gardens.

This is one of the best regions in which to gain an understanding of the cotton culture. You will see fields of cotton alongside the road. Several cotton gins welcome visitors and provide a window on the past. Watching the ginning process, it's hard not to think back to the time when cotton was picked by hand, row after row. Now huge multi-row pickers can clear a field in a fraction of the time. The Calhoun County Museum and Sumter County Museum both have exhibits on cotton, and other local industries, along with their historical and cultural collections.

Even most historians are unaware that this is the location of the country's first dug channel canal—Old Santee Canal. An innovatively designed visitors center presents the story of the canal and also the saga of one of the first semi-submersible torpedo boats, the Little David, that was built here. There is also a good bit of early history at Santee National Wildlife Refuge where you will see a prehistoric Indian mound and the site of a Revolutionary War fort.

Calhoun County Museum

All in the Family

Family is important in the south and in many of the rural communities people are united by bonds of kinship. Visitors should remember this before they comment on colorful characters they encounter. At **Calhoun County Museum**, the family link is particularly strong. The museum was established in 1952 as a history room by Jean Ulmer, the mother of the current director Debbie Roland.

Jean Ulmer began collecting items that reflected the history and culture of the county and its people. Visitors will find all kinds of artifacts, ranging from military uniforms to children's toys and from farm equipment to oversized kitchen napkins. Debbie Roland believes that if a visitor doesn't have fun at the museum the staff hasn't done its job. Exploring the museum, now located in a former pecan factory, is a different experience for everyone. Explanations given to young children who are touring their first museum differ from those given to an out-of-towner trying to gain an understanding of Calhoun County.

Most of the pieces in the museum have fascinating stories, such as the one about the portrait of Catherine Kinseler Kaigler. When Sherman's soldiers were moving through the state, they camped on the grounds of the Kaigler estate in Sandy Run. When Catherine was ordered to leave her house, she refused. She barred the door saying that her father and grandfather had been born in the house and she would not abandon it. According to the story, she so reminded the commanding officer of his mother, that he allowed her to stay and didn't burn her home. But his men did enter the house, vandalizing and stealing the family belongings. They couldn't reach Catherine's portrait because it was hanging high above the mantle, so they tried to poke the face out with their bayonets. You can still see the gouges they made. They did manage to steal a portrait of Katherine's two sons, but it was returned. The repentant thief sent it to the Mayor of Columbia and asked that it be returned to the family. The museum's display has Catherine's second-day wedding dress as well as her granddaughter's. These are just two of the museum's fashion items. There is an exhibit section called *Fashions of Yesterdays* with wedding dresses, day dresses and even mourning jewelry.

The museum's Lawrence Keitl collection includes items associated with a local gentleman who was picked as one of the ten most influential men in the state between 1850 and 1860. Keitl was a friend of President Van Buren. Items exhibited include a dressing robe and other personal memorabilia. Uniforms, munitions and personal mementoes are all part of the military collection. There are also period rooms featuring children's toys, kitchen items and household articles. Another exhibit traces the African influence in South Carolina while another concentrates on prehistoric people and Native American culture. The shelves and storefront of A. O. Rickenbacker's general store from nearby Cameron have been moved to the museum so that visitors can see a genuine old-fashioned store complete with pot-bellied stove. Finally, there is a large area with an extensive array of farm equipment and vehicles.

Those doing family genealogy can use the museum's extensive archives for their research. Local and regional artists frequently mount temporary exhibits in the museum's gallery space. The Calhoun County Museum is open at no charge Monday through Friday from 9:00 A.M. until 4:00 P.M.; if you plan to do research in the archives call ahead for an appointment at (803) 874-3964.

Directions: From I-26 traveling south from the Columbia area, take Exit 136, Route 172 east to St. Matthews. Traveling north on I-26 from the Charleston area, take Exit 145, Route 601 north. In St. Matthews the museum is located at 303 Butler Street.

Cotton Fields and Cotton Gins

Picking and Ginning

If cotton is no longer "king," it is still indelibly linked with the south and the Santee Cooper region remains a big cotton producer. Driving along the highways and back roads, you see cotton fields stretching for miles. Fields adjacent to cotton gins that are open to the public, often allow you to try your skill at picking cotton. It's not hard to pluck one of the soft fleecy bolls from its prickly holder, but imagine picking three hundred pounds of cotton bolls in one day. Before the days of the one-row and multi-row pickers, good field hands would make that their daily quota.

The business of cotton, or what was once called white gold, is becoming more mechanized but there are still older-style cotton gins where the process has changed little over the decades. One such operation is the **Lowder Brothers Gin Company**, on Route 401 outside Sumter. Tourists check in at the main office, and are welcome to observe the ginning process. Ginning is done September, October and November during the work week from 7:30 A.M. until NOON and from 1:00 to 5:00 P.M.

Farmers, as in days gone by, bring trailers loaded with cotton to the gin. The difference is that the lines are shorter now. The trailers pull alongside the gin and are unloaded by a suspended metal pipe that sucks the cotton up into the metal containers of the gin. The farmers swing the huge vacuum pipe back and forth across their trailers until all the cotton is funneled up.

Inside, the gin processes the cotton and sends the seeds from each boll to the seed house. The farmer leaves his baled cotton at the gin to be shipped to market but refills his trailer with his seeds to plant the next year's crop. If you watch the ginning operation closely you will see that there are seven stages of cleaning before the cotton is baled. The material eliminated from the cotton, called cull, is used for cattle feed. Everything inside most cotton gins is covered with a patina of cotton fuzz. Even some of the workers sitting beside the machines seem to have a coating of cotton dust. The rafters and pipes have cotton cascades like white Spanish moss. The machinery keeps up a steady rhythm that makes conversation impossible, so if you want the process explained you'll have to step outside. At Lowder's, they still bale the cotton in burlap.

Another cotton gin that opens its door to the public is **Vallentines** in Cope. Here you will find an old general store, farm and cotton gin that were established in 1911. When J. L. Vallentine opened the store, he advertised, "Everything from

Visitors can paddle or stroll through a black water wonderland at Cypress Gardens. Cypress trees tower over the garden's colorful azaleas, camellias, spring bulbs and native wildflowers.

horse collars to crochet needles." Today you can buy stick bologna and hoop cheese, cotton souvenirs and collectibles. From the store you can walk to the adjacent cotton gin and view the ginning process. Here the 500-pound bales are plastic wrapped. Vallentines is open Monday through Saturday from 10:00 A.M. to 5:00 P.M.

While in the general store or the area's museum shops, try to pick up a small book called *Barefoot-n-Cotton*. It's written and illustrated by Patsy P. Lewis, the director of tourism in Sumter, and provides a glimpse of what it was like to grow up on a cotton farm in the south.

Directions: From I-95 take Exit 135, Route 378 west to Sumter. For Lowder Brothers Gin Company, turn north off Route 378 onto Route 401. For Vallentines, if you are traveling on I-95 head south to Exit 86, where you will pick-up I-26 toward Columbia. Take Exit 146 and head south on Route 601/301 through Orangeburg. Continue south on that road for another 13 miles to Cope. The cotton gin is one mile off Route 301; make a right onto Route 332 and the gin is on the right.

Cypress Gardens

Water Wonderland

Many of the state's verdant gardens are former rice plantations. **Cypress Gardens** was reclaimed in the late 1920s on the site of a failed plantation that had lapsed into its natural state, replete with giant swamp cypress and overgrown weeds and vines.

Benjamin Kittredge purchased the old Dean Hall rice plantation, which had flourished from the late 18th century until the Civil War. While hunting wild turkey within this watery jungle-like habitat, it occurred to Kittredge that the area would be particularly interesting if it could be cleared and presented as a natural garden. He realized his concept and created a 162-acre swamp garden that opened to the public in 1932.

The Gardens are open year round and there is always something in bloom. The blooming season reaches its peak in March and April with a profusion of azaleas, dogwoods, daffodils and wisteria. Before this spring bonanza, visitors will be able to enjoy the huge camellia bushes that flank many of the trails. Native wildflowers also brighten the trail.

Cypress Gardens is accessible by 2½ miles of trails that weave through this swamp garden, providing a close look at the blossoms; you can also explore by boat. The entrance fee includes use of a flat-bottomed boat you can paddle yourself through the easily negotiable circular water trail. The trip takes approximately 30 minutes to navigate. Though the dark depths seem fathomless, the water is actually only two feet deep in most places. If you prefer you can relax and let one of the garden's boatmen take you around.

The naturalistic gardens are a popular spot with bird enthusiasts, who frequent the two nature trails that meander through the more isolated sections of the swamp. Pileated woodpeckers, barred owls, wood ducks, herons, osprey and egrets are just some of the species you may spot. You may even see an alligator or otter as you explore the trails.

Harkening back to the garden's earliest days, a small working rice field reveals the old methods. Depending on the time of your visit you may watch the field being planted, tended or harvested.

The visitor center has interpretative material on the terrain including a fresh-water aquarium, reptile exhibits and a butter-fly house. Cypress Gardens is open daily 9:00 A.M. to 5:00 P.M. Admission is charged.

Directions: From I-26 take Exit 199B and head north on Route 17A. Turn right on Cypress Gardens Road and you will see the gardens entrance on the right. If you are traveling on I-26 from Charleston, take Exit 208, Route 52 and continue past Goose Creek. Turn right on Cypress Gardens Road and right again at the garden entrance.

Edisto Memorial Gardens and Horne Wetlands Park

Augmenting Nature

Orangeburg is called the "Garden City," due in large part to the lovely **Edisto Memorial Gardens**, a 150-acre, city-owned free garden on the banks of the north branch of the Edisto River. The garden started in the early 1920s with a five-acre azalea plot and has expanded over the years.

The rose garden was added in 1951, and now it's an All-American Rose Selections Display Garden, with between 4,000 and 5,000 plants representing at least 75 labeled varieties of roses. This is one of only 23 official test gardens in the country. Up to five of the best hybrid roses are selected each year from the test garden for inclusion in the display garden.

Beneath giant oaks and century-old cypress trees, the colorful azaleas and huge camellia bushes add bright splashes of color to the garden. Peak spring bloom is from mid-March to mid-April. In the spring 200 Yoshino cherry trees add to the beauty of the scene. At dusk, the floating fountain in the garden pond is lighted, creating a focal point for visitors. There is also an outdoor butterfly garden and a sensory garden with a Braille trail.

The last full weekend in April marks the South Carolina Festival of Roses, a celebration listed as one of the top 20 tourism events by the Southeastern Tourism Society. Edisto Memorial Gardens has hosted this event since 1972 and it grows more popular each year. Roses bloom at Edisto from the middle of April until the first killing frost of November.

Adjacent to the gardens is the **Horne Wetlands Park** where a 2,600-foot boardwalk takes visitors into this tupelo-cypress wetlands. A self-guided tour along the Edisto Memorial Gardens Nature Trail identifies native trees and plants in this wetlands park. (You can pick up the tour brochures at the Orangeburg Chamber of Commerce office at 250 John C. Calhoun Drive just outside the garden gates or at the Orangeburg Arts Center in the gardens.) The boardwalk, which is accessible to the disabled, permits visitors to get an up-close look at the plants and wildlife found in the wetlands along the banks of the Edisto River. Two hundred miles long, it's the longest black water river in the world. (See Edisto River Canoe and Kayak Trail selection.) Visitors can even access the park by water since the boardwalk has a dock area where canoeists and kayakers can tie up.

Long-range plans call for exhibit boards in an interpretative shelter and labeled plantings along the boardwalk. One curious feature you will see on the river is the water wheel, which supplies water to the nearby pond. It is similar to Oriental rice paddy irrigation wheels.

At the entrance of the gardens is a fountain that was erected in memory of soldiers who died in World War I and II, the Korean War and the Vietnam Conflict. When this statue was added in 1950, the gardens added "memorial" to its name.

From late November until January the gardens are alight with the Children's Garden Christmas. Animated displays, 50 lighted cherry trees and a nativity scene add to the gardens' appeal. There is no charge for this holiday celebration which is open from 5:00 until 10:00 P.M.

Directions: From I-26 take Exit 154, the Orangeburg exit, Route 301/601 south. Edisto Memorial Gardens are on Route 301 just four blocks from the downtown area. From I-95 take Exit 97, Route 301 west to Orangeburg.

The I.P. Stanback Museum and Planetarium

Artistic Stars and Heavenly Bodies

The South Carolina State University is a historically Black college once called The Colored Normal, Industrial, Agriculture and Mechanical College. Now the arts have a firm foundation on the campus in Orangeburg as you will see when you visit **The I. P. Stanback Museum and Planetarium**.

In pursuing the college's mission of establishing a culturally diverse model for its students, a museum and planetarium were built in the early 1970s. Art was first exhibited in the college library's basement-level Whittaker Gallery, but in 1980 the present facility was built. It was named in honor of prominent Columbia businessman and philanthropist Isreal Pinkney Stanback, the first African American chairman of the University's Board of Trustees who served from 1966 to 1982.

The museum's permanent collection includes both African and African-American work. Tribal art by the Mende, Bambara and Yoruba people is featured. The staff interprets the work so that visitors understand the significance of the exaggerated features on some of the tribal figures like the Nimba Figure done by the Baga People of West Africa and the Janiform Bundu Mask done by the Sande Society Mende People of Sierra Leone. There is an extensive collection of photographs from South Carolina and from Harlem. Works by Gordon Parks, James Vanderzee, Lloyd Yearwood and Addison Scurlock are owned by the museum. Prints and paintings in the permanent collection include works by Romare Bearden, Jacob Lawrence, Ellis Wilson and William H. Johnson, plus sculpture done by Charleston's Phillip Simmons. Frequent traveling exhibits and work by students and faculty is shown at the museum.

Across the foyer from the exhibit galleries is the planetarium with its 40-foot dome. Shows change monthly and their themes often focus on current space news as well as general astronomy subjects. This is the second largest facility in the state, and more accessible to the public than the larger Roper Mountain Science Center in Greenville. The facility has a Minolta IIB planetarium projector in its 82-seat auditorium. It is also a NASA Regional Teacher Resource Center and can be accessed on the Internet via http://www.draco.scsu.edu. This computer site will give you information on current shows plus a wide array of additional data.

When you visit you will also see an exhibit area for the college's science collection including African gemstones, meteor fragments and replicas of communications satellites. Hours are

Monday through Friday from 9:00 A.M. to 4:40 P.M. There is no charge to visit, however there is a nominal charge for planetarium programs. Planetarium programs are given on the first Sunday from October through April at 3:00 and 4:00 P.M. For a schedule of programs call (803) 536-7174.

Directions: From I-95 and I-26 take Route 301 exit and head west to the South Carolina State University campus. The I.P. Stanback Museum and Planetarium is at 300 College Street on the campus.

Lake Marion and Fisheagle Tours

Bird's Eye View

Boaters can navigate a 122-mile inland water route, via lakes and canals, from Columbia to Charleston. **Lake Marion** is at the upper end of this route. There are two interesting parks on the lake, the 50-acre Taw Caw Creek Park (a county park) and the 2,496-acre Santee State Park.

Taw Caw Creek Park, on Goat Island, offers visitors a boardwalk and nature trails through marshy terrain. The park also has a fishing pier, launching ramp and picnic facilities. The larger **Santee State Park** has a fishing pier and rents fishing boats (you do need to bring your own gas engines) and pedal boats. It has a swimming area, playground and tennis courts. Santee has 174 campsites in two lakefront campgrounds and 30 cabins. A restaurant and park store add to the convenience of this scenic park. The park is open daily 6:00 A.M. to 10:00 P.M. The restaurant is open Thursday through Sunday for breakfast, lunch and dinner. Campsites are on a first come/first serve basis but cabins can be reserved by calling (803) 854-2408.

Lake Marion is a fisherman's paradise. Numerous tournaments are held here and the catch includes catfish, largemouth and striped bass. Some of the best catches are made by the waterfowl who make the lake their home. The best way to observe the diverse bird population is by taking one of the lake and swamp wildlife scenic tours offered by **Fisheagle Tours**. Their pontoon boats, open sided in pleasant weather and closed in the cooler months, get you close to nature.

Lake Marion—at 100,000 acres it's the state's largest lake—is unique because of the many trees that were left standing in the submerged soil when the lake was formed. These trees continued to flourish despite their flooded environment. These islands of plant life provide natural habitats that are ideal for the numerous species of birds who make their home here. The Spanish-moss draped bald cypress provide a splendid setting as the pontoon boat floats slowly under their limbs.

Dianne and Francis Burn and their son, Randal, run Fisheagle Tours and they offer insightful, educational and thoroughly enjoyable two-hour narrated tours that give passengers a genuine sense of appreciation for this unique ecosystem. Be sure to bring a camera as the pontoon boat offers close-up views of herons, ospreys, anhingas, cormorants, egrets, sunning turtles, alligators and a wide variety of other waterfowl. They impart interesting information such as the fact that Native Americans used Spanish moss as diapers for their young. You'll also learn all about "frustration nests" that are built by ospreys when their young die. Instead of devoting their time to feeding their offspring they build these unnecessary nests.

Fisheagle Tours operate from March through October. For the current schedule, rates and reservations call (800) 967-7739 or (803) 854-4005. Passengers 90 or older are given a free ride, as are children under six. There are seats in the pontoon boat and the ride is smooth enough for all ages. In November, the boat is moved to Old Santee Canal State Historic Site (see selection) and tours are given of the Tailrace Canal. These excursions include riding 75 feet straight up the Pinopolis Lock, one of the tallest locks in the world. Along this route, you are apt to see bald eagles, ospreys, pelicans, cormorants and otters.

Directions: From I-95 take Exit 98 at Santee and take Route 6 for 3 miles northwest of Santee. For Taw Caw Creek Park take Exit 108, the Summerton exit, off I-95 and follow signs east for 6 ½ miles to Goat Island.

Old Santee Canal State Historic Site and Berkeley Museum

America's First Summit Canal

Getting cotton from the fertile uplands of South Carolina to Charleston's bustling harbor prior to 1800 involved either a long haul by wagon, or a boat trip down the Santee River into the unpredictable waters of the Atlantic Ocean and on into Charleston. Innovative thinkers decided that a canal linking the Santee and Cooper rivers, which were only 22 miles apart, would provide a far better route to Charleston, and would avoid the cargo loss so often suffered when plying the open sea from the mouth of the Santee to the safety of Charleston's harbor.

Alhough the difference in elevation between the two rivers was only 35 feet, this canal was still an engineering achievement. It traversed swamp and forest land, with three locks to lift boats from the Santee River to the summit level, and seven locks to descend down to the level of the Cooper River.

Work began on the Santee Canal in 1793. One enthusiastic booster was General George Washington (who also supported the more northern Chesapeake & Ohio Canal, built about 30 years later). Seven hundred workers labored seven years to construct the canal, which began operating in 1800. At that time General William Moultrie was governor and he became the first president of the Santee Canal Company.

Originally mules or horses on tow paths pulled canal boats and barges along both sides of the 30-foot-wide canal. But later crewmen with poles pushed the boats through the 5½-foot deep water. The canal was utilized from its first days, and before long it began showing a profit. But in 1817 and 1819, severe droughts dried up the canal. Corn was planted in the summit bed of the canal to take advantage of the fertile soil. The canal quickly rebounded and 1830 was its busiest year with 700 barges and boats traveling through the locks. In 1840, a railroad was built between Columbia and Charleston. As the railroad expanded the canal declined until it was finally closed in the early 1850s.

Today most of the canal lies beneath the waters of Lake Moultrie, but at **Old Santee Canal State Historic Site,** located where the southernmost section of the canal entered Biggin Creek, you can see visitor center exhibits that show exactly how the canal was constructed and operated. Be sure to notice that you enter the center through replicas of canal lock doors and there is a trough of water on both sides of the walkway that extends into the exhibit area.

The center has a composite model of the Santee Canal and you will discover fascinating details about the construction of the canal. Many of the men and women who labored to build it were slaves. Their owners were paid a yearly sum of $120 for men and $100 for women. The men were required to fill 54 wheel barrows a day with rock and dirt as they dug the canal bed by hand.

If a portion of the swamp was tamed for the canal, a great section remained in its natural state. The visitor center's exhibits also focus on the natural environment. A 30-foot live oak tree reaches upward two stories. Within its boughs and beneath its limbs are a wide variety of wildlife that visitors are encouraged to identify—bobcat, river otter, gray fox, squirrel, great blue heron, eastern garter snake and others. A chart is close by to help those less familiar with these local species. A limestone cave theater shows nature programs and movies associated with the history of the region.

This area has enumerable historic connections. During the Civil War, gunpowder was made in the vicinity. The CSS *Little David*, a semisubmersible Confederate torpedo boat, was built on the property by Dr. St. Julien Ravenel, owner of the plantation at Stony Landing. He based his design on a model created by

Ross Winan, a northern sympathizer from Baltimore. The *CSS Little David* was five feet in diameter, 48½ feet long and 18 feet at the middle, both ends tapered to a point. In 1863, the *CSS Little David* made the first successful torpedo attack on a warship, the *USS New Ironsides*. After ramming the warship, a column of water came down the smokestack and put out the fire operating the semisubmersible. Three of the four crew members jumped overboard, while the remaining member, the pilot, who could not swim, stayed with the vessel. The *CSS Little David* began to drift away from the *USS New Ironsides*. The pilot was able to restart the engine fires. The first assistant engineer noted this and swam back to the vessel and the two men were able to safely return the *CSS Little David* to Charleston. The visitor center has a ⅜th scale model of this historic vessel.

After exploring the center take time to walk along the four miles of boardwalk that lead out into the marsh, swamp and along the scenic bluff habitats. Observation points along the boardwalk provide glimpses of ever-present wildlife. You may want to bring a camera. You can also rent canoes at the park and paddle along Biggin Creek and into the old canal itself. It is a sobering statistic that 85% of park visitors nationwide never get more than 500 feet from their car. This significantly reduces the experience as part of the thrill of this historic site is the natural wonders such as alligators, otters, deer, beaver and herons along the swamp, creek or canal walks.

There is also an historic plantation house within the park, **Stony Landing Plantation**, built around 1840 on the high bluff at the headwaters of the Cooper River. This was a crossroads of early commerce and there were earlier buildings here. The one that has been restored was built by merchant John Dawson, who purchased 2,319 acres on March 26, 1839 and built his home facing the Congaree Road. The house is built on brick pillars that raise it off the ground. These pillars and the arches that support the fireplaces are original. This height allowed breezes to cool the house in the summer, while fireplaces in each room provided warmth in colder seasons.

Adjacent to this historic site is **Berkeley Museum**. On the grounds outside the museum is a full-size replica of the *USS Little David*. The first thing you notice when you enter the museum is the striking painting of General Francis Marion at the Battle of Eutaw Springs. The work was commissioned by the late Russell Blackmon and painted by Major Robert W. Wilson. Also in the museum entrance is a case with the 1991 world record catfish caught in the Cooper River by George A. Lijewski. This enormous catfish weighs 109 pounds, 4 ounces. Exhibits in the museum trace the region's earliest inhabitants. There are artifacts from the Paleo-Indian period—arrowheads, cattail leaf mats, archaic implements and fish traps. Native American artifacts are also exhibited and there are examples of colonial industries. Berkeley County's swamps were familiar territory for Francis Marion, the famed Swamp Fox. The museum traces the American Revolution's impact on this region and then the later impact of the Civil War. There is a nominal charge for this museum that is open Monday through Saturday from 9:00 A.M. to 5:00 P.M. and Sunday 1:00 to 5:00 P.M.

If you're in the Moncks Corner area around meal time, a great place to stop is **The Dock Restaurant** overlooking the Tailrace Canal. Here too you will see a stuffed replica of George Lijewski's prize-winning catfish. That's appropriate as catfish and hush puppies are the restaurant's specialties. Hours are Sunday through Thursday 11:30 A.M. to 9:30 P.M. and Friday and Saturday until 10:30 P.M.

Thirteen miles southeast of Moncks Corner is **Mepkin Abbey**, now a monastery but originally the home of Henry Laurens, an American patriot who was imprisoned in the Tower of London. His estate was burned by the British. Another plantation house was built on the grounds and it was burned during the Civil War. Before being given to the Catholic Church, the estate was the home of Henry and Clare Booth Luce. You can see their graves as you explore the tranquil gardens on the banks of the Cooper River. The gardens and chapel are open to the public at no charge daily from 9:00 A.M. to 4:30 P.M.

Old Santee State Historic Site is open from 9:00 A.M. to 5:00 P.M. during the winter months and until 6:00 P.M. in the summer. The visitors center closes at 4:30 P.M. in the winter and 5:30 P.M. in the summer. The park has a small gift shop.

Directions: From I-26 take Exit 208, Route 52 north to Moncks Corner. Old Santee Canal State Historic Site is located off Route 52 Bypass (R.C. Dennis Boulevard) on Stony Landing Road. The Dock Restaurant is off Highway 52 in Moncks Corner. For Mepkin Abbey take Route 402 from Moncks Corner; the monastery is on River Road.

Poinsett State Park, Palmetto Trail and Poinsett Bombing Range

Upcountry Terrain/Lowcountry Vegetation

The 1,000-acre **Poinsett State Park** is in the High Hills of the Santee, an area that resembles the rolling countryside of the mountains. Some of the vegetation seems the same, including the mountain laurel and hardwood trees. But the Spanish moss-draped cypress are a reminder of the adjacent Wateree Swamp.

153

Poinsett, open from 9:00 A.M. to 9:00 P.M. during the summer and until 6:00 P.M. in the winter, offers a wide array of recreational options. One of the most enjoyable is the equestrian trails. Unfortunately, it is strictly BYOH (Bring Your Own Horse). They rent pedal boats in the summer months and fishing boats all year long so visitors can access the lake. The park has 50 camp sites and four cabins. There are picnic facilities, a playground and a nature center with exhibits on the flora and fauna you will discover if you explore the park's nature and hiking trails.

Poinsett State Park is one of the access points for the **Palmetto Trail**, which will eventually stretch across the state. Another nearby access point is in **Mill Creek Park**, where a signboard shows the route of the *High Hills of Santee Passage* portion of the trail. This is one of the few sections of the trail where horseback riding is permitted. There are stables at this park where horse-owners can bring their mounts and enjoy the many trails through Manchester State Forest and nearby Poinsett State Park. Mill Creek also has a lake, picnic areas and campsites. For information call the Sumter County Recreation Department at (803) 436-2248.

Joel Poinsett, for whom the state park is named, introduced the Euphorbiaceae plant into the country. Poinsett, a Charleston-born diplomatic, served as the country's first minister to Mexico from 1825 to 1829 and was President Van Buren's Secretary of War. It was in Mexico that Poinsett saw the showy flowers of the Euphorbiaceae plant. When he returned he introduced this popular plant, that now bears his name, to cultivation. Poinsett is buried at the nearby **Church of the Holy Cross**. It's worth visiting this Gothic Revival church built in 1850, by a congregation that dates back to 1770. The church is noteworthy as it is built of *pise de terre* or "rammed earth." Notable architectural features include corner towers, pointed arches and the Bavarian-made stained glass windows. The church has one of the few operational organs made by renowned 19th-century New York craftsman Henry Erben. The church is open by appointment; call the pastor at (803) 494-8101.

Also named for Poinsett is the bombing range near the park. Bleachers are provided for visitors who want to watch the Air Force's military exercises. You have to call ahead at (803) 668-3620 for the day's schedule of activities. If you are lucky you'll get to see A-10s and F-16s perform tactical maneuvers. After bombing designated targets, the planes rapidly disappear into the bright blue sky.

Directions: From I-95 take Exit 119, Route 261 west to Pinewood, where the road turns north. Stay on Route 261 through the Manchester State Forest and there will be an entrance to Poinsett State Park on the left. For Mill Creek Park turn left on Route 808; it will take you to Route 51 and the entrance to the park. The Poinsett Bombing Range is on Route 261 near Wedgefield.

Santee National Wildlife Refuge

Pre-colonial and Colonial Reminders

The 15,000-acre **Santee National Wildlife Refuge**, along 18 miles of Lake Marion's northern shore, has four separate units: Bluff, Dingle Pond, Pine Island and Cuddo. These units encompass diverse habitats including pine and hardwood forests, marshes, croplands, impoundments, ponds and open water. Nature is not the only attraction at the refuge; this is the location of the **Santee Indian Mound** and the site of **Fort Watson**.

Prehistoric tribes were in the Santee River area between 1200 and 1400 A.D. The region was part of the Province of Cofitachiqui, a tribal priestess who was visited by Hernado De Soto during his 1540–1542 expedition. The Santee Mound culture used these earthen pyramid-shaped, flat-topped mounds as ceremonial sites, not for burials. There would have been a small temple on top of this 30-foot high mound on the banks of Scotts Lake. By the time the British traders arrived in the 1700s, these ceremonial centers were abandoned. There is a walkway that you can take to an observation point at the top of the mound.

In 1780, British soldiers under the command of Colonel John W.T. Watson built a small fort on top of the Santee Mound. In April 1781, Colonel "Light Horse" Harry Lee (the father of Robert E. Lee) and General Francis Marion, the Swamp Fox, laid siege to Fort Watson. Their goal was to take control of British supply lines and break the British stranglehold on river traffic. They were under orders to provide support for Major Nathaniel Greene's engagement with the British at Camden.

Lee and Marion arrived at Fort Watson on Sunday, April 15, and trapped 120 British within the post. One of their men, Major Hesekiah Mahan, suggested building a log tower from which they could fire down into the fort and force the British to surrender. The 40-foot pine tower gave the colonials the necessary advantage, and the British Garrison Commander Lieutenant James McKay ended the siege after eight days.

This historic site is located in the Bluff Unit, where you will also find the visitors center overlooking Lake Marion. The center provides an orientation to the refuge with dioramas of native wildlife and an aquarium of native fish. The center is open Monday through Friday from 8:00 A.M. to 4:00 P.M. The historic points of interest are along the Wright's Bluff Nature Trail; you can also drive to a parking lot beside the information signs explaining these historic sites.

This varied landscape of Santee National Wildlife Refuge provides a home and resting spot for a wide variety of wildlife. From November through February, approximately 8,000 Canada geese and 50,000 ducks are at the refuge. Whistling swans can be seen along the bluff during December. Sparrows, juncos and finches are found in the forests during the winter months. Largemouth bass, striped bass and catfish are plentiful in December and the striped bass school in January. Activity can be seen around the nesting boxes in February when wood ducks, purple martins and bluebirds start arriving.

Spring is an active season in the habitats. Raptors arrive in March and this is the month when alligators again can be seen sunning themselves and largemouth bass are plentiful. There's plenty of color in the wild in April—butterflies are everywhere and buntings, orioles, tanagers, vireos and blue grosbeaks seek the forested areas. Spring migration and nesting continues in May.

Newcomers in June include hummingbirds, titmice and chickadees. This is also the month when white bass begin schooling. With nesting completed, shorebirds can be seen along the pond and lake shore in July teaching their young. Summer warblers migrate here in August. This is also a time to be generous with bug repellent when visiting the refuge as redbugs, biting flies and mosquitos are plentiful.

Fall songbird migration peaks in September, while in October raptors, cormorants and waterfowl arrive. This is an excellent time for catfishing. November is the best month to spot bald eagles. Lucky visitors have even spotted the peregrine falcon at the refuge.

There are public boat launching ramps in the Cuddo Unit (Route 260 at Taw Caw Creek) and in the Pine Island Unit (east end of Route 400) and in the Bluff Unit (Route 257 and Routes 301/15). The Bluff area ramp is only open March through October; the others are year round. Fishing and hunting are permitted with the appropriate license. A special refuge permit is needed for hunting. For additional information call (803) 478-2217.

Directions: From I-95 take Exit 102, west on Route 301/15 to Santee National Wildlife Refuge visitors center and historic areas.

Sumter County Museum and Sumter Gallery of Art

Summons to Sumter

Opening the door of the Williams-Brice House provides entry into the past at this elegantly restored Edwardian house. It's now the **Sumter County Museum**. Even before you step inside, you're greeted by a pair of antique cast iron lions flanking the doorway.

The original house was built in 1845 by successful Jewish merchant Andrew Jackson Moses and his wife Octavia, and it was here they raised their 14 children. In 1915, the Moses's granddaughter, R. Virginia, and her husband, Aaron Cohen Phelps, inherited the house. It was their intention to renovate the original structure, but they found it to be in such poor condition they demolished it. They built a new brick home on the same site. One of the personal touches added at that time was A.C. Phelps's monogram in the mosaic tile of the vestibule. The family sold the house in 1922 to O.L. Williams, a wealthy Sumter industrialist. The house was inherited by his daughter, Martha Williams Brice. It was her nephews and heirs, Thomas and Philip Edwards who, in 1972, gave the house to the Sumter County Historical Society to use as a museum.

The museum combines period rooms on the main floor with exhibit and period rooms upstairs. Some furnishings are family pieces and others are from the Sumter area. A notable example is the square grand piano in the double parlor that was specially built for James H. Aycock of Wedgefield. The decorative arts and furniture are a mixture of Rococo Revival and Empire styles. The dining room wall is graced with romanticized female portraits depicting the four seasons painted in the 1850s.

A number of intriguing portraits hang on the walls including one of Revolutionary War hero General Thomas Sumter, by Rembrandt Peale, and former house owner O.L. Williams, painted by Charles Mason Crowson. Robert E. Lee is captured by Albert Caper Guerry. The Sherman Smith Gallery features changing exhibits related to the history of the area.

The Myrtis Ginn Osteen War Memorial Room has artifacts from the Revolutionary War through Desert Storm. Be sure to note the inscription on the Confederate Bowie knife made in England; it reads: "Home of the Brave, Land of the Free." Another room features children's period furniture, dolls and toys. The museum has one of the finest textile collections in the state, and exhibits vintage clothing from 1840 to 1940 and quilts and coverlets dating from 1820. Every six months a new textile exhibit is mounted. Tucked away in the museum is a 1930s watch repair shop, while another room displays the contents of Lenoir's country store from Horatio.

One portion of the grounds was designed, in the 1960s, by one of the leading landscape gardeners in the southeast, Robert Marvin. In the William Dinkins Building you will discover the **Morgan Collection of Country Life** with a wide array of household items, building tools, agricultural equipment and farm machinery. Also on the museum grounds is the **Backcountry Homestead**. The buildings reveal the simple, strenuous life of settlers in this region. Buildings are in the process of being moved here from elsewhere in the county. Already in place is a settler's house and commissary. Plans call for the addition of a log cabin, barn, smoke house, corn crib, wash house and other outbuildings.

Museum hours are Tuesday through Saturday 10:00 A.M. to 5:00 P.M. and Sunday 2:00 to 5:00 P.M. There is no admission fee, but donations are requested. One downstairs room has been converted to a gift shop with an interesting array of hand-crafted items. In the museum annex located in the 1917 Sumter Carnegie Public Library is the museum's **Genealogical and Historical Research Center**. If you are doing research on your family history, this is an excellent resource. The center has abstracts of state courthouse records, funeral home records, census data, an extensive photographic collection and a wealth of old diaries, letters and family records. The archives are open Tuesday through Saturday from 10:00 A.M. to 5:00 P.M. There is a nominal per day research fee. Both are closed on holidays.

While in town you should also visit the **Sumter Gallery of Art**, located in the historic Elizabeth White house. The Greek revival cottage was the home of this renowned Sumter artist and it now provides an ideal setting for her work. Elizabeth White lived from 1893 until 1976. She inherited the house from her grandfather and it was her home for many years. White taught art in Sumter's public schools in the 1920s and later taught at the University of South Carolina. It was while traveling in Europe in 1927 that she conceived the idea of creating postcards with her etchings of Southern scenes. This work garnered her an invitation to join the MacDowell Colony in Peterborough, New Hampshire, a group that included Willa Cather and Thornton Wilder. White's etchings were exhibited at the Smithsonian Institution in Washington, D.C. in 1930 and as part of that year's New York World's Fair Art Exhibition.

In addition to the permanent collection of White's work, the Sumter Gallery of Art has a touchable collection for the visually impaired. Several galleries feature changing exhibits of work by local, regional and national artists. A gift shop offers the work of more than 100 regional artists. The gallery also offers workshops and art classes; call (803) 775-0543 for a current schedule. Gallery hours are August through June, NOON to 5:00 P.M. Tuesday through Friday and 2:00 to 5:00 P.M. on weekends. It is open in July by appointment only, primarily for group tours. There is no admission fee, but donations are gratefully accepted.

Directions: From I-95 take Exit 135, Route 378 west to Sumter. Take the Oswego exit off Route 378. Turn left on North Main, then right on Calhoun Street and left onto Washington Street. The Sumter County Museum is at 122 N. Washington Street. The Genealogical and Historical Research Center is at 219 West Liberty Street; from Washington continue past the museum and make a right on Liberty Street. To reach the Sumter Gallery of Art from Calhoun Street, make a left on Main Street; the museum is at 421 N. Main Street.

Swan Lake Iris Gardens

No Ballerinas but Plenty of Beauty

What an incomparable setting this would be for Tchaikovsky's romantic ballad *Swan Lake*—it seems a place where magical spells are possible. The inky-black water of the 45-acre lake is surrounded with a border of colorful iris in the summer months, while in the spring azaleas, yellow jessamine and wisteria imbue pastel hues. In the fall and winter, camellias and holly add bright notes of color.

In **Swan Lake Iris Gardens** exotic water lilies float on the mirror-like surface of the water during the summer months, and small islands abloom with iris seem thrown into the lake like brilliant jewels. Actually, many of these iris were thrown here by a disgruntled gardener. Hamilton Carr Bland was so disgusted with his non-blooming exotic Japanese iris, he threw them into the moist low-lying land beside a grist mill lake he had bought in the early 1900s for fishing. The next year Mr. Bland noticed that the flowers that never bloomed in his landscaped home garden were flourishing alongside the lake. He began designing and developing an extensive area which became the Swan Lake Iris Garden.

Mr. Bland's iris were Kaempferi, or Japanese iris, and they thrive on moist soil. Bland gave his original section of the garden to the city and another larger section across the highway was donated by another Sumter businessman, A.T. Heath. Now 150 acres, the gardens have over 25 varieties of iris, making it one of the most extensive plantings of Japanese iris in the United States. The huge iris blooms from six to ten inches in diameter and range from pure white to pinks, blues and purples with striped combinations and color mixes. Peak blooming period is the last week of May, but they start in mid-May and extend through June.

Swan Lake Iris Gardens is one of the few places in the world where visitors can see all eight species of swans. Adding to the appeal of the gardens are glorious masses of colorful iris in the summer and brilliant azaleas, wisteria and jessamine in the spring.

SOUTH CAROLINA DEPARTMENT OF PARKS, RECREATION AND TOURISM

Pathways wind around the lake and a rustic bridge takes you over the water onto some of the larger islands where Spanish moss bedecked oak and cypress grow. During the summer the blooming calendar includes gardenia, crepe myrtle and a host of annuals. There are benches throughout the garden where you can sit and enjoy the vista.

The gardens are a great birding spot, but the most dramatic are the swans that make their home here. This is one of the few places in the world where you can see all eight species of swans. The swans have been gathered from North and South America, Australia, England and Europe. It's fascinating to see the ranges of coloration and behavior traits. The Royal White Mute (the species immortalized in the classic ballet) lives up to its name, while it's easy to see how the Trumpeter got its name. Another noisy variety is the Whooper, a fluffy white species with a bright yellow beak. The Black Australian has a royal red beak. The Coscoroba have pink beaks and legs. Black Necked swans also hail from South America. Swans with a black beak and a yellow dot below the eye are native North American Whistler. From the Russian Arctic are Bewick swans that look very similar to the Whistler.

You can bring bread or crackers to feed the friendly swans. The only time to be cautious is in early spring during mating season when some of the males are apt to be territorial. There is a breeding program at the gardens and the babies stay in "swandominiums" until they are big enough to survive among the older fowl.

The gardens host three special events. The first is the late spring when the Iris Festival celebrates its namesake. The Fall Fiesta of the Arts is held the third weekend in October, and the entire month of December finds the gardens alight for the Swan Lake Christmas Fantasy of Lights.

Swan Lake Iris Gardens is open year round at no charge (there is no charge for the special events either) from 8:00 A.M. until sundown. The gardens also has a boardwalk trail that leads into an undeveloped cypress swamp. Visitors are welcome to picnic in the gardens and children can enjoy the playground, where they will discover a vintage 1920 fire engine. There are also tennis courts at the gardens. No dogs, bikes, radios, music, jogging or alcohol are permitted. A picturesque, old-style covered bridge takes visitors over the highway from one section of the garden to the other. The physically challenged can use the elevators built on both sides of the highway.

Directions: From I-95 take either Exit 135, Route 378 or Exit 122, Route 521 into Sumter. Both will intersect Route 76. Take Business Route 76 into Sumter (Route 378 actually merges into this). Turn west on Liberty Street and the Swan Lake Iris Gardens will be on the left at West Liberty Street.

Woods Bay State Park

The Carolina Bay Phenomena

Along North Carolina, South Carolina and Georgia's coastal plains there are a series of elliptical depressions that geologists cannot definitively explain. **Woods Bay State Park** is the site of one of these formations, called Carolina Bays. All the formations are oriented in a northwest/southeast direction. Along the southeast rim of the depression at Woods Bay, you can see a sandrim, which is usually the most visible feature of these formations.

There are four theories about how Carolina Bays were formed. One school of thought is that when the ocean covered this area, large springs under the water dislodged sediment and currents deposited them elsewhere. When the ocean receded the areas where the sediment was removed formed a natural depression, or bay. Another theory is that a gigantic bombardment of meteorites collided with earth and formed these depressions. A third idea is that tidal eddies moving in circular directions could have scooped out the sandy bottom of lagoons leaving oval depressions when the ocean receded. Finally, there are those who believe that artesian springs bubbling up through soft sandy soil of nearby lakes and ponds created the bays.

It is difficult for the uninitiated eye to spot a bay, but this is a good place to try. This is also an excellent vantage point to spot alligators as the 1,541-acre park has a boardwalk through the cypress/tupelo swamp and shrub bog. You can rent canoes Thursday through Monday from 9:00 A.M. to NOON and 1:00 to 4:45 P.M. and follow a canoe trail into the bay; 85% of Woods Bay is under water. This is also a popular fishing spot.

Woods Bay State Park is open Thursday through Monday 9:00 A.M. to 6:00 P.M. It is closed on Tuesday and Wednesday. Office hours on days the park is open are from 11:00 A.M. until NOON.

Directions: From I-95, Exit 135, take Route 378 east to Turbeville. Then take Route 301 north for five miles; turn left at the park sign and continue for two miles and you will see the park on the left.

Santee Cooper Country Regional Tourism Contacts (Area Code 803)

SANTEE COOPER COUNTIES PROMOTION COMMISSION
U.S. 301/15 & Route 6
P.O. Drawer 40
Santee, SC 29142
854-2131 or outside SC
(800) 227-8510

BERKELEY COUNTY CHAMBER OF COMMERCE
P.O. Box 905
Nesbitt House
Moncks Corner, SC 29461
761-8238, (800) 882-0337

CALHOUN COUNTY CHAMBER OF COMMERCE
P.O. Box 444
St. Matthews, SC 29135
874-3791

CLARENDON COUNTY CHAMBER OF COMMERCE
P.O. Box 1
Manning, SC 29102
435-4405

ORANGEBURG COUNTY CHAMBER OF COMMERCE
P.O. Box Drawer 328
Orangeburg, SC 29116-0328
534-6821, (800) 242-3435

GREATER SUMTER CONVENTION & VISITORS BUREAU
P.O. Box 1449
Sumter, SC 29151
773-3371, (800) 688-4748, fax: 778-2025

TRI-COUNTY CHAMBER OF COMMERCE
P.O. Box 175
Harleyville, SC 29448
496-3561

Santee Cooper Country Calendar of Events
(Area Code 803)

Late March

Elloree Trials. Spring thoroughbred and quarterhorse racing. Elloree, 897-2616.

Mid-April

Clarendon County Striped Bass Festival. One of the highlights of community-wide street festival is a catfish wrestling match. Manning, 435-4405.

Late April

South Carolina Festival of Roses. At Edisto Memorial Gardens spring roses provide the backdrop for this arts & crafts festival with canoe and kayak races, foot races and even rubber duck races. Orangeburg, 564-6821.

Late May

Carolina Back Country. A day on an early 1800s farm with candle making, dulcimer music, blacksmithing and other period demonstrations. Sumter County Museum, 778-5434.

Iris Festival. Swan Lake Iris Gardens hosts the highly popular festival of arts and crafts, featuring garden tours, parade, concerts and a food fair. Sumter, 775-9742.

Early July

Fabulous Fourth in the Creek. An old-fashioned family festival with crafts, games, concessions, fireworks and a mini-fest for children. Goose Creek, 572-1321.

Early October

Sumter County Fair. Farm animal competition, competitions for jams, jellies and other homemade items, carnival rides, and all the other components of an old-fashioned country fair. Sumter, 778-5848.

Fall Carolina Back Country Harvest. Sheep shearing, basket weaving and harvesting activities combine with old-fashioned music and food. Sumter County Museum, 778-5434.

Mid-October

Octoberfest Southern Style. Barbecue cook-off, children's games, entertainment and sports events at Dillon Park highlight this event. Sumter, 436-2248.

Holiday Arts and Crafts Fair. More than 100 artists and craftsmen demonstrate and sell their wares at the fairgrounds. Orangeburg, 536-1636.

Late October

Fall Fiesta of the Arts. Swan Lake Iris Gardens hosts a visual and performing arts fest. Sumter, 436-2260.

Octoberfest Southern Style. Regional barbecue cook-off, entertainment, military displays, fireworks as well as arts and crafts make this a popular event. Sumter, 436-5434.

December

Swan Lake Christmas Fantasy of Lights. Month-long celebration finds the gardens alight with holiday decorations. Sumter, 436-2260.

Children's Garden Christmas. Edisto Memorial Gardens has animated displays, lighted trees and a nativity scene during their month-long celebration. Orangeburg, 564-6821.

Early December

Holiday House Tour and Christmas Tea. Seasonally decorated private homes and gardens, tours of the Sumter County Museum and an afternoon tea highlight this event. Sumter, 778-5434.

Eight Swans A Swimming Candlelight Tour of Homes. Bed & Breakfasts open their homes to tours of their holiday decorations. Sumter, 778-5434.

Boykin Christmas Parade. On December's second Sunday farm machinery and other intriquing elements parade through Boykin's short main drag; adding to the fun is musical entertainment at the old Swift Creek Church. Boykin, 778-5434.

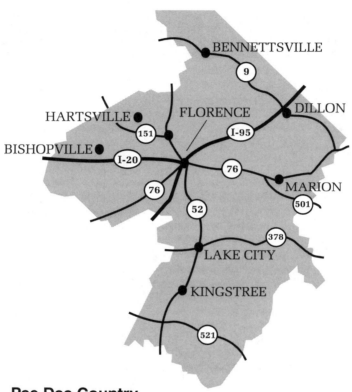

Pee Dee Country

Pee Dee Country

It is in small towns, like those in the seven counties that comprise the Pee Dee Country region, that the warm, welcoming hospitality so closely associated with the south is most often felt. If you spend a few hours in Bishopville, Hartsville, Marion, Latta or Florence you will begin recognizing faces and responding to a steady stream of greetings.

The pace of this agricultural region is slower, except at Darlington Raceway where death-defying speeds are achieved during the racing season. Highlights of these and other races are spotlighted at the NASCAR Stockcar Hall of Fame. At other sites in the region, the achievements that are celebrated are earned over time with the slow progression of the seasons. The long-time dominance of cotton in this part of the south is catalogued at the South Carolina Cotton Museum in Bishopville. The story of indigo is revealed at the Dillon County Museum in Latta.

The region is named for the river that takes its name from the indigenous population that once inhabited this northwest corner of South Carolina. The river narrowly missed life-long recognition, as the original lyrics of the renowned Stephen Foster song were, "Way down upon the Pee Dee River." Despite Foster's substitution of the Suwanee River, the Pee Dee River is one of the south's great river systems.

The river's swampy back areas gave rise to the legends surrounding one of the most renown Revolutionary War heroes, Francis Marion. A statue of the Swamp Fox stands in the town that bears his name and his exploits are part of the story at the Museum of Marion County.

The marsh and Black Creek bluff outside Hartsville has been transformed into the verdant Kalmia Gardens of Coker College, and a neighborhood yard in Lee County into the unusual Fryar's Topiary Garden. The marshy area even gave rise to the elusive Lizard Man, who terrorized those who sighted him at various spots in Lee County in 1988.

Dillon County Museum, Latta and Abingdon Manor

Quintessential Down Home Hospitality

Exhibits on county founder J.W. Dillon are just part of the story at the **Dillon County Museum**, a museum that also includes medical, military, historical and agricultural exhibits. During a right-of-way dispute as the Atlantic Coastline was laying tracks through the area, enterprising merchant Dillon obtained options on 50 acres of land through which the railroad ultimately passed. In 1888, the town of Dillon was established. Shortly after that, the nearby area of **Latta** became a railroad loading station. Interestingly, Latta was named for the railroad surveyor who laid it out instead of any of the locally prominent families.

The Dillon County Museum is in the restored 1915 office of one of Latta's prominent physicians, Dr. Henry Edwards. It and the Edwards family residence next door (the first two-story house in town) are on the National Register of Historic Places. The first exhibit room in the museum is a recreation of Dr. Edwards's turn-of-the-century office with his original phone and other memorabilia. A taped introduction to the room is provided by docent Francis Lane, who was delivered by Dr. Edwards. Elsewhere in the museum is his son Luther's dental office.

The next room runs over with military uniforms, weapons and other artifacts described by a young relative of State Senator James H. Manning, a pivotal figure in area politics in the early 1900s. Visitors also learn about James Dudley Haselden, a native who attended the U.S. Naval Academy and was killed in a submarine accident in 1920 and John David of Dillon who was the first South Carolina officer killed in World War I.

The agricultural room has displays on cotton and tobacco. In 1908, the largest tobacco market in the state was in Latta. One room is entirely devoted to the growth of indigo in the region. This crop was first planted in this country in 1741, since conditions in this part of South Carolina were favorable for its cultivation. You'll see indigo-dyed cloth from India and Africa as well as what the plant looks like and how it was grown. There is a lovely painting by Lorna Shanks (who amassed this indigo collection) of Eliza Lucas, the daughter of the governor of Antigua, who married Charles Pinckney. Eliza grew indigo on her Wappoo plantation, near Georgetown, but when she sided with the Patriots during the American Revolution, the British destroyed her plantation. She spent the last 20 years at Hampton (see Hampton Plantation State Park selection). Eliza Lucas Pinckney's son Thomas was the first governor of South

Carolina. The indigo exhibit ends with a collection of indigo-dyed Levi Straus jeans, which were sold as early as 1879.

The museum is open Tuesday and Thursday from 10:30 A.M. until NOON and again from 1:30 to 4:30 P.M. Saturday hours are 10:30 A.M. to 4:30 P.M. and Sunday 1:30 to 4:30 P.M. Donations are gratefully accepted. The adjacent Edwards residence is being restored and will be used as museum exhibit space. The Dillon County Museum also mounts rotating exhibits from the South Carolina State Museum (see selection). James Dillon's house in Dillon is open by appointment; call (803) 774-8496.

A burgeoning art community is developing in Latta, as you will see when you stroll down Main Street. Stop in **Different Strokes Gallery**, owned and operated by Eddie Watson, an accomplished painter whose work captures scenes from his childhood as an African American growing up in the south. He grew up on a farm outside Latta. Watson's gallery showcases his work as well as that of other artists. **Weatherly Gallery** features fine prints, limited editions as well as original art. This gallery, on Main Street just before entering the downtown area, has workshops and programs with visiting artists. **Lorna Shanks Studio** in Latta is in the home she shares with husband and fellow artist James Meekins. You can arrange to see her studio by appointment; call (803) 752-7376. Her work is also exhibited at The South by Southwest Gallery in the Red Barn in Florence. Lorna's home studio provides this gifted painter with space to work on her commissioned portraits of people, pets and homes. Consignment artwork, crafts and gourmet treats can be found at **RJK Frames and Things**, a shop that specializes in custom framing in addition to being a comfortable meeting spot for those in need of a cup of coffee or snack. The shop also sells the adorable Ma Morgan dolls, life-like little figures with their heads in their crossed arms. Once seen these captivating dolls are hard to resist—like the Cabbage Patch dolls, it's called adopting, not buying.

Latta has two historic districts. Architectural points of interest include the McMillan House, one of the few French Second Empire houses in the state; the classic antebellum E.B. Berry house, the 1888 one-room post office and the Federalist style, two-story brick building that is featured in Ripley's *Believe It Or Not* as the smallest block in the state. In all there are 64 properties on the National Register of Historic Places.

The most elaborate is the estate of Senator James H. Manning, which takes up a whole block. The Greek Revival house, built between 1902 and 1905, is known as the house of 40 columns. The Ionic columns were constructed from trees cut from the Manning's 7,200-acre plantation. There are expansive porches and verandas around the first floor and off the hallway on the second floor. You can enjoy the hospitality of Latta's largest and most lavish home as it is now the **Abingdon Manor**, a small, luxury inn with four guest rooms and an elegant suite. The rooms are exquisitely decorated and each has its own fireplace and private bath. Sleeping in the huge feather beds feels like floating on a drifting cumulus cloud. In 1997, the inn was awarded a four diamond rating by AAA, one of the few in the state.

Current owners, Michael and Patty Griffey bypassed the problems of many innkeepers because they purchased the property after it had been converted and furnished as a bed and breakfast. The estate had passed out of the Manning family in 1972, after a temporary period when it was a bridal shop. It was transformed into a bed and breakfast in 1992. The Griffeys changed the name to that of one of their favorite English country estates, once frequented by King Henry VIII. The service they provide is certainly fit for royalty. Patty prepares an elegant gourmet breakfast that is served in the formal dining room, or in pleasant weather, on the verandah. She grows herbs that she uses in her omelets and salads and, with advance notice, prepares tasty, tempting five-course dinners. For information and reservations call (803) 752-5090.

For the outdoor lover, another option is camping at the 835-acre **Little Pee Dee Park**, whose terrain ranges from a small river swamp to bottomland hardwoods and pine and scrub oak sandhills. A nature trail winds through the various habitats and leads to a beaver pond. A tract featuring one of the unique Carolina Bays (see Woods Bay State Park) was recently acquired by the Heritage Trust. The park is popular with fishermen trying their luck in its 55-acre lake.

Directions: From I-95 take Exit 181, Route 38 east. When the road intersects with Route 917, take that for five miles into Latta. Route 917 becomes Main Street, the Dillon County Museum is on the right at the first traffic light, at 101 South Marion Street. For Abingdon Manor turn left from Main Street on Marion Street. At the Methodist church take the right fork, which is Church Street and follow to the end. Abingdon Manor is on the left at 307 Church Street.

Fryar's Topiary Garden and Lee County

Explore the Highways and Byways

Lee County celebrates the past with its historical driving tour, but current residents are also providing points of interest. Just outside Bishopville is **Fryar's Topiary Garden**, where one man's hobby has become a community treasure. African-American Pearl Fryar had never heard of topiary art when he saw a sheared plant at a local nursery. After inquiring how to achieve such a result, he returned to his home determined to try it in his garden and hopefully win the local "Yard of the Month" award. He did far more than simply win the award; over time his creation expanded and so did his fame.

Fryar's garden covers three acres and is filled with whimsical creations and exotic designs featuring green swirling arches, spirals and geometric forms. With no training he has achieved a garden that causes landscape specialists to marvel. Mr. Fryar has appeared on *The Victory Garden* and been the subject of countless newspaper and magazine articles. Visitors are surprised to learn that the gardens are not watered, sprayed or fertilized. The plants are surrounded by pine straw to help keep them moist and prevent weeds. It is unexpected to see this unusual garden in the midst of a residential area. The garden is at 165 Broad Acres Road.

Another Interstate 20 exit brings you to **Lee State Park**, the closest park in the state to an interstate. There is a five-mile loop road within this 2,839-acre forested park through which the Lynches River flows. There are nature trails, six miles of horse trails, a 10-stall barn and a horse-show ring. You can rent a horse from the livery. The park also offers 30 camp sites, picnic shelters, swimming and fishing.

Another recreational area, **Ashwood Lake**, offers fishing, boating and picnicking facilities. Ashwood Community is of historical interest as only ruins remind travelers of this United States government pilot project begun during President Franklin D. Roosevelt's administration. In 1935, needy families from all over the United States were resettled in this part of Lee County. This was an early experiment in communal living; each tenant was given ten acres, a mule, cow and hogs. Today cotton fields cover the land where the community once stood.

Details of the past abound in the **Lee County Historical Society**'s self-guided driving tour that takes you past 13 historical markers. These designate houses of note, locations of skirmishes and battles from the American Revolution and the War Between the States, and the site of the last duel fought in the state.

Unfortunately there's no driving tour for the more than 15 sites around the county where, in 1988, various individuals spotted the "Lizard Man." International media attention focused on Sheriff Liston Truesdale as he hunted the elusive seven-foot, scaly creature. The creature was never found, although thousands flocked to the area in hopes of spotting the phenomenon.

Media attention has also focused on another local personality, the "Button Man." Dalton Stevens suffered from insomnia and wiled away the long nights sewing thousands of button on a suit and other apparel or gluing them on various items like his guitar and a hearse. The Button Man has appeared on all the major talk shows and has clippings from newspapers and magazines around the world. He is often on hand for events like the annual Lee County Cotton Festival, held in October.

Directions: From I-20 take Exit 116, Route 15N toward Bishopville. Turn left on Broad Acres Road and you'll see Fryar's Topiary Garden on your left. For Lee State Park, take Exit 123 from I-20; the park is located just north of the interstate. Ashwood Lake is eight miles south of Bishopville on Route 15.

Hartsville Museum

"All America City"

You can get a sense of Hartsville, the Pee Dee Region and indeed the entire state in the restored 1930 post office that now houses the **Hartsville Museum**. Fanlights above the doors, windows and high ceilings make this a bright exhibit space. Be sure to look up as you enter to appreciate the restored original skylight, augmented by artistic stained-glass panels representing the cotton plant, long-leaf pine, magnolia, yellow jessamine, the Carolina wren and kalmia—all closely associated with the region.

From the region's earliest days there are Native American arrowheads and other artifacts found along the Pee Dee River. There is even a box of arrowheads that young visitors can touch. It's worth remembering that archeologists say that the way to identify an arrowhead is to feel the sharp edge of both sides. Nature often creates one such sharp side but not two. The exhibit also includes examples of Catawba pottery (see Catawba Cultural and Research Center selection).

Just as the Native Americans were close to the soil, this part of South Carolina is strongly agricultural; there are tools of the trade on exhibit. You can see a cotton plant, the tools used to plant and harvest the crop, the scales used to weigh the hand-picked cotton and the spinning wheel and loom where earlier generations took the raw material and made cloth and useful household items. Visitors are fascinated with the new colored cotton. Many visitors did not realize before seeing this exhibit that cotton can now be grown in colors, such as the brown and green cotton seen in this museum (see South Carolina Cotton Museum selection). There are photographs from the days when Hartsville was a major cotton market; at one time it was the largest long staple market east of the Mississippi River.

One photograph captures a youthful David R. Coker, founder of the Coker Pedigreed Seed Company. Coker's successful experimentation with cotton led to a strain resistant to the boll weevil. Eventually, Coker expanded his work to include other field crops and vegetables. By 1963, 65% of the cotton acreage of the southeast was planted with Coker seeds; so also was 80% of the oat acreage, 75% of the flue-cured tobacco and 40% of the hybrid corn. (A marker at the Coker Experimental Farms on Fourth Street indicates the fields of one of the few agricultural spots in the country designated as a National Historic Landmark.)

Young visitors gravitate to the Elizabeth B. Coker hat collection and an old trunk filled with items that children are invited to try on. A strategically placed mirror gives them a glimpse of the past as they preen in faded finery.

If dress-up entertains the young, South Carolina's first automo-

The museum for Hartsville, an "All America City," reflects the richness of the town's past. Multi-sensory exhibits introduce visitors to cotton cultivation; the town's baseball hero, Bobo Newson; and the Eastern Carolina Silver Company which operated briefly in Hartsville.

bile captivates the males in the family. The 1899 Locomobile Steam Car was the country's best selling car in 1900. James L. Coker, Jr. purchased the car in Massachusetts, where it was made by the same company that produced Stanley Steamers. Coker had the car shipped to Virginia; Duncan Gaym, Coker's brother-in-law, drove the automobile from Norfolk to Hartsville. You can see that there's not much protection from the elements in this automobile. The high-pressure boiler used to fuel the car had a tendency to explode periodically. Since it was located directly underneath the car's seat, these explosions were always memorable.

Many of the women who visit the museum find their interest captivated by the display case filled with silver made by the Eastern Carolina Silver Company that operated in Hartsville from mid-1907 through 1909. The company's catalog listed 150 pieces, each marked with a small palmetto tree on the bottom. A design of the cotton plant was the company's most unique motif.

For many years day-to-day life in Hartsville was captured in photos by Claude Hart. He was born in North Carolina in 1881 and was no relation to the Harts who established the town. Hart moved to the community in 1909 and set up the first photography tent. He eventually moved to a studio, that was in business until 1948. On display is his Kodak field camera and photographs that chronicled Hartsville's growth.

One individual that helped put Hartsville on the map was Bobo Newsom, the town's most famous sports hero. During his 20 years in baseball's major leagues, Bobo changed uniforms 17 times and played for 8 teams. The Washington Senators bought and sold him four times, the St. Louis Browns three times and the Brooklyn Dodgers and Philadelphia Athletics twice. Newsom's long career in the majors allowed him to pitch to Babe Ruth in the 1920s and Mickey Mantle in the 1940s. In 1940, he pitched in the World Series for the Detroit Tigers. His father was on hand to watch Bobo win the first game, but later that night his father had a heart attack and died. Detroit lost the Series. The museum has a life-size cut-out of Newsom in the permanent exhibit that highlights his career.

Up to this point, all the senses have been covered in the museum except hearing; wait 'til you hear the player piano. It has only one level of volume—loud!

A changing exhibit area showcases regional artists, hobbyists and historical exhibits. The museum is open at no charge Monday through Saturday from 10:00 A.M. to 5:00 P.M.

On the back of the museum brochure are walking tours of this "All America City's" two historic districts. Each walk begins at the museum and is approximately 1.5 miles long. Founders' Pathway has 15 points of interest. This route takes you past numerous private homes on East Home Avenue as well as sever-

174

al churches and **Coker College**. Founded in 1908 by Major James Lide Coker, this was the first college in the state established east of Columbia and north of Charleston. Davidson Hall, built in 1909, is listed on the National Register of Historic Places. This route also takes you past the home of David R. Coker founder of Coker Pedigreed Seed Company. Coker's wife, May Roper Coker, established Kalmia Gardens (see selection).

City Pathway takes you past 12 spots of interest in the West College Avenue National Register Historic District. Many turn-of-the-century homes are architecturally interesting. Hartsville is proud of its 1996 designation as an "All America City. "

Directions: From I-20 take Exit 116 and follow Route 15 north through Bishopville and on to Hartsville via Business Route 15, which becomes South Fifth Street. The Hartsville Museum is at 222 North Fifth Street. From I-95 take Exit 164 in Florence and follow Route 52 north toward Darlington. Take Route 52 Bypass and Route 151 into Hartsville, where it will become Fourth Street. At the end of Fourth Street turn left onto Home Avenue. The museum is on the far left corner of the next intersection. There is parking and handicapped access behind the building.

John Lide Hart Cottage and Jacob Kelley House

Hartsville's First Families

Captain Thomas E. Hart of Society Hill purchased land from Rosier Kelley along the Black Creek in 1817, land that is now Kalmia Gardens (see selection). Among his eight children was John Lide Hart, born in 1825, the third son of Thomas and Hannah. Thomas Hart was financially ruined in the panic of the mid-1830s, and died in 1842. In 1850, John, age 20, purchased 491 acres of virgin pine forest from his brother-in-law Colonel Thomas C. Law.

John established the Hartsville Plantation on his land, which ran along what is now Hartsville's East Home Avenue to Fifth Street. Local lore claims that John cut timber on his property and personally helped construct the Federal-style **John Lide Hart Cottage** that was his home from 1846 to 1855. You can see the hewn timber frame inside the cottage. The ceilings, with their original whitewash, were retained during the cottage's restoration.

John Hart definitely made an economic contribution to the community. He established a carriage factory (the town's first industry), a steam-powered sawmill, gristmill, workers' homes, a store, post-office, school (The Academy) and church (Hartsville Baptist Church, now the First Baptist Church).

John Hart suffered business failures, but not to the extent of his father's reverses. His carriage company faltered and he sold it, along with the plantation, to Caleb Coker, whose wife was Hart's first cousin. John Hart moved to Darlington and became a partner in a carriage manufacturing company. Hart belonged to the South Carolina militia and was killed on May 16, 1864 at Drewry's Bluff during the Richmond campaign. James Lide Coker, whose father had purchased John Hart's business and plantation, was severely wounded in the Civil War. James Lide returned to his home town and was given one-half interest in the Hartsville Plantation. He set about reversing the economic hardships that befell the town during and after the war.

There are plans to furnish John Lide Hart Cottage with period pieces and memorabilia from the town's earliest families. The house, at 116 East Home Avenue (so called because Thomas and Hannah Hart had the public road built to shorten their journey home to Society Hill). Costumed docents give tours from February through November on the first Sunday of the month from 3:00 to 5:00 P.M.

The **Jacob Kelley House** predates the Hart cottage. This farmhouse was built around 1820 by farmer and landowner, Jacob Kelley, for his bride Charity Hearon. The house was originally a single-story log cabin but it grew as the Kelleys' five children were born. As you face the house, the oldest section is on the left; inside this section is the parlor. On the right side of the house you'll see the carved fireplace mantel that survived the March 1996 fire that greatly damaged the house. The house has been completely restored and is again filled with handcrafted regional pieces from the 19th century. You will see portraits of three of the five Kelley children: James, Robert and Elizabeth Kelley Brown (not represented are Sarah and Rosier). Be sure to notice the joggling board on the porch, a fixture at many southern homes since the early 1800s. This lightly bouncing long board provides gentle exercise that is much enjoyed by children, courting couples and seniors.

During the Civil War, Jacob Kelley's house had a brush with history on March 2 and 3, 1865. The house became the headquarters of a scouting party under the command of Major General John E. Smith, commander of the Third Division of the Fifteenth Army Corp. His men scoured the area for livestock and provisions for General Sherman's army. Elias Kelley, age 10, put his 85-year-old grandfather and the family's valuable possessions in a buckboard and fled to the safety of an island in nearby Segars Mill Pond. The Union troops did not burn any buildings in the area.

In 1969, Mrs. Caroline Will, a descendant of Jacob Kelley, gave the house to the Darlington County Historical Commission.

Graham Segars, her brother, whose idea it was to restore and preserve the house, was in charge of the restoration. Gradually, pieces suitable to the period were purchased. The house, on the National Register of Historic Places, is open February through November on the first Sunday of the month from 3:00 to 5:00 P.M. In the back yard you will see a log smokehouse, cookhouse and privy. During the first weekend in March there is a living history demonstration in the house and on the grounds that features Civil War re-enactors. In early December there is a Christmas Open House; call (803) 332-6401 for details.

Directions: From I-20 take Exit 131, Route 15 north. At the intersection with Route 151 head into Hartsville. For the Jacob Kelley House from Route 15 north make a left onto the Route 151 Bypass. Continue on the bypass to Kelleytown Road and turn left. Kelley House is on the left. One mile from this intersection, bear right on Route 151 and head into Hartsville.

Kalmia Gardens of Coker College

Miss May's Fabulous Folly

The 30-acre **Kalmia Gardens of Coker College** is uniquely situated—a north-facing 60-foot bluff above the flood plain of Black Creek provides a fertile growing area for a splendid diversity of plant and animal life. The terrain is uncommon in this part of the state and results in abundant mountain laurel, the *Kalmia latifolia*, for which the garden is named. From mid-April until late May, the steep hillside looks like it has its own fluffy white cloud. Spring is a splendid time at Kalmia because, in addition to the indigenous laurel and wildflowers, there are massed plantings of camellias, azaleas and wisteria. There is always something of interest and the welcoming kiosk adjacent to the parking lot has a monthly list of must-see plants for your visit.

Since the garden peaks in May, it is singularly appropriate that the garden creator was "Miss May," May Roper Coker (whose father was Secretary of Treasury under President Woodrow Wilson). If you look on the back of a ten dollar bill you will see the Roper family car parked in front of the Treasury building. May was the wife of David Robert Coker, the founder of Coker Pedigreed Seed Company (see Hartsville Museum selection). David's brother, Dr. William Chambers Coker gave the property along the bluff to his sister-in-law because of her enthusiasm for gardening. Dr. Coker, the head of the Botany Department at the University of North Carolina, wrote a book about the plant life of Hartsville and, in particular, this bluff. When he purchased the property, part of it had become a dump site and the natural growth was endangered.

This land changed hands many times between 1772, when King George III granted 200 acres to Benjamin Davis, and 1817 when a small portion was acquired by Thomas Edwards Hart. Hart built a home on the bluff from timber cut on the property. Each of the four original rooms has paneled wainscoting and mantels carved by Hart. Hart's family and property grew—he had eight children and ultimately 1,223 acres on which he planted cotton, tobacco and other crops. Hart was active in the developing community, serving as the area's first postmaster, justice of the peace and captain of the local militia. By 1837, the settlement was known as Hartville or Hartsville. One of the newcomers was Major James Lide Coker, who helped transform the settlement into a city.

Captain Hart's fortunes plummeted in the panic of the late 1830s and his death at age 46 in 1842 was believed to have been hastened by his financial reverses. His wife, Hannah Hart continued to live in the house on the bluff until 1859. His son, John Hart, in 1846 built a cottage in town (see John Hart Cottage selection). Dr. William Chambers Coker and David Robert Coker were sons of the major who transformed Hartsville.

But it was Miss May who transformed this small portion of the area into a scenic attraction that lures visitors to Hartsville. Many in the community did not see how she could take a neglected wilderness miles from town and make it into a garden oasis—especially not during the Great Depression. The project became known as "Miss May's Folly." With a few workmen and a mule, she created trails leading down the bluff to the creek. Exotic plants were added to the natural foliage, such as bald cypress, pines, white oak and beeches, to create a garden. Atlantic white cedar, now uncommon to this region, was protected along Black Creek. A pond, fed by an artesian well, was added to the garden. Since 1935, the garden that Miss May established has been open to the public. In 1965, Miss May gifted Coker College with the garden in memory of her husband.

Coker College was established in 1908 by Major James Lide Coker. It was formerly the Welsh Neck High School but with mandated public high school in the state, the private secondary school was no longer necessary. Major Coker had long felt that education was vital for women because, in his mind, when women were educated, a family was educated. Coker transformed the facility into the first college for women in this part of the state. The college became coed in 1968 and now has approximately 900 students. Visitors are welcome to drive around the campus located on East College Avenue.

Kalmia Gardens is open year round at no charge from dawn until dusk. There are eight trails and six specialty gardens as well as the noted Kalmia and daylily collections. The Captain Thomas

Edwards Hart House is open to the public on special occasions.

Black Creek separates the gardens from **Segars-McKinnon Heritage Preserve**, a 707-acre tract along the north bank of the creek. Plans call for trails through the swamp to provide public access to the preserve.

Canoes may be rented in Hartsville. They are owned by the city; call (803) 383-3020 for more details. Visitors can enjoy paddling from Lawton Park to Kalmia Gardens. There is also a bicycle path from the city to the gardens.

Directions: From I-20 take Route 15 north to Hartsville. Turn left on Business 151, West Carolina Avenue, for Kalmia Gardens, which is inside Hartsville city limits. If you want to bypass Hartsville, turn left on Route 151 Bypass, right at the traffic signal on Kelleytown Road, then left on Business 151 and Kalmia Gardens will be on your right.

Museum of Marion County and Florence

Lair of the Swamp Fox

It is appropriate that the pre-Revolutionary village of Marion, like the county, bears the name of the legendary general Francis Marion, who was dubbed the Swamp Fox by Banastre Tarleton. The young British officer vainly pursued the fearless riders and deadly marksmen who made up Marion's brigade. Marion's surprise attacks bedeviled the British forces as did his ability to escape into the swamps and forests of his native state.

Across from the Robert Mills-designed courthouse in downtown Marion, is a statue of the Swamp Fox standing sentinel over the ground he defended. The **Museum of Marion County**, housed in the Marion Academy Building, has a replica of this statue and a portrait of Francis Marion, born near Georgetown in 1792. The museum has furnishings and memorabilia contributed by area residents. The second floor has a school room, a model of a log cabin, a turpentine still and agricultural tools. There are also two rooms of changing exhibits at this museum that is open Tuesday through Saturday from 9:00 A.M. to NOON and 1:00 to 5:00 P.M.

Much of Marion is a National Historic District with a wealth of beautifully restored buildings. One is the lovely **Rosewood Manor**, an 1895 mansion that takes up an entire city block. Built for Seaboard Railway director William Stackhouse, it was deemed too big for his family and so Stackhouse traded homes with grocer McCoy Rose. The manor's size is a benefit now that it has been transformed into a bed and breakfast inn (803-423-5407) under the direction of owner Thomas Griggs. He not only oversaw a painstaking restoration but, when it was finished, he filled the rooms with his treasured collection of antiques. In the parlor there is a rosewood chest that belonged to Melvin Purvis, the FBI agent who killed John Dillinger (see South Carolina Criminal Justice Hall of Fame selection). The Sheraton table in the dining room and Victorian breakfront in the breakfast room are striking pieces. The music room has a grand piano, Baroque harp, violins and music box.

Between Marion and Florence, if you take a slight detour up Route 327, there is another interesting old home, **The Columns**, in the area's last working plantation. The Rankin-Harwell plantation was built in 1857 for Dr. William Rogers Johnson. All the materials to build the Greek Revival house were from the grounds. Bricks were manufactured and used to form the inside of the 22 giant free-standing Doric columns. Throughout the year various events are scheduled on the grounds of this 1,500-acre estate including Civil War re-enactments; call (803) 669-6703 for a schedule or to arrange a house tour.

If you continue on to Florence at the regional airport you can visit **The Florence Air and Missile Museum** with aircraft from World War II through Vietnam. Items of interest include a 98-foot Titan intercontinental ballistic missile, a Gemini capsule, moon

At the Florence regional airport visitors can see a collection of aircraft from World War II through Vietnam. The space-related exhibits include Pee Dee native Dr. Ron E. McNair's space suit.

rock and Pee Dee native son Dr. Ron E. McNair's space suit. Another point of interest is **The Florence National Cemetery**, the smaller of two such cemeteries in the state (see Beaufort National Cemetery selection). The Florence cemetery is ¼ mile north of the Florence Confederate stockade. Many of the Union soldiers imprisoned here died of war injuries and disease and were buried in trenches on the grounds of James H. Jarrott's plantation. The first casualties were interred on September 17, 1864 and a year later the grounds were declared a National Cemetery. One of the soldiers buried here is the first woman buried in a National Cemetery. Florena Budwin disguised herself as a man and enlisted in the Union Army in order to follow her husband, a captain from Pennsylvania. Her husband was killed and she was captured. It was then that her deception was discovered, but she stayed in the camp to nurse the prisoners until she died on January 23, 1865. The cemetery is at 803 E. National Cemetery Road in Florence.

Directions: From I-95 take Exit 157 (Route 76) or Exit 164 (Route 52/301) into Florence. For Marion head east on Route 76/301.

NASCAR Stockcar Hall of Fame and The Darlington International Raceway

The Flag is Up!

During any visit to the **NASCAR Stockcar Hall of Fame**, you can watch a race. Videos of famous races—and famous crashes—play continuously in this museum which sits outside the gates of **The Darlington International Raceway**. Twice a year on "The Track Too Tough To Tame," there is live action. In mid-March the Transouth 400 is run and on Labor Day weekend the Mountain Dew Southern 500 roars off. The latter is the largest one-day tourism attraction in the state.

The museum has the world's largest collection of stock racing cars and information about the drivers who raced them. Notable cars include: a 1950 Plymouth raced by Johnny Mantz in the first NASCAR superspeeding event, a 1951 Hudson raced by Herb Thomas, a 1963 Ford raced by Fireball Roberts, a 1964 Mercury raced by Joe Weatherley (for whom the museum was originally named), a 1966 Ford raced by Fred Lorenzen, a 1991 Chevrolet Lumina crashed and rolled by Darrell Wartrap and many others. The Hall of Fame has photographs and biographical information on all the inductees. There is also memorabilia from many of these drivers.

The museum is open daily year round from 9:00 A.M. to 6:00

There's action twice a year at Darlington International
Raceway, "The Track too Tough to Tame."

P.M. Admission is charged. There is a well-stocked gift shop with
everything from racing jackets to postcards.

While in Darlington drive through the downtown area to see
the **Blue Sky mural** painted in the 1930s on a town square building. It was done after the old courthouse was torn down and features this now long-gone building and a street scene from by
gone days.

Directions: From I-20 take Exit 131, Route 401 north to
Darlington. When you intersect Route 52, turn left and the
NASCAR Stockcar Hall of Fame will be on Route 157 in
Darlington.

South Carolina Cotton Museum

You'll Cotton to this Museum

The 1930s Copeland Grocery Store on North Main Street in
Bishopville is now the home of the **South Carolina Cotton
Museum**. Old shelves preserve the appearance of a general store.
Joining grocery items and patent medicines from times past are
cotton wreaths, ornaments and other collectibles appropriate to
this museum that celebrates the days when cotton was king.

Many of the young visitors to the museum delight in touching the fluffy cotton. For some it is their first hands-on experience of the crop that precipitated so much of the south's economic, political and military history. You will see tools of the trade, dating back to a pre-Civil War spin ginner, a hand-cranked machine that could, in one day, turn raw cotton into enough yarn to make between seven and ten yards of cloth. This spinner is one of the museum's most unique items, since only seven of these are known to survive. The museum also exhibits several variations on Eli Whitney's cotton gin, another inestimable labor saving device. Mechanical pickers greatly increased the amount that could be picked (see Cotton Fields and Cotton Gins selection). Old photographs show various phases of cotton growing, harvesting and processing.

It's fascinating to read in a museum display that from one bale of cotton, weighing about 500 pounds, it would be possible to make either 300 pairs of men's jeans, 1,200 men's t-shirts, 750 men's dress shirts, 875 women's woven blouses, 350 women's dresses, 525 women's skirts, 350 women's jeans, 3,000 baby diapers, 750 terry bath towels, 7,800 men's handkerchiefs, 475 men's dress trousers, 350 men's work trousers, 200 sheets or 1,200 pillowcases.

Early agricultural tools were mule-powered. A popular exhibit features Mr. T, a mechanical mule, donated as all the exhibits have been. The mule comes from the Tapp family who owned now-closed department stores in Columbia. While not mechanical, the oversized model of a boll weevil also gets a reaction from young visitors. Beside the weevil is a cotton mopper, used in the early 1900s to poison the boll weevil. The mop was coated with black strap molasses and arsenic which was brushed over the cotton plant.

Visitors are sure to learn something new as they explore the exhibits. Few realize before touring that 75% of the material found in dollar bills is cotton fiber. Also surprising to many is the fact that cotton can be grown in colors. This technique is not new; over 1,000 years ago the Incas of South America grew delicately hued cotton. Unlike dyed yarns, natural color deepens, not fades, with time and washings. The museum has examples of red, ivory, green and brown cotton grown locally. There is a different meaning to the little poem hanging in the museum that reads in part: "First day white, next day red, third day dead." This refers to the short life of the cotton blossom.

You'll see the top hat and carrying case of renowned South Carolina politician Ellison Durant "Cotton Ed" Smith. His incredible 36-year tenure as U.S. Senator has only recently been surpassed by another native son, Strom Thurmond. On display is a painting of Smith's birthplace and home **Tanglewood Plantation**, located just south of Bishopville on Route 341 (if you take Exit 120 off I-20 it is three miles south of Lynchburg and 15 miles from the exit). The house, listed on the National Register of Historic Places, can be toured. There is a smokehouse (believed to be the oldest standing log structure in the state) plus an art gallery and visitors center.

The South Carolina Cotton Museum is open for a nominal charge Monday through Friday from 10:00 A.M. to 5:00 P.M. The museum is always popular during the Lee County Cotton Festival the third week in October. During this event local history buffs re-enact the Cash-Shannon Duel (an historical marker on Route 15 north just across the Lynches River bridge from Bishopville commemorates the Cash-Shannon duel). Fought on July 5,1880 it was the last duel in South Carolina.)

Directions: From I-20 take Exit 116, Route 15 north to Bishopville. Route 15 becomes Main Street in Bishopville. The South Carolina Cotton Museum is on the left at 115 North Main Street.

Pee Dee Country Regional Tourism Contacts (Area Code 803)

PEE DEE TOURISM COMMISSION
3290 Radio Road, P.O. Box 3093
Florence, SC 29502
669-0950, 800-325-9005, fax: 665-9480

DILLON COUNTY CHAMBER OF COMMERCE
P.O. Box 1304
Dillon, SC 29536
774-8551

DARLINGTON CHAMBER OF COMMERCE
P.O. Box 274
Darlington, SC 29532
393-2641

FLORENCE CONVENTION & VISITORS BUREAU
3290 Radio Road
Florence, SC 29502
664-0330

GREATER FLORENCE CHAMBER OF COMMERCE
P.O. Box 948
Florence, SC 29503
665-0515

GREATER HARTSVILLE CHAMBER OF COMMERCE
P.O. Box 578
Hartsville, SC 29550
332-6401

GREATER LAKE CITY CHAMBER OF COMMERCE
P.O. Box 669
Lake City, SC 29560
394-8611

LEE COUNTY CHAMBER OF COMMERCE
P.O. Box 187
Bishopville, SC 29010
484-5145

MARION CHAMBER OF COMMERCE
P.O. Box 35
Marion, SC 29571
423-3561

MARLBORO COUNTY CHAMBER OF COMMERCE
P.O. Box 458
Bennettsville, SC 29512
479-3941

MULLINS CHAMBER OF COMMERCE
P.O. Box 595
Mullins, SC 29574
464-6651

GREATER WILLIAMSBURG COUNTY CHAMBER OF COMMERCE
130 E. Main Street
P.O. Box 696
Kingstree, SC 29556
354-6431

Pee Dee Country Calendar of Events (Area Code 803)

Late March

Mark III Vans 200. NASCAR racing event featuring the rising stars of racing in the first race of the Busch Grant National Series. Darlington, 395-8892.

Transouth Financial 400. 400 drivers race 400 miles in a Winston Cup race. Darlington, 395-8892.

Mid-April

Southern Plant and Flower Festival. Blooming plants, flowers, trees and gardening equipment for sale at the Pee Dee State Farmers Market. Florence, 665-5154.

Bar B Q Shag Festival. A celebration of the state's distinctive food and dance. Hemingway, 558-2751.

Nike South Carolina Classic. Annual race always draws a crowd. Florence, 669-1838.

Late April

Arts Alive Festival. A wide range of music highlight this festival. Florence, 661-1385.

May

Jubilee Arts Festival. Artists and craftsmen demonstrate and sell their work. Bennettsville, 479-6982.

Late August

Gatorade 200. A fall classic on Labor Day weekend, and the last race for the Busch Grant National Series. Darlington, 395-8892.

Southern 500 Winston Cup Race. The crowds always come for this race. Darlington, 395-8892.

Late September

Golden Leaf Festival. Country music, arts and crafts, regional food and a husband hollerin' contest are features of this event. Mullins, 464-6651.

Mid-October

Lee County Cotton Festival. Parade, races, arts and crafts, entertainment, carnival rides, antique car show and family activities blend to celebrate the cotton crop. Bishopville, 484-5154.

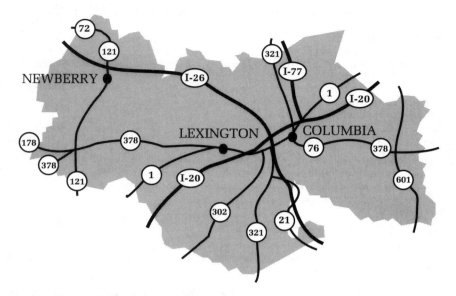

Capital City & Lake Murray Country

Capital City & Lake Murray Country

Local legend proclaims that five inches from General Wade Hampton I's grave at Trinity Church's cemetery is the exact center of South Carolina (it's actually 13 miles southeast of Columbia near Hopkins). When the capital was moved inland from Charleston in 1786, this centrally located spot on the Congaree River was designated the new seat of government and the two-square-mile town of Columbia was laid out. The town has grown and lived up to the expectations of its founders. It is the center of government, if not the center of the state, and a hub of arts, education, history and recreation.

Columbia wears its history proudly. Bronze stars mark cannon hits from Sherman's forces when they burned most of the city to the ground. Restored homes of regional and national historic figures and the extensive Lexington County Museum complex provide a layered look at the region from the early Saxe-Gotha settlement through the Civil War. For a comprehensive look at Columbia and the state from an historical, economic and scientific point of view there is no better resource than the South Carolina State Museum.

This urban inland city boasts an amazing array of nearby natural attractions from the ageless wetlands of the Congaree Swamp National Monument to Peachtree Rock, a prehistoric sandstone outcropping. Adventure Carolina and other outfitters offer a wide array of water excursions, including after-work canoe trips. Many Columbians desert the city early for the recreation at Lake Murray. Outstanding city parks such as Finlay Park and Riverfront Park offer a green getaway in the heart of the city.

Adventure Carolina

Fitness is Fun!

Did you know that Columbia is one of the top ten canoeing towns in the country? *Paddler Magazine* gave this distinction to Cayce, one of Columbia's suburbs, because it is the location of **Adventure Carolina.** The magazine noted, "Just about any water in the state is within striking distance of Cayce. There's the Edisto and the Saluda, and there's also the local favorite, the Congaree, formed when the Broad and the Saluda meet in Columbia."

With over 30 years experience as guides and outfitters, Adventure Carolina can provide outings for novices and experts. Many introductory classes and workshops are free and all basic equipment is provided. The paddling school teaches whitewater and flatwater canoeing, whitewater kayaking and sea kayaking. They schedule canoe trips for all ages and levels; there are even after-work canoe trips. These three-hour trips begin at 6:00 P.M. and offer a marvelous antidote to a stressful day. There are also full moon trips and camping trips. For those who want to start their day exercising, they have sunrise paddles. A series of all-women adventures includes canoeing, kayaking, sea kayaking and camping. If you want to get out on your own they rent canoes, provide drop-offs and pick-ups and furnish canoe trail maps.

Adventure Carolina has the largest selection of outdoor-oriented books in the state as well as the largest selection of climbing gear. Behind the store they have a 25-foot climbing wall used for instruction. They sell or rent equipment needed for an amazing array of outdoor activities. For more information call (803) 796-4505 or visit the store from 10:00 A.M. to 6:00 P.M. Monday through Saturday.

Directions: From Columbia take I-321/176/21 across the Congaree River. You will be on Knox Abbott Drive; make an immediate left on State Street. Adventure Carolina is at 1107 State Street in Cayce.

Cayce Historical Museum

From Prehistory to Present

At the **Cayce Historical Museum** they feel that "to lose your beginnings is to lose your future." Beginnings here go back to man's earliest days on this continent. Native Americans from all eras of prehistory hunted and camped in this part of South Carolina. The oldest Clovis point arrowheads date back thousands of years.

The museum's Saxe Gotha/Granby Room delves into these early years. Artifacts from the Native American village on the west bank of the Congaree River fill several cases. Members of the Congaree tribe were on hand to greet Captain Juan Pardo and his army of 125 men when they marched from Santa Elena, the Spanish settlement on Parris Island (see selection). Pardo and his men arrived in November 1566 to establish a mission for the indigenous population and to explore for minerals. By 1718, a trading post was established to protect the early traders at the Congaree village.

Saxe Gotha Township was established in 1733 by fewer than a hundred men. In 1748, a second fort was established to protect the Saxe Gotha settlers from the Iroquois. Included in the exhibits are dioramas of both forts and a 1733 map of Saxe Gotha.

The museum is located in a replica of the two-story trading post that was built here in 1765. The British seized the trading post during the Revolutionary War and fortified it, calling it Fort Granby. Between February 1781 and July 4, 1781, there were battles around the fort. In July, it was under the command of Lord Francis Rawdon when General Nathaniel Greene and his troops recaptured it.

During this engagement 18-year-old Emily Geiger became a heroine. One room at the museum is devoted to Emily's saga. The Patriots under General Greene needed to get a message to General Sumter but it was deemed suicide for any man to carry it through the heavily patrolled British lines. Emily volunteered to carry the message but was captured by the British on July 3, 1781 and taken to Rawdon's headquarters. She was held in the same room that serves as her exhibit room in the reconstructed building. Emily knew that they had sent for a woman with Tory sympathies to search her, so Emily memorized the note, then swallowed it. When the search proved futile, she was released and continued on her mission, delivering the message to Sumter verbally. Sumter arrived in time to combine forces with Greene and defeat the British. The room contains a field bed such as commanders would use during campaigns and a trunk that belonged to Emily's cousin, Abraham Geiger. There is a bust of Emily Geiger in South Carolina's State House (see selection).

In 1781, ferry service started across the Congaree River. The operation was situated within sight of Fort Granby. Following the war, the fort was purchased and converted to a private residence by Major Daniel Tateman and his wife, Ann Geiger, who was Emily's first cousin. The Tateman's daughter, Elizabeth, married James Cayce and the house became known as the Cayce House.

This leads to the Victorian era and a museum room with exhibits from this period, including a mannequin in a fashionable dress from the 1800s. One case is filled with delicately-made crocheted, tatted and embroidered pieces. Civil War exhibits include Confederate money, weapons and other memorabilia. There are also reminders of the 1865 Union prisoner camp, Camp Sorghum, where 1,400 officers were held. The camp name was derived from the rations of sorghum molasses and uncooked corn meal that the prisoners were fed.

The final exhibit room within the museum is the Cayce Room with local history covering the first half of the 20th century. Education and transportation are major themes of this exhibit. Attention is also paid to the civic leaders of Cayce.

The museum grounds has an 18th-century kitchen and old smokehouse. The kitchen dates back to the 1750s and is furnished with original pieces that reflect an earlier era. Notice the tree trunk vegetable holder and the husk broom. Part of this structure served as quarters for the house slave. Nearby is a milk house and behind the kitchen is an 1820 smokehouse with butchering equipment, salt boxes and smoked hams hanging from the rafters.

A red caboose reflects Cayce's railroad history. Hanging here are photographs of almost 200 locals associated with the railroad; they are part of the **Cayce Railroad Hall of Fame**. The Dixieana Depot, a stop on the route from Savannah to Columbia, still contains its old desk and equipment, including a pot-bellied stove.

A portion of the grounds is the **Granby Historical Garden** with plants the settlers might have grown in 1737. Bridges and boardwalks make it easy to explore this garden oasis. Adjoining the museum grounds is Granby Garden Park with playground equipment and picnic facilities.

Cayce Historical Museum is open Tuesday through Friday from 9:00 A.M. to 4:00 P.M. and weekends 2:00 to 5:00 P.M. It is closed on Mondays and holidays. There is a small admission charge. Begin the tour in the main musum. A tour guide at the entrance will greet you and stay with you throughout your tour or, if you prefer, you may browse on your own after a brief introductory overview is given by the tour guide.

Directions: From I-26 take the Cayce exit, Route 321. Once in Cayce, turn right on 12th Street. The Cayce Historical Museum is at 1800 12th Street Extension in the Cayce City Hall Complex.

Columbia Museum of Art

Main Stream Art on Main Street

The **Columbia Museum of Art** opened in 1950 and in 1998 moved to spacious new quarters on Main Street. The museum continues to be a center for exhibitions, lectures, concerts and other cultural events.

Exhibits are mounted chronologically with decorative arts and paintings of the same period displayed together. There is a small but fascinating collection of classical art. One of its highlights is a late Archaic Greek black-figured vase, called the Craft Vase in honor of the museum's first director Dr. John Richard Craft, who acquired this work for the museum. The vase is believed to be produced in the area around Athens (called Attica) around 510 B.C. This single-handle 14-inch-high container is a lekythos used to hold perfumed oil. The story told on the vase concerns the Greek siege of Troy during the Trojan War. Achilles and Ajax are playing a game oblivious to the imminent attack of the Trojan soldiers, but the Goddess Athena is on hand to warn them of their danger. Some scholars believe the vase conveys a message that even great heroes can be caught with their guard down.

The museum has galleries exhibiting the Samuel H. Kress Collection of Baroque and Italian Renaissance Art. Samuel H. Kress, the founder of the S.H. Kress stores, divided his collection among museums in cities where he operated his stores. Among the many outstanding works is a painting attributed to Canaletto (Giovanni Antonio Canal). Canaletto began painting opera backdrops with his father but soon found his metier in large canvases of his beloved Venice. The museum's painting is one of his favorite views of the city with the front of the Doge's Palace and the Church of S. Maria Della Salute in the distance. Another view of Venice is captured by Francesco Guardi with his 1770 work of the Grand Canal and the Dogana (Harbor Custom House). Guardi was called, "The poet who sang of Venice in colors." Representing the French Impressionists is Claude Monet's *L'Ile Aux Orties, Giverny,* its delicate colors and fluid style giving it an interplay of light and water that is masterful.

Sandro Botticello's *The Nativity* is an excellent example of the religious theme of so much Florentine Renaissance art. Botticelli gives us the traditional nativity scene in a theatrical manner with the angel announcing the birth to the shepherds, the caravan of the Magi and two elegant Florentine youths. A 1723 painting by Francois Boucher, *Joseph Presenting his Father and Brothers to Pharoah*, was believed lost for decades but was identified in 1953 and acquired by the museum.

Portraiture was another popular artistic subject and the museum has a strong representative sampling of this genre. Thomas Sully was an outstanding portrait painter and his painting of his daughters *Blanche and Rosalie* demonstrates his powers. Born in England, Sully eventually settled in Charleston where he became friends with Charles Fraser. Fraser's miniature of *Judge Abraham Nott* is also in the museum's collection. In addition, the museum has Gilbert Stuart's *Mrs. Samuel Savage* done in 1810. Stuart is best remembered for his portrait of George Washington, a work that was never finished. The museum also has a growing collection of works by contemporary American artists. One worth noting is Alison Saar's *Snake Man*, which reveals the artist's fascination with the traditions and mythologies of the African-American community.

The Columbia Museum of Art is justifiably proud of their glass collection, including the 55 pieces of Tiffany glassware in the Maurice B. Bradley Collection. The items date from 1900 to the late 1920s and reveal the scope of Louis Comfort Tiffany's visionary impact on American home decor. Included among the items is an unusual Moorish-influenced lamp and fanciful iridescent tableware. There is also a substantial collection of 18th-, 19th- and 20th-century decorative arts and furnishings. One unusual piece is the *Cross Check* armchair designed by Frank O. Gehry. This bentwood chair is structurally expressive and quite decorative. Throughout the year the museum mounts four to six temporary exhibitions.

The Columbia Museum of Art is open Tuesday through Friday from 10:00 A.M. to 5:00 P.M. and weekends 12:30 to 5:00 P.M. Admission is charged. There is a museum shop and library which are open during regular hours.

Directions: From I-26 take I-126 to the Huger Street exit. Continue on Huger Street to Gervais Street and make a left. Take Gervais past the State House (on the right) and make a left on Main Street. The Columbia Museum of Art is on the corner of Main and Hampton streets.

Congaree Swamp National Monument

Lions, Tigers and Leopards—oh, my!

That's ant lions, clymene tiger moths and southern leopard frogs—all part of the amazing diversity of wildlife that makes its home at **Congaree Swamp National Monument**. Many visitors are curious to know why a swamp is designated as a national monument. This diversity is part of the answer. In June 1983, Congaree Swamp, already protected by its inclusion in the national park system, was designated part of the United Nations International Biosphere Reserve Program. Identification lists point out some of the more than 320 plants, 41 mammals, 24 reptiles, 52 fish and 200 bird species identified at this park.

This diversity provides a genetic library and a warning system—botanists, biologists, and others are alerted to potential hazards by careful observation of the life cycles in this rich natural environment which includes the last great river bottom hardwood forest in the country. There is a sense of stepping outside of time, certainly stepping back in time perhaps, to the era of the giant reptiles and dinosaurs. Here you'll see 90 tree species as well as some of the tallest trees on the east coast (although nine national champions were lost during Hurricane Hugo). Another facet of the swamp that makes it unique is its muck, specifically Dorovan muck. The muck is significant because the bacteria in the muck eats CFC's (chloroflorohydrocarbons), which cause holes in the ozone layer.

Several trails provide access into various parts of the park. The 4.6 mile Weston Lake Loop Trail is the most popular long trail in the park; it takes you into the old growth forest where the trees form a high canopy. You're apt to spot wildlife along the bank of Cedar Creek while hiking this trail. A three-to-four-hour hike through part of the old-growth forest can be taken on the 7.5 mile Oakridge Trail. Be alert for wild boars as you cross the floodplain's "guts," the small streams that carry high water in and out of the swamp. To reach remote parts of the swamp take the 11.1 mile Kingsnake Trail; here too there will be good opportunities for spotting wildlife. There's also a 1.6 mile Bluff Trail that circles the Ranger Station and provides access to the two boardwalks. The trail also leads up to a small cliff on the edge of the floodplain. Another alternative is to take the 10.4 mile River Trail along the banks of the Congaree; the river is the lifeblood of the swamp. This trail can be extremely wet, as floodwater from the river covers 80% of the park on an average of ten times a year.

Most visitors take the .7-mile self-guided boardwalk tour that extends through the loblolly pines into the swamp itself. The boardwalk is built roughly six feet above ground. The loblolly pines also harken back centuries. Many of these massive trees are more than 10 feet in circumference and 150 feet in height. Fifteen points of interest are pointed out along this walk, including an example of poison ivy that grows abundantly in the park. Visitors who take a guided nature walk will learn how to tell the poisonous vine from the Virginia creeper with the following rhyme, "leaves of three, let it be; leaves of five, let it thrive." The trail guide also points out a green shrub called "hobblebush." Leucothoe became known by this common name because bear hunters' dogs would get hobbled in this shrub while the bears ran right through. The trail ends at Weston Lake where there is a link with the 1.1-mile low boardwalk. This walkway takes you through a primeval swampy flat where you'll see bald cypress and water tupelo trees. The quintessential swamp appearance is created by the cypress knees, part of the tree's root system, that protrude from the wet, swamp ground. The low boardwalk ends up back at the parking area.

The park can also be explored by canoe, although it's BYOC— bring your own canoes and life preservers (a first aid kit and water are also advisable). There are marked canoe trails and canoes can be rented from Adventure Carolina (803-796-4505, see selection) and River Runners (803-771-0353). It is also possible to get a free permit for primitive camping.

Remember that this park is a protected natural sanctuary and visitors should not remove any plant or animal specimens. The park ranger office is open daily (except Christmas Day) from 8:30 A.M. to 5:00 P.M. There is no admission to the park. During mosquito season visitors should apply repellant before hiking. Just behind the ranger station there is a native plant butterfly garden with plants you might see on your hikes on the bluff or floodplain.

Directions: From I-77 on the outskirts of Columbia, take Exit 5, Route 48 east. When the road forks, bear right and follow the directional signs to the entrance of the Congaree Swamp National Monument. It is approximately 20 miles from Columbia.

Fort Jackson Museum and Sesquicentennial State Park

ATTENTION!

Soldiers began training at Camp Jackson in 1917. Since that time, infantrymen, cavalrymen, paratroopers, aircraft pilots, balloon pilots, war dogs and carrier pigeons have been trained at Fort Jackson. Today drill sergeants receive their instruction at the fort. No marching, drilling or military decorum is demanded of visitors to the **Fort Jackson Museum**.

Fort Jackson, named for Andrew Jackson, the seventh president, is the army's largest and most active initial entry training center. As the country entered World War I, the citizens of Columbia purchased the land for the camp and gave it to the Federal government. In six months 10,000 workers constructed 1,500 structures. So great was the rush, most of the men in the artillery trained with wooden sticks; they didn't receive their weapons until they arrived in Europe. Major General Charles J. Bailey was commander at Fort Jackson, as well as the head of the 81st Division. The men in his unit had a felt patch with a wildcat sewn on the shoulder of their uniforms. General Pershing thought that the patches increased esprit de corps and thus the tradition of wearing a shoulder sleeve insignia was launched.

The museum's uniformed mannequins include combat wear from the American Revolution, Civil War and the Spanish American War. Uniforms, helmets and weapons are displayed from World War I. Also exhibited is a Cooper Bomb; British airmen held this bomb outside the window of their plane and dropped it on enemy targets. There is also a Browning automatic rifle that General James C. Dozier, the Adjutant General of South Carolina and commandant at Camp Jackson, brought back from Europe in WWI.

From 1925 to 1939, the camp was used by the South Carolina National Guard but it was reactivated at the onset of World War II when 500,000 men were trained at Fort Jackson. There is a full-size exhibit of a barrack from this period. This era saw a number of well-known visitors including President Franklin D. Roosevelt, General Dwight D. Eisenhower, Betty Grable and Joe Louis. There are weapons and munitions from the United States, Germany and Japan.

Exhibits reveal details of more recent conflicts; for example there are photographs and a replica with uniformed mannequins of the BauBang village built to familiarize soldiers with Vietnam. There is also a display of hand-made weapons used by the Vietcong. Another exhibit concentrates on Desert Storm; there is even a Coke bottle with Arabic writing. Larger munitions and aircraft are displayed on the grounds around the museum.

Fort Jackson Museum is open at no charge Tuesday through Friday from 10:00 A.M. to 4:00 P.M. and Saturday from 1:00 to 4:00 P.M. It is closed on Sunday, Monday and Federal holidays.

Not far from Fort Jackson is the 1,419-acre **Sesquicentennial State Park** (locals shorten the name to Sesqui). The park, on the outskirts of Columbia, was donated to the state in 1937 in commemoration of the city's 150th anniversary. When you visit this park you will quickly realize why the area is called the sandhills. The name refers to a 20-to-30-mile strip that extends from North Augusta to Cheraw. The sandy soil in the region makes you expect a beach. While there is no breaking ocean today, there once was. Over a million years ago the ocean extended inland to Columbia, so this may well have been ocean-front land. Sandhills resulted from the four occasions when the ocean receded, then returned to this area.

Today at Sesqui there is the gently lapping water of the 30-acre lake. Recreational options include swimming, fishing and pedal boats. There are picnic areas along the lake and two nature trails. The Jackson Creek Nature Trail is a quarter-mile self-interpretation trail that leads to the dam. A second trail leads away from the dam through the pine-scrub oak forest. It crosses several creeks that feed into the lake and ends near the refreshment stand in the day-use area. Near the conference center there is a small cedar bog. If you spot a plant or animal you don't recognize, drop by the nature center and check the exhibits. They have live specimens from the park and park personnel are available to answer questions.

In addition to walking trails there is a four-mile jogging trail and an exercise course. There are also bike trails. Eighty-seven campsites amid the pine trees offer inviting getaway options on a first come/first served basis. Groups can rent the conference center for meetings and special events. Near the conference center is a 1756 log house that was relocated at the park and now serves as an art studio and gallery. The park has a playground and athletic fields. Park hours are daily 7:00 A.M. to 9:00 P.M. from April through October; at other times hours are 8:00 A.M. to 6:00 P.M.

Directions: For Fort Jackson take I-77 to Exit 12. Enter at Gate 2 and take a right on Jackson Boulevard. Turn left at Fornay Street and the museum will be on the corner of Fornay Street and Jackson Boulevard. For Sesquicentennial State Park, from I-77 take U.S. 1 exit and head west toward Camden. The entrance to the park will be on the right. From I-20 take Exit 74, U.S. 1 for three miles. The park can also be accessed from I-26 by either taking I-20 west or U.S. 1 west.

The Governor's Mansion and State House

Halls of Power

South Carolina's capital is Columbia and the government is centered in two locations: **The Governor's Mansion** and the **State House**. The executive mansion was built in 1855 but not as an official residence. It was to house officers of the Arsenal Military Academy, a two-year school that prepared students for the Citadel. Fortuitously, the building escaped Sherman's fires that burned so much of Columbia. Since 1868, it has served as the home of all but six governors, who chose to maintain their own residences in Columbia. The house is now the center of Governor's Green, which includes a fountain, beautiful gardens and two additional houses used for visiting dignitaries, special functions and tours: the 1855 Lace House and the 1830 Caldwell-Boylston House.

When you tour The Governor's Mansion, even the public rooms reveal that this is a home. As your tour takes you through the large drawing room, dining room, library and other public

Bronze stars on the State House's western wall mark the location of cannon damage from the Sherman's attack during the Civil War. A massive renovation project has returned this 1855 building to its former splendor.

areas, your attention will be directed to individual pieces of furniture or art that were given to the mansion by former residents. The piano was a birthday gift to Governor James F. Byrnes' wife, Jane. During one memorable evening after a concert in Columbia, Leonard Bernstein sat at the piano for hours and entertained guests of Governor Hollings. The 66-piece silver set in the state dining room was commissioned for the battleship *USS South Carolina* in the early 1900s. When the ship was decommissioned in the 1920s, Senator Thurmond had the silver sent to the Governor's Mansion when he became governor. The wallpaper, chosen by Governor Donald S. Russell's wife, Virginia, is decorated with palmettos, the state tree. The plasterwork medallion is from an old mansion in Columbia. There is also a small family dining room on the first floor that opens onto a private courtyard.

In the Hall of Governors, there is a photograph of all but three of South Carolina's governors. Here, too, are the flags from the first *USS South Carolina* loaned to the mansion by the Daughters of the American Revolution. Off this hallway are guest rooms. The Middleton Bedroom has a bed that belonged to Declaration of Independence signer Arthur Middleton. The bed was part of Middleton's baggage during his military service in the Revolutionary War. A framed note in the guest room from President George Bush says that the "mansion is a joy to behold and stay in." Additional public rooms include a cozy ladies' parlor and a library with pictures of the homes of four South Carolina signers of the Declaration of Independence.

Appointments must be made to tour the Governor's Mansion; call (803) 737-1710. There is a gift shop in the basement of the Caldwell-Boylston House.

The State House reopened in 1998 after a $33-million renovation project. The building has a stormy history. The legislative building was constructed in 1855 and shelled by Union troops in 1865. Bronze stars mark where cannon shells damaged the western wall. The corner stone of the State House was laid on December 15, 1851. Construction was fraught with difficulties. The two-year effort of the first architect was found defective and the building was dismantled under a new architect. This delay may have proved worthwhile because when the work began again the building had been shifted so that it had a north and south exposure at the intersection of Senate and Main streets. Work was suspended on the uncompleted building when Sherman's army marched into Columbia in February 1865. Worse damage was done to the old state house by a fire later that year that destroyed the library, offices and workshops. Work resumed on the state house in June of 1885, but various setbacks delayed construction until about 1891. The last architect,

Charles C. Wilson, appointed in 1904, said the State House was "one of the most notable buildings of the world." Its Corinthian capitals were, according to Wilson, "wonderful, nothing finer in France or Italy." At 43 feet high, these monolithic (cut from a single piece of stone) columns are among the largest in the world. The State House was finally completed in 1907.

There are two bodies of the legislative branch—the Senate and the House of Representatives. On the capitol grounds there is a replica of the Liberty Bell. On the north side of the State House is a statue of the first governor elected after Reconstruction, General Wade Hampton. It is open weekdays from 9:00 A.M. to 5:00 P.M.

Directions: From I-26 take I-126 which becomes Elmwood Avenue. Take a right onto Lincoln Street (two blocks beyond overpass). The Governor's Mansion is in the second block on the right. From I-77, take Route 277 to Calhoun Street. Turn right on Calhoun and continue to Lincoln Street; then make a left. The Governor's Mansion is in the second block on the right. For the State House, from Elmwood Avenue turn right on Assembly Street and a left on Gervais Street. The State House is on the right. From I-77 take Route 277 to Elmwood and turn right. At Main Street turn left. The State House is at the end of Main Street.

Hampton-Preston Mansion and Garden

First Family of Columbia

Ainsley Hall, who built the **Hampton-Preston Mansion** in 1818, was not a lucky man. His wife loved the house, but so did Wade Hampton I. In 1823, Hampton made Hall an offer of $35,000 to buy the house and he just couldn't turn it down. Hall told his wife he would build her an even grander house across the street (see Robert Mills Historic House selection), but he died before that house was completed.

Wade Hampton I and Mary Cantey, his third wife, had six children. They were married in 1801 when he was 50 and she was 22. She lived in the Hampton-Preston mansion until her death in 1863. Her daughter Caroline Hampton Preston was the next to reside here. After Caroline married John Preston in her girlhood home in 1830, she returned in 1832 to bear Charles, her first child. The Prestons lived in this Columbia mansion from 1835 until 1873; they remodeled the house in mid-century to accommodate their family. Two of the children died at an early age, but the others, ranging in age from 3 to 14, spent most of their childhood years at the Hampton-Preston mansion. During the Civil War, Wade Hampton Manning was an orderly for General Wade Hampton III and later served as secretary for Governor Hampton. Neither Wade Hampton II or General Wade Hampton III ever

201

lived at the Hampton-Preston mansion.

During the Civil War, for a short time in February 1865, the house served as headquarters for Union General J.A. Logan. According to local legend, the reason that the Hampton-Preston mansion survived the burning of Columbia is that when the troops were burning the city, Sherman found a Roman Catholic nun and the children from her convent school hiding in a graveyard. Sherman told her she could have any house in Columbia and she picked the Hampton mansion, so Logan was forced to leave his headquarters and the house was secured.

In 1873, the mansion passed out of the family when it was purchased by Governor Moses's wife for $42,000. From 1890 through the 1930s, the property was used by a succession of female educational institutions. The house is now operated by Historic Columbia Foundation.

Touring the mansion provides a glimpse of one of South Carolina's most prominent antebellum family. The Hampton and Preston families had a great influence on the politics and economy of South Carolina. The mansion's rooms are filled with family pieces that reflect their taste and affluence. Portraits of the three Wade Hamptons hang in the gentlemen's sitting room. Many of the small items in the room such as the umbrella, dominoes, lap robe and books belonged to family members. The elegant parlor has a marble bust of Sarah Buchanan Preston, who it is claimed lost more suitors during the Civil War than any other woman in the country—it was not a lucky thing to win her affections during those tumultuous years. She eventually married after the war. During the war, when Union troops moved through South Carolina, Wade Hampton III's sisters took down the drawing room curtains at Millwood, their family plantation house, and wrapped them around the family silver, china and other valuables and put them on a farm wagon to be moved to safety. The draperies in the parlor are reproductions of those at Millwood and the china and crystal are from the plantation, which was destroyed by fire during Sherman's march.

The Hampton-Preston Mansion is open Tuesday through Saturday from 10:15 A.M. to 3:15 P.M. and Sunday 1:15 to 4:15 P.M. The house is closed on major holidays. Admission is charged.

Directions: From I-26/126 head into Columbia and turn right on Bull Street, then make a left on Blanding Street. The Hampton-Preston Mansion is at 1615 Blanding Street. Tickets are obtained across the street in the gift shop of the Robert Mills House.

Historic Horseshoe of the University of South Carolina

Make a Wish!

In 1801, South Carolina College (today the University of South Carolina) was established and its educational buildings were designed in a horseshoe shape with a lush backdrop of old trees. During the Civil War, many of the facilities served as hospitals for the armies of the North and South. At the head of the **Historic Horseshoe** is **McKissick Museum.**

The museum, established in 1976, features six major exhibit areas. Financier Bernard Baruch, born in nearby Camden in 1870, gave the University his outstanding collection of silver services and other silver items which are displayed in the museum. There are photographs of Baruch's South Carolina home and details of his long service as an adviser to presidents Wilson and Roosevelt. Included in the art gallery, that features state and regional artists, is the Mandell Art Nouveau Collection. Another outstanding exhibit features Native and African-American artifacts, traditional pottery, baskets and quilts. Also popular is the J. Harry Howard Gemstone Collection with approximately 3,500 exquisitely-cut jewels including brilliant amethysts and aquamarines. Adding to this is the Thomas Cooper Collection of Minerals with a special gallery for fluorescent minerals from which light glows from within. McKissick Museum has a number of exhibit rooms that detail the history of the University of South Carolina and its athletic record, including the 1980 Heisman Memorial Trophy won by South Carolina star George Rogers. Finally, the University has an extensive collection of Twentieth Century-Fox Movietone newsreels. The museum also has radio broadcast materials from outstanding South Carolina broadcasters.

McKissick Museum is open at no charge Monday through Friday from 9:00 A.M. to 4:00 P.M. and weekends 1:00 to 5:00 P.M. It is closed on major holidays. In addition to the museum's permanent collection, McKissick hosts changing exhibits of art, science, regional history and folk art. If you are doing research you can make an appointment to use the Folkarts Resource Center and the Broadcasting Archives.

On the corner of Sumter and Pendleton streets is the **Confederate Relic Room and Museum** with artifacts and memorabilia from the colonial period to the space age. The museum's primary thrust is on South Carolina during the Civil War. There are uniforms, weapons, battle flags, newspaper clippings, currency and personal mementoes. This museum is open at no charge Monday through Friday from 9:00 A.M. to 5:00 P.M.

Also on the Horseshoe is the **South Caroliniana Library** whose reading room is copied from Bulfinch's Library of Congress. This was the first separate college library building erected in the country when it was built in 1840. This library is a repository of state history and genealogy. The library is open Monday through Friday from 8:30 A.M. to 5:00 P.M., and until 8:00 P.M. on Thursday. Saturday hours are 9:00 A.M. to 5:00 P.M.

Directions: From I-76 feed into I-126 to Columbia; exit at Huger Street (feeds directly onto this street, no turning) and continue to Gervais Street and turn left. Take Gervais Street past the State House to Sumter Street and make a right. The Historic Horseshoe will be on your left on Sumter Street.

Lake Murray and
Dreher Island State Park

Islands in the Sun

The 50,000-acre **Lake Murray**, with 520 miles of shoreline, was completed in 1930 to provide hydroelectric power and water-oriented recreational opportunities for South Carolina's mid-lands. When the dam was finished it was the world's largest earthen dam in cubical content for power purposes. The dam is 208 feet high and 1½ miles long. At it's widest point, Lake Murray is 41 miles long and 14 miles wide and covers a total of 78 square miles. During World War II, the area was used for training exercises by the Army Air Corps.

One of the public access spots along the shores of Lake Murray is **Dreher Island State Park**. The 12 miles of shoreline within the 348-acre park offer a myriad of recreational options. The park is actually three islands linked by a causeway and two bridges. Campers particularly enjoy this park because of the numerous lakeside campsites. In all, there are 97 sites with hookups and 15 tent sites at the park (the park takes reservations for 40 camp-sites). For more luxurious overnighting, make reservations to stay at one of the five island villas. Each has a fireplace, a screened porch overlooking the lake, as well as an upstairs balcony. They have all the amenities of upscale villas and are a real bargain, but they fill up fast (reservations are taken a year in advance). During the summer they are rented on a weekly basis, at other times there is a two-night minimum. For more information call the park office between 11:00 A.M. and NOON or 4:00 and 5:00 P.M. at (803) 364-4152.

Dreher does not have a supervised beach, so swim at your own risk. They also do not rent boats, although there are six boat ramps and rental slips for boats. The lake is popular with fishermen and the park has a tackle shop and general store. Lake Murray is home to numerous fish species but its most abundant catch is striped bass, largemouth bass, bream and crappies. Dreher is the launching site for more than 100 fishing tournaments annually.

Another place you can access Lake Murray is from either side of the dam. South Carolina Electric and Gas has a small sandy swimming beach with picnic facilities that is open at a nominal fee. This is a day-use only area. The company has seven additional park sites and recreation areas around the lake. There are three rental sites on the lake: in Chapin, The Lake Connection (803-781-8083) rents pontoon boats; Putnam's Landing (803-345-3040) rents power boats, while in Ballentine, Lake Murray Marina (803-781-1585) has boat rentals.

You need a boat to get to one of Lake Murray's hidden treasures, the **Purple Martin Audubon Sanctuary** on Lunch Island, between Shull Island and Snelgrove's Landing. In the 1940s Lunch Island was known as the Bombing Range Island because the Army Air Corps practiced dropping dummy bombs at this target, severely damaging the vegetation. The bamboo, low shrubs and other vegetation that grew back make the island an ideal roosting habitat for the purple martin. The sanctuary's establishment was a cooperative effort between the South Carolina Electric & Gas, the Columbia Audubon Society and the South Carolina Department of Natural Resources. This is the first sanctuary in the country established exclusively for the purple martin.

Today this tranquil island, much enjoyed by fishermen, picnickers and bird watchers, is the state's largest known purple martin staging area. It's from here that purple martins began their annual migration to Brazil. The isolated location of the island protects the birds from predators and there are abundant feeding opportunities on and around the island. Purple martins, the largest swallow species in North America, arrive in June in enormous bands of 20,000 to 40,000 birds. They gather at dusk and depart at dawn to feed. These vocal songbirds are highly social and seem to prefer to nest close to man. Even Native Americans encouraged purple martins by putting gourds near their gardens. An often repeated myth is that purple martins eat mosquitos. They don't, although they eat other insects including dragonflies, grasshoppers, Japanese beetles, wasps and butterflies.

Directions: For Dreher Island State Park from I-26 take Exit 91, and head west toward Chapin on Route 48. Turn right on Route 76 for a short distance, then take Route 26, St. Peter's Church Road, until you see the sign for Dreher Island Road off of Route 231. Turn left on Route 571, State Park Road. This will take you into the park; about 12 miles from the I-26 exit.

Lexington County Museum

Grasping the Past

Many stories are told at the **Lexington County Museum**, an amazingly comprehensive collection of buildings that reflect the history of this area from colonial time through the Civil War. Various local residents' daily lives are interpreted through a narrated tour that takes visitors around the grounds and to a number of houses and dependencies. The Antebellum tour reveals everyday farm life in the pre-Civil War period, including a visit to the **John Fox House** and the loom room. Also available with advance reservations is a Colonial South Carolina tour and a Loom House tour each with their own emphasis.

The town of Lexington grew out of the Royal township of Saxe Gotha established in 1735. King George II wanted to encourage back country settlement to provide a buffer between the settled lowcountry plantations and the powerful Native American tribes that roamed the western frontier and whose trails crossed this region. The settlement's name honored the marriage of the Prince of Wales to Princess Augusta of the German state of Saxe Gotha.

The settlement was endangered by the Cherokee War of 1760 and the unrest that followed. In 1718, a fort had been built on the Lexington side of the Congaree River where the Occaneechi Path, which traveled south from the Virginia colony, met the Cherokee Path of South Carolina. For the most part, the Native Americans in this region were peaceable and settlers continued to farm the region growing corn, wheat, tobacco, hemp and flax. Several skirmishes were fought in the area during the American Revolution and at its conclusion in 1785, the area's name was changed to Lexington. The town, established in 1820 as the seat of county government, first consisted of a court house and a few houses. But by 1861, when the town was incorporated, it was a bustling community of tradespeople and professionals. The Civil War was hard on this area and the town was virtually destroyed by General Sherman's western flank.

The oldest documented house in the town of Lexington, the **Lawrence Corley Log House**, is part of the museum complex. Corley built his house in 1772 near Twelve Mile Creek and E. Main Street. Corley served in the Revolutionary War and married twice; his second wife outlived him by 30 years. The 1790 census, the first taken in the new country, indicated eight people lived in this house along with one African-American slave, indicating that the Corleys were a middle class frontier family. But theirs was a difficult existence and the rustic interior reveals the paucity of their possessions. The house has only two rooms: a main room downstairs and a sleeping loft. Authentic 18th-century furnishings, such as might have been used, are in evidence.

Built two years after the Corley house is the Swiss-style **Heinrich Senn House.** The early settlers built river houses with logs for the framework and boards that covered the exterior instead of mud chinking. Saxe Gotha had saw mills by the 1740s. The museum uses this house as a **Loom Room.** Before the early 1820s settlers generally used flax. After that time they used cotton—growing the crop, picking, carding, spinning and weaving it into clothes. Edwin J. Scott, writing of Lexington in the 1820s, said, "Everybody wore homespun except the clergy, the officers of Court and those of the militia, whilst acting in their official capacity." The loom room has antique looms, spinning wheels and quilting frames.

The four-room **Hazelius House** dates from before 1820 and speaks of a more affluent era. In 1834, the house was purchased by the Lutheran Synod of South Carolina, enlarged to eight rooms and used as a seminary. It is the second oldest seminary in the country (the oldest is in Gettysburg, Pennsylvania). The seminary headmaster was Dr. Ernest Hazelius, and it was in this office long after Hazelius's death that Charlie Tillman wrote the words of a revival song he had heard sung by African-Americans who attended his tent show. The song he wrote is the spiritual, *"Give Me That Old Time Religion."*

Also from the 1820s is the **Oak Grove Schoolhouse.** Discipline was so stringent that the students staged a rebellion and locked the teacher out until they were promised better treatment. This happened on more than one occasion and the teacher often retaliated by putting a board over the chimney and smoking the students out. Schools of this type were called field schools because they were placed in fields no longer used for crops. One room accommodated students from 7 to 14, although most girls dropped out by age 10 so they could help at home. Lexington had 12 schools in 1813, with a student population of approximately 200; this from a community population of 5,000 free whites. African-Americans were not taught in schools.

Dr. Simmon's medical office built in 1820 at 102 Gantt Street, is now located at the Lexington County Museum. The office was used as the Lexington post office from 1866 to 1880 and individuals would pay for their mail when they picked it up rather than putting stamps on the correspondence.

The Antebellum tour spends a great deal of its time exploring the John Fox House and its dependencies. The house was built around 1832 and inhabited by the family for more than 100 years. John Fox (1805-1884) was a prosperous farmer and industrious public official in Lexington County. Although Fox did not favor secession, once South Carolina left the Union he supported the war effort. According to family stories, "When Sherman came through Lexington County some of the Yankees hung John Fox three times to make him give up his money." He ultimately did reveal where he had buried his papers and currency.

At the John Fox House, fully furnished with locally-made pieces from the mid-1800s, you get a close-up glimpse of home life before the Civil War. The parlor was for entertaining guests, not family relaxing. Guests would play the piano, fiddle or banjo. Conversation was important as a means of learning the latest news. Refreshments would be hot drinks and food. The dining room had to accommodate the roughly 15 people who lived and worked on this site. There were also 15 African-American slaves who ate in the kitchen. A cupboard holds the colorful company china, tilted forward so that it would not gather dust. The pie safe was locked, although the doors to the house were almost never locked. One interesting observation is that the chairs around the table were lower than they are today so that the diners were less likely to spill their food because they were closer to their plates. This was important since, like most of their contemporaries, they only had three changes of clothes. There is also a downstairs front bedroom, one of eight in the house. The Foxes often hosted overnight guests and even rented rooms to students attending the Lutheran seminary across the street. The upstairs has family bedrooms. Two bedrooms are used to exhibit museum collections: one has Indian artifacts, the other Lexington County articles. The house also has the second largest collection of quilts in the state; these are displayed on a rotating basis in the bedrooms.

A covered breezeway links the house with the kitchen and cook's room. Food was prepared almost constantly to serve at the three daily meals. Meats were always cooked a long time to prevent spoilage. The main meal was at midday, leaving the afternoon for chores such as candle-making, churning and preserving.

The yard was a work area, not a landscaped showplace. Outside the Fox house, museum visitors see winter and summer dairy sheds, a smoke house, an oven used for heavy baking, a well and wash pot for cleaning clothes, beehives, a rabbit box, herb garden and a three-seater privy. In the courtyard, replacing the original dependencies, are historic structures from the area including slave quarters, a potato house, the loom room and a cotton gin house that houses a collection of farm tools.

The Lexington County Museum is open Tuesday through Saturday from 10:00 A.M. to 4:00 P.M. and on Sunday 1:00 to 4:00 P.M. The last tour begins at 3:00 P.M. If you want to schedule a tour other than the basic Antebellum tour, call ahead at (803) 359-8369.

Directions: From I-20 to Lexington take U.S. 1 into Lexington. From U.S. 1 turn right onto Columbia Avenue and the museum will be on your right behind the Lexington Paint Company and Ace Hardware.

Peachtree Rock Preserve

Natural Oddity

Columbia has an advantage many cities envy: within 20 miles of its downtown area are amazing natural retreats such as Congaree Swamp National Monument (see selection) and **Peachtree Rock Preserve**.

Peachtree Rock Preserve encompasses diverse ecosystems within its 306 acres. It was acquired by The Nature Conservancy in 1980. A mile-and-a-half trail lets you explore a terrain where the vegetation changes from mountainous to desert-like plant communities. The trail leads from a small dirt parking area downhill through typical sandhill shrubs, pines and turkey oaks. There are rough steps to help negotiate the short, but steep incline down to the bowl-shaped swampy area where you'll find the remarkable sandstone outcropping known as Peachtree Rock as well as other formations.

The rock for which the preserve is named seems to be balanced on a small inverted triangle. Upon this seemingly fragile base the massive outcropping rests like a giant bowl. The formations date back 40 or 50 million years to the Eocene Epoch when oceans covered this region. Within the rock are marine fossils, particularly the tube-like burrows of a marine animal called Calianassa major.

Near another sandstone outcropping is a waterfall where clear, cool waters provide a welcome respite on a warm summer's day. The waterfall is created by a perched water table, meaning that the water falls from a layer of impervious rock that is higher than the surrounding area. Lichens cover the rocks. In pockets of soil on the rocks near the waterfall, you can spot four species of fern: the wooly lipfern, the blunt-lobed woodsia, resurrection fern and ebony spleenwort. Near the stream are cinnamon fern, royal fern and netted chain fern.

You will not be surprised to learn that in earlier days this remote location was the site of numerous illegal whiskey stills. The area was popular because of the availability of fresh spring water and the thick, evergreen shrubs that camouflaged the operations. Moonshine activity occurred in this area as late as 1965. The remains of two stills can be seen along the trail.

The trail continues for another ¾ mile past the Peachtree Rock area to the second sandstone outcroppings. It is a fairly arduous uphill hike joining an old road along the ridge. Collecting turpentine from longleaf pines was at one time an economic boon to this area. Early practices involved cutting a cup-size cavity at the base of the tree to trap the tar, making the tree vulnerable to disease and creating a build-up of combustibles leading to a high incidence of forest fires. Tin cups were used after 1901 and did far less damage to the pines.

Those who trek to the second group of rocks will have a splendid view across the valley. Here, too, you will see one large rock standing tall and separate, although this time it does not perch as precariously as its more accessible outcropping. Mountain laurel cover the slopes of these rocks.

Continuing along the path brings you to another plant ecosystem, a desert-like area where the oaks are dwarfed and twisted and the vegetation sparse. There are even small rosemary bushes, the farthest north it is known to grow. Leaving this stark area, you'll return to the pines and oaks and back to the creek that flows from the waterfall. The trail does not parallel the creek but you will see intermittent glimpses before you spot the familiar contours of Peachtree Rock.

A second short half-mile trail leads down from the rock to an unusual outgrowth of galax. This plant, with its shiny round leaves, is customarily found in cool mountain habitats and this is the only known occurrence in the sandhills area. Continuing on the path you will come to a patch of woody goldenrod, which flowers in late October. This is found in few other areas of the state.

The reserve is popular with bird watchers. Brown-headed nuthatches can be seen year round and the low areas are home to tufted titmice, chickadees, rufous-sided towhees, cardinals and brown thrashers. Summer species included red-eyed vireos, white-eyed vireos, crested flycatchers, summer tanagers and wood thrush. Winter brings dark-eyed juncos, white-throated sparrows, yellow-bellied sapsuckers and ruby-crowned kinglets.

Directions: From I-26 take the Airport exit, Route 302 west. Continue past the airport and past South Congaree and the Edmund community. Turn left on Route 6, where it veers off from Route 302. Once on Route 6, watch for the second paved road; the sign will indicate this is the turn for the Bethel United Methodist Church (the first paved road has a sign for the Bethel Independent Church). Once on the paved road, turn right at the stop sign on to a dirt road; there is a parking lot on the left and a small sign for Peachtree Rock Preserve. For additional information on the preserve call The Nature Conservancy, South Carolina Chapter at (803) 254-9049.

Riverbanks Zoological Park and Botanical Garden

Diverse Delights

"Never a day passes but that I do myself the honor to commune with some of nature's varied forms," said noted African-American agricultural experimenter George Washington Carver (1864–1943). Following his advice is easy at **Riverbanks Zoological Park and Botanical Garden**, a 170-acre park sprawling on both sides of the Lower Saluda River. You'll see more than 2,000 animals in natural habitat exhibits and a wide array of botanical specimens in a walled garden that is slightly larger than a football field.

Riverbanks houses approximately 200 mammals, 300 birds, 300 reptiles and 1,300 fish and invertebrates. Boulders, ledges, pools and flowing water provide barriers separating animals from visitors, giving the zoo a natural look and allowing the animals to move about freely and recreate their wild behavior. You'll feel like you're on safari, visiting the plains of Africa or exploring the wilds of South America. Riverbanks has achieved international recognizition for its breeding programs for endangered species.

Since Riverbanks opened in 1974, it has become the largest public attraction in the state with more than 13 million visitors. It is one of the 20 most visited zoos in the country. Shortly after opening in 1990, the Aquarium Reptile Complex (called ARC and pronounced "ark") was named one of the top three new zoo exhibits by the American Zoo and Aquarium Association. The Southeast Tourism Association has voted Riverbanks, "Travel Attraction of the Year" twice and the zoological park has received the Governor's Cup Award from the South Carolina Chamber of Commerce, as the state's most outstanding attraction.

The award-winning Aquarium Reptile Complex has four galleries: South Carolina, the desert, the tropics and the ocean. Large naturalistic dioramas are just part of the creative educational graphics that enhance the ARC's popularity. The South Carolina gallery follows the state's waterways from the Blue Ridge mountains to the coastal wetlands. Moving across the country, the desert gallery reveals the desert's varied reptile life. This exhibit also represents the savannah and grasslands. The air is moist and warm in the lushly vegetated tropical habitat. Here visitors find Amazon pools with piranha and electric eels, a stream with huge anacondas and false gharial crocodiles believed to be extinct in the wild. Finally, more than 15 aquariums reveal the ocean world. A 55,000-gallon Indo-Pacific coral reef tank has an observation area where visitors can watch twice-

Black-footed penguins are among the crowd pleasers at Riverbanks Zoological Park, one of South Carolina's largest and most popular attractions that is ranked as one of the top ten zoos in the country.

daily feeding. At 11:00 A.M. and 2:00 P.M. divers feed hundreds of fish, including sharks and moray eels. Elsewhere in the zoo there are daily sea lion feedings.

Another popular daily occurrence is the tropical rainstorm in the birdhouse at 11:00 A.M., 1:00 and 3:00 P.M. on weekdays and 11:00 A.M. and hourly from 1:00 to 4:00 P.M. on weekends. Also in the birdhouse, the penguins are fed at 11:30 A.M. and 3:30 P.M. At Riverbanks Farm, goats, sheep and pot-bellied pigs mingle with visitors. There is a milking demonstration at 10:00 A.M.

With the opening of the Botanical Garden, Riverbanks virtually doubled its size. Visitors stroll on a bridge over the Lower Saluda River to the west bank. There is a ½-mile river and woodland trail that affords scenic views. It leads past a spot where Sherman is reputed to have slept. Legend has it that Sherman spent the night sleeping in a cave-like area beneath a giant boulder before crossing the river and burning much of Columbia. Some disgruntled citizens are still heard to mutter: "Of course he slept under a rock, where else do snakes sleep?" The trail also leads to the ruins of one of South Carolina's first water-powered textile mills. The trail can be picked up after you cross the bridge or from the walled garden. Those choosing the latter option should be aware the trail down to the river's edge is very steep. Access to the visitors center and walled garden is also available by a free tram that runs continuously.

The walled garden is the horticultural jewel of the complex. An eight-foot brick wall, that suggests an English walled garden, encloses a delightful floral hideaway with plants from all over the world. Running through the center of the garden is a 300-foot-long canal featuring cascades and pinwheel fountains, while brick paths lead to speciality areas such as the berry garden, the art garden and the midnight garden. There are borders with seasonal plants and others planted with color themes. An arched passageway leads to an amphitheater. Adjacent to the walled area is a cottage-style rose garden. Other gardens in the planning stage are an island bed garden, shade garden, home landscape idea garden and children's garden.

Riverbanks Zoological Park and Botanical Garden is open daily except Thanksgiving and Christmas Day. Hours are 9:00 A.M. to 4:00 P.M. on weekdays and until 5:00 P.M. on weekends. Admission is charged. There are several dining options and three gift shops. A picnic grove along the river is accessible from the parking lot; this area is just outside the zoo since no food or drinks may be carried into the zoo. Annual events at the zoo include "Springtime at the Farm" in late March, "Taste of Columbia" in April, "Conservation Day" in late May and "Lights Before Christmas" throughout most of December. For information about Riverbanks call (803) 779-8917.

Directions: From I-126 in Columbia take Greystone Boulevard to the zoo turnoff. Riverbanks is at 500 Wildlife Parkway.

Riverfront Park & Historic Columbia Canal, Finlay Park, Memorial Park and Tunnelvision

Afternoon Delights

You'll feel like you are on the brink of civilization at **Riverfront Park**, on the city's edge where the Broad and Saluda rivers meet to form the Congaree. Wildlife is abundant. In the tall grass along the river, you're apt to see herons, since they're native to South Carolina's wetlands. There are yellow-bellied turtles sunning themselves on exposed tree limbs and you may glimpse paw prints from nocturnal raccoons. The park's levee road has several shaded river overlooks where you can picnic or just sit and observe nature. Signs describe the flora and fauna you're apt to see. There is a walking, jogging and bicycling path along the levee road.

The rivers were South Carolina's earliest transportation. Settlers followed the rivers and then sent their commerce and trade along these water routes. The only impediment to this method was the rock-strewn shoals where the Saluda and Broad rivers met, so in 1824 the state built the **Columbia Canal**. Barges loaded with cotton traveled this one-mile channel and several mills were built along the canal before the railroad supplanted the river as the primary trade route.

During the Civil War, a powder mill was built along the river, using the water as the source of power. Sherman burned this mill when he marched through Columbia. In the 1890s, the canal, which had fallen into disrepair, was rebuilt and sold to the Columbia Water Company. Water-generated electric power soon powered the lights of the city. The world's first electrically-operated textile mill was powered by water from the canal (see South Carolina State Museum selection, the museum is located in the former textile mill). In 1906, Columbia's public waterworks, one of the first of its kind in the country, was moved from Assembly Street to the banks of the Columbia Canal, where the **Waterworks** can be seen today. The facility initially filtered up to seven million gallons of water daily. Now it exceeds 70 million gallons of water a day. Signs tell the story of the Waterworks. Once you cross the pedestrian bridge from the parking lot into the park you will see the **Pump House**, the heart of the old waterworks system. You can see the interior of the old pump house, now supplanted by a more modern facility. At the south end of this old facility, a set of sliding doors leads to a wide balcony with a view of the cascading spill gates and a dramatic expanse of river.

Riverfront Park and Historic Columbia Canal is open at no charge daily from 10:00 A.M. to 6:00 P.M. from March through Thanksgiving. Near the Pump House is a statue of Christopher Columbus. Columbia was the first North American city named in his honor. Just off the parking lot you will also see the Little Red Schoolhouse, a facility that dates to 1867 and was in use until 1913.

Riverfront is on the edge of Columbia, while **Finlay Park** is in the heart of the city at the base of Arsenal Hill where the Governor's Mansion sits (see selection). The 17.5 acre park sprawls around its centerpiece, a 1.5-acre lake called the Little Congaree. Water flows into this lake from a stunning cantilevered waterfall that features two cascades. It is one of the most photographed sights in Columbia. Special lighting after dusk illuminates the waterfall. The park has over 40 varieties of flowers, but one of the most striking effects is created on the northern slope beside the falls. The hillside is covered by yellow jessamine, South Carolina's state flower. Along the path, overlooking the waterfall and the lake, are contoured swings where you can relax and enjoy the view. For younger visitors who enjoy more action, there is a children's play area. Residents and visitors alike flock to the park, a popular lunch spot for picnickers. The **Watermark Cafe** serves lunch.

A wide array of festivals are held at the park where an amphitheater provides a scenic setting for summer concerts on Saturday evenings, children's activities and multi-cultural entertainment. Finlay Park (originally Sidney Park but renamed for popular Columbia mayor, the late Kirkman Finlay) is open daily at no charge.

Just two blocks away is **Memorial Park**, which has the largest monument of its type outside of Washington, D.C., honoring the 980 South Carolinians who died in Vietnam. It is a replica of the capital's tribute.

While not a park there is one additional scenic spot in the capital that should not be missed—**Tunnelvision**. This striking mural painted by South Carolina artist Blue Sky creates a clever optical illusion. There seems to be a tunnel running through the wall of the Federal Land Bank Building at Taylor and Marion streets. You will probably want to go around the block several times to fully appreciate the effect of this giant mural.

Directions: From I-126 head into Columbia and bear right on Huger Street. At Laurel Street turn toward the river; the park entrance is behind the Southern Bell office on Huger Street.

Finlay Park is at the corner of Laurel and Assembly streets. For Memorial Park, turn on Hampton Street and go two blocks to Gadsden Street. For Tunnelvision, from Laurel Street turn right on Marion and proceed two blocks to Taylor Street.

Robert Mills Historic House and Park and Mann-Simons Cottage

First Federal Architect

South Carolinian Robert Mills designed numerous courthouses and public buildings throughout the state (although he constantly went over budget). He also designed the Washington Monument, the Treasury Building Arcade and the Old Patent Office (now the National Portrait Gallery) in Washington, D.C. Though he did private residences, this is the only documented one still standing. That is why the **Robert Mills Historic House** is on the National Register of Historic Places and is recognized by the United States Park Service as a National Monument.

Mills incorporated many innovative designs in the stylish Neo-classical two-story brick house he built in 1823 for Ainsley Hall, a prominent Columbia merchant. Before the house was finished Hall died (he is buried in the First Presbyterian Church yard) and it was auctioned off in 1827. (See Hampton-Preston Mansion selection.) The property was purchased by the Presbyterian Theological Seminary (where Reverend Joseph Wilson taught; see Boyhood Home of Woodrow Wilson selection) and was later the home of Columbia Bible College.

The house was one of the lucky Columbia structures that survived the ravages of the Civil War. But in the 1960s the house was slated for demolition. The Ainsley Hall Foundation (which soon changed its name to Historic Columbia Foundation) was formed and saved the house. In 1967, the house opened as a decorative arts museum, showcasing the arts of the first third of the 19th century. The house reflects the period, not a particular Columbia family. A formal garden of the period has been planted as a setting for this historic house. Several of the flanking dependencies, such as the carriage house, were in Mills' plans but were not built. They have been reproduced using Mills' drawings.

When you tour the Robert Mills House you can't help but be impressed by the seven-bay, arcaded porch that extends across the back of the house. The front is quite formal with an Ionic portico raised on a brick arcade. The windows also differ in the front and the back. The front windows are in recessed brick arches, while the rear has three-part Venetian windows that are trimmed with pilasters on the first floor. When you step inside, the entranceway is laid out in a unique manner with no visible staircase and a circular hallway with six doors leading to various downstairs rooms. One door is a false door, added to achieve symmetry. The rooms are furnished with period pieces. The two formal parlors can be joined by sliding open the dividing panel; they both have numerous windows creating a light, airy effect. The Marquis de Lafayette visited the Mills house in 1825.

The Robert Mills Historic House and Park is open for guided tours Tuesday through Saturday from 10:00 A.M. to 4:00 P.M. and Sunday 1:00 to 5:00 P.M. The house is closed on major holidays. Admission is charged and there is a gift shop in the ticket office in the flanker next to the house. This serves the Woodrow Wilson House, Hampton-Preston Mansion and Mann-Simons Cottage as well as the Mills House . The carriage house and grounds can be reserved for private functions; call for additional information and rental fees, (803) 252-1770.

Far more modest than the Mills house, but no less historic is the white-frame **Mann-Simons Cottage**, built in 1799 for Celia Mann. Celia Mann was a slave in Charleston until she gained her freedom. According to family tradition, she walked to Columbia where she earned her living as a mid-wife. When Celia died in 1867, after bearing four daughters, her industry enabled her to have an estate of $1,500.

The house was left to her daughter, Agnes Jackson Simons, born in 1831. Agnes was a baker and laundress; she married twice and was twice widowed. Her second husband, Bill Simons, was a prominent local musician. Agnes's descendants lived in the house until 1970 when it was sold to the city and eventually became part of the Historic Columbia Foundation. There are only a few family pieces in the house; the basement has exhibits that trace the building of the cottage and the family history. The First and Second Calvary Baptist Church was founded in this cottage basement, as was Zion Baptist Church. After the Civil War, African-Americans began worshiping together here. The furnishings represent the time when Celia Mann lived here and there is a photograph of Agnes on the wall in the parlor.

The Mann-Simons Cottage: Museum of African-American Culture is open Tuesday through Saturday from 10:15 A.M. to 3:15 P.M. and Sunday 1:15 to 4:15 P.M. It is closed on major holidays. Admission is charged.

Directions: From I-26/126 head into Columbia and turn right on Bull Street, then make a left on Blanding Street. The Robert Mills Historic House and Park is at 1616 Blanding Street. The Mann-Simons Cottage is two blocks away at 1403 Richland Street.

South Carolina Criminal Justice Hall of Fame

Hands Up!

The **South Carolina Criminal Justice Hall of Fame** is *the* spot for those fascinated by law enforcement. It's also a great spot to teach children about police officers' responsibilities. At the entrance is a memorial to South Carolina police officers killed in the line of duty.

Exhibits include an extensive array of firearms, uniforms and photographs of the jails and courthouses throughout the state. There are examples of law enforcement equipment such as radios, radar, hand-cuffs and a breathalyzer. A uniformed mannequin stands beside a 1955 highway patrol car. There is a wall covered with license plates from years past, plus patches from all the counties and cities in South Carolina.

An intriguing exhibit places photographs of suspects beside the drawings done by police artists. It is interesting to see how close the drawings are to the individuals being sought. Young visitors enjoy this display and the games and toys associated with law enforcement from Dick Tracy and Dragnet to G-Men games.

Not all the attention is given to the good guys. There's a moonshine still, illegal gaming wheel and an array of clippings on the capture of "Pretty Boy" Floyd and the shooting of John Dillinger. Melvin Horace Purvis, the FBI agent who headed the Chicago office and was called the "nemesis of public enemies," was born in Florence County, South Carolina. His exploits are vividly recalled through photographs and memorabilia. His fame was such that he was considered one of the most outstanding personalities of 1934 along with President Roosevelt and the Dionne Quintuplets. Several weapons that belonged to Purvis are on display, as is a ceremonial sword presented to him by Hermann Goering during the trials after World War II when Goering was indicted as a war criminal and sentenced to death. Goering took his own life before the sentence was carried out. The South Carolina Criminal Justice Hall of Fame is open at no charge Monday through Friday from 8:30 A.M. to 5:00 P.M.

Directions: From downtown Columbia take I-26 across the Congaree River, then head east on I-20 and exit on Broad River Road north. The South Carolina Criminal Justice Hall of Fame is on the right at 5400 Broad River Road beside the Criminal Justice Academy.

South Carolina State Museum

Nothing Could be Finer

After exploring the **South Carolina State Museum**, visitors are left with a sense of wonder that so many historic events happened in the state and so many influential figures were either born in South Carolina, or call the state home. State residents are filled with a sense of pride as they discover their roots. Four floors of museum exhibits cover South Carolina art, history, natural history, science and technology.

The museum's biggest artifact is the building in which it is housed, the 1894 Columbia Mill, the world's first totally electric textile mill. Bricks to build the mill were fired at Columbia's Guignard Brick Works, the country's oldest continuously operating brick works. The original three-foot brick walls and heartpine beam ceiling can still be seen.

On the first floor, the Lipscomb Art Gallery has changing exhibits featuring artists who were born in South Carolina, or who have worked in the state. A hands-on "please touch corner" features activities associated with the gallery's temporary exhibits. One perennial favorite is African-American artist Philip Simmons's wrought iron gate with its palmetto tree, egrets and intricate designs (see Philip Simmons's Garden selection).

Another popular favorite is the life-size replica of a giant white shark in the natural history gallery. Stavros Chrysostomedes, an American sculptor of Greek descent, built this 43-foot replica in a rented garage. It's made of aluminum and fiber glass, with a steel rod down the middle. On February 10, 1988, the South Carolina National Guard transported the shark to the museum on two flat-bed trucks. These now-extinct sharks lived 20 million years ago and weighed up to 28,000 pounds. A case beside the model gives visitors a chance to touch a 20-million-year-old tooth from a giant white. A reproduction of the shark's three layers of teeth hangs on the wall, while the 22½-inch-wide jaw with the real teeth of a modern-day great white shark is protected in a case. The teeth are serrated on the side like a steak knife.

As you look at a lighted map of the state, it is hard to believe what the next exhibit reveals—500 million years ago parts of South Carolina were volcanic islands. Fossils found in limestone quarries show life forms from the region's earliest years. Like archaeologists, you can read the rock and learn about life during the Upper Cretaceous period. There are models of some of the species that roamed this region during the Ice Age: mastodons, giant beavers, Harlan's ground sloths and glyptodonts, which were related to the armadillo. Included in this exhibit area are

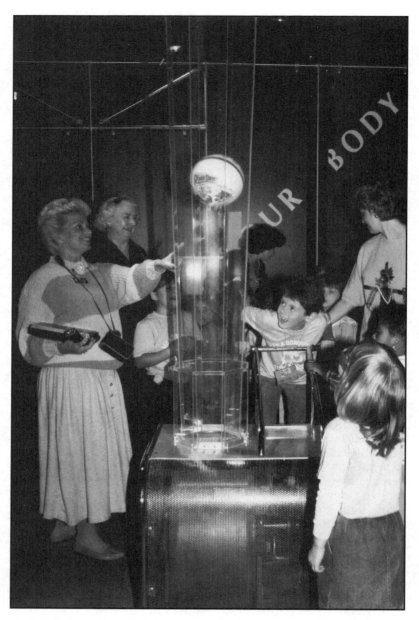

A ball flies high as this young man makes wind with bicycle pedals in one of the many hands-on exhibits at the South Carolina State Museum.

natural habitats from around the state: the Piedmont, sandhills, riverbottom forest, saltmarsh and back yards. Young visitors are fascinated by these habitats because hidden in the background of each mural painted by Kent Pendleton, which serve as backdrops for the three-dimensional displays, is a leprechaun.

The museum's third floor is devoted to science and technology. One of the most popular exhibits is a life-size reproduction of the *Best Friend of Charleston*, the first American-made locomotive. It was cast in New York and assembled in Charleston and made its inaugural run in 1830. Before the advent of this locomotive, backcountry farmers had floated their goods down the Savannah River to Savannah, but the loss of business to the Georgia city, prompted Charleston businessmen to support the 135-mile railroad line from Hamburg, located on the Savannah River, to Charleston. At the time it was finished, it was the world's longest railroad line. Six months after the *Best Friend* began running, a new engineer shut the steam exhaust valve and resulting pressure blew up the train. Local lore even claims the engineer sat on the valve, causing the explosion. Some parts of the train were salvaged, and a new locomotive called *The Phoenix* was subsequently built.

Nearby a model train runs through a Lowcountry background that suggests the 1880s. There are farms, a meandering river and busy railroad yard. A second model runs through terrain that suggests the Upcountry, circa 1920s. This model includes a small airport, a bustling town and a far more elaborate rail yard.

This exhibit area also includes a room that reminds visitors of its former use as a textile mill. A small mirrored spinning room creates the illusion of row after row of equipment from 1915. When the mill was built in 1893, General Electric was just a fledgling company. Up to this time the company had only made a 10 horsepower engine, but it committed to making an engine 6½ times bigger for this factory. Some G.E. executives weren't even sure they could make an engine that powerful. You can see one of these prototype 65-horsepower engines in the exhibit. This textile mill was one of the first major industrial installations for General Electric. The bell that rang to announce the lunch break for mill workers was, as you can see, only slightly smaller than the Liberty Bell.

Within this area there are a wide variety of vehicles, including a 1913 Model T Ford that has only been driven 25 miles. Elijah Hall, a farmer in Lexington County, bought the car and drove it off the road on his first trip. He put it in his barn and it was never driven again. It stayed in the barn for decades, and only the tires needed to be replaced because they had rotted. Another unique vehicle is the 1938 John Deere tractor with steel wheels to grip the sandy South Carolina soil.

Another exhibit focuses on aviation. In 1942, Doolittle's Raiders began their training in Columbia before heading south to Florida. In 1944, Skunkie, a B-25 training plane, crashed in Lake Greenwood. Local lore claimed the pilots were buzzing the beach looking for sun bathing girls. In 1983, Skunkie was reclaimed from the lake and presented to the museum, but all that is exhibited is a propeller. A small airplane, built between 1927–1929 by six Clemson University students who each contributed $35, hangs from the museum's ceiling. Clemson is thought to be the first college to form a student aviation club. Reflecting their long-standing rivalry, University of South Carolina fans are apt to say that its present position is as high as it ever got.

The museum reveals that South Carolinians are responsible for an amazing array of inventions. Samuel Morse, who was a portrait painter in Charleston before turning to more technical matters, invented the telegraph. Charles H. Townes won a Nobel Prize (which is on display) for inventing laser technology. Joseph Goldstein, another native, also won a Nobel Prize for discovering how cholesterol enters human cells. In 1849, Henry Fitz produced the first observation telescope for Erskine College in Due West, S.C. Until recently, South Carolina produced more astronauts than any other state. General Charles Duke of Lancaster walked on the moon as part of the Apollo 16 mission. The space suit he wore is on display, as is a piece of moon rock. South Carolinian Ronald McNair was killed in the Challenger disaster in 1986.

The fourth floor has historical exhibits including a fully-stocked country store and an original one-room schoolhouse. An intriguing display delves into funeral practices with a cooling board, coffin and mortuary art. There is also a slave cabin and a taped rendition of a story read in the Gullah dialect used by African-Americans on South Carolina's Sea Islands (see Gullah 'n' Geechie Mahn Tours selection).

A life-size model of the *CSS Hunley*, the first submarine to destroy an enemy ship at sea can be seen on the fourth floor. In 1864, it sank the *USS Housatonic* before also sinking in Charleston harbor. Popular novelist Clive Cussler has provided the coordinates for its current position in the Charleston Harbor. You'll learn that the palmetto became the state symbol after the British attacked Fort Moultrie (then called Fort Sullivan) on Sullivan's Island off Charleston. Built of palmetto logs, the fort simply absorbed the cannon shot into its soft and spongy wood and the American forces withstood the attack.

The South Carolina State Museum is open Monday through Saturday from 10:00 A.M. to 5:00 P.M. On Sunday it opens at 1:00 P.M. It is closed on Thanksgiving, Christmas and Easter.

Admission is charged. The Cotton Mill Exchange museum shop, one of the largest museum shops in the southeast, is open during the same hours.

Directions: From I-26, take the I-126 spur into Columbia. Exit onto Huger Street and continue several blocks until you reach Gervais Street. Turn right on Gervais and the museum is one block on your right beside the historic Gervais Street bridge.

Trinity Cathedral and Churches of Columbia

Centered in South Carolina

After the American Revolution, the Episcopal Church, the successor to the Anglican Church, was in dire straits. Many of the church's clergymen were British supporters who fled at the end of the war. Churches were burned and the Anglican Church itself was disestablished. There were virtually no congregations outside of the Lowcountry area, so members from that region formed the Episcopal Society for the Advancement of Christianity in South Carolina. **Trinity Cathedral**, founded in 1812, was the first church constructed with the help of this group.

A small wooden cruciform church was built on the corner of Gervais and Sumter streets. Its dedication in 1814 was the church's high point. From that year on its membership steadily declined until the church could no longer support a resident rector. This was the situation when Peter Shand, a lay reader from Charleston, arrived in 1833 and began a 52-year rectorate at Trinity. His arrival signaled a new era for the church.

By 1845, the then sizeable congregation enlisted Edward Brickell White to design a new church. The church you see today (minus the transepts, apse and Seibels Chapel) was his design. White modeled Trinity after England's York Cathedral. Disregarding the turmoil of the Civil War, the transepts were added and the chancel extended in 1861-62. Trinity even managed to escape the fiery fate of one-third of the city on February 17, 1865 when General Sherman's troops burned Columbia, although the rectory and parish house were destroyed. The Seibels Chapel was dedicated in 1958 as a memorial to the Seibel family. In 1977, Trinity became the Cathedral Church of the Diocese of Upper South Carolina.

The "jewels of Trinity" are its stained glass memorial windows; those on the altar sanctuary were given to the church by the congregation in remembrance of Dr. Shand. As you enter the church you can pick up a small pamphlet that explains the

Biblical reference, or themes, of the stained glass windows.

Other features of note include the original closed rental pews, the carrara marble altar and marble tablets in the sanctuary and the baptismal font designed by sculptor Hiram Powers. Be sure to gaze up at the carved wooden ceiling. The embroidered linens and needlepoint cushions were done by parishioners or given in their memory. The altar silver was also given in memory of parishioners. It was stolen from Dr. Peter Shand in 1865 by Union soldiers. In the 1890s, the rector asked his parishioners to contribute any silver they had managed to save. The donated pieces were melted down and remade into two of the chalices used to this day in the Sunday services at Trinity.

No visit to Trinity Cathedral is complete without spending time in the churchyard. Beneath the ancient oaks and sprawling magnolias are the graves of illustrious South Carolinians. A map of the cemetery in the vestibule of the church helps pinpoint the resting place of these famous figures. Three Wade Hamptons are buried here: General Wade Hampton I (1751-1835), hero of the American Revolution and the War of 1812; Colonel Wade Hampton (1791-1858), wealthy planter and great horse enthusiast and Lieutenant General Wade Hampton (1818-1902), who served in the Confederate army, then as governor and United States senator from South Carolina. In all six governors are buried here. In addition to Hampton, they are: Richard Irvine Manning, his son John Lawrence Manning (who later became a U.S. senator), Richard Irvine Manning III, Hugh Smith Thompson and James Francis Byrnes. The latter also served as U.S. congressman and senator, associate justice of the Supreme Court, secretary of state as well as other government posts.

Also buried in the churchyard are seven bishops of the Episcopal Church and Dr. Peter Shand. There are monuments for soldiers of the American Revolution as well as later struggles including the Civil War. One unusual marker departs from the norm; it reads "Scared to the memory of Henry G. Green," instead of the more traditional "sacred." Some markers tell a story. Popular during the Civil War was a broken column crowned with a laurel wreath, indicating the death of a young man but signaling the victory of life after death. An example of this marks the grave of General States Right Gist who died in battle at age 33. The only walk-in vault in the cemetery belonged to the Parr family. When the last family member was buried in 1847, the will requested that the key to the vault be thrown away. Many individuals and groups come to do rubbings of the interesting memorials in Trinity's Churchyard.

While Trinity escaped the fire of 1865, two of Columbia's churches did not. The Washington Street United Methodist Church, 1401 Washington Street, was burned by Sherman's men. The current church, built in 1872, is the fourth church on this site. The Ebenezer Lutheran Church, 1301 Richland Street, was also destroyed in the fire, and a new sanctuary built on the same spot in 1870. Had Sherman realized that the First Baptist Church, 1306 Hampton Street, was the site of the first Secession Convention in December 1860, he would have certainly burned it as well. It, along with Trinity, is listed on the National Register of Historic Places. The Catholic church, St. Peter's, 1529 Assembly Street, was built in 1906 to replace the 1824 edifice that was lost to fire in 1865 when this entire end of town was destroyed by a fire that got out of control.

The first Presbyterian congregation in Columbia was organized in 1795. In 1853 the First Presbyterian Church, 1324 Marion Street, was erected. It was enlarged in 1925. For a time, the church's 188-foot steeple made it the city's tallest structure. In 1838, the First Presbyterian Church established a Sunday school for African-Americans. In 1896 the Ladson Presbyterian Church, 1720 Sumter Street, was built for its African-American congregation.

Directions: From I-26 feed onto I-126 into Columbia and exit on Huger Street. Make a left on Gervais Street and continue past the State House to Sumter Street. Make a right on Sumter and you will see Trinity Cathedral.

Woodrow Wilson Boyhood Home

Teenage Tommy Wilson

Thomas Woodrow Wilson was born in Staunton, Virginia's Presbyterian manse on December 28, 1856. A year later Reverend Joseph Wilson was offered a larger and more prosperous church in Augusta, Georgia. The Wilsons remained in Georgia from late 1857 until 1870. Years later in a speech Wilson said, "My earliest recollection is of standing at my father's gateway in Augusta, Georgia, when I was four years old, and hearing someone pass and say that Mr. Lincoln was elected and there was to be war. Catching the intense tones of his excited voice, I remember running in to ask my father what it meant."

Tommy Wilson spent the Civil War years in Augusta, but he spent the reconstruction years in Columbia where his family moved when he was 13. He had two older sisters, 18-year-old Marion and 15-year-old Anne Josephine, as well as a 3-year-old brother Joseph Ruggles, Jr. Reverend Wilson accepted an influential position on the faculty of the Columbia Theological Seminary and agreed to serve as interim minister of the First Presbyterian Church. But after only four years, the Reverend became involved in a controversy. He wanted to have separate chapel services for the seminary students and this was an unpopular position. Consequently, Wilson left to take another position in Wilmington, North Carolina.

In that same year, 1874, Woodrow Wilson left home to attend Davidson College in North Carolina. After a year, he transferred to Princeton, where his father studied, and where he would eventually teach and ultimately serve as university president.

The Woodrow Wilson Boyhood Home is the only house the Wilsons ever owned. With his church and seminary salary, Reverend Wilson decided he could afford to build a house. Adding to the family finances, Mrs. Wilson received a bequest from the estate of her younger brother. Mrs. Wilson supervised the construction of the cottage-style Tuscan villa, designed at a cost of $8,500 after the popular Downing style. Typical of this design are arches in the front door, hall, windows, porch rails and lattice work as well as bay windows. Surrounding the house were gardens that Mrs. Wilson laid out on their block-long lot. The care, attention and finances that went into this home indicate that the Wilsons expected to remain in Columbia.

As you tour the house, you will only see a few Wilson family pieces, although several of these have great significance. The period pieces illustrate the life style of a middle-class Presbyterian family during the 1870s. The antique gaslight fixtures in the parlor are original to the house. Columbia's gas works were destroyed during the Civil War, and rebuilt in 1871. This was one of the first houses piped for gas. The company turned on the gas two hours each evening. After nine o'clock kerosene and other light sources had to be used.

In the parlor corner are graduated boxes of Delftware with blue and white scenes of ships and windmills. While an adolescent in Columbia, Tommy Wilson became fascinated with ships, nautical adventures and ship construction. He could identify the rigging of different ships, the different class of ships and the location of every spar, sheet and shroud on them. He read Marryat's tales of the sea. He had been late to learn to read, perhaps suffering from a form of dyslexia. But in Columbia, studying with Professor Charles Barnwell, he learned Latin, Greek and other subjects. His religious training was under the guidance of seminary student Francis Brooke, and it awakened his spiritual nature. It was in Columbia that Tommy Wilson applied for membership in the First Presbyterian Church. Bible reading and personal prayers remained important to him for the rest of his life.

Mrs. Jessie Wilson was a well-educated, well-read woman who was very close to her son. The letters she sent him at Davidson College indicate her concern for his health and well-being. In the dining room you will see a mahogany sideboard that belonged to Mrs. Wilson's family. Notice the furry paw feet on the front legs and the columns carved with pineapples, the symbol of hospitality. The bay window offered an expansive view of the garden with its vegetables, fruit and flowers.

Upstairs in the bedrooms is the bed in which Woodrow Wilson was born. Wilson's niece sold the bed and bureau to the house (to the great envy of the Birthplace Home in Staunton which would dearly have loved to display the bed in the room where he was born). In later years when speaking of his boyhood room in Columbia, President Wilson said, "Why I could walk it blindfold."

The Woodrow Wilson Boyhood Home is open Tuesday through Saturday 10:15 A.M. to 3:15 P.M. and Sunday 1:15 to 4:15 P.M. It is closed on major holidays. Admission is charged.

Directions: From I-26/126 head into Columbia and turn right on Bull Street. Then make a left on Blanding Street. Tickets for the Woodrow Wilson House are sold at the gift shop on the grounds of the Robert Mills House, one of four properties under the umbrella of the Historic Columbia Foundation.

Capital City and Lake Murray Country Regional Tourism Contacts (Area Code 803)

LAKE MURRAY TOURISM & RECREATION ASSOCIATION/LAKE
MURRAY COUNTRY VISITORS CENTER
2184 N. Lake Drive (SC Route 6), P.O. Box 1783
Irmo, SC 29063
781-5940, (800) 951-4008, fax: 781-6197

BATESBURG-LEESVILLE CHAMBER OF COMMERCE
P.O. Box 349
Batesburg, SC 29006
532-4339

CHAPIN CHAMBER OF COMMERCE
P.O. Box 577, 200 Clark Street, Suite 200
Chapin, SC 29036
345-1100, fax: 345-0266

COLUMBIA METROPOLITAN CONVENTION & VISITORS BUREAU
1200 Main Street, 9th Floor, P.O. Box 15
Columbia, SC 29202
254-0479, (800) 264-4884, fax: 799-6529

COLUMBIA METROPOLITAN VISITORS CENTER
1012 Gervais Street
Columbia, SC 29201
254-0479, ext. 1, (800) 264-4884, ext. 1, fax: 929-3510

GREATER COLUMBIA CHAMBER OF COMMERCE
P.O. Box 1360
Columbia, SC 29202
733-1110

IRMO CHAMBER OF COMMERCE AND VISITORS CENTER
1246 Lake Murray Boulevard
Irmo, SC 29063
749-9355, fax: 732-7986

LEXINGTON CHAMBER OF COMMERCE
P.O. Box 44
Lexington, SC 29072
359-6113

NEWBERRY COUNTY CHAMBER OF COMMERCE
P.O. Box 396
Newberry, SC 29108
276-4274

SALUDA COUNTY CHAMBER OF COMMERCE
Law Range, Saluda, SC 29138
(864) 445-3055, fax: (864) 445-9495

WEST METRO CHAMBER OF COMMERCE
1006 12th Street
Cayce, SC 29033
794-6504, fax: 794-6505

Capital City & Lake Murray Country Calendar of Events (Area Code 803)

Mid-March

St. Patrick's Day Celebration at Five Points. A parade, entertainment, arts and crafts, regional cuisine and children's activities are part of the event. Columbia, 770-8203.

Late March

Palmetto Sportsmen's Classic. Wildlife and hunting exhibits plus demonstrations of archery, hunting and fishing. Columbia, 734-4008.

Springtime at the Farm. Special farm demonstrations at Riverbanks Zoo. Columbia, 779-8717.

L "Eggs"ington Easter Eggstravaganza. Hunt Easter eggs, enjoy egg races and other festive events. Lexington, 359-0964.

Kids Day Columbia. Games, art and crafts for children. Finlay Park, Columbia, 343-8750.

Mid-April

Riverfest/Riverrun. Live entertainment, crafts, children's activities, a bike race and 5K race enliven this event. Bank of the Congaree River, Columbia, 733-6210.

Taste of Columbia. City's finest restaurants offer their specialties at Riverbanks Zoo. Columbia, 779-8717.

National Timber Festival and Exposition. Wagon-led parade, logging demonstrations celebrate the timber industry. Saluda, 445-3055.

Early May

Mayfest. Hundreds of craftspeople and regional entertainers make this one of the state's largest arts and entertainment festivals. Columbia, 343-8750.

Mid-May

SC Poultry Festival. A parade, craft exhibits, entertainment, regional cuisine and a chicken-calling contest enliven this festival. Batesburg-Leesville, 532-9273.

Canoe-A-Thon. Paddle ten miles along the Saluda River. West Columbia, 771-7715.

Early July

Lake Murray's July 4th Celebration. Approximately 100 boats decked out in patriotic colors parade the lake and there is a firework display. Lake Murray, 781-5940.

Lexington County Peach Festival. A 4th of July festival featuring arts and crafts, entertainment and regional peach specialties. Gilbert, 892-2473.

Mid-September

Jubilee Festival of Heritage. African-American arts, crafts, food, storytelling and entertainment event. Mann-Simons Cottage, Columbia, 252-1770.

Early October

SC State Fair. Grandstand entertainment, midway games of chance, art exhibits, agricultural judging have made this a popular event for over 125 years. Columbia, 799-3387.

Mid-October

Civil War Reenactment. Siege of Lexington by General Sherman is recreated, exhibits of firearms and memorabilia plus a Civil War ball and a tea highlight event. Lexington, 356-6931.

Mid-November

Veteran's Day Parade. High school marching bands, military bands,

229

martial equipment and marching installations from around the state make this a colorful event. Columbia, 343-8750.

Early December

Lights Before Christmas. Riverbanks Zoo has hundreds of lighted holiday displays. Columbia, 779-8717.

Christmas Light Boat Parade. Lake Murray is brightly lit by decorated boats. Columbia, 781-5940.

Carolina Carillon. Holiday parade featuring top marching bands, floats and roving entertainers. Columbia, 779-1770.

Christmas Candlelight Tours. Historic homes are decorated and showcased for the holidays. Columbia, 252-3964.

Late December

First Night Columbia. Music, dance, art and fireworks mark the New Year. Columbia, 799-3115.

The following region, Thoroughbred Country, doesn't march to its own beat—it trots, paces and canters. Some streets remain unpaved to protect the horses and at McGhee's Mile Track visitors will spot this unique stop sign.

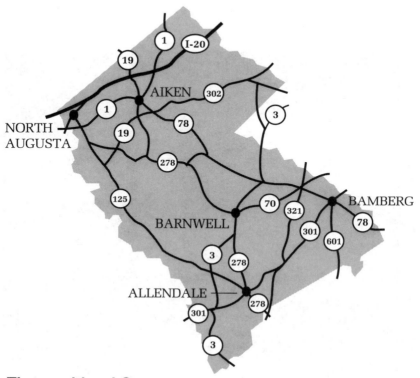

Thoroughbred Country

= Thoroughbred Country =

Thoroughbred Country doesn't march to its own beat; it trots, paces and canters. The region revolves around horses, from thoroughbred tracks in Aiken to work horse stables in the rural areas. In Aiken, many streets remain unpaved to protect horses's hooves. Traffic signals are controlled by buttons, not at pedestrian height, but at a spot convenient for riders. Horse and buggies have the right of way on the city's Main Street. Visitors will learn a new vocabulary in this region: like "breezing" while watching morning exercise sessions at the McGhee's Mile Track where Kentucky Derby contenders train and "chukker" while observing the action of international polo teams on the Whitney Polo Field. You can learn the Chitlin' Strut in Salley during the November festival or enjoy the country's largest urban forest at Hitchcock Woods.

Many towns in this region were settled along the Charleston-Hamburg Railway, the country's first commercial railway and, in its day, the world's longest commercial railway. You can trace this railroad heritage in Bamberg, Denmark, Blackville, North Augusta and Aiken. The South Carolina Heritage Corridor connects the region.

The one park in the state that commemorates the Civil War is Rivers Bridge State Park, where Sherman's troops met their only major resistance as they headed from Georgia to Columbia. The turmoil of the Civil War was also felt at Redcliffe Plantation.

Aiken County Historical Museum

"Rich" History

Aiken has an abundance of lavish "cottages" built by the Winter Colony, wealthy seasonal residents, but none are open to the public. You can't visit a house museum, but you can enjoy the grounds and exteriors of these magnificent estates. **Banksia**, within the heart of the historic Winter Colony District, is the one exception. This mansion can be explored, as it is now the **Aiken County Historical Museum**.

The first house on the Banksia block dates back to the early 1860s, but it wasn't until 1869 when William Hutson Townsend began acquiring the land that the entire block came under one owner. The land passed through the Harrington family and then to Richard Flint Howe who began, in 1931, a major remodeling effort, to the estate he called Banksia. The house, which incorporates the original frame portion, has an imposing front entrance with columns, window medallions and elaborate decorative touches including a bronze fox head as a door knocker. The sprawling white house harmoniously fits the contours of the hillside on which it is built and it is surrounded by one of Aiken's distinctive serpentine walls. The house passed from the Howe family in 1951 and was for a time a boarding house, then a college campus and finally a public library before being acquired as the Aiken County Historical Museum.

You may want to scatter bread crumbs as you wander through the labyrinth of Banksia—room follows room and you climb up

Banksia, the home of the Aiken County Historical Museum, is the only lavish "cottage" open to the public in the town's historic Winter Colony Historic District.

and down steps exploring every nook and cranny of the house. Off the entrance foyer are several furnished rooms. In the parlor there is a portrait of Nancy Potter Bourne McKim, a Winter Colony resident. This painting was used in the 1930s for the Ponds face cream magazine ads. The piano still has period sheet music, including Irving Berlin's *You Forgot to Remember* and *Dixie Lullaby*. There is a collection of china and silver. The study, or library, has several ship models including an 18th-century clipper ship and the *USS Constitution*. In the furnished bedroom there are wedding dresses from four generations of one family. There is also a children's bedroom filled with antique toys. The other rooms have exhibits covering such topics as natural history, agriculture, textiles, medicine, the military, regional history, transportation, African-Americans, archaeology and others. There is a complete line of goods from the former Moody's Drug Store in Dunbarton that reflects buying opportunities in 1950. Aiken County is the only part of South Carolina with kaolin deposits. Mining of this resource began in the 1850s and still continues, as you will learn from the in-depth exhibit on this fine white clay used as a filler in textiles, paper, rubber and porcelain production.

On the top floor there is a delightful miniature circus, the Polidor and Schreadley's miniature Ringling Brothers, Barnum & Bailey Circus with 1,000 Lilliputian people, 600 intricately crafted animals and 100 colorful wagons. Polidor, the International Clown, whose real name was Edward Guillaume, performed for over 30 years. He met Roy Schreadley in 1927 while playing Philadelphia. Schreadley began building circus miniatures and the following year gave his first miniature wagon to Polidor. The miniature so impressed the famous clown that he began sending pictures of the circus and eventually even measurements to Schreadley, who used them to create his miniature masterpieces.

There are two additional structures on the grounds of Banksia that are part of the Aiken County Historical Museum. The first is the **Ergle Log House**, circa 1808, which provides a glimpse of settlers' existence in the 19th century. The log house is furnished and there is a wide range of kitchen utensils and tools. From a slightly later period is the 1890 **China Springs School**, a one-room schoolhouse from the region. Inside are student's desks and supplies.

The museum is open at no charge Tuesday through Friday from 9:30 A.M. to 4:30 P.M; weekend hours are 2:00 to 5:00 P.M. The museum is closed on national holidays.

Directions: From I-20 take Route 19, Laurens Street, into Aiken. Turn left on South Boundary Avenue and then make a right on Newberry Street. The museum is at 433 Newberry Street, SW.

Aiken Historic District

Newport of the South

Local legend claims that Andrew Dexter, one of the two engineers working to lay out the South Carolina Canal and Railroad line, fell in love with Sarah Williams, whose father had a plantation in this part of South Carolina. Colonel Williams is said to have told Dexter that he couldn't marry Sarah unless he brought the railroad through this area. The height of the land and the clay soil were not ideal, but the town of **Aiken**, named for the president of the railroad William Aiken, was laid out around Williams' property in 1828 by Dexter and his fellow engineer C.O. Pascalis.

You'll hear more stories like this on the 90-minute guided tour of Aiken given on Saturday mornings at 10:00 A.M. The tour bus leaves from the front of the Aiken Municipal Building in the Alley. These tours provide an opportunity to hear the stories behind the serpentine gates, since none of the homes are open for tours, although **Banksia** has been converted to the Aiken County Historical Museum (see selection). Advance reservations for tours are highly recommended and there is a nominal charge; call (803) 641-1111 for more information.

The town that Andrew Dexter laid out in 1834 has wide boulevards arranged in a checkerboard pattern with streets running north and south and avenues named for South Carolina counties running east and west. In the center of the wide streets, parkways were planted with flowering trees and shrubs. Aiken, to this day, looks the way it did when Dexter drew his plans. To recognize the city's unique heritage, in 1995 a city-wide arboretum was established. As you drive around Aiken take note of the magnolias along Park Avenue and the canopy of live oaks along South Boundary. There is a **Colleton Avenue Trail Guide** which lists 48 trees of note along Colleton and several nearby streets. Of course, there is also Hitchcock Woods (see selection), which is the largest urban forest in the United States.

Almost from its inception, Aiken was recognized as a health resort and a part-time getaway. The first to avail themselves of its year round charm were the lowlanders. These seasonal residents came in the summer to escape the heat and malaria and other diseases prevalent on the coastal plantations and the surrounding marshland. Later the **Winter Colony** led to Aiken's Golden Era in the 1890s.

The Winter Colony were wealthy northerners who built walled estates and entertained each other, but kept aloof from the town. When they left, however, they gave land to the city for parks, churches and other public uses. The newcomers realized the

236

Aiken landscape was ideal for polo matches, drag hunts, steeple-chases and rides in the town's urban woods. Aiken became one of the most horse-friendly cities in America. Horses always have the right away, many of the roads are unpaved out of deference to the horses, the traffic signal boxes are at rider level and tracks and training farms abound. (See Thoroughbred Racing Hall of Fame selection.)

The winter visitors built lavish estates, which they called "cottages," on Hayne Avenue, Colleton Avenue, South Boundary and Whiskey Road and nearby streets—all well worth exploring. A map of Historic Aiken pinpoints 78 points of interest. All historic sites are marked by a brass numbered plaque. As you explore remember the homes are not open for tours and

Aiken is one of the most horse-friendly cities in America. Carriages were once common along the tree-lined streets, now visitors are likely to sightsee from the windows of a car or tour bus.

many residents prefer that visitors do not stop at their gates to snap photographs. One of the most photographed landmarks in Aiken is the street sign at the intersection of Whiskey Road and Easy Street.

Aiken is known for its architectural diversity. As you drive its tree-lined streets you will have a mini-course in architectural styles. The house at 424 Barnwell Avenue is an Adams-style Colonial. Note its symmetrical two-story facade and arched entranceway, including the double window with wood pediment and dentil mold at the cornice. Rose Hill, a Winter Colony cottage, has gambrel roofs and a gable-end facade and is an excellent example of shingle-style architecture. This is one estate where you can drive, or walk, onto the grounds as it now serves as a college. The grounds contain a delightful Victorian garden with beds laid out in little "rooms."

Three homes along Hayne Avenue, the oldest residential street for Aiken merchants, are of note. The house at 718 Hayne represents the Italian Renaissance style, not commonly found in the south. Notice the hipped tile roof with wide eaves and the large first floor windows with arched openings of cast stone. Nearby at 734 Hayne is a Colonial Revival residence with a symmetrical facade, large one-story porch and third floor dormers. Another shingle-style house, 611 Hayne, has a steep roof and turret.

Gregory White Smith and Steven Naifeh, Pulitzer Prize winning authors from New York, restored Joye Cottage, one of Aiken's most magnificent estates. They wrote a book about their project, *On a Street Called Easy, In a Cottage Called Joye*, which is subtitled "A Restoration Comedy." This gives a humorous account of transforming a 60-room "handyman special from hell" into the palatial estate it was when William C. Whitney bought a modest house from Miss Sarah Joye and enlarged it to a 50-room vacation "cottage." Whitney, a New York banker, served as Secretary of the Navy in Grover Cleveland's cabinet. Across the street is Joye Cottage Stable, where 30 horses were once stabled. It is now a separate private residence.

Also on Easy Street is the fabled Pink House, designed by Mrs. Thomas Hitchcock's son-in-law Julian Peabody, who trained at the Ecole des Beaux Arts. This estate extends a city block and has an elegant ballroom. Another Aiken home that fascinates visitors is at 494 Powder House Road. The highly decorative wood detailing mark this as a Folk Victorian residence.

A selection of these private homes are open during the spring for the St. Thaddeus Episcopal Church's House Tour. Aiken's oldest church at 125 Pendleton Street, S.W. is a Greek Revival structure built in 1842 and remodeled in 1926. Behind the sanctuary are the graves of botanist Henry Ravenel and the poet James Mathewes Legare. Soldiers of the Union and Confederate armies who died in the 1865 Battle of Aiken are interred in the cemetery. It was the summer residents from the Lowcountry who initiated the drive to build this church. The Winter Colony needed a school and in 1916 Mrs. Thomas Hitchcock founded the Aiken Preparatory School at 619 Barnwell Avenue, N.W. Originally a boy's preparatory school, it now is coed. Fred Astaire's son attended this school and there are legends about the Astaires's visits to Aiken. Another school established by the colony was the Fermata School for Girls, founded in 1919 by Marie Eustis Hofmann, the wife of world renown pianist Josef Hofmann. Fire destroyed the school's main buildings on Summerall Court in the 1940s.

In addition to education and religion, the Winter Colony residents added recreational options to Aiken (see Thoroughbred Racing Hall of Fame selection) including 16 polo fields, training and race tracks, hunting preserves and golf courses. One of the oldest golf courses in the country is **Palmetto Golf Club and Course** whose first four holes were laid out by Thomas Hitchcock in 1892. Three years later five more holes were added and William Whitney donated enough land to complete an 18-hole course which was designed by Alistair McKenzie, noted designer of America's earliest courses. The original greens were not grass but sand. This is a private course but you can drive in and see the rolling fairways and challenging greens. In 1898 the Winter Colony denizens also formed The Aiken Club, an exclusive men's club that built its own court tennis facility in 1902. Court tennis originated in France over 700 years ago and never achieved wide popularity in the United States. This facility at 146 Newberry Street, S.W. is one of only nine indoor courts currently in use in the country. Court tennis was the predecessor of lawn tennis, squash and raquetball. The sport developed in 13th-century French monastaries, although early versions were played in Egypt and Persia around 450 B.C. Henry VIII was quite fond of this game.

Not all the Winter Colony people had their own estates in Aiken and when the homes of their friends were filled the wealthy sought the hospitality of the **Willcox Inn.** The inn was established in 1900 by Frederick Willcox, who had worked as a caterer at the Highland Park Hotel before it burned to the ground in 1898. His Highland Park position had brought Willcox in contact with numerous Winter Colony residents and he became friends with many, including Mrs. Thomas Hitchcock. It was with their encouragement that he opened his inn. It was immediately popular and additions were made at regular intervals. The Willcox reputedly had the first bathtub in the south to have hidden plumbing. Local legend claims that in the Golden Age of the Winter Colony, the Willcox doorman would not admit gentlemen unless their shoes shined and were of the "proper" quality.

Distinguished guests included Franklin D. Roosevelt, Harold Vanderbilt, Governor Averell Harriman, Elizabeth Arden, Count Bernadotte of Sweden and the Duke of Windsor. The Aiken County Historical Museum (see selection) has guest registers from the Willcox dating from 1920 to 1940. The Willcox Inn was restored to its former luster in 1985 and has regained its reputation for outstanding cuisine. Be sure to dine in the Pheasant Room and wander through the public rooms even if you do not overnight at this lovely inn; call (800) 368-1047 for more information or for reservations.

Another restaurant with a history is **No. 10 Downing Street**, 241 Laurens Street, S.W. It's in the Legare-Morgan House, a one-story white clapboard cottage built in 1837. The house was owned by the family of noted South Carolina poet, artist and inventor James Mathewes Legare. In 1871, it was purchased by Thomas C. Morgan, a British naval officer. One of the house specialties is Scotch Eggs (these are hard-boiled eggs wrapped in sausage and deep fried). The restaurant is popular so reservations are recommended. Call (803) 642-9062 for reservations. It is closed on Sundays and Mondays. There is an abundance of good restaurants in Aiken. In The Alley you can walk back and forth checking the crowds and the menu at Up Your Alley (803-649-2603) and The Bowery (803-648-2900). There is also Olive Oils Italian Cuisine at 233 Chesterfield Street (803-649-3726) and Malia's Restaurant at 120 Laurens Street, S.W. (803-643-3086), a very popular spot with the lunch crowd.

Both The Alley and Laurens Street are great for browsing. They have a plethora of fascinating boutiques and antique shops. Be sure to stop in the **Aiken Center for the Arts**, 122 Laurens Street, where you'll find regional artist's work. The center's gift shop has hand-crafted items, art and jewelry. The center offers workshops and classes for all ages and levels.

Directions: From I-20 take Route 19 into Aiken. It will become Laurens Street.

Bamberg and Denmark

Small Town Charm

The tracks brought commerce and development to the villages along the route of the South Carolina Canal and Railroad Company. One village where the trains stopped, or turned out, was called Simmonds Turnout. In 1831, community leaders gave the railroad, for no compensation, 50-foot right of ways and the right to clear 100 feet on each side of the proposed railroad line.

The railroad could also cut timber without paying. For a time, the railroad's 137-mile track was the longest in the world, and the railroad ran the first commercial locomotive *The Best Friend of Charleston.* Now that railroad line is a National Historic Civil Engineering Landmark.

Simmonds Turnout changed its name to honor Major William Seaborn Bamberg, who moved to the community in the 1840s. The houses that community leaders built along Railroad Avenue and the adjacent streets reveal the town's history. Fifty-two of the town's buildings are on the National Register of Historic Places, and there is a roughly three-block **Bamberg Historic District**. A walking tour brochure provides details on the architecture and owners of 65 sites in Bamberg.

There are eight properties that South Carolina's Archives and History department pinpoint as "defining the historic character of the district." One so noted is the one-and-one-half story 1897 house at 403 Railroad Avenue. The upper level porch reveals elaborate carpenter's ornamentation and the prominent lower porch is attractively rounded. The Hooten House, built in 1898 at 508 Railroad Avenue, is another key structure. So is the 1888 Folk Zeigler House, at 503 Railroad Avenue, with its ornamental trim and millwork, hand-turned at the nearby sawmill. The brick Trinity Methodist Church, at 416 Railroad Avenue, is noted for its hip-roofed main block with projecting gabled wings and tall bell tower. Another notable church is the Bamberg First Baptist, Railroad Avenue at Carlisle Street. This has an imposing doorway, having three two-story Tuscan arches with entrances in each of the three. Three more private residences are noted by South Carolina Archives and History: the 1913 two-story frame house at 310 Railroad Avenue with a Neo-classical portico, the 1901-04 two-story frame house with a two-tier porch across the facade at Midway and South Carlisle streets and the 1898 frame house at 224 Midway Street with its irregular V-shaped central entranceway.

There are two public buildings on the walking tour that should be noted. The 1938 Bamberg Post Office has a 6' x 12' mural by Dorothea Mierisch, titled *Cotton the World Over*, that was one of 16 murals done in the state as part of the New Deal Art Program. It was also during the Depression that the ladies of the Friday Afternoon Book Club established Bamberg's first library, which opened in 1934 and was maintained by the club until 1945 when it became part of the county library system. The Old Library, now used by the County Council, is on North Street.

Tours and overnight accommodations are available at the **General Bamberg Inn**, 217 N.E. Railroad Avenue, the home of General Francis Marion Bamberg, for whom the county is named. (He is related to Major William Seaborn Bamberg for whom the town was named.) General Bamberg served with Hart's Battery. When Bamberg returned from the Civil War, he built this Victorian Queen Anne residence in 1870. The house remained in the family until 1981 when it was sold to Mrs. H.M. Wheeler.

The 64-year old Mrs. Wheeler and her daughter, Diane, spent the next 11 years restoring the house. They purchased the house sight unseen, after reading a real estate advertisement which said "colonial home may need a little work." They did 90% of the work themselves and it is an impressive accomplishment. The original plaster ceiling medallions, brass and crystal chandeliers and wide-board flooring are restored to their former glory. The 12-foot-high ceilings make the rooms imposing, and antique furnishings and eight working fireplaces reinforce the old world charm. There are five guest rooms; for information call (803) 245-5964.

Four miles south of Bamberg on Route 78 is **Woodlands Plantation**, the home of author and poet laureate William Gilmore Simms. The house can be toured by appointment, call (803) 245-4624. Seven miles north of Bamberg is the town of **Denmark**, where your first stop should be the Denmark Depot & Museum on Route 78. Visitor information and train exhibits can be found in the Amtrak station, which now also serves as the home of the Denmark Downtown Development Association.

An artists, craftsmen and antique-collectors cooperative called **The Caroline Collection** is housed in the nearby American Telephone & Telegraph Building on Palmetto Avenue. It's open Tuesday through Saturday from 10:00 A.M. to 5:00 P.M. and Sunday 1:30 to 5:00 P.M. All communications in the southeastern United States went through this building once it was operational in 1923. The first transcontinental telephone call went through this Denmark landmark. Iron gratings were placed over the windows and the building was guarded during World War II to prevent sabotage. Some of the telephone operators actually lived in this building.

One of Denmark's most appealing features is its business district with establishments that have been in town for generations. Brooker Hardware is just one of these long-term community stores, now run by the third generation of Brookers. Here you can find a wide array of items from lumber to fine crystal. Across Palmetto Avenue (the town's main street) is Poole's 5 & 10, which is a throwback to the 50's dime stores. Poole's was established in 1939 and still has its old wooden floors and wide array of goods.

Continuing down Palmetto Avenue you will pass the restored Dane Theater, now serving as a community cultural center. Across the street is the popular Wee Bake Bakery, where you can buy mouth-watering morsels Thursday through Saturday. On the corner of Palmetto is **Jim Harrison's Art Gallery**, where the native son and world-renowned artist has a gallery of his work from signed prints to originals. A glance in the display window reveals one of Harrison's main interests, a collection of Coca-Cola memorabilia. One exterior wall of the gallery/studio has a Coca-Cola mural done by Harrison who is one of the few independent artists licensed to use the soft drink name in his calendars and prints. He was 14 when he started painting these advertising signs alongside his 70-year-old sign-painting mentor J. J. Cornforth. Together they traveled the county painting barns and the sides of stores and gas stations. When Cornforth retired Harrison inherited the Coca-Cola business, maintaining the wall bulletins and painting new ones. Harrison is considered one of the country's best advertising artists. He is also noted for his studies of Americana, farm landscapes, nature studies and small towns.

Directions: From I-95 take Exit 77, Route 78 west through Branchville to Bamberg, then on to Denmark. From I-20 take Exit 22, Route 1 south to Aiken. Then take Route 78 east to Denmark and on to Bamberg.

Healing Springs and Barnwell

God's Little Acre

Lute Boylston, a deeply religious farmer, willed the acre on which the healing springs stands to God, stating that no earthly owner may ever again possess or control its water. This generous gesture keeps the area open, but unfortunately has left no one directly responsible for its upkeep and maintenance. (Locals claim that the year after Boylston died, tax forms for the land were sent out to "God Almighty, in care of the Boylston family.") The Barnwell Historical Society is in the process of trying to become the legal guardian of **Healing Springs** and, if successful, plans to improve the surroundings.

The history of the curative powers of this spring is traced back to the early 1700s. The indigenous Native Americans considered the waters sacred and sought their healing power when sick or wounded. An Irish trader named Nathaniel Walker succeeded in getting the tribal chief to break the taboo against revealing the secret of the springs to an outsider. Local stories claim the chief traded the healing springs to Walker for maize. What really persuaded the chief to make the trade will never be known, but the following day the entire tribe left the area never to return.

The healing effects of the spring water became a matter of record during the American Revolution after the Battle of Slaughter Field in August 1781. Four mortally wounded British soldiers were left in the care of two slightly wounded men beside the bubbling spring waters. The two expected to recover were ordered to return to their Charleston garrison once their comrades had died and been buried. Six months later all six men rejoined their company, reporting the "healing" powers of the springs.

The pure artesian water has been analyzed by companies in the United States and abroad. It contains approximately 14 minerals and chemicals. Virtually everyone in Barnwell County can recount a story about someone they know, or have heard about, who has used the water and been cured. When you visit, you'll see people filling bottles and large containers from four pipes that now bring the water to the surface. Visitors arrive with trucks and cars full of empty bottles and spend hours filling their containers.

Adjacent to the springs is Healing Springs Baptist Church, established in 1772 on land given by Nathaniel Walker, a member of the English "Dunkers." The practice of holding religious services at the springs began on January 14, 1770.

In 1960, a Mennonite community was established in the Healing Springs area. One member of that community owns and operates the popular **Miller's Bread Basket** in the former Blackville opera house. The restaurant serves freshly baked bread, hot pastries and other home-cooked favorites. There is an adjoining shop that sells hand-crafted quilts and other crafts. It's also worth checking out the old Southern Railway depot that now serves as a library and museum. In Blackville you can see the railroad bed of the *Best Friend of Charleston*, the first commercial railroad in America and the longest commercial line. The train ran through Blackville on its journey back and forth from Charleston to Hamburg (see South Carolina State Museum selection).

Ten miles south of Blackville is **Barnwell** which, although on the path of Sherman's march through South Carolina, does have a number of surviving churches. The oldest in town is the 1831 St. Andrews Roman Catholic Church on Academy Street. One of the few pre-Civil War churches organized by and for African-Americans is the Bethlehem Baptist Church on Wall Street. The church was built in 1829, but the present building was reconstructed in 1889 using material from the original. The Episcopal Church of the Holy Apostles was built in 1856–1857 with the financial support of the English Reverend Edwin A. Wagner who donated the lot and money for the construction of this typical Gothic English parish church. The church was built of cypress wood with virgin heart pine pews for a congregation of 35 white and 10 African-Americans who took part in the services from a gallery. A medieval font given by Reverend Wagner is at the door. During the Civil War when Kilpatrick's Cavalry marched into town, they stabled their horses in the church and reputedly allowed the animals to drink from the font. Church members had removed and buried the stained glass windows; they were reinstalled after the war. The altar window was a gift of Governor James Hammond. The church is on the National Register of Historic Sites. Buried in its cemetery are civic and state leaders as well as local personalities. One final church to survive, a Presbyterian Greek Revival church built on Academy Street in 1848, now serves as the Circle Theatre. For theater performance information call (803) 259-7046.

Barnwell is also noted for its vertical sundial, the only one in the country. It's located in front of the courthouse and was built in 1878–1879. Made in Charleston on the orders of Captain Joseph D. Allen, the sundial is within two minutes of Eastern Standard Time, although it was erected two years prior to the establishment of that time standard. When you see the clock, try to figure out what all the markings mean—it's a challenge.

Seven miles northeast of Barnwell, is the 307-acre **Barnwell State Park**. Two fishing lakes attract sportsmen. There is a designated swimming area and a nature trail. Overnight visitors can stay at one of the 25 camp sites or, with advance planning, in one of the park's five vacation cabins. The park is open 9:00 A.M. to 9:00 P.M., except from November through March when it closes at 6:00 P.M.

Directions: From I-20 take Aiken Exit 18, and head south on Route 19, then pick up Route 78 east to Blackville. For Healing Springs take Route 3 north for three miles. From Blackville take Route 3 to Barnwell.

Hitchcock Woods, Hopeland Gardens and Rye Patch

Nature's Triple Crown

By the 1890s, Aiken began to attract wealthy seasonal residents who came south to escape the winter weather. It was Mr. and Mrs. Thomas Hitchcock who lured their New York friends to Aiken's temperate climate. Mrs. Thomas Hitchcock was an enthusiastic horsewoman and she fell in love with Aiken, realizing it would be an ideal spot to enjoy a five-to-seven-month sporting holiday. The Winter Colony built magnificent homes and estates with elaborate stables so they could ride to the hounds and play polo. Polo was introduced in Aiken in 1882, six years after it was first played in the United States (see Whitney Polo Field selection).

The nearly 2,000-acre wooded preserve known as **Hitchcock Woods** was the domain of the winter colonists. Here the Hitchcocks, Whitneys, Iselins, Von Staes and their friends enjoyed riding and hunting. In 1939, the Hitchcock family donated 1,200 acres (more acres were subsequently added) to the newly created Hitchcock Foundation, on the provision that it be open to the public. Hitchcock Woods is two-and-a-half times the size of Central Park and the largest urban forest in the country. Horses and hikers share the trails in this urban oasis, so there are some trail rules to observe. Horses have limited vision, so if you are walking and spot a horse approaching, stand in a visible spot, do not step off the trail to a more obscure position as this could spook the horse. Stand still and speak to the rider as they approach but do not touch the horse unless invited to do so.

There are a number of points of interest, including the Memorial Gate added in Francis R. Hitchcock's memory in 1929. Native Americans who once roamed this area told stories about the river of sand that winds through the forest. The Bebbington Springs area of the preserve has plants normally seen in more mountainous regions, while the Lowcountry Ride is a hilly trail where abundant wildflowers bloom in early spring. The Kalmia Trail follows a ridge that from late April to mid-May is abloom with pink clouds of kalmia. Another fascinating trail is the Ridge Trail that Thomas Hitchcock laid out in the 1920s. He used this track for training his race horses. Another trail with history is Cathedral Aisle, which follows the railroad bed of the South Carolina Canal & Railroad Company, the longest line in the world when it was completed in 1833.

Hiking or riding (it's strictly BYOH, that's bring your own horse, as there are no rental facilities available) you are sure to spot a wide variety of birds, mammals, a few reptiles such as lizards and turtles, and amphibians like several species of frogs.

A smaller, more manicured 14-acre park was given to Aiken by Mrs. C. Oliver Iselin. **Hopeland Gardens** is hidden by one of the distinctive serpentine brick walls that once protected the Iselin mansion, which is no longer standing. Oliver Iselin inherited a fortune made in the railroad and coal mining industries. His wife, Hope Goddard Iselin, maintained racing stables in the United States and England. She was a close friend of members of the British Royal family and in fact shared their horse trainer. Mrs. Iselin did much for Aiken before dying at age 102. She organized the group that helped build the city's first hospital and she helped found the Fermata School for Girls, a private school adjacent to Rye Patch. She served as a director of a private school for African-American students.

Under a canopy of ancient oaks, deodara cedars and magnolias is a garden of fountains, reflecting pools, statuary and judicious plant arrangements. Beside a small lake is an Italian rotunda of delicate wrought iron and marble dedicated to Aiken resident Joan Tower. There is also a lake-side natural amphitheater where free performances in the park are given every Monday evening from May through August. Bring a chair or blanket and enjoy local and regional artists.

The garden also has a Touch and Scent Trail with Braille plaques. The Doll House, a playhouse for Mrs. Iselin's daughter, is now the headquarters for the Aiken Garden Club Council. At Christmas this is decorated as part of the festive open house at Hopeland Gardens. Beside the Doll House is a historic camellia garden. There is also a Thoroughbred Racing Hall of Fame (see selection).

The 14-acre Hopeland Gardens was a gift to Aiken from Mrs. C. Oliver Iselin. The family's estate no longer stands but visitors can see the Doll House, a former children's playhouse. The gardens are laid out beneath ancient oaks, deodara cedars and magnolias.

A walk through the wetlands area and across a picturesque bridge leads to **Rye Patch**, a neighboring estate owned by Dorothy Goodyear Rogers. This 10-acre estate was donated to the City of Aiken in 1982. A lovely Rose Garden was planted in memory of Mrs. Rogers' granddaughter Patricia Goodyear, 1949-1988. While at Rye Patch you can also visit the **Clifford S. Gerde Carriage Museum** where you will see a collection that includes a Kentucky Breaking Cart, a surrey with the fringe on top, buckboard phaeton, Rockaway and several other carts and wagons. You can arrange to hold special functions in the Rye Patch mansion. From spring through fall you can enjoy lunch from 11:30 A.M. to 2:00 P.M. at the **Guest Cottage Restaurant**, where pictures from Rye Patch's past adorn the walls.

Hopeland Gardens and Rye Patch are open daily from 10:00 A.M. to sunset. Admission is free.

Directions: From I-20 take Route 19, Laurens Street, to South Boundary Avenue and turn left. From South Boundary Avenue turn right on Whiskey Road for the entrance to Hopeland Gardens and Rye Patch which is between Dupree Place and Berrie Road.

Montmorenci Vineyards

Grape Scott!

Viticulture in the Aiken area dates back to 1858, when the Aiken Vine Growing and Horticultural Association was formed, although grapes were grown in the region even before that time. Several years later, wine fanciers were visiting the area to sample an Isabella grape claret made by the Benson and Merrier's Winery. The blue Isabella grape, a Concord variety, was indigenous to the Carolinas and began being used for wine around 1816.

A current award-winning winery is located just outside Aiken in the small community of Montmorenci, named by James Archille de Caradeuc for his ancestral French homeland of Montmorenci. De Caradeuc grew up on a plantation near Charleston but in 1840 he acquired this land and attempted to grow grapes. The Scotts have succeeded where the Frenchmen failed. That's not a national distinction because it is Robert Scott Sr. and his son Bobby who are the owners of the new Montmorenci Vineyards.

For the Scotts, wine making was a hobby that turned into a business. For years they made wine for family and friends. Scott Sr., a chemical engineer with Gulf Oil Company, experimented until he found the grapes that did the best on their 16 acres of reddish clay soil. He obviously succeeded. The winery's first vintage in 1989 won a bronze for its hybrid dry red wine at the International Eastern Wine Competition in Watkins Glen, New York.

Visitors can taste the wines of Montmorenci at the sales center visible from Route 78, located in a 1931 stucco Tudor home, the same one pictured on all the winery's labels. You can see the vineyard from the windows on the west side of the main room. There are approximately 40 varieties of grapes.

The Montmorenci Visitor Center is open Wednesday through Saturday from 10:00 A.M. to 6:00 P.M. It is closed on major holidays and the first two weeks in January. You can taste the various wines at the center and purchase your favorites.

Southern Moon Pottery is virtually across from the winery off Route 78 on Woodward Drive, an oak-lined street that runs parallel to the highway. Inside is a studio and teaching facility offering unique items for purchase. Studio hours are 9:00 A.M. to 5:00 P.M. Monday through Saturday.

Directions: From I-20 take Exit 22, Route 1 south to Aiken, then follow Route 78 east to Montmorenci. The visitor center will be on your left.

North Augusta

It's Another State

North Augusta is embarking on a 15-year development plan that includes a recreational and tourism complex along the Savannah River with bike paths, a golf course and perhaps a hotel and convention center. North Augusta is also part of the newly-formed South Carolina Heritage Corridor (see selection).

But as North Augusta looks to the future, it isn't forgetting its past. The earliest community, initially called Hamburg, was incorporated in 1827. It was a thriving river port and the western terminus of the South Carolina Canal & Railroad Company. In 1813, the town founder Henry Schultz, with business partner Lewis Cooper, built a toll bridge across the Savannah River connecting Augusta, Georgia with South Carolina. Schultz's financial reverses (plus his habit of not allowing individuals to cross the bridge because he didn't like their looks or some other pet peeve) caused Georgia to seize his bridge in 1821. In retaliation Schultz established Hamburg with the hope of ruining Augusta.

The city you see today was really launched in the late 1800s when James Urquhart Jackson purchased 5,600 acres of land and formed the North Augusta Land Company. Another bridge was built over the Savannah River in 1902 and a trolley line connected Augusta with Aiken. By the early 1900s, North Augusta was a resort town for wealthy northerners.

One of the most luxurious properties in town was the sprawling Hampton Terrace Hotel, the world's largest wooden hotel, which burned in 1916. The guest roster included president-elect Howard Taft, John D. Rockefeller, Harvey Firestone and other luminaries. **Seven Gables**, also called Palmetto Lodge, was built as a men's club house for guests of the famous hotel, but later served as a private residence. For a time it was the home of author Edison Marshall. Now a restaurant, Seven Gables, at 1724 Georgia Avenue, serves delicious continental cuisine. Another site associated with the hotel was the Rutland Tea Room, 124 Arlington Heights, which lost its clientele after the fire and was converted to a private residence.

North Augusta's Georgia Avenue/Butler Avenue/Carolina Avenue Historic District has a number of historic homes of note, though most are in private hands and not open for tours. One house you certainly should drive past is the 1860 Star of Edgefield, 111 Butler Avenue, with its elaborate ironwork on the first and second floor porches. All the walls, both inside and out, are 24-inch-thick brick. But for the Civil War, the estate would be even more elaborate. A ship carrying a matching iron fence sailed from England but was sunk by a Union gunboat in Charleston Harbor. The Butler house, as it was also called, served as a hospital during the Civil War.

North Augusta also has several independent listings on the National Register of Historic Places. Two of the town's most elegant estates are now European style inns: **Lookaway Hall**, 103 Forest Avenue West, built around 1895 by Walter Jackson; and **Rosemary Hall**, corner of Forest and Carolina avenues, built in 1902 by James U. Jackson, one of the original developers of North Augusta. To experience a feeling of yesterday's grandeur, have afternoon tea at Rosemary Hall or Lookaway Hall. Reservations must be made 24 hours in advance; call (800) 531-5578.

Sesame Lodge, 1008 West Avenue, originally a bed-and-breakfast inn, was built in 1902 by Budd C. Wall and designed by his daughter Martha Wall Andrews, an early female architect. On the outskirts of town at 908 W. Martintown Road is the Hammond Home; the rear portion, built in 1790, is the town's oldest structure. Hammond was a planter and merchant. The front portion of the house was built by his grandson in 1840. The Hammond Family Cemetery adjacent to the house has a pyramid-shaped monument dedicated to the Hammond family members who served in the Revolutionary War, plus a gravesite holding the remains of soldiers who died in the war. Elm Grove, 1065 West Martintown Road, built in 1842 on part of an original land grant from King George III, was built and designed by Major Andrew Jackson Hammond, one of the signers of the Ordinance of Secession.

If you want to take a walk or bike ride, head for North Augusta's **Greeneway**, a 3.2-mile trail (to be extended to 8 miles) following an abandoned railroad line. The trail passes through **Riverview Park** where you will find tennis courts, baseball and soccer fields, hiking trails, horseshoe pits, picnic areas and an activities center. In the spring, the Greeneway provides a glimpse of the elusive *relict trillium*, an endangered wildflower. Another city park, **Wade Hampton Veterans Park** on Georgia Avenue, has monuments honoring American veterans.

For unique shopping don't miss the **Royale Boutique Gallery**, 320 Georgia Avenue (behind the Veterans Park) which offers limited editions, a wide variety of work by local and nationally known artists, art jewelry and accessories. For a unique, hand-crafted gift be sure to stop at David Stuart's **Wild Hare Pottery**, 1627 Georgia Avenue (corner of Alpine Avenue). Here locals can sign up for lessons, but travelers have to be content with purchasing Stuart's artistic creations.

A delightful dining spot is **B.C. Davenport's**, 301 Georgia Avenue. The restaurant, originally the home of Joe and Ethel Davenport, was built in 1905 (a year before the town of North Augusta was established). Joe Davenport, the town's first fire chief, never lived down the fact that he slept through the Hampton Terrace Hotel blaze. He was also a pharmacist known far and wide for his "Frog Pond Elixir" reputed to cure everything from colds to constipation. Mrs. Ethel Davenport, the first woman ever elected to the North Augusta town council but more well-known for her green thumb, grew flowers of all kinds. Today's restaurant owner has made a tribute to this love of flowers with delicate floral murals throughout the establishment.

North Augusta also boasts an old-fashioned ice cream parlor, the **Pink Dipper** at 501 Georgia Avenue. For another nostalgic experience stop at the **Sno-Cap Drive-In**, 618 West Avenue, for lunch or a snack.

For further information stop at the Greater North Augusta Chamber of Commerce, 235 Georgia Avenue. You can pick up brochures and maps for a self-guided tour of North Augusta.

Directions: From I-20 take Exit 5, Route 25 south which will become Georgia Avenue in North Augusta. You can also take Exit 1 from I-20, which will bring you into town on Martintown Road.

Redcliffe Plantation State Park

Managing Editor's Home Offers the Time of Your Life

The brief state park information sheet about **Redcliffe Plantation State Park** refers to the colorful Hammond family who owned the estate. That hardly does justice to the complexity of the four generations who owned and lived at this antebellum plantation house. It would be hard to find a more striking difference between two generations than there was between James Henry Hammond and his eldest son, Harry.

James Henry Hammond almost destroyed his political career by his inappropriate behavior toward his nieces, the daughters of South Carolina political giant Wade Hampton II. Throughout his life, James Henry had a series of illicit liaisons. He instructed his son, Harry, that women were "made to breed," to serve as "toys for recreation," or for economic purposes to bring men "wealth and position." Harry, according to accounts left by his son Henry Cumming Hammond, had "...the best woman in the world for a companion, for a friend, for a coworker, for a cosufferer, for a wife."

The senior Hammond was a strong proponent of states rights, southern nationalism and secession. He believed that slavery was the cornerstone of the agrarian south and argued that the south would be strong. He declaimed, "No, you dare not make war on cotton. No power on earth dares to make war on it. Cotton is king." After the devastation of the Civil War, with finances at Redcliffe strained and cotton prices low, Harry declared, "Cotton will never be called King again."

James Henry Hammond achieved his lifelong ambition when he was elected U.S. Senator in 1857. His first public office was as U.S. Congressman in 1834, but he resigned for health reasons and traveled to Europe with his wife of three years and their son, Harry. In 1842, he was elected governor for one term. During his term of office he reputededly attempted to seduce Wade Hampton's daughters. Hammond's wife left him after discovering an ongoing relationship with two slave women. During this period of separation Hammond purchased land six miles north of the property he already owned. He intended to build an impressive family home, designed not as a working plantation but as a showplace. While Hammond served as U.S. senator, Redcliffe was constructed under Harry Hammond's supervision and was completed in 1859. Hammond resigned his senate seat two days after Lincoln was elected president, vowing to support the newly formed Confederacy "with all the strength I have." But he soon became critical of the southern government and died before the war ended.

Harry did not share his father's interest in politics. He served in the Confederate Army, earning the rank of major and surrendering his troops as part of Lee's Army of Northern Virginia at Appomattox on April 9, 1865. As he left the army he said all that he owned was "a pipe, some tobacco, and literally nothing else." But he did own Redcliffe, although he had to divide the property among his family, leaving Redcliffe and 400 surrounding acres to his mother. Most of the slaves, roughly 300, stayed. That was a mixed blessing, as it maintained the number of people that needed to be supported by the plantation's crops. It was financial help from Harry's wife, Emily Cumming Hammond, that sustained the family.

The third generation at Redcliffe was Harry and Emily's third daughter Katharine Fitzsimons Hammond who married Dr. John Sedgwick Billings, a physician she met while studying nursing in Boston. Their 28-year-long marriage began on April 20, 1897. Katharine was always happiest when she was at Redcliffe. Her son, John Shaw Billings, shared his mother's love for Redcliffe, where he was born. In 1935, he bought the estate for $15,000 from a family member to keep it intact. John had married a local girl and their wedding reception was at Redcliffe. John was an editor of *Time* and *Life* magazines. When he acquired his family estate, John wrote, "I long to chuck my job and go to Redcliffe for good." His love of the property prompted him to undertake a major restoration effort. In 1954, Billings retired to Redcliffe. Having no direct heirs, Billings gave Redcliffe to the state at his death on August 27, 1975.

When you tour this two-story Georgian Lowcountry-style house you will see reminders of the 120 years of Hammond family ownership. The heart pine flooring and plasterwork ceilings are original as are the native sycamore doors, mantles, banisters and library shelves. Hammond's desire to demonstrate his financial standing is reflected in the sterling silver door hinges. Every piece of furniture is connected to the family and many have fascinating histories. The elaborate wood-grained piano in the parlor was purchased in 1843 for $11.00. One parlor wall is covered with a massive copy of a Raphael, acquired by Harry Hammond on his Grand Tour in 1855. The Tiffany and Sheffield silver in the dining room are original and some pieces date back to the 17th century. A Buddha in the corner is just one of the objets d'art that were given to John Shaw Billings's grandfather, a highly respected physician. The library strongly recalls the presence of Billings with bound copies of *Life* and *Time* filling the shelves. Bedrooms upstairs reflect the successive generations.

On the grounds is a slave quarters that was converted into a garage and an example of one of the slave cabins that once stood on the property. The grounds were landscaped by Louis

Berckman, a Belgian horticulturist who lived in Augusta and whose nursery grounds became the renowned Augusta National Golf Club. Remnants of Berckman's plantings can still be seen on the course and at Redcliffe, including the banks of azaleas and clusters of camellias. One of Redcliffe's most noted horticultural touches is the mile-long avenue of southern magnolias that connected the plantation with Glen Loula, the home of Paul Hammond, one of James Henry Hammond's sons. The grounds have a number of foreign trees including a Japanese parasol tree, Chinese pistachio and cork tree.

The 369-acre Redcliffe Plantation State Park is located at Beech Island, so named not because there is a beach or an island but because when the region's Swiss and German settlers pronounced the name of the nearby farming community Beech High Land (named for the Beech trees on the high terrain), it sounded like island. There is a nature trail, but visitors are warned during the summer months to watch out for snakes on the path and to check for ticks after their hike. The park is open Thursday through Monday year round from 9:00 A.M. to 6:00 P.M. The house can be toured Thursday, Friday, Saturday and Monday from 10:00 A.M. to 3:00 P.M. and Sunday NOON to 3:00 P.M. A nominal fee is charged to tour the house. A series of innovative programs are scheduled year round; call (803) 827-1473 for information.

Aiken State Park is just a short distance from Redcliffe. This 1,067-acre park is popular with fishermen who try their luck in the four spring-fed lakes and in the Edisto River (see Edisto River Trail selection). You can rent canoes, fishing boats and pedal boats. A nature trail winds along the edge of the river swamp through the sandhills terrain. There are 25 camp sites, a playground area, picnic facilities and lake swimming.

Directions: From I-20 take Exit 1, Route 230 south to the intersection with Route 125. Turn left on Route 125, which will merge with Route 278. Redcliffe Plantation State Park is three miles southeast of Beech Island off Route 278; follow state park signs. For Aiken State Park, head east on Route 278 and then north on Route 302; signs mark the park entrance. The park is also accessible via Route 78 just 16 miles east of Aiken.

Rivers Bridge State Park and
Broxton Bridge Plantation

All Fall Down

Sherman was determined to punish the state that, in many soldiers' eyes, was responsible for the Civil War. South Carolina was, of course, the first to secede from the Union and the location of the war's opening shots. Sherman commented in later years that "somehow our men had got the idea that South Carolina was the cause of all our troubles...I would not restrain the army lest its vigor and energy should be impaired; and I had every reason to expect bold and strong resistance at the many broad and deep rivers that lay across our path." But as Sherman marched through South Carolina in January and February of 1865 the only major armed resistance he encountered was along the Salkehatchie River.

Sherman's march toward the capital at Columbia was held up for two days, February 2nd and 3rd, at three crossings along the Salkehatchie: Rivers Bridge, Broxton Bridge and Buford's Bridge. The crossings, spaced at six-mile intervals, had a main bridge as well as smaller bridges over streams, creeks and swamps. At the first two of these crossings, visitors can still see the breastworks behind which the valiant and outnumbered Confederates held the Union troops at bay. The odds were fierce at Rivers Bridge. Roughly 800 to 1,500 Confederates delayed the advance of 7,000 to 9,000 Union soldiers. (In all there were about 60,000 Federals spread out over a 40-to-60-mile stretch.) Union casualties at Rivers Bridge were 16 dead and 85 wounded, while the Confederates had 8 killed, 44 wounded and 45 captured.

The action at Rivers Bridge was on terrain where the Salkehatchie resembled a swamp more than a river. An Ohio soldier remembered the river "ranging from knee-deep to waist-deep, full of fallen trees, cypress vines, and deep holes which, with the tangled underbrush and vines that grew between, made anything but pleasant marching." When Broxton Bridge was burned, Rivers Bridge became the primary crossing point across the Salkehatchie. Here the Confederates held the high ground, entrenched on a ridge along the north bank of the river. From this vantage point they could fire down at the Union troops trying to cross the plank causeway that led to the bridge. All during a chilly, rainy February night, the Confederates fired on the Union troops standing in the swamp or lying against tree stumps in the damp marsh grass. Before dawn the northern troops started building corduroy roads, resting planks on logs laid across the bridge's causeway. Alhough their position was unbreachable, the Confederates lacked the manpower to protect their flanks and were forced to evacuate after holding the Federals at bay for nearly two days. The Confederates barely vacated the breastworks before their former positions were overrun by a force ten times their size. The Southern force retreated roughly 30 miles northwest to Branchville.

When you visit **Rivers Bridge State Park** you not only see the breastworks that guarded the crossing, you also see a common grave where in 1876 Confederates killed during the Battle of Rivers Bridge were reburied near the battlefield. At the only state park in South Carolina commemorating the Civil War, the monument that stands over the soldiers' mass grave reads:

> "Soldiers rest, your warfare o'er,
> Sleep the sleep that knows not breaking.
> Dream of battlefields no more,
> Days of danger, nights of waking."

There are also World War II graves and monuments at this park, as well as more traditional recreational options like picnicking, camping, fishing in the Salkehatchie, hiking on the nature trail and enjoying the playground equipment. The park is open April through October daily from 9:00 A.M. to 9:00 P.M. It is open Thursday through Monday, from November through March only until 6:00 P.M. The park office is open on days when the park itself is open from 11:00 A.M. until NOON. The 25 campsites are on a first-come, first-serve basis.

Breastworks remain from the skirmish on February 1st at the Broxton Bridge crossing. The battlefield is on the southern end of the **Broxton Bridge Plantation**. The plantation is now a bed & breakfast inn with guests accommodated in five bedrooms in the rustic 1850s Kite Kinard house. You can still see the faded imprints of soldiers' names written by Northern troops who crossed the Salkehatchie. Broxton Bridge plantation has remained in the extended Broxton-Varn family for nine generations. You can hear Civil War stories from the current owner on a guided tour of the battlefield. Call (800) 437-4868 for advance reservations.

Broxton Bridge is also noted for its two 100-shot sporting clay courses and opportunities to hunt quail, deer, turkey, ducks over decoys and continental tower shoots by reservation. The plantation has 7,000 acres of hunting land plus a ten-acre lake stocked with bream, bass and catfish.

Directions: From I-95 take Exit 57, Route 64 west toward Ehrhardt. Before reaching this community, bear left on Route 641. Rivers Bridge State Park is off Route 641, on Route 8. To reach Broxton Bridge Plantation, from Route 64 you will bear left on Route 641, then left again on Route 601. The plantation will be on your right.

South Carolina Heritage Corridor

The Good Earth

In 1993, the **South Carolina Heritage Corridor** was created linking 14 counties from Charleston to the mountains of Oconee County. This 240-mile corridor gives visitors a look at the landscape, history and culture of the Upcountry and Lowcountry. The winding trail is a time machine taking visitors along the Great Wagon Road that settlers traveled, past Revolutionary War battlefields and pre-Civil War plantations that recall a vanished way of life. The corridor is divided into four regions, each with its own Discovery Center. The corridor follows Highway 78, which, wherever possible, parallels the 136 miles of South Carolina Railroad tracks that the *Best Friend*, the country's first commercial steam locomotive, traveled in 1833. The Aiken/Bamberg area is one of the four regions (others are Oconee, Edgefield and Charleston).

The Aiken/Bamberg section is strongly rural, interspersed with county seats like Barnwell and railroad towns like Olar and Blackville. Contributing to the unsettled quality of this region is the heavily wooded 400-square-mile tract appropriated for the Savannah River Site, a nuclear weapons facility.

The Discovery Center is right off Route 78 at the Clemson Edisto Research & Educational Station, part of Clemson University. The Discovery Center orients visitors to the corridor's cultural, historical and recreational points of interest and to the Heritage Byways that loop off the main route. Beside the center is an agricultural museum with larger pieces of equipment on the grounds in front of the center. Because this is an educational center, there is an operational farm that tests various row crops. Visitors have the opportunity to compare state-of-the-art farming with demonstrations of old methods and equipment from earlier eras. Fields are labeled so that interested visitors can identify the various crops. A heritage vegetable and herb garden displays vintage produce. You can also see new crops such as the hybridized cotton that comes in a variety of colors.

Directions: Region Three's Discovery Center is just outside the Blackville city limits on Route 78. For more information on the Heritage Corridor call the South Carolina Department of Parks, Recreation and Tourism at (803) 734-0122.

Thoroughbred Racing Hall of Fame, Whitney Polo Field and McGhee's Mile Track

A Run for Your Money

Aiken is a horse town. It's not a one-horse town, but more like a thousand-horse town. The street signs all have small horse heads in the corner. At certain intersections, the signal switches are at the height of a mounted rider, not at a pedestrian's. Many of the city's roads are unpaved because hard-packed dirt is easier on horses' hoofs. From the end of November until the middle of April, there are approximately 1,500 horses in Aiken county. This figure includes the 350 thoroughbreds and 125 standardbreds stabled within Aiken city limits.

In its heyday, Aiken was the "Polo Center of the World." There were once 16 polo fields in town. Whitney Polo Field boasts the distinction of having the longest continuous period of play of any field in the country.

Aiken's ascendancy as the playground for the racing set can be traced to the arrival of Mr. and Mrs. Thomas Hitchcock in the 1890s. The city's rich equine heritage is detailed at the **Thoroughbred Racing Hall of Fame** at Hopeland Gardens (see selection). This repository of racing history is housed in what was once the Iselin carriage house, which was flanked by stalls for their horses. The space where Mrs. Iselin parked her Rolls-Royce now has a gallery with photographs, ribbons, racing silks and memorabilia featuring champion thoroughbred flat racers and steeplechase horses trained in Aiken from 1942 until the present. Forty American racing champions have trained at the Aiken Training Track including 1981 Kentucky Derby winner, Pleasant Colony; 1990 Preakness winner, Summer Squall; 1993 Kentucky Derby winner Sea Hero; and the latest inductee, Stormy Song, the 1996 Breeders' Cup Juvenile Fillies Winner. There is also an extensive collection of Engelhard silver trophies.

The upstairs gallery focuses on polo, which was introduced in Aiken in 1882, a few short years after it was first played in this country. In 1889, the Aiken Polo Club became the tenth member of the United States Polo Association and for a long time Aiken was the "Polo Center of the World." There are also trophies and photographs about horse activity in Aiken. The facility is open Tuesday through Sunday afternoons from 2:00 to 5:00 P.M. from fall through spring.

Polo is still played in Aiken at **Whitney Polo Field**, which can boast the longest continuous period of play of any field in the country. At its zenith there were 16 polo fields in Aiken. When a tournament is being held, there may be as many as 250 polo ponies in Aiken. A polo match has six chukkers, or periods, each seven minutes. There are no time outs during these periods except if a player is injured or if there is a rules violation. The play is strenuous and ponies are changed after each period, although a pony may be used later in the same game. Good players need to have at least four ponies per game and players will readily concede that a good mount is about 75% of the game. A polo pony is actually a horse, usually with thoroughbred breeding and race track experience. The object of the game is to score goals and each team consists of four players (three in arena polo).

Aiken's polo season runs from September through November and March through July. Games are held, weather permitting, on Sunday at 3:00 P.M. at Whitney Polo Field. This field was built by Thomas Hitchcock, one of America's first ten goal players, and then acquired by William C. Whitney. The field was deeded by Whitney to a board of trustees so that polo could continue in Aiken. During the season United States Polo Association sanctioned tournaments are played here in April and October. Admission to the games is $2.00 per person; for additional information call (803) 648-7874. Parking is available along the sides of the fields. Be sure to park at least ten yards away and avoid the ends of the field. The south side of the field is reserved for members and guests of the Polo Club. After the third period at half time, spectators are invited to do the "Aiken Stomp" getting out onto the playing field and stomping down divots of turf dug up during play.

Aiken's love of horses reaches a crescendo with the **Aiken Triple Crown**, three successive week-ends of events beginning with the Aiken Trials, then the Aiken Steeplechase and the Aiken Harness Races. The **Aiken Trials** take place in mid-March at the **Aiken Training Track**. Since 1942, these have provided the first "public" viewing of promising young racing thoroughbreds. The young two-and three-year-old horses take part in timed "trials" under full grandstand conditions. The public is welcome and tailgate parties are a time-honored feature of this family-oriented event.

Since it was established in 1941, the Aiken Training Track has enjoyed a reputation as one of the world's finest thoroughbred training grounds. Since 1990, Aiken-trained Grade 1 winners have earned an average of $4 million annually. Visitors can watch the training sessions, which begin around 6:00 and continue until about 9:30 A.M. The etiquette of track-side behavior is to stay out of the way, don't wear a hat that may blow off and spook the horses and don't reach out to pet a passing horse. Just park and watch the horses "breezing," which is what they call the morning work out. The **Track Kitchen**, at Mead and Marion avenues, is open from 7:00 A.M. to 2:00 P.M. and you're welcome to drop in for a hearty breakfast or a great hamburger and fries. The kitchen is run by James "Pockets" Carter, who knows everybody at the track. The walls are filled with photographs of champion Aiken horses.

The second event of the Triple Crown, the **Aiken Steeplechase**, is held in late March at Ford Conger Field. The National Steeplechase Association has sanctioned the Aiken Hunt Meets as the first and last event in the steeplechase calendar. Steeplechasing originated in England in the early 1700s, when races would stretch "from this point to that church steeple yonder." The riders jumped all the obstacles in their way on the shortest route to their objective, thus races where horses jumped hurdles were called a "steeplechase." Some of the country's finest thoroughbreds test the jumps at the Aiken course.

The final race in the Crown is the **Aiken Harness Race** in early April at the **McGhee's Mile Track**, established in 1936 by Dunbar Bostwick. He is credited with reviving an interest in harness racing, which was introduced when horse racing was considered frivolous and the horses were kept to a prescribed pacing gait. The privately-owned McGhee' s Mile Track on Banks Mill Road is a training center for standardbred horses. In a humorous nod to equine lingo, the "STOP" sign on the premises, reads "Whoa."

Directions: From I-20 take Route 19, Laurens Street to South Boundary Avenue and make a left. From South Boundary Avenue turn right on Whiskey Road for the entrance to Hopeland Gardens and the Thoroughbred Racing Hall of Fame. For Whitney Polo Field continue on Whiskey Road to Mead Avenue and turn left. For the Aiken Training Track make a left from Whiskey Road onto Grace Avenue. McGhee's Mile Track is on Banks Mill Road off South Boundary Avenue.

It's not just the horses that set a fast pace in Aiken. It was also the Winter Colony residents who influenced the town's tempo.

Thoroughbred Country Regional Tourism Contacts (Area Code 803)

THOROUGHBRED COUNTRY
P.O. Box 850
Aiken, SC 29802
649-7981, fax: 649-2248

AIKEN CHAMBER OF COMMERCE
P.O. Box 892
Aiken, SC 29802
641-1111, fax: 641-4174

THOROUGHBRED COUNTRY
P.O. Box 850
Aiken, SC 29802
649-7981, fax: 649-2248

AIKEN COUNTY PARKS, RECREATION & TOURISM
828 Richland Avenue West
Aiken, SC 29801
642-7559, fax; 643-1992

ALLENDALE COUNTY CHAMBER OF COMMERCE
P.O. Box 517
Allendale, SC 29810
584-0082

BAMBERG COUNTY CHAMBER OF COMMERCE
Route 3, Box 215 A
Bamberg, SC 29003
245-4427

BARNWELL COUNTY CHAMBER OF COMMERCE
P.O. Box 898
Barnwell, SC 29812
259-7446

GREATER NORTH AUGUSTA CHAMBER OF COMMERCE
235 Georgia Avenue
North Augusta, SC 29841
279-2323, fax: 279-0003

HOSPITALITY BYWAYS ASSOCIATION
P.O. Box 527
Allendale, SC 29810
584-3950

MIDLAND VALLEY AREA CHAMBER OF COMMERCE
P.O. Box 305
Clearwater, SC 29822
593-3030, fax: 593-6526

Thoroughbred Country Calendar of Events
(Area Code 803)

February
   Polo. Winter colony sports enthusiasts enjoy a long tradition of matches at the Whitney Polo Field on Sunday at 3:00 p.m. through July. Aiken, 641-1111.
Early February
   Battle of Rivers Bridge Re-enactment. Realistic Civil War encampment and lantern tours. Ehrhardt, 267-3675.
Late February
   Battle of Aiken. Re-enactments of Civil War 1865 cavalry battle. Montmorenci, 648-6729.
Early March
   Storytime in the Gardens. On Tuesday at 4:00 p.m. from March through May and again in September and October, senior volunteers read children's stories for those eight and under. Children should be accompanied by an adult; be sure to bring a blanket. Hopeland Gardens, Aiken, 642-7648.
Mid-March
   Aiken Triple Crown. Three successive March weekends have trial, steeplechase and harness races. Aiken, 641-1111.
   Arts Alive. Musical and theatrical performances combine with children's theater, craft demonstrations and art exhibits. Bamberg, 245-3038.
Early April
   Dogwood Festival. A parade, street dances, arts and crafts, food and a tour of homes mark this event. Denmark, 793-3676.
   Spring Cooter Festival. A cooter (turtle) race, parade, petting zoo, art show, carnival rides, food and crafts mark this spring celebration. Allendale, 632-2025.
Early May
   Wonderful Day in May. An air show, family entertainment, food and crafts highlight this day-long event. Arnwell Airport, 259-7446.
   Funfest. Celebrates the town's heritage with entertainment, carnival rides, games and a parade. Wagener, 564-6380.
   Lobster Race. Though not a beach community, Aiken has an annual lobster race, a take-off of the Kentucky Derby, with beach music and lots of family fun. Aiken, 649-9500.
   Hopeland Gardens Summer Concerts. On Mondays at 7:00 p.m. from May through August there are al fresco concerts; be sure to bring a blanket or lawn chair. Aiken, 642-7648.
Late May
   Beech Island Heritage Day. Living history re-enactments bring Beech Island's past to life. Redcliffe State Park, 827-0184.
Late June
   Experience Aiken Craft Show. A family festival with carnival games and rides, a craft show and entertainment. Aiken, 642-7648.
Late August
   Schuetzenfest. German hunter's festival with folk dancing, German heritage events and cuisine and a volkslauf, or people's run. Ehrhardt, 267-3531.
Early September
   Whiskey Road Race. T-shirts proclaim, "We run on Whiskey" at this race that includes a 10K road race, a two-mile race, a one-mile race

and a tot trot. Aiken, 642-7652.

Late September

Aiken's Makin'. This craft fair and children's festival includes a waiters' and waitresses' race. Aiken, 641-1111.

Early October

Whiskey Road Fox Hunt. In the sand hills and wooded areas of Aiken, Edgefield and Saluda there are live hunts on Tuesday afternoons and Thursday, Saturday and Sunday mornings from October through March. Aiken, 641-1111.

Mid-October

Colonial Trades Fair & Militia Muster. Re-enactments demonstrate how settlers lived in colonial South Carolina; event includes a court re-enactment. Living History Park, North Augusta, 279-7560.

Heritage Festival. Mennonite food and crafts, parade, antique cars and family entertainment mark this autumn celebration. Blackville, 284-2444.

Late October

Jack-O-Lantern Jubilee. Costume contests, pumpkin carving, games, rides and entertainment mark this holiday celebration. North Augusta, 441-4290.

Late November

Chitlin' Strut. Noshing on chitterlings is only one part of this fun-filled festival; there are crafts, carnival rides and entertainment. Salley, 258-3485.

Blessing of the Hounds. On Thanksgiving morning in Hitchcock Woods the Blessing of the Hounds opens the meet of the Aiken Drag Hunt for the Aiken Hounds. Aiken, 641-1111.

Holiday Arts & Crafts Fair. Seasonal and traditional items done by local crafters. Allendale, 584-4207.

Early December

Christmas Craft Show. More than 200 craftspeople exhibit at this event. Aiken, 642-7630.

Holiday Home Tour. A self-guided candlelight tour of homes in Aiken's Historical District. Aiken, 641-1111.

Late December

Christmas in Hopelands. Pathways and buildings are strung with lights, the garden is bedecked with decorations and there are Christmas concerts and refreshments. Aiken, 642-7630.

First Night Aiken. Welcome the New Year with music, dance, art and magic. Aiken, 641-9094.

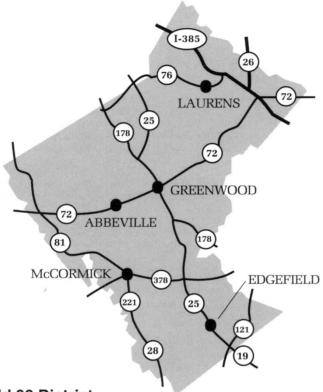

Old 96 District

Old 96 District

Old 96 District is named for the British frontier settlement that withstood a 28-day siege by Patriots in the spring of 1781. The region that once belonged to the Cherokees is rich in history from Long Cane, where first Native Americans and settlers fought, then British fought Patriots, to significant Civil War sites. Abbeville is called the "birthplace and the deathbed of the Confederacy." The Burt-Stark House is an integral part of that story, for it was here that Confederate President Jefferson Davis held his last Cabinet meeting. Oakley Park Museum highlights stories of the Red Shirt movement that flourished here during Reconstruction.

The economic history of the region can be discovered at the Old Edgefield Pottery, where a unique skill is still being practiced, and at Dorn Mill, where an unusual architectural property is being restored and interpreted. Two current commercial concerns in the region merit attention: the Park Seed Company, with its nine-acre trial gardens and Emerald Farm, with its restorative goat milk soaps and herbal products.

Significant as all these attractions are, it is perhaps the natural beauty of the area that is best known. The region calls itself the "Freshwater Coast" and boasts five major lakes with 3,000 miles of shoreline. In all there are 109,600 acres of water; including the Savannah River, a National Wild and Scenic River. There are a myriad of state and local parks, the 116,000-acre Sumter National Forest and the Savannah River Scenic Highway. This abundance creates a wide variety of recreational options: hiking, hunting, fishing, horseback riding, boating, swimming and camping.

Abbeville and Belmont Inn

Town Square but Attitude Hip

Abbeville's Court Square, with its park benches, fountain, trees and grassy area, is the center of the town's restored historic district as well as its bustling commercial center. Preservation work has uncovered brick streets around the square and restored an historical look to the store fronts.

The restoration creates a 19th-century appearance in this thriving 20th century community, but settlement goes back to the 18th century. A frontier village was established in the 1730s by Patrick Calhoun, father of John C. Calhoun, a future U.S. vice-president. When the time came to found a town, the village doctor, Dr. John de la Howe, chose the name Abbeville, in honor of the French city that was once his family's home. The town figured prominently in the Civil War. Prior to the outbreak of hostilities, the first organized meeting to adopt an Ordinance of Secession was held in Abbeville. The last meeting of Confederate President Jefferson Davis's war council was held at the Burt-Stark Mansion (see selection). Abbeville is called "the birthplace and deathbed of the Confederacy." The town square has a **Confederate Monument**. The original 1906 obelisk given to the city by the Daughters of the Confederacy was destroyed by fire in 1991. A "new" monument that duplicates the old was dedicated on December 14, 1996.

"King Cotton" and the railroad brought prosperity to Abbeville. By the early 1900s, an ornate opera house (which also served as the city hall) stood on the town square beside the court house. Performers on trains from New York to Atlanta stopped in Abbeville. Drama, dance and music entertained the local gentry. The Ziegfeld "Follies" played Abbeville, as did Jimmy Durante, Groucho Marx and Fanny Brice. By the late 1940s, movies were running in the aging theater. In 1968, a major restoration effort was launched and today the Opera House Players perform year round in the opera house's George Settles Theater. Free tours are given daily except when the company is rehearsing.

During the railroad heyday, touring actors and traveling salesmen stayed at the Eureka, a stately turn-of-the century hotel built in 1903 on the edge of the town square. The hotel gradually declined and was eventually abandoned, though never demolished. In 1983, the hotel was purchased by Mr. and Mrs. Joseph C. Harden and restoration began. Renamed the **Belmont Inn**, with 24 guest rooms, it opened in 1984. Renovated again in the mid-1990s, each guest room features period reproductions that suggest old world elegance. The public rooms have an inviting warmth and there is a casual Tinkers Alley Bar & Grill on the lower level. For elegant dining it would be difficult to surpass Timothy's, where the chef is gaining a reputation throughout the state. For information and reservations call (864) 459-9625.

You'll see a number of architecturally interesting private homes on a walking tour of Abbeville. Pick up a brochure at the Chamber of Commerce offices on the square. If the town looks familiar to you, although you are sure this is your first visit, it may be because it served as the location for the Julia Roberts movie, *Sleeping with the Enemy*. The 1888 **McGowan-Barksdale-Bundy House** is now the headquarters of the Abbeville County Historical Society. When restoration is complete, it will become the Jane Greene Derrick Center for the Arts. This Queen Anne style house was built for General Samuel McGowan, who was present at the capture of Fort Sumter and commanded a South Carolina brigade during the Civil War. When his house was finished in 1888 it was called the most expensive house in town. Ornamentation abounds both inside and out. Even the outbuildings are decorated; three boast sawed Gothic Revival bargeboards, ornately cut roof trim. Later the house was the residence of General W.E. Barksdale, who served in World War II. In addition to fascinating private homes, there are 36 churches within the city limits. Several churches date from the 19th century such as the Trinity Episcopal Church on Church Street, the oldest church in the city, built in 1859-1860.

While strolling Abbeville's streets, stop at the Abbeville County Library to see the **Poliakoff Collection of Western Art**. Abbeville native Dr. Samuel Poliakoff amassed a note worthy collection of contemporary Native American ceramics, bronzes, weavings and paintings. The collection can be viewed at no charge Monday, Wednesday and Friday from 10:00 A.M. to 5:00 P.M. and on Tuesday and Thursday until 7:00 P.M. Saturday hours are 10:00 A.M. to 1:00 P.M.

One spot to glimpse mementoes from the town's past is the **Abbeville County Museum**, located in the 1850s jail house. It was founded in 1976 by the late Helen Ladd Neuffer with the assistance of the local American Legion Post. Within the museum is the counter and sales case from the Old Gable Store in Antreville, a nearby town. Residents have donated a wide range of items that remind visitors of the past, including old photographs of the town and surrounding countryside, a Confederate Catechism of Secession and a horn used to call slaves from the fields. On the museum's second floor, there are clothes and accessories, toys, books, tools, glassware and kitchen articles.

The 1839 Creswell Cabin, on the museum grounds, was moved from the Troy area to its present location. Inside the cabin are furnishings and articles representing rural life in the 19th century. The museum at Poplar and Henry M. Turner streets is open by appointment; call (864) 459-2696.

In addition to dining at the Belmont Inn, locals frequent the Veranda Cafe and the Village Grill. Visitors often flock to town during May for the annual **Abbeville Spring Festival**, a family-oriented event featuring a parade, a tour of selected private homes, live entertainment, an antique car and collector show, crafts, food and rides for the children. For details call (864) 459-4600.

Directions: From I-26 take Exit 52, Route 72 south to Abbeville, where it will become Greenwood Street. Turn right on Main Street for Court Square.

Burt-Stark Mansion

"Deathbed of the Confederacy"

The **Burt-Stark Mansion** has an indelible link with the past—this *is* a house where history happened. In the parlor, Jefferson Davis, with his cabinet and war generals, held the Confederacy's last council of war. Although President Davis was loathe to acknowledge it, his advisors to a man voiced the opinion that the resources of the South were exhausted and to continue fighting would be futile and just bring more misery. Only General Lee and his Army of Northern Virginia had surrendered, so with great regret discharges were signed for the soldiers of the Confederacy and the war was officially ended.

The route to this residence was fraught with danger. Davis and his cabinet, accompanied by approximately 3,000 soldiers, fled Richmond, traveled through North Carolina—Greensboro and Charlotte—then into South Carolina's Waxhalls and on to the home of Davis's close friend Major Armistead Burt. Traveling with Davis was Secretary of State Judah P. Benjamin, Secretary of War John C. Breckenridge, Secretary of the Navy S. R. Mallory, and Post Master General John H. Reagan. Also with the party were generals W.C. Breckenridge, Basil W. Duke, J.C. Vaughn, George C. Dibrell, S.W. Ferguson and Braxton Bragg. Davis's wife, Varina, and their children had arrived at the house two weeks earlier.

The group, after riding hard, arrived around noon on May 2, 1865. After resting for part of the afternoon and eating a meal sent over by neighbors who had learned of the distinguished guests at the Burt House, the men adjourned to the parlor for their final cabinet meeting. Davis argued forcibly for continuing through Georgia to Mississippi and joining with Confederate forces there to continue the fight but his advisors dissuaded him.

The Burt-Stark Mansion is called the "Deathbed of the Confederacy" because it was in this parlor on May 2, 1865 that Confederate President Jefferson Davis and his cabinet and generals had the last council of war before they disbanded their armies.

A disheartened Davis spent the night at the Burt house before riding out with his advisers before dawn. The troops riding with Davis carried $500,000 in gold and the Seal of the Confederacy. Somewhere along their journey both disappeared—neither have ever been recovered.

When you visit the Burt-Stark Mansion you will see the parlor exactly as it was when President Jefferson Davis, his cabinet and generals met here. Although the furniture was sold at auction, it was recently returned to the house, intensifying the sense of history that visitors feel when they gaze around the room. At the welcome center on the square in Abbeville there is a mural of this historic final meeting, but it is even more moving to stand in the very room where the Confederacy ended.

The other rooms of the two-story, weather-boarded Greek Revival-style mansion, built in 1830, are filled with original pieces representing five generations of the Stark family. The last surviving member of the family who purchased the house in 1900, Mary Stark Davis, gave the house and all of its artifacts to the Abbeville County Historic Preservation Commission. Tours are conducted by a friend of this generous benefactress, Margaret Bodie. She speaks of Mary with such familiarity and fondness, visitors often feel that Mary has just stepped out and will soon return. She quotes Mary as telling her, "You better have the house exactly as I left it. I want it to look like I'm coming home." The house is open Friday and Saturday afternoons from 1:00 to 5:00 P.M., and is closed in January. Other times it is open by appointment; call (864) 459-4297. Admission is charged.

Directions: From I-26 take Exit 52 south through Greenwood to Abbeville. The Burt-Stark Mansion is located on North Main and Greenville streets in Abbeville.

Dorn Mill and MACK

Building on Gold

The town of McCormick was built on top of gold mine tunnels. Gold-bearing rock formations stretch across three state lines in the Piedmont region—North Carolina, South Carolina and Georgia. Excavation of these deposits has taken place since the 1790s. No one knows the exact date William Burkhalter Dorn spent $1,200 to buy 1,263 acres of land in western South Carolina from Dr. John Wardlaw Hearst, a relative of the Hearst family of newspaper fame.

Dorn began mining for gold on his land and was nearly out of capital when the mine struck in 1852. Dorn used slaves to excavate the dirt and operated several different types of mills to process his gold. By the late 1850s, when the vein was exhausted, he had excavated nearly one million dollars in gold. Dorn lost most of his fortune after the Civil War. In 1869, Dorn sold the mine to inventor Cyrus McCormick, who had a summer home in Aiken. McCormick spent over $200,000 trying to find another rich vein of gold but, by 1882, gave up the search and began selling the land, which became the town of McCormick. The **Dorn Gold Mine** site is used during Gold Rush Days in late June, when exhibits on mining are displayed there.

In 1898, **Dorn's Flour and Grist Mill** was built (it is in the process of renovation and interpretation). The 2½ -story red brick structure, originally a cotton gin, still has steam engines, boilers and machinery in place from its days as a grist mill. It is the only steam-powered mill in the state and one of the few in the country. The mill, which operated until the 1940s, ground corn meal for store sales, flour for local farmers and feed for their animals. Much work remains to be done before this outstanding example of rural industrial architecture can open its doors for tours. There are five rooms on the ground floor and two rooms in the upper section. The main room downstairs had two large mill stones within a wooden platform. There is also an intricate system of pulleys and belts as well as a grain cleaner and sacking machinery. Dorn's Flour and Grist Mill is at 206 North Main Street, the northwest end of the street.

McCormick offers old-fashioned pleasures such as the hand-dipped ice cream cones at Strom's Drugstore, founded in 1911. Before World War II, the store even offered curb service. If you want a full meal head for **Fannie Kate's Inn and Restaurant** at 127 South Main Street. Originally opened in 1884 as the McCormick Hotel, a temperance establishment for railroad passengers and traveling salesmen, it became McCain's Boarding House in 1905. Fannie Kate, the granddaughter of owner Mrs. J. M. Marsh, eventually ran the hotel. Years later in 1992, long after it ceased to operate, the McCain family donated it to the town. In 1995, it was purchased and restored as Fannie Kate's by Barbara and Lou Roberts. There are nine guest suites and a dining room featuring traditional Southern dishes. There's a pub on the lower level for informal relaxing. For information or reservations call (800) 965-0061 or (803) 465-0061.

Just down from this establishment, at 115 South Main Street, was a second hotel serving the eight passenger trains that brought customers into McCormick in the 1880s. In those days, it was the Carolina Hotel. Salesmen, called drummers, would display their wares in designated rooms of the hotel. In later years, it was known as the Connor and the Keturah Connor, taking on the name of the last family owners. This property, on the National Register of Historic Places, is now the home of the

McCormick Arts Council at the Keturah, known as **MACK**. In addition to gallery space where changing exhibits showcase the work of local artists, there is a well-stocked Gallery Shop where you can find unique items. MACK sponsors workshops, classes, and field trips. MACK founded the Savannah Valley Heritage Festival, held on the last Saturday of September, which celebrates folklife, music and customs of the region.

Directions: From I-20 take Route 28/211 north to McCormick.

Emerald Farm and Park Seed Company

Working Wonders with Nature

Two very different family-owned operations can be visited in the Greenwood area; one is a goat and herb farm, the other one of the world's best known seed companies. **Emerald Farm** is small but fascinating. You can learn a great deal about how to take care of yourself from owner/manager Kathy Zahn. She raises goats and makes goat milk soap and a wide array of herbal products. Kathy can advise you on what herbs to take to lose weight, knock out the flu bug, soothe aching muscles and remedy a host of other problems. She makes specialty soaps that are whimsical and medicinal—her "Happy Feet" soaps are shaped like a foot and made with goat milk and peppermint, guaranteed to comfort sore feet. The gift shop stocks herbal bath vinegars, moisturizers, natural powders, facial masks, bath salts, massage and bath oil, skin toners, body gel, herbal shampoo and the wide assortment of soaps all made at the farm's small soap factory.

Younger members of the family will enjoy stopping by the barn to see the goats. The farm also has sheep, cows, chickens and honey bees. Nutritious milk from the Saanen goats is bottled at the farm and visitors are invited to help milk the goats.

Emerald Farm is open at no charge, although there is a charge for guided tours, arranged by appointment. The farm is open 9:00 A.M. to 5:00 P.M. Monday through Saturday. The farm also does a thriving mail order business; you can call (864) 223-9747 for a catalog.

If you head north of Greenwood, you'll discover **Park Seed Company** with a nine-acre trial garden featuring the newest hybrids. Each year they have 3,200 individual trials with more than 700,000 plants, all hand-planted and hand-tended. The outdoor trials run from March through November, while those in the greenhouses continue year round. Gardeners get a wealth of ideas from these test gardens. Many of the plants can be ordered in the gift shop and picked up immediately. The shop fills orders from Park Seed Company catalogs and from Wayside Gardens' catalog. The gardens are in bloom from spring until fall while the two greenhouses are in perpetual flower. You will find an incredible variety of seed packages including flowers, vegetables and herbs. There are also garden books and a wide range of horticultural and gardening gadgets, tools and decorative items. You can tour the seed room and packaging plant Monday through Friday at 10:00 A.M. and 2:00 P.M. Park Seed Company is open at no charge daily from 9:00 A.M. to 5:00 P.M. One of the garden's biggest events is the Festival of Flowers in June, a month-long celebration that involves all of Greenwood. Flower Day is the last Saturday in June and it is the high point of the festival.

While in the area, stop at **Greenwood Museum**, located in a 1930s furniture store in the "Uptown" shopping area. The downstairs concentrates on natural history with cases filled with rocks, minerals, shells and other scientific collections. Here you also see Native American artifacts, a munitions collection and an exhibit on inventor, Thomas Alva Edison. There are museum rooms from the 1900s that recreate a drug store, general store, a fully-equipped kitchen, a music room, school room and a doctor's office complete with operating table. The lower level exhibits focus on textiles, transportation and communication, while upstairs there is an art gallery, with an area that features Edgefield pottery (see Old Edgefield Pottery selection) and an international collection including the Gertrude Morse Collection from Africa. The museum is open Wednesday through Saturday, 10:00 A.M. to 5:00 P.M. There is a nominal admission, except for the first Saturday of each month when admission is free. Just inside the entrance is a museum shop.

If you get hungry while exploring, stop at one of the most popular spots in town, the **Little Pigs Barbecue** at 414 Montague Avenue. Their barbecue is terrific and at lunch time the tables are often filled with locals grabbing a bite. For those who want to stay overnight in Greenwood, you can't beat **Inn on the Square**, 104 Court Street. Forty-six guest rooms are filled with antique reproductions. The inn's restaurant features boutique wines and distinctive dining. For more information call (800) 231-9109 or (803) 223-4488.

Directions: From I-26 take Exit 9, Route 221, south to Greenwood. Take the Greenwood bypass south and make a left on Cambridge Avenue. Continue toward Ninety Six on County Farm Road for a short distance, and make another left on Emerald Farm Road. For Park Seed Company, take the bypass north instead of south (Routes 25/178/72) until you reach Route 254, and head north for a short distance. The Greenwood Museum is at 106 Main Street. From Main Street turn left on Montague Avenue for Little Pigs Barbecue.

Long Cane Massacre Site and Troy

Living on the Edge

When white settlers first arrived in the hardwood forests of western South Carolina, the huge trees stood far enough apart that the abundant deer and buffalo could be seen from great distances. There was no underbrush to obstruct the view. It wasn't uncommon for settlers to see a hundred buffaloes grazing on a single acre. Deer traveled in herds of 60 or more and bear were also numerous. In 1797, the last reported panther in the region was killed along Long Cane Creek.

The abundant wild game, fish and bird population along **Long Cane Creek** made this an appealing spot for a settlement. In 1756, the Calhoun clan settled here, including John C. Calhoun's grandmother, Catherine Calhoun and her four sons James, Ezekiel, William and Patrick. The family also included her widowed sister Mary Calhoun Noble and cousin Hugh Calhoun. The family left Ireland to escape the dual threats of famine and religious persecution. Within two years the Province of South Carolina had granted the Calhouns two huge tracts of land (between 300 to 750 acres in each) along a branch of the Little River.

This land grant, however, conflicted with a treaty South Carolina had made with the Cherokee Nation in 1740, which granted all land west and north of Long Cane Creek to the Cherokees. The land granted to the Calhouns was closed to white settlers. The Cherokees had friendly relations with settlers up until the onset of the French and Indian War in the 1750s, but they were becoming increasingly uneasy about settlements encroaching on their land.

The Calhouns were part of that threat. Other settlers, fleeing the unprotected frontiers of Pennsylvania and Virginia, joined the Calhouns. By 1760, it is estimated there were between 150 to 250 settlers in the Long Cane area. The Cherokees became convinced that the English were going to continue expanding into their territory, a realization heightened by the construction of Fort Loudon, so they planned an attack on the Ninety-Six Fort (see selection). The route to this fort lay through the Long Cane settlement. Somehow the settlers were alerted to the impending attack and attempted to flee to Augusta's Fort Moore, but the loaded wagons got bogged down along the soggy banks of Long Cane Creek. The Cherokees caught up with them on February 1, 1760 and attacked so swiftly and unexpectedly that the men were not able to reach the guns they had packed in the wagons. Some settlers escaped into the canes, others were captured and between 20 and 50 were killed. When the settlers returned after the attack they buried 23 victims, including Catherine Calhoun, in a mass grave a quarter mile from the massacre site (the gravesite, with a stone marker erected by Patrick Calhoun, and massacre site are indicated by a historical marker). Ann Calhoun, William's daughter, was taken prisoner and lived with the Cherokees for several years before being reunited with her family.

When the settlers returned they exercised greater care, living within stockades for protection. Calhoun's Fort, also called Fort Long Cane or Fort Boone, was reportedly controlled by Patrick Calhoun and sheltered approximately 140 settlers. The threat of attack did not end until 1785 when a treaty was signed between the Cherokees and the United States.

There was yet another fight in this area, and the **Battle of Long Cane** was between the British and the Patriots. The Patriot force, led by Scottish immigrant Lt. Col. James McCall, along with Col. Elijah Clarke and his men, were joined by Col. Benjamin Few with refugees from Georgia. The growing Patriot presence at the Long Cane settlement was unsettling to the British who decided to drive them out before they grew stronger. Col. John Harris Cruger, commander of the British at Ninety-Six Fort, sent 450 troops to eliminate the patriots. Three miles from the Long Cane camp the two forces met on December 11, 1780. The patriot force, numbering only 100, was not able to withstand the British attack. After 21 casualties, the Patriots retreated. McCall and the Long Cane Militia headed north and on January 17, 1781 they fought with Daniel Morgan in the Battle of Cowpens (see selection), a British defeat that was one of the major turning points of the Revolutionary War.

Each October on the weekend before Halloween there is a reenactment of the Battle of Long Cane with living history camps, bayonet and tomahawk contests and a musket firing competition. At other times, visitors need their imagination to fill the countryside with combatants. There are no exhibits, no visitors center, no guided walking paths—just a marker to indicate what transpired on this ground. The site is on Route 117, a dirt road just outside of **Troy**.

For a pictorial map of Troy covering the historical and cultural points of interest stop at the Southernwood Greenhouses on Old Charleston Road in Troy next to the Troy Baptist Church. The self-guiding map lists a number of the local churches, the two-cell brick jail built before 1910, a 19th-century log cabin and the ruins of Bradley's Mill, a late 1700s grain mill on Long Cane Creek and the ruins of Bradley's covered bridge.

Directions: From I-20 take Exit 18 and head north on Route 25. Make a left on Route 378 to McCormick, then take Route 221 north. Turn left again on Old Charleston Road, which will become East Main Street in Troy. The Southernwood Greenhouses is on the right.

Magnolia Dale and
Oakley Park Museum

Antebellum Ambiance

In 1839, Connecticut native Samuel Brooks built **Magnolia Dale** on land that was part of the 1758 royal land grant to John Lamar. Edgefield attorney Alfred J. Norris purchased Magnolia Dale in 1872. Portraits of Norris and his wife, Mary Fox, still hang in the house. Their daughter, Mamie Norris, married James Hammond Tillman, the nephew of political boss "Pitchfork" Ben Tillman. James Tillman served as the state's Lieutenant Governor from 1901 to 1903.

When Kendall Company, the local textile mill, bought the property in 1930 they built residential houses on the estate but preserved the lovely old historic house. In 1959, after years of urging by Mrs. Mamie Tillman, the company gave the home to the Edgefield County Historical Society and it now serves as their headquarters. The reception rooms, furnished with select pieces of period furnishings, are used for meetings and there are exhibits in the upstairs rooms. You will see a 1772 portrait of Arthur Simkins, considered the "Father of Edgefield" because of his contributions to its early development, and of his wife, Margaret Dalby. Their plantation Cedar Fields on the banks of Log Creek was one mile from the town square in Edgefield. Simkins was an ardent patriot during the American Revolution and after the war he served as a judge in the local court. The walls of Magnolia Dale are also graced with portraits of the four daughters of Governor Francis W. Pickins, one of the ten state governors to come from Edgefield. The foyer features a sideboard that once belonged to Governor George McDuffie, who, as a state congressman, led South Carolina's Nullification Movement which in turn led the way to the hostilities that divided the country. Upstairs the Strom Thurmond Room has memorabilia, photographs and furnishings from this noted native son.

Magnolia Dale is open Monday through Friday by appointment; call (803) 637-2233, 637-5306 or 639-5239. There is a nominal admission fee.

General Martin Witherspoon Gary's 1835 home, **Oakley Park**, is the only shrine in the world dedicated to the Red Shirt Movement and Reconstruction. General Gary lived here during the Reconstruction era when the government in South Carolina was run by northerners who had come down to the south after the Federal government established Radical rule. Southerners derided these outsiders as "carpetbaggers" and "scalawags." The Red Shirt movement (named for the brightly colored shirts members wore), which General Gary headed in the Edgefield area, worked to elect Wade Hampton governor in 1876, ending the power of the Reconstructionist.

From the balcony of his house, Gary rallied 1,500 followers. Governor Pickens' daughter Douschka Pickens, referred to as South Carolina's Joan of Arc, also rallied the crowd. Gary and his supporters headed into Edgefield Village in 1876 to monitor the polls and make sure the white southerners' vote was counted. When you tour the house, you will see a display case with one of the original red shirts worn by Gary's enthusiastic followers. There are also Confederate flags, currency, swords and other relics.

The house is furnished with period pieces, as well as seven items that belonged to General Gary including the dresser, bedside table and wash stand in the master bedroom. Governor John Gary Evans, the general's nephew, deeded the estate in 1941 to the town of Edgefield. The house is maintained and operated by The United Daughters of the Confederacy.

Oakley Park Museum is open Wednesday, Thursday and Friday from 10:00 A.M. until 4:00 P.M. and at other times by appointment; call (803) 637-3233. Admission is charged.

If touring plantations makes you long to overnight in such antebellum splendor, then stop by **Cedar Grove Plantation**, just five miles north of Edgefield. This 1790 house built by John Blocker, one of the oldest in the state, is now on the National Register of Historic Places. It's noted for its unique barrel-vaulted ceiling in the entry hallway, the hand-painted French wallpaper and the hand-carved mantels and moldings. The heart of pine wood used in the house was cut from trees on the 2,000-acre plantation. Each room has a fireplace and the furnishings suggest old world elegance. The original kitchen and slave quarters still stand on the grounds. Two rooms are available for overnight guests. Amenities include a gourmet breakfast, served either in the ornate dining room or on the back porch overlooking the in-ground swimming pool (surrounded by flowers and herb gardens and which guests may enjoy). Cedar Grove Plantation Bed & Breakfast, operated by Sandy and John Whitehouse, will with advance reservations give tours to interested travelers; call (803) 637-3056.

Directions: From I-20 just north of Aiken, take Route 19, which will merge with Route 25 in Trenton as it heads northwest to Edgefield. Route 25 becomes Main Street in Edgefield. Turn left on Bacon Street; continue until it dead-ends on Norris Street at Magnolia Dale (320 Norris Street). Oakley Park is in Edgefield at 300 Columbia Road, off Route 25. Cedar Grove Plantation Bed & Breakfast is just north of Edgefield on Route 25.

Ninety Six National Historic Site

A Star Attraction

Traders in the early 1700s estimated that it was 96 miles from the Cherokee Village of Keowee in the upper South Carolina foothills to the English village that was soon simply called **Ninety Six**. A number of inland trading paths intersected here and it became a convenient stop-over point and trading hub. Leather and belts were traded for guns, powder, rum and other supplies. Robert Gouedy, a veteran of the Cherokee trade in Tennessee, was the first settler here and he established a trading post at Ninety Six in 1751. When he died in 1775 he owned in excess of 1,500 acres and approximately 500 people owed him money.

Relations between the Cherokees and the settlers were not good, and the latter built Fort Ninety Six for their protection. The fort was actually constructed around Robert Gouedy's barn. It was needed since in March 1760 over 200 Cherokees attacked the fort. There had been an attack the month before which destroyed Gouedy's trading post. In 1761, a treaty was signed greatly limiting the Cherokee's hunting privileges and prohibiting them from traveling south of the Keowee settlement without permission. This encouraged settlers and by the early 1770s the community had grown to at least a dozen buildings including a courthouse and jail, blacksmith shop, four mills, a trading post and houses. Over a hundred people lived in Ninety Six, or in its vicinity.

By 1775 the combatants had changed, when the first battle of the American Revolution fought south of New England was waged at Ninety Six. The forces were uneven, as there were 1,800 British Loyalists and only a third of that number under command of Patriot Major Andrew Williamson. The battle began on November 18th and lasted several days before ending in a truce. The British realized the strategic significance of this out-post. In 1780 when Colonel John Cruger took command, he strengthened the defenses, added a stockade on the west and a star fort on the east. It was good that the British took that action because from May 22 to June 18, 1781 American Patriot leader General Nathanael Greene laid siege to the fort and its 550 Loyalist defenders under the command of Colonel John Harris Cruger. This was the longest, although ultimately unsuccessful, siege of the American Revolution. It left the village a smoking ruin. The British abandoned the fort in July and moved to the coast, ending their control of South Carolina's interior.

The best place to gain an overview of the historic events that occurred at Ninety Six is the visitors center with its video, exhibits and collection of Revolutionary War artifacts. A National Park Service ranger is on hand to answer questions. Next, take the mile-long trail that heads into the woods and across Spring Branch Creek. The first point of interest is the sunken roadbed of Island Ford Road, cut to its present depth by decades of travel. If you followed the road north for seven miles, you would see the Saluda River crossing at Island Ford. It was here the road joined thoroughfares leading to Charlotte and Camden.

You cannot find a better example of 18th-century siege lines anywhere in the country. The siege lines survived and archeologists were able to restore virtually all the old outlines, although they could not make them the exact contours and heights as the originals. Polish military engineer Thaddeus Kosciuszko, an aide to General Greene, directed the construction of the siege lines with three parallels deep enough for infantry. There were also zigzag approach trenches, called saps, which could not be penetrated by enemy fire. The third parallel was supported by a rifle tower and was only yards from the star fort, whose outline can still be seen. The fort employed a number of defensive measures including a deep ditch surrounding it, a palisade of sharpened stakes midway up its outer wall and a protective wall of sandbags on the parapet to protect defenders. A covered way allowed the Loyalists to move from the star fort to the village of Ninety Six where you can see the site of the two-story brick jail, built in 1772. Another covered walkway led west of the village to the stockade fort, built originally as protection from the Cherokees. The fort, which encompassed the only reliable water supply for the village, has been reconstructed.

The last site marked on the walking trail is the site of Cambridge, the town that grew up in 1783 when settlers began returning to the region. In hopes that their community would become a center of learning, it was named for the English university town. An epidemic in 1815 decimated the community and Cambridge became a rural crossroads fading away in the 1840s. Now Black Swan Tavern, a 1787 log structure from Greenwood, has been relocated near the Cambridge site. The tavern has reconstructed artifacts that suggest the frontier period and is used for living history programs.

A second more primitive trail, the one-mile Gouedy Trail, gets you off the beaten trail and onto a "nature" trail (this trail branches off the paved interpretive trail in the village). The first significant site on this trail is the depression that indicates the location of the brick-lined cellar of Robert Gouedy's first trading post. Next you will see a grave marker, indicating where Major James Gouedy, Robert's son is buried. He died at age 56 in March 1816. It is believed that Robert Gouedy lies in an unmarked grave somewhere in the vicinity. Approximately 50 people are buried in a colonial era cemetery, although there is no information on who lies buried here. The trail also takes you on what was once the Charleston Road, perhaps the oldest road in upper South Carolina. It led from Charleston to the back country.

Ninety Six National Historic Site is open daily from 8:00 A.M. to 5:00 P.M. It is closed on Thanksgiving, Christmas and New Year's Day.

Directions: From I-26 take Route 34 to the present town of Ninety Six, then take Route 248 south for two miles to Ninety Six National Historic Site.

Old Edgefield Pottery

Mud Pots Stand the Test of Time

A stoneware tradition arose in the **Edgefield** area that combined Native-American techniques, Chinese techniques, English traditions and African slave labor. This mix provided a cross-fertilization of techniques, and the Edgefield area was thus called the "crossroads of clay."

Paleo-Indians fired the muddy clay they gathered from the banks of the Savannah River into a stone-like consistency, shaping the earliest known pottery vessels on the continent some 4,500 years ago. To make these first containers, Spanish moss and palmetto fibers were mixed with the clay. When the European settlers arrived, the Native Americans were still using these time-tested methods to make pottery. Their techniques were copied by the African slaves who made pots to use on the plantations.

Utility was the objective when pottery making began in earnest around 1800 with the Landrum family's first pottery manufacturing operation. It was designed to do more than supply the plantation; the kitchen and smokehouse jugs and pots made at Landrum's pottery were sold to the backcountry settlers of South Carolina and the settlers traveling west. Only rarely did this pottery make tableware. By 1850, the Landrum family owned three potteries, each producing thousands of pieces of pottery. One of the most commonly produced items was a storage jug, ranging in size from a half gallon upward to a 30-gallon capacity.

Edgefield pottery is noted for its "alkaline" glaze. It is this glaze that harkens back to Chinese methods. The technique was carried to the west by French Jesuit priests, who traveled from the Orient to the New World. Edgefield potters used materials that were similar to those employed by Chinese potters: feldspars, wood ashes, lime and sand. They ground and blended these to form a celadon glaze. All the ingredients needed for pottery making were abundantly available in west central South Carolina: kaolin, feldspar and sand.

By the 1840s, there were so many potteries in the Edgefield area and such competition that decorative touches were used to differentiate the works. The swag and tassel motif was an Edgefield tradition. Some potters added figures, depicting both white and black subjects. Most of the work was unsigned. An exception is the work of a slave named Dave, who was called Dave Pottery. He had been trained to set type at Dr. Abner Landrum's Pottersville newspaper, so he could read and write. He signed, dated and often wrote verses on his huge 20- and 30-gallon jugs and jars.

Old Edgefield Pottery has a collection of old pieces, including several by Dave. On one he wrote: "A better thing I never saw, when I shot off the lion's paw." Potter Stephen Ferrell, who practices the old methods in Old Edgefield Pottery, points out the little dots next to Dave's name. They indicate how much the vessel will hold; for example, five dots translates to five gallons. The shelves of this pottery factory also contain "face jars" which reflect African traditions. White kaolin clay is used for eyes and teeth on the faces.

By the Civil War, the pottery tradition had declined, but continued through the 1930s, when flower pots were the big item. Edgefield proved a training ground for potters who migrated west and south. In 1992, the Old Edgefield Pottery was founded. Potter Stephen Ferrell, who had published articles on early South Carolina pottery techniques and organized the first museum show of Edgefield pottery, became the resident potter.

The Old Edgefield Pottery, at 230 Simkins Street, has exhibit areas and a small selection of items for sale. In the back are the kilns where Ferrell fires his work. Visitors usually find him hard at work on his latest creations, but his new work is fashioned using the old methods. Edgefield County Historical Society, who established this pottery, hopes to encourage the pottery tradition throughout the county. The society's goal is to educate the public on the importance of alkaline-glazed pottery as a uniquely southern art form. The pottery is open Tuesday through Saturday from 10:00 A.M. to 6:00 P.M., or by calling (803) 637-2060 or 637-5306 for an appointment. There is a nominal charge for tours.

While in Edgefield be sure to notice the courthouse. It was built in 1839 and designed in a style inspired by Robert Mills. Inside you'll see portraits of ten South Carolina governors from Edgefield. On the town square there is a statue to native son Strom Thurmond.

Continuing traditions that made Edgefield the "crossroads of clay," Old Edgefield Pottery makes, displays and educates visitors about alkaline-glazed pottery.

Directions: From I-20, take Route 19 north toward Edgefield. It will merge with Route 25 which becomes Main Street in Edgefield. Old Edgefield Pottery is down Potters Alley off Main Street at the Courthouse Square.

Thurmond Lake
and McCormick County

Freshwater Coast

South Carolina's western region is called the "freshwater coast" because visitors are never far from the recreational opportunities offered by creeks, the Savannah and other rivers, or a chain of lakes. **Thurmond Lake**, the state's second largest, was created by Thurmond Dam. This construction project was one of the largest undertaken by the Corps of Engineers east of the Mississippi River.

Thurmond Lake, built between 1946 and 1954, covers 70,000 acres and teems with bass, catfish, trout, bream and crappie. The lake has a 1,200 mile shoreline and serves as the boundary between South Carolina and Georgia. More than 100 islands are scattered throughout the lake providing an exceptionally rich environment for waterfowl and wildlife. Small game hunting on the lake shore is a popular activity. The J. Strom Thurmond Dam Visitors Center is open daily from 8:00 A.M. to 4:30 P.M. Free tours of the power plant are given on Friday at 10:00 A.M. and on weekends at 3:00 P.M. Within the visitors center there is a diorama showing the lake's recreation area, an aquarium stocked with fish found in the lake and hands-on exhibits that encourage young visitors to explore the region's natural history.

If you want to spend more than a day in the area, there are accommodations at three state parks and four Army Corps of Engineers campgrounds: Modoc, Hawe Creek, Leroy's Ferry and Mount Carmel as well as private campgrounds near the lake. **Hickory Knob State Park** is the state's first resort park. It boasts an 18-hole golf course, fishing, skeet shooting (by reservation only), tennis and swimming, as well as a variety of accommodations including cabins, an 80-room lodge and camping. In the park, another overnight option is the historic **Guillebeau House**. This log house is the only remaining documented structure built by the French Huguenots in South Carolina's Upcountry. The house's two bedrooms can accommodate four guests and has a fully-equipped kitchen, fireplace and other amenities including telephone and television. For information and reservations call (800) 491-1764 or (864) 391-2450. The park also has a nature center with year round interpretive programs, nature trails, two boat docks, boat rentals, a tackle shop and a restaurant and gift shop.

Baker Creek State Park is located within Sumter National Forest on an offshoot of Thurmond Lake. This 1,305-acre park is in a heavily wooded area with nature trails that wind through the forest and along the shore. Jutting out over Little River is a pavilion, inspired by Japanese architecture. Renting a pedal boat provides the best perspective to appreciate this graceful structure. There is miniature golf, a playground, a bathhouse and areas designated for swimming, picnicking and camping.

Twelve miles south of the town of McCormick is **Hamilton Branch State Park**, a 731-acre park on a peninsula jutting into Thurmond Lake. The choice pick among the 200 campsites are those along the lakefront. There is a boat ramp, playground and picnic area.

Just north of McCormick is yet another park, **Calhoun Falls State Park**, located on Lake Russell another popular fishing spot in Abbeville County. Catches include largemouth bass, bluegill, crappie and catfish. The lake is also ideal for sailing, water skiing and power boating. Within the park there are nature trails, wildlife observation areas, a bathhouse near the lake swimming area, boat ramps, a fishing pier, playground, picnic facilities, and 41 campsites. The park is on Route 81, **The Savannah River Scenic Highway**, which continues as Routes 81 and 28 merge and parallel Lake Thurmond. The route takes you through **Mt. Carmel**, a National Historic District established in 1884; **Willington**, a town founded by Moses Waddel, the first president of the University of Georgia; **McCormick** (see Dorn Mill selection); **Plum Branch**, named for the fruit that grew near the original site of the town; **Parksville**, which has the distinction of being the only town actually on Thurmond Lake; **Modoc**, named for an indigenous Oregon tribe; and **Clarks Hill**, the location of the Lake Thurmond Dam. At the lower end of McCormick County the scenic highway crosses the Savannah River.

When you are in the Clarks Hill area try to schedule your day so you can enjoy dinner at **La Cantina Restaurant**. Dining here is more than a meal, it's an experience. Gourmet southwest cuisine is prepared in taste tempting fashion. The restaurant was built by Rusty Lindberg and Laura Buchanan, who own and operate it. Much of the food is prepared in a beehive-shaped brick oven that Rusty built, called a horno (pronounced OR-no), adjacent to the picturesque side porch with its heavy wooden beams and stone floor. You can sit and watch Rusty wield a long pole to reach the iron skillets he has carefully placed in the fire. Each room is decorated in a distinctive manner, so be sure to take a look around the entire establishment. The restaurant is open Thursday through Saturday from 4:00 to 11:00 P.M. If you time your visit well, Rusty may pull out his guitar. He's a talented classical guitarist and his music adds another magical dimension to an evening at La Cantina. The restaurant is extremely popular so you might want to call for reservations (864) 333-5315.

One of the few lodging options available on Thurmond Lake is **Savannah Lakes Village**. This retirement/recreation community has an 80-room lodge that offers accommodations to the public. If you are a lodge guest you can enjoy the 18-hole golf course, tennis courts, swimming pool and other facilities. You need not be a guest to stop for breakfast, lunch or dinner at **The Cove Restaurant**, which overlooks Lake Thurmond.

Directions: From I-20 take Route 28/221 north to McCormick. You will be skirting the lake on your left once you reach the intersection with Route 221. Hamilton Branch State Park is 12 miles south of McCormick on Route 221. Baker Creek is three miles west of McCormick on Route 378. Hickory Knob State Park is eight miles west of McCormick on Route 7, north of Route 378. For Calhoun Falls State Park take Route 28 north out of McCormick to Route 81. Go north on Route 81 for two miles past the community of Calhoun Falls (there are no waterfalls in this town or in the park). La Cantina Restaurant is 19 miles south of McCormick. Take Route 28/221 to Clarks Hill, then turn on Route 533/88 (opposite the post office). Cross the railroad tracks and turn left; the restaurant is on the left in less than a quarter of a mile. For the Lake Thurmond Visitors Center in Clarks Hill, turn west on Route 221 and you will see the sign for the center.

Old 96 District Regional Tourism Contacts (Area Code 864)

OLD 96 DISTRICT TOURISM COMMISSION
104-½ Public Square
P.O. Box 448
Laurens, SC 29360
984-2233,   fax: 984-0096

ABBEVILLE COUNTY DEVELOPMENT BOARD
P.O. Box 533
Abbeville, SC 29620
459-2181

GREATER ABBEVILLE CHAMBER OF COMMERCE
107 Court Square
Abbeville, SC 29620
459-4600

EDGEFIELD COUNTY CHAMBER OF COMMERCE
P.O. Box 23
Johnston, SC 29832
(803) 275-0010

GREENWOOD COUNTY CHAMBER OF COMMERCE
P.O. Box 980
Greenwood, SC 29648
223-8431

LAURENS COUNTY CHAMBER OF COMMERCE
P.O. Box 248
Laurens, SC 29360
833-2716

MCCORMICK COUNTY CHAMBER OF COMMERCE
P.O. Box 938
McCormick, SC 29835
465-2835

NINETY SIX CHAMBER OF COMMERCE
P.O. Box 8
Ninety Six, SC 29666
543-2900
Old Edgefield District

COURTESY CENTER/ARCHIVES
104 Court House Square
Edgefield, SC 29824
(803) 637-4010

Old 96 District Calendar of Events (Area Code 864)

Early April

Peach Blossom Festival. Parade down Main Street, crafts, games, rides and family entertainment highlight this event. Johnston, (803) 637-5304.

Mid-May

Abbeville Spring Festival. Arts and crafts fill the town square; a parade, antique car show and entertainment enliven this festival. Abbeville, 459-2211.

Springtime in the Falls. Arts and crafts and entertainment are part of this town-wide yard sale. Calhoun Falls, 447-8512.

Late May

Catfish Festival. Catfish dishes and other food, arts and crafts, carnival rides and entertainment are featured. Wareshoals, 456-7478.

Early June

Dairy Festival. John de la Howe School presents a day filled with traditional life skills, demonstrations, food, entertainment and art and crafts. McCormick, 391-2131.

Late June

S.C. Festival of Flowers. Park Seed Company's garden invites visitors to celebrate the beginning of summer. The gardens are in full bloom, there's plenty of music, a sports tournament and a flotilla on Lake Greenwood. Greenwood, 223-8411.

Gold Rush Days Festival. This event features a parade, food, arts and crafts, entertainment including an evening show and a dance. McCormick, 465-2516.

Ridge Peach Festival. Children's rides, antique cars, live entertainment, food and games contribute to a celebration of a "family day in a family town." Trenton, (803) 275-4616.

Late September

Savannah Valley Heritage Festival. Folk Festival with history demonstrations, music, arts and crafts and regional food. McCormick, 465-3216.

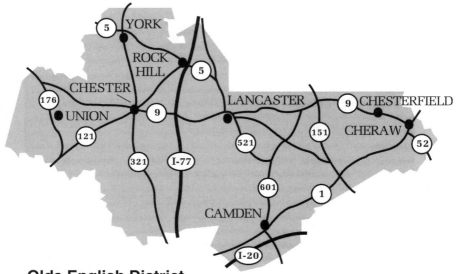

Olde English District

═ Olde English District ═

The north central portion of South Carolina witnessed a great deal of action during the American Revolution. Reflecting these Revolutionary War battles and the earlier settlements of British colonials in the mid-1700s, this area is called the Olde English District.

When the British settlers arrived they supplanted the indigenous population, a story told at the Catawba Cultural and Research Center and the Museum of York County. Andrew Jackson State Park reflects the rugged pioneer times in which this American statesman was born, while Historic Brattonsville reveals the political loyalties in the New Acquisition, as this part of South Carolina was called immediately prior to the Revolution.

The very names of the region's towns reveal their British antecedents: York, Lancaster, Chesterfield, Chester and Camden. When hostilities broke out, Lord Cornwallis and his troops were headquartered in Camden for a protracted stay as you will learn at the Historic Camden Revolutionary War Site. Battles were fought near Brattonsville and at Kings Mountain.

Transportation was important to this region in order to get goods to markets in the Lowcountry. Two dimensions of this story are revealed at the Landsford Canal State Park and the South Carolina Railroad Museum.

Three large river systems flow through the region: Pee Dee, Catawba-Wateree and Broad. These rivers and the lush growth of the Upcountry offer a wide range of recreational options. Cheraw State Park, Sandhills State Forest, Carolina Sandhills National Wildlife Refuge, Lake Wateree State Park and Chester State Park are all appealing choices. You can soar like the birds at the Bermuda High Soaring School, skim over the water like flying fishes at the McGregor Ski Center, watch horses race like the wind at Springdale Race Course, or defy gravity on the thrill rides at Paramount's Carowinds theme park.

Andrew Jackson State Park

Seventh President South Carolina Native Son

Andrew Jackson was born on March 15, 1767, just days after his father's death, in rugged pioneer country that once belonged to the Waxhaw Indians. In a letter Andrew Jackson wrote on August 11, 1824 he stated, "I was born in South Carolina as I have been told at the plantation wherever James Crawford built about one mile from the Carolina road." (North Carolina also claims the area where Jackson was born.) Jackson spent his early years in this rough environment and received virtually no schooling; even as an adult he was never able to write correct English.

When the Revolutionary War came in 1776, the Waxhaws were invaded by the British and the 13-year-old Jackson was taken prisoner. He was ill-treated during his imprisonment in Camden and his two brothers lost their lives in the war. His mother died as a result of hardships she encountered while traveling to Charleston to help Patriots imprisoned there. These experiences left Jackson strongly anti-British.

A museum at **Andrew Jackson State Park** has a small collection of exhibits connected with the pioneer period when Jackson's family lived in the Waxhaws. There are frontier kitchen implements, farm tools and bedroom furniture. You'll see copies of Jackson letters and papers, some with references to his birth in South Carolina, and Indian arrowheads. Mounted on a rock in front of the museum is an imposing statue by Anna Hyatt Huntington depicting a young Andrew Jackson sitting astride his horse.

Every Friday in May the park hosts a living history program about young Andrew Jackson. School children are interested in the one-room log schoolhouse, and park personnel talk about the way school was conducted when all grades met in one room. On the last Saturday night in May the program is presented for the general public. Throughout the year there are other interpretive programs at the park; call (803) 285-3344 for the current schedule.

There are two trails at this 360-acre park, a one-mile trail winds around the fishing lake. The 18-acre lake is a popular fishing spot and boats may be rented. A second mile-long trail extends through the wooded part of the park. There are also 25 camp sites, a picnic area and playground equipment.

Andrew Jackson State Park is open daily April through October from 9:00 A.M. to 9:00 P.M. and from 8:00 A.M. to 6:00 P.M. the rest of the year. Museum hours are weekends only year round from 1:00 until 5:00 P.M. and at other times by appointment only. Camp sites are on a first come/first serve basis.

Directions: From I-77 take Route 5 east, then take Route 521 north to Andrew Jackson State Park. It is virtually on the border between South Carolina and North Carolina.

Bermuda High Soaring School

Silent Running

Have you ever watched a bird riding the wind's currents and wished you could experience the joy of flight? Have you thought it would be fun to soar effortlessly among the clouds buoyed by the breeze? You certainly can't capture that feeling on a commercial flight. Even small planes fail to provide a sense of being one with the elements. But there is a way to know what a bird's flight is like and that is to go soaring. There are roughly 4,000 registered sailplanes in the country and soaring is enjoyed in every state of the union. Unlike ultralights and hang gliders, sailplanes are regulated by the Federal Aviation Administration, and therefore the planes are inspected and the pilots licensed.

There are about 180 soaring clubs across the country; many are associated with flight training facilities. One of the largest soaring operations east of the Mississippi River is the **Bermuda High Soaring School** started by Stan Hoke in 1963 in Chester, but now owned and operated by Jayne and Frank Reid at its new home in Lancaster County.

The school has introductory rides and instructional flights. FAA certified commercial pilots or flight instructors take the planes aloft. It's an experience you will remember and one that many want to repeat. Sailplanes use no fuel, have no engine and no propeller. Instead, they use gravity and rising thermals. A crop duster plane pulls the sailplane into the air and then releases it.

Enthusiasts say the experience is always different and always exhilarating. When soaring, participants deal only with the "now"—all thought processes are involved in the moment. Glider pilots speak of entering the third dimension when they are soaring. The experience evokes strong emotional reactions from participants. Of course, the overwhelming emotion of first-timers is apprehension, but most are soon converts. To give a student the necessary hours in the air to enable him to solo takes a student 30 to 35 flights with an instructor and costs about a thousand dollars.

Bermuda High Soaring School is open Wednesday through Sunday from 10:00 A.M. to 5:00 P.M. and offers introductory rides (for those who want to enjoy a unique experience), instruction and sailplane rentals. The school can be contacted at: Thermal Trail, P.O. Box 1510, Lancaster, SC 29721-1510 or by calling (803) 475-7627. The school will not take anyone under

12, but students can solo when they are 14. Reservations are necessary for flights; you can also arrange to set up a camp and overnight beside the glider field. Visitors are welcome to watch the action at the glider field. You can obtain additional information on the Internet at www.glider.org.

Directions: From I-20 heading east toward Camden, take the Lugoff exit for Route 601 (this is before the exit for Camden). Take Route 601 north into Route 1, still heading toward Camden. Follow Route 1 past the Dupont Plant on your right and over the Wateree River Bridge. Take a left at the next light onto Springdale Road (there is a shopping center with a Wal-Mart at this intersection). Follow Springdale Road until it turns from a four- to a two-lane road. Then continue through the light and take a left at the second light onto Route 601/521 and continue for two miles. There is a sign for North Central High School on the left side of Route 601; take a right at the sign onto Lockhart Road and follow for 15 miles to the intersection with Route 341. Turn right on Route 341, then take the first left onto Mt. Pisgah Road and continue for eight miles. At the intersection with Route 903 turn right. Take Route 903 until you cross the county line to Lancaster County. There will be a fork in the road with a sign for Bermuda High Soaring. Take the right fork and your first right on Thermal Trail. Follow Thermal Trail along the field and turn left on Lift Lane to the entrance.

Boykin Mill and General Store

Vision of the Past

In 1755, William Boykin II settled, with his sons, in central South Carolina. His two-year-old son Burwell grew up to become a prosperous farmer in the region. He enlarged the family's holdings, obtaining land on the north and south banks of Swift Creek. The Boykins established a mill that became a community focal point.

Boykin Mill still uses water power and hand-dressed mill stones to grind whole-grain, meal and freshly milled grits as it has for over 200 years. In the early years, the Boykins also had a cotton gin and sawmill beside the gristmill. Today, there is a picnic area alongside the picturesque mill pond. You can purchase all the ingredients for your al fresco meal at the **Boykin Mill General Store**. The store's floor-to-ceiling wooden shelves are filled with an intriguing array of fresh farm products and gourmet jellies, jams and candies as well as freshly-ground grits and cornmeal from the Boykin family mill. There are a few tables plus some rocking chairs on the porch. Manager Alice Boykin, daughter of the wife and heir of Lemuel Whitaker Boykin II, prepares delicious southern-style breakfasts or lunches. The store is open Monday through Saturday from 7:00 A.M. to 6:00 P.M.

Across the street is the **Mill Pond Restaurant**, one of South Carolina's best dining spots. Like the mill and country store, it is on the National Register of Historic Places. The restaurant doesn't look imposing from the outside as it sprawls across three old buildings—a former post office and country store. But inside, the main dining room provides a splendid view of the pond. At sundown, you're apt to see waterfowl, including egrets and ibis. The middle building is a smaller dining room with a marble fountain counter that serves as a bar. The former post office is now the kitchen. The restaurant is open Tuesday through Saturday from 5:00 to 10:00 P.M.; for reservations call (803) 424-0261.

If you call ahead (803-424-4731) you can arrange to see the inside of the **Swift Creek Baptist Church** just up the road from the mill and country store. The two-story Greek Revival church, built in 1827, was renovated under the auspices of the South Carolina Department of History and Archives. The elegance of the church is in the simplicity of its design. The church is no longer consecrated and is used for meetings as well as weddings and concerts.

Boykin was the location of the last Civil War battle fought in South Carolina. A monument commemorating those who fought here on April 18, 1865 was erected by the 54th Massachusetts Infantry on the occasion of the 130th anniversary re-enactment. The battle was an uneven match between local Confederate forces and the numerically superior 2,500-man Federal force. Among the dead was the last Federal officer killed in the Civil War, Lieutenant E.L. Stevens. Burwell Boykin, a 15-year-old volunteer with the South Carolina Home Guard, fought in this battle. Boykin's father was Confederate Colonel Alexander Hamilton Boykin.

A 1760 slave house beside the mill has been converted to a shop called **The Broom Place**. Brooms are made with 100-year-old equipment. The brooms range in color and style, some purely decorative and others designed for hard use. You can purchase the brooms and other craft items Monday through Friday from 10:00 A.M. to 5:00 P.M. and Saturday 10:30 A.M. to 2:00 P.M.

Directions: From I-20 take Exit 98, Route 521 south. Bear right on Route 261 for four miles to Boykin and turn on Boykin Mill Road. You will be able to see the country store and mill from Route 261.

Camden Archives and Museum, Fine Arts Center of Kershaw County and Bonds Conway House

Rooting for the Past and Drawing Upon the Future

Camden, South Carolina's oldest inland city, is justifiably proud of its past. An overview of the city's history and heritage can be gleaned at the **Camden Archives and Museum**, ensconced in a 1915 Carnegie Library that served the public until 1973. Here they are not content with old photographs of popular landmarks—they have the actual items! You'll see the original town clock made by Isaiah Lukens of Philadelphia in 1825. There is also the life-size weather vane of King Haigler, Chief of the Catawbas from 1750 to 1763. He befriended the settlers of what was originally called Pine Tree Hill. This is one of the earliest tributes to a Native American in the country. A replica of this weather vane stands atop the tower of what was once the 1886 Opera House, but is now a downtown department store at 950 Broad Street.

The museum's collection includes a small case of prehistoric and early tribal artifacts including examples of Catawba pottery. There are also Civil War exhibits including reminders of the six Confederate generals from this part of South Carolina: Joseph Brevard Kershaw, James Chesnut, Zachary Cantey Deas, John Doby Kennedy, James Cantey and John Bordenave Villepigue. Another section of the exhibit space concentrates on the *Carolina Cup* and the *Colonial Cup* which are run in Camden (see Springdale Race Course selection). There are other local memorabilia including photographs of hotels that enjoyed a vogue during Camden's resort era, 1883 to 1944.

Many visitors plan a visit to the Camden Archives to do genealogical research. The collection includes manuscripts, city records, other public and private records, books, pamphlets, photographs, maps, newspapers and reference material for Camden, Kershaw County and South Carolina. In addition to genealogy, the archive covers architecture, biography, Camden authors, military, southern studies, cultural studies and health/medicine issues. Research requests by mail are handled by the staff for a nominal fee.

The Camden Archives and Museum is open Monday through Friday from 8:00 A.M. to 5:00 P.M. and on the first Sunday of the month from 1:00 to 5:00 P.M., except holiday weekends.

A few blocks away is the **Fine Arts Center of Kershaw County**, the only arts agency in the county. The center mounts 12 to 15 art exhibits annually plus presents a season of theatrical performances and musical programs. They offer two professional productions and two community efforts. The center also has classes and workshops in art, music and dance.

You can stroll across an expansive grassy field to the adjacent **Bonds Conway House**, built around 1812 by the first black citizen in Camden to buy his freedom. Bonds Conway was born in 1763 and was the property of Edwin Conway, who arrived in South Carolina in 1792 from Virginia. Bonds was the body servant of Edwin Conway's son, Peter.

In 1793, Conway sold Bonds (who was then 30 years old) to Zachariah Cantey, a prominent citizen of Camden. Attached to the bill of sale was the following affidavit: "I hereby acknowledge that I purchased the within named Negro man, Bonds, with his own money, of Mr. Edwin Conway, and do relinquish any title or claim to him." Bonds made his living as a skilled carpenter, purchased land and built this cottage. At his death he divided his land between his four surviving children. In 1977, the Bonds Conway House was purchased by the Kershaw County Historical Society and it was moved to its present location at 811 Fair Street, behind the arts center. The house was restored and serves as the society's headquarters. It can be toured on Thursday from 1:00 to 5:00 P.M.

If you are looking for a spot to dine in Camden, head for **Lucy's,** a local favorite at 1043 Broad Street. The restaurant is open for lunch Tuesday through Friday from 11:30 A.M. to 2:30 P.M. and for dinner Tuesday through Saturday from 6:00 to 10:00 P.M. The restaurant gets its name from a mysterious mannequin who is involved in a continuing window-front drama. Locals are alert to all the nuances of Lucy's romance with an admirer named Jeffrey, who is often found in the adjoining window. The two have even taken part in local parades. This is the local version of the popular coffee commercial with its long-running romantic entanglements.

The restaurant is decorated with family possessions of owners Billy Silver; his sister, Toni Partridge, her husband, Vint; and their son Prentiss Cook. The restaurant's namesake was Billy and Toni's mother. The focal point of the establishment is the soaring antique bar that came from the Willard Hotel in Washington, D.C. The menu changes daily and offers an enticing array of options. Often it includes the chef's signature dish Veal Lucy's, a delicate meat topped with sweet marsala and boursin cheese.

Directions: From I-20 take Exit 98, Route 521/601 north to Camden. The Camden Archives and Museum is on Route 521 which becomes Broad Street, at 1314 Broad. For the Fine Arts Center of Kershaw County make a right turn on Rutledge Street and a right on Lyttleton Street; the center is at 810 Lyttleton. The Bonds Conway House is behind the arts center.

Catawba Cultural
and Research Center

Ye Iswa

The earliest inhabitants of what is now known as Rock Hill, were part of the Chiefdom of Cofitachequi, an early name for the Catawbas. The first contact between the Catawbas and the Spanish was in 1521, when a Catawba speaker, Francisco of Chicora, was captured during a slave raid on the Cofitachequi. A Spanish trading expedition under Lucas Vasquez de Ayllon made contact with the Cofitachequi in 1526. By the time Hernando De Soto, the discoverer of the Mississippi River, headed north from Florida in 1540, the Catawbas were familiar with European trade goods and many had succumbed to European diseases. During the early years, settlers in the region abandoned the term Cofitachequi in favor of the term Catawba Nation. In 1715, during the Yamassee War when fighting broke out between the settlers and the Tuscarora and Cherokee tribes, the Catawbas fought with the Europeans.

Following the defeat of the warring tribes, the Catawbas offered sanctuary to those Native Americans whose tribes were so decimated by war they could no longer survive. Remnants of about 30 different groups joined the Catawbas including the Waxhaws, Watertee, Sarahs and the Sugaree. The Cheraw merged for a time but later reestablished their own group.

The loyal support of the Catawbas brought them close ties with the British, resulting in more trade but also in devastating diseases for the indigenous population. By the time of the American Revolution the territory of the Catawbas had been reduced from 55,000 square miles to a 144,000-acre reservation. During the American Revolution and the Civil War, Catawbas served in the military and were scouts for such illustrious generals as Francis Marion, Sumter and Lee.

Under the 1840 Nations Ford Treaty, the Catawbas surrendered their 144,00 acre reservation to South Carolina. Under the terms of the treaty, the Catawbas would be removed to an area far removed from settlement. In return they would receive a cash payment. No removal was ever instituted and no payment ever made since the U.S. Senate never ratified the treaty. Although the treaty was never implemented, the Catawbas had surrendered their land. A 630-acre tract of land, part of the original 144,000 acres in South Carolina, was purchased back by the tribe and set aside as the Old Reservation. It has been home to the Catawba Nation since the late 1850s. Visitors can learn more about the Catawbas when they visit the **Catawba Cultural and**

Research Center at the Old Reservation.

The Catawba Center has a small on-going exhibit with ceremonial tribal items and outstanding examples of Catawba pottery. The Catawbas are the only Native Americans east of the great Pueblos that has retained its aboriginal pottery-making skills in an unbroken line of succession. Catawba pottery can be traced to the Archaic period, circa 2,500 B.C. The methods used by the Catawbas utilize construction techniques from the Woodland and Mississippian periods. A unique element of the pottery is that it is made with clay taken from two distinctly different ancestral clay holes. Potters use the coiling method to make a pot or bowl then, after it is shaped, a rubbing stone creates the unusual velvet-like finish. The Catawbas do not fire their pottery in a kiln, but use the older method of burning it in a bonfire, sometimes repeating this step two or three times.

Catawba pottery has become increasingly valuable as purchasers realize the distinct craftsmanship involved in its creation. Catawba potters make animal effigies and animal effigy pots. The most traditional is the snake pot. Pottery is sold at the center's gift shop (which also has Native American books, literature and other crafts) and at the Museum of York County. The center is open Monday through Saturday from 9:00 A.M. to 5:00 P.M. Visitors are welcome to watch a video about the Catawba Indian Nation and are also able to do research at the Catawba Nation Archives.

The center holds educational programs for visitors and for Catawbas in the area. Here the tribal members study the remnants of their native tongue and attempt to pass their cultural traditions on to the next generation. There are currently 2,165 Catawbas on the official tribal rolls. The majority live on the reservation or within a 20-mile radius. Close to 100 families live on the reservation.

Visitors are welcome to take the half-mile nature trail after stopping at the center. The trail leads down to the river. There is an archeological site just off the trail. One of the best times to visit is the Saturday after Thanksgiving when the Yap Ye Iswa (The Day of the Catawba) Festival is held. This is the time to see ceremonial dances, hear traditional music and see crafts and exhibits. To find out more details call the center at (803) 328-2427.

Directions: From I-77 take Exit 79 (from I-77 north that will be toward your right, from the south toward your left). Take Dave Lyle Boulevard to Springdale Road and turn right. Continue on Springdale for approximately 1⅓ miles to Hopewell Road and turn left. Take Hopewell Road to Needy Store Road, approximately one mile, and turn left. Take Needy Store Road to Reservation Road and turn right. Continue on Reservation Road, and make a left on Indian Trail Road. Take Indian Trail Road to

Tom Steven Road and turn left. The Catawba Cultural and Research Center is the white building on the right at 1536 Tom Steven Road.

Cheraw Historic District and Cheraw State Park

"The Prettiest Town in Dixie"

In the northeast corner of South Carolina, a collection of towns and villages were, for a time, grouped together as the Old Cheraws and the "queen city" was **Cheraw**. A reporter once called it "the prettiest town in Dixie." Before 1700, there was a well-fortified Cheraw Indian hilltop village positioned where navigation began on the Pee Dee River. By the time a trading post was established around 1740, the village was virtually abandoned. Cheraw was settled by English and Irishmen who moved up river. An influx of Welsh Baptist settlers from Pennsylvania moved in some miles south of Cheraw. By 1750, Cheraw was one of six villages in the state to be noted on English maps of the colony.

Other immigrant groups also migrated to the region, a large section of which the British government granted in 1766 to Joseph and Eli Kershaw. The Kershaw brothers laid out Cheraw with broad streets and a town green. By 1830, triple rows of elms lined the streets. You can still see some of these trees on the median, particularly on Third Street. Many were cut when the water lines were added at the turn-of-the-century. Local lore has it that in its early days, Cheraw had a law ordering any drunk or disorderly person to dig up an elm from the forest and plant it in town. If that method was used to achieve the long line of trees, the town population must have been heavy drinkers.

During the American Revolution, Cheraw was occupied by British troops under Major McArthur. Conditions in Cheraw affected the soldiers and many Redcoats were stricken with malaria and smallpox and were treated in a hospital set up in **Old St. David's Church** by the 71st Highlanders. Many did not recover and are buried in a mass grave in the church cemetery; the officers were buried individually. General Nathaniel Greene's Patriot force camped across the Pee Dee River from Cheraw. His men, too, were treated in a make-shift hospital they established in the church. Old St. David's was the last Anglican church in the colony authorized by King George III. It was built between 1770 and 1774 (services began in 1772) on land Eli Kershaw set aside for that purpose. Thanks to reconstruction efforts, the interior with its box pews looks much as it did in its

Cheraw's Old St. David's Church, built between 1770 and 1774, was the last Anglican Church in the South Carolina colony to be authorized by King William III. During the American Revolution at different times the church was used as a hospital by British and Patriot troops.

earliest days. The church was disestablished in 1785 when British practices were unpopular. For several decades the church was used by the Baptists and Presbyterians—in fact, there was once an unseemly race between the two preachers to see who would arrive first and have the use of the church. In 1819 the Episcopal Church reclaimed Old St. David's.

The church was once again used as a hospital by both armies during the Civil War. Drawings from the period show rows of tents among the graves. General Sherman and 60,000 troops with 20,000 camp followers (more than were in any other South Carolina town) occupied Cheraw for several days while they waited for the Pee Dee River to drop so they could cross into North Carolina. Sherman, who made his official headquarters in what is now the Matheson Memorial Library, did not burn the town. Some think it was because there were so many Northern troops he was afraid his men would be harmed. In early March 1865, there was an accidental munitions explosion that destroyed the business district and even did some damage to Old St. David's. In 1867, the world's first Confederate monument was erected in the church cemetery, while Union troops still occupied the town. You can see the church's interior by picking up a key at the Greater Cheraw Chamber of Commerce at 221 Market Street.

More than 50 antebellum buildings survive in the 213-acre National Register Historic District. All of Cheraw's early public buildings survived the war and four of the most significant stand on the **Town Green**, the public space given to the community in 1768 by Eli Kershaw. In 1858 the Masons, the Cheraw Lyceum and the town built a two-story wooden **Town Hall**, though the weatherboards were cut to give the appearance of stone blocks. Four Doric columns extended up both stories in the front. The Masons met on the second floor. An opera house was downstairs. During the Civil War this building was also used as a hospital. You can see the interior during normal business hours.

The gentlemen of the Lyceum, who helped fund the town hall, were given a small brick building on the Green, formerly used as a chancery court. Here the Lyceum organization met and collected books for a town library. During the Civil War, the Lyceum served as a Confederate telegraph and quartermaster's office, then Union soldiers used it during Reconstruction. In 1962, the town gave the United Daughters of the Confederacy the use of the building as a museum. After renovation, exhibits were installed covering the Cheraw Indians, early settlement and shipping on the Pee Dee River as well as agricultural, industrial and domestic life in the 19th century. From the modern era, there is memorabilia from Cheraw's native son Dizzy Gillespie, the "King of Bebop" who was born here in 1917.

The 1836 **Market Hall,** also on the Green, resembles St. Peter's Catholic Church because they both were designed by Conloy Peter Lynch. The market has four Doric columns, a double stair leading to the second floor porch and a steeple. The first floor was a bricked open-market where crops and livestock were sold. Upstairs, the Chancery courts for the Old Cheraws met. The restoration work on this building received an award of excellence from the South Carolina Chapter of the American Institute of Architects.

The final, more modest, structure on the Green is the **Inglis-McIver Law Office**. It is not known when this tiny clapboard office was built, but in 1850 Alexander McIver purchased it. His son, Henry McIver, was Solicitor of the Judicial Court until the Civil War. After the war, he practiced law in Cheraw until he became an Associate Justice of the Supreme Court. His son, Edward McIver, who became a circuit judge, used this building as an office. The small office also served J. A. Inglis, a law partner of Chief Justice McIver. Inglis was chairman of the committee that drew up the Ordinance of Secession for South Carolina and introduced the resolution that South Carolina seceed from the Union.

Another Cheraw law office is worth a visit. You enter the **Pee Dee River Artifacts Room** through the Ingram Law Office at 204 Market Street. This one-room museum, open at no charge Monday through Friday from 9:00 A.M. to 5:00 P.M., exhibits objects recovered by scuba dive enthusiast Miller Ingram, Jr. He explored the wreck of the steamboat *SS Robert Martin* and displays its treasures, including a 300-pound anchor. British china from the 1740s and other items are also on display along with reminders of Sherman's brief occupation of Cheraw.

Many antebellum homes survive in Cheraw. The town's oldest house is "The Teacherage" at 230 Third Street. For many years it was a teachers' boarding house. Another house of note, the Lafayette House at 235 Third Street, was built in 1823 by Dr. William Ellerbe. Two years later, during General Lafayette's triumphant return to the United States, a public reception was held here for the French hero. Several of the houses in the old part of town are now bed and breakfast establishments. One is the antebellum mansion built by Civil War Captain John Craig Evans at 501 Kershaw Street; for lodging information call (803) 537-7733. This inn has private baths, working fireplaces and antique furnishings. Another B&B from the 1850s is called 505 Market Street; for details you can call (803) 537-9649. A third choice is 314 Market Street, a colonial revival house. To obtain more information about accommodations call (803) 537-5797. For a chance to explore some of the lovely private homes in the historic district, plan to visit the first weekend of April, when Historic St.

David's Parish has their Annual Spring Home Tour. For schedule details on this event call the Cheraw Visitors Bureau at (803) 537-8425 or the Chamber of Commerce at (803) 537-7681.

South Carolina's first state park is **Cheraw State Park** with its 360-acre Lake Juniper, a major draw for fisherman, swimmers and boaters. A championship 18-hole golf course skirts the lake and extends into the hardwood/pine forest. The longleaf pine is home to the endangered red-cockaded woodpecker. The upper end of the lake has towering trees and a cypress swamp; be sure to head in that direction if you rent a boat (though a pedal boat would be too much of a trip by foot power). Picnic facilities near a sandy beach are popular with area families. There are cabins, available by advance registration, and lake side campsites available on a first come/first serve basis; call (800) 868-9630 for additional information and cabin reservations.

Naturalists may also be interested in stopping at the **Cheraw Fish Hatchery and Aquarium**, six miles south of Cheraw. The hatchery raises large and smallmouth bass, channel and blue catfish and sunfish.

A short distance south of the fish hatchery, near the town of Patrick, is **Sand Hills State Forest**, that sprawls on both sides of Route 1. Its most unique feature is **Sugar Loaf Mountain**, which towers a hundred feet above the surrounding countryside. In early May the mountain laurel adds color along the forest trail. There are hiking, biking and horse trails, although there is no livery or mount rentals.

Continuing south on Route 1 to just north of McBee is the 45,586-acre **Carolina Sandhills National Wildlife Refuge**, where hiking trails provide an opportunity to spot and photograph a wide range of wildlife including the red-cockaded woodpecker, quail, wild turkey, pine barren tree frog, white-tailed deer and other native species. There are observation towers and photography blinds as well as interpretative displays.

Directions: From I-95 take Route 9 northwest past Bennettsville to Cheraw. Cheraw State Park is four miles southwest of Cheraw on Route 52. Cheraw Fish Hatchery and Aquarium is southeast of town on Route 1. If you are traveling from the south on I-95, exit at Florence and take Route 52 north.

Chester State Park, McGregor Ski Center, Cruse Vineyards & Winery and Callahan Farms

Outdoor Recreation and Sustenance

The 523-acre **Chester State Park** was once farm land but the gentle hills have been reclaimed by the forest and hardwoods are gradually replacing pines. The Caney Fork Falls Nature Trail leads through the forest to a man-made falls created by the dam that resulted in the 160-acre lake fishermen enjoy. Bass, brim, crappie and catfish can be caught here. Boat rentals let visitors get out in the lake and try their luck. There is also a fishing pier near the campground that has 25 sites available on a first/come, first/serve basis.

Chester State Park's recreational options include an equestrian show ring, an archery range with 28 field targets, a playground and a picnic area with shelters. There is no swimming in the park and no horse rentals. The park is open daily April through September from 9:00 A.M. to 9:00 P.M. The rest of the year it closes at 6:00 P.M. The office is open year round from 11:00 A.M. until NOON.

If you want to get out on a lake, stop at **McGregor Ski Center** just outside Chester. On a 120-acre private lake, where there are no other boats to interfere with the training sessions, water skiers, both beginners and tournament competitors, receive instruction. You can learn the basics or perfect stunt maneuvers. The center uses a MasterCraft Prostar 190 and the facility includes an electronically timed slalom course. There are private and group classes as well as slalom course pulls; to obtain additional information call (803) 581-3605.

After the activity at the state park or on the lake, you can relax and sample the gold medal wines at nearby **Cruse Vineyards and Winery**. Try their Chardonnay and Pinot Noir, or newer labels like the Seyval Blanc, Vidal Blanc and Chambourcin. Cruse's wine master also makes a line of blends. The winery is open 3:30 to 6:00 P.M. on Fridays and NOON until 6:00 P.M. on Saturdays.

Now that you have acquired wine to add to your dining pleasure, stop at **Callahan Farms** to pick your own fruit, flowers, herbs and seasonal vegetables to make your meal complete. The season starts on May 15th and continues through the fall. The farm also has a roadside market so you can just purchase fresh-picked produce. There is a gift shop with herbal products and locally made crafts. The dairy barn has been converted to a Scavenger's Den, rather like a permanent garage sale.

Directions: From I-77 take Exit 65, Route 9 west to Chester. Once in Chester, pick up Route 72; the park is three miles southwest of town. To reach the McGregor Ski Center, from Chester continue west on Route 9 until you see the sign indicating the ski center. Cruse Vineyards and Winery are off Route 9 before you reach Chester. From Route 9, turn right on Cedarhurst Road and then right again on Woods Road. Callahan Farms is three miles north of town at 1310 Peden Bridge Road.

Glencairn Garden and
Rock Hill Telephone Museum

A Rock in the Foothills

Rock Hill was named when the Columbia-to-Charlotte railroad was being cut through the white flinty rocks of the foothills. The newest and largest town in northern York County abounds with civic pride, in fact, there is a monument called Gateway in the town's center. A circular intersection is surrounded by terraced gardens. There are four 13-foot "Civitas" statues by artist Audrey Flack representing the civic spirit of residents past and present. Completing this city monument are two sixty-foot historic Egyptian Revival columns.

In Cherry Park, another city green space, there is a 14-foot bronze sculpture done by Mark Lundeen of the *Mighty Casey*, the legendary ballplayer immortalized in Ernest Lawrence Thayer's poem "Casey at the Bat." Appropriately, it stands at the entrance to the park's softball field.

If this is the most imposing public space, the most inviting is the award-winning six-acre **Glencairn Garden**, named for the ancestral home of garden donors, Dr. and Mrs. David Bigger. When this oasis was their private domain, it was surrounded by a six-foot fence that protected the deer and other animals living in their garden. A gift from a friend of an azalea plant introduced them to a species they grew to love. They ultimately collected over 3,000 bushes. The garden, which also has massed dogwoods and flowering shrubs, is at its best the last week of March through mid-April. Dr. Bigger opened it on Sunday afternoons as early as 1940. The Biggers deeded it to the city and it became a public garden in 1958. It remains as Dr. Bigger envisioned, except for the city-commissioned additions of a tiered fountain, a Japanese footbridge and the paved area. Depending on the time of your visit you may see massed camellias, irises and grape hyacinths, tulips, day lilies, wisteria, pansies, petunias, periwinkles and water lilies in bloom. The gardens are open daily at no charge.

In the downtown area you'll find the **Rock Hill Telephone Company Museum**. The best introduction is the eight-minute film about the history of the telephone industry and this independent company. The story starts in 1894 with the operation of a single telephone line between a local buggy company and the depot; soon there were 25 lines and the Rock Hill Telephone Company was established on December 10, 1894. The museum was once the company's central office and has an eclectic collection of old equipment, including a turn-of-the-century magneto telephone that visitors can use to talk to someone else in the museum. Young visitors enjoy trying their skills as an operator on a 1940s switchboard. Exhibits provide a glimpse of a century of changing communication technology extending up to fiber optics and fax machines. The museum is open at no charge on Monday, Wednesday, Friday and Saturday from 10:00 A.M. to 2:00 P.M.

If you want to obtain more information on the area stop at the visitors center at 201 E. Main Street. You'll find racks of brochures plus an engaging exhibit called "How We Got Here From There." This is an overview of transportation to and in the region starting with the rivers used by the Native Americans and progressing to the settlers' buggies. You'll see a dugout, covered wagon, locomotive, buggy and an Anderson automobile, built in 1916 by the former Rock Hill Buggy Company. The Anderson cost roughly $1,600 at the same time that Henry Ford's Model T was selling for $343. It's interesting to see the luxury car of its day. There are also photographs spanning Rock Hill's development.

Just six miles north of Rock Hill on the west shore of Lake Wylie is the **Catawba Nuclear Station**, named for the Catawba River that feeds the lake. The station's information center **EnergyQuest** is open to the public at no charge Monday through Saturday from 9:00 A.M. to 5:00 P.M. and Sunday NOON to 5:00 P.M. The center has film, exhibits and video games to explain nuclear power. On the second and fourth Wednesday of every month there are tours of the nuclear station for visitors over 18. For information, call (803) 831-3612. Another tour available upon request is of the Lake Wylie hydro facility. Tour participants walk the catwalk the length of the dam and then take an elevator down into the facility to see the working turbine and generator. You can also arrange an Operator Simulator Tour, which gives you a chance to watch nuclear operators and trainees practice in a control room simulator that is an exact replica of the Unit I Control Room. Outside the center there are picnic areas and nature trails.

Directions: From I-77 take Exit 79, the Dave Lyle Boulevard toward downtown Rock Hill. After about 3.5 miles, turn left onto

Main Street. Make the next left onto Caldwell Street. The visitors center and "How We Got Here From There" exhibit are in the Federal Building on the corner of East Main and Caldwell streets. For Glencairn Gardens return to Main Street and then make a left onto Elizabeth Lane, which will turn into Charlotte Avenue. Glencairn Garden is on the corner of Edgemont and Charlotte on the right. For the Rock Hill Telephone Company Museum, from I-77 take the Dave Lyle Boulevard for 3.7 miles and turn left onto Black Street. The museum is 100 yards on the left. To reach EnergyQuest, take Route 901 north from Rock Hill and it will merge with Route 161 eventually. Make a right onto Route 274 and, after traveling across Allison Creek Bridge, look to the right for Route 1132 and the Catawba Nuclear Station and its information center.

Historic Brattonsville

Doorways in Restored Village Open Into the Past

The Piedmont region of the Carolinas was the "back country " trade route for travelers from Pennsylvania and Virginia to North and South Carolina. The border between the Carolinas was unclear, since both colonies gave land grants in the same territory. The Catawba Indian Nation (see Catawba Cultural and Research Center) also had land holdings in this disputed area. A boundary survey was made in 1772. When the border was clearly established, the South Carolina portion was called the "New Acquisition" territory.

It was in this newly designated South Carolina land that William Bratton owned 200 acres (purchased in 1765). Bratton and his wife, Martha, moved to the region 25 years after the first settlers established a foothold in present York County. Some time between 1774 and 1780, the Brattons built a small pine and oak log cabin. Although they weren't the oldest residents, their house is the oldest surviving in the county. The two-room cabin was built on the Scots-Irish plan with a front door and an opposite door in the back wall. **Colonel Bratton's Home** was on a high ridge, with two springs located close to the cabin. There were gun ports in the loft, reflective of the lingering unrest and violence in the back country.

During the American Revolution, William Bratton was a South Carolina militia leader. He served in the field against the Cherokee and then was promoted to major when the Southern campaign began. This campaign was launched after the British captured Charleston on May 12, 1780. Despite Bratton's misgivings, the New Acquisition section of South Carolina was the only part of the state that did not accept British protection after the fall of Charleston. The Tories under the command of Captain Christian Huck of the Rocky Mount garrison were ruthless in their suppression of the Patriots. Huck destroyed Colonel

Glimpse what village life was like from the 1750s to 1850s at Historic Brattonsville. Visitors see a restored backwoods cabin, plantation house and 19th-century doctor's office. Sheep shearing is just one of the agricultural methods of the period that are recreated.

SOUTH CAROLINA DEPARTMENT OF PARKS, RECREATION AND TOURISM

William Hill's Iron Works, burning the iron works, the mills, plantation house and even the slave quarters. Huck also burned the residence of the pastor of the Fishing Creek Presbyterian Church and its library. His actions inspired hatred for him personally and for his troops. On July 11, 1780, Huck and his force, estimated at between 90 and 150 men, arrived at the Brattons' log house seeking Colonel Bratton. When Martha, who had insisted she did not know of her husband's location, replied that she would not tell them if she did, a reaping hook was placed at her throat. Only the intervention of Captain John Adamson, a Tory militia officer from Camden, prevented her death. She was viewed as a heroine for refusing to answer even in the face of death.

Huck and his men traveled north to the neighboring cabin of James Williamson who, along with his sons, were camped with the Patriots. Huck spent the night in the empty cabin and the following morning a battle was fought along the fence line outside the cabin. The Battle of Williamson's Plantation, is more popularly known as the Battle of Huck's Defeat. Many were killed while they slept and Huck himself perished in the fight. Martha Bratton saved the life of Captain Adamson, by telling the men how he had saved hers the night before. Although it had little significance in the larger campaigns of the war, this battle had a strong effect on the morale of Patriot and British supporters. Some historians consider this victory the first link in the chain of events in the south that led to the surrender at Yorktown; locally it culminated at the Battle of King's Mountain (see selection).

After the war, William Bratton became politically active, holding at least eight county or state offices. Martha bore eight children. During the late 1780s, Bratton operated a tavern in his home. Martha inherited the property at William's death in 1815. When she died a year later, their son Dr. John Simpson Bratton inherited the self-sufficient farm. His business acumen led to his eventual accumulation of over 8,000 acres of land, with cotton being the cash crop, and a sizeable slave holding. He also built a substantial frame house, the **Homestead**, with flanking brick cabins, including a detached brick dining hall at a cost of $1,650.00, a considerable amount for the time. He added a large number of log work buildings, including a building that housed the plantation's cotton gin, to the estate. With his wife, Harriet Rainey, they raised 14 children.

Dr. John Simpson Bratton ran his cotton plantation, served as a banker for his neighbors, maintained a medical practice and established a general store and post office at **Brattonsville**; the family holding had become a village. With seven girls to educate, Dr. Bratton remodeled his father's Revolutionary house, where he had been raised, into a girl's school that opened in 1840. A teacher moved to the village and the school grew to such an extent a new brick house (it was eventually a post Civil War home for Dr. Bratton's youngest son, Napoleon Bratton) was built.

When Dr. Bratton died in 1843, he failed to leave a will and an inventory was taken to divide the property between his wife and 13 of the surviving children.

In the 1840s, approximately 185 people lived in the village of Brattonsville. Among this number were family members, slaves, the overseers' families, teachers, students and skilled artisans. As the Civil War approached, Dr. Bratton's widow and children were all financially comfortable, although none had Dr. Bratton's wealth and prominence. In the 1850s, J.S. Bratton II built Hightower Hall, an imposing residence (not open for tours) which, like all the buildings in **Historic Brattonsville**, is on the National Register of Historic Sites.

Since the mid-1970s the village of Brattonsville has been under a preservation and reconstruction plan under the direction of the York County Historical Commission. Living history not only brings the social and political history to life, it also focuses on the agricultural life of the 1850s. Restored buildings include a backwoodsman cabin, McConnell Cabin, the 1780 Colonel Bratton Home, the 1823 Homestead House, slave cabins, brick kitchen, medical office and other support buildings. The buildings are filled with period furnishings and the grounds maintained as they once might have been.

Historic Brattonsville is open from the first Sunday in March through the last Saturday in November. It is closed on holidays. Tours are given Tuesday through Saturday from 10:00 A.M. to 4:00 P.M. and on Sunday from 2:00 to 5:00 P.M. A tour fee is charged. There is a well-stocked gift shop in the village. Throughout the year there are special programs and events in the village. Highlights include a reenactment of the Battle of Huck's Defeat in July, the Red Hills Heritage Festival on the second Saturday in October and Christmas Candlelight Tours in December.

Directions: From I-77 take Exit 82B, west on Chevy Road to Route 322. Eight miles south of Rock Hill make a left on Brattonsville Road and it will take you into the village.

Historic Camden
Revolutionary War Site

Cornwallis Comes to Town

Camden was established during the winter of 1733-34 as a frontier settlement called Pine Tree Hill. In 1758, Joseph Kershaw established a store in the village for a Charleston mercantile firm. By the 1760s, Kershaw had added grist and flour mills and a sawmill. This now thriving inland trade center was, at the suggestion of Kershaw, renamed Camden in honor of Charles Pratt, Lord Camden, a British Parliamentary champion of colonial rights.

Kershaw, one of the most prosperous men in town, began construction in 1777 of an elegant three-story home on Pine Tree Hill, a gentle rise overlooking Pine Tree Creek. In June 1780 before the house was completely finished, British Commander Lord Charles Cornwallis marched into town with his army and commandeered the Kershaw house for his headquarters though the Kershaw family was already in residence. Several days later, Cornwallis departed, leaving Lord Francis Rawdon in charge. Colonel Kershaw was taken prisoner and deported to Bermuda, while his family was for a time consigned to an upstairs room, then later moved to one of the outbuildings that had been used by a smallpox victim.

Camden was not a Loyalist stronghold when Cornwallis arrived. In fact, so strong was the town's Patriot sentiment, it had been selected in 1777 as a site for one of the state's powder magazines, which was built under Joseph Kershaw's supervision. The magazine was fortified by a moat and an earth wall, but these proved no match against Cornwallis' forces.

Two months after the British took over Camden, on August 16, American General Horatio Gates, with his Continental forces supported by militia, tried to retake the town. A battle seven miles north of Camden resulted in one of the worst defeats of the Revolution. Many of the untrained militia ran from the field. Gates also left the battlefield; only the Continental troops under Baron Johann de Kalb held their positions. De Kalb was mortally wounded with "eight wounds of bayonets and three musket balls." After the battle he was brought to Camden where he was treated for three days before he died. The British buried him with honors. He was initially laid to rest in the backyard of the "Blue House" then, in 1825, he was reinterred in front of Bethesda Presbyterian Church.

Although they handily won the Battle of Camden, the British did not rest on their laurels; instead they actually increased the fortifications around Camden. They built a new stockade wall around the town and added five small forts, or redoubts, around the perimeter. This effort paid off because in April 1781, when the new Southern Commander of the Continental army, General Nathaniel Greene, saw the strength of the British position, he decided against attacking. But Lord Rawdon and 900 men left the protection of Camden and attacked Greene's forces a mile north of town on Hobkirk Hill. This was a hard-won British victory. So great were the losses that the British abandoned Camden within days, setting fire to most of the town as they left.

You can see reminders of these tumultuous times at the **Historic Camden Revolutionary Site**. Pick up tour tickets and maps at the 1840 Cunningham House. Like many of the structures in this Colonial-era village, it was moved here from another location. The nearby 1789 one-room Craven House is post-Revolutionary War Georgian architecture. Architectural details like the window frames, closet doors, wainscoting and chimney wall paneling are original. A portrait of Baron de Kalb hangs in this building. You can see a ten-minute slide presentation in a replica of a colonial-era barn, complete with dogtrot, or open walkway, between the two wings.

The 1800 **Bradley House**, which originally stood nine miles east of Camden, is typical of early construction in the Pine Creek area. It retains many of its original features including flat sandstones, uncommon for the area, used in the chimney and the detailed dovetailing of the logs. Most of the 12-inch wide flooring is original to the house. Exhibits and dioramas on Camden's early history up to the time of Cornwallis' arrival are exhibited in the Bradley House.

The 1812 **Drakeford House** is another log structure. It is appropriate that Camden's role in the Revolution and the city's occupation be revealed in this home of a "gallant patriot soldier." Richard Drakeford lived 12 miles north of Camden and he prospered after the war. The house's inventory at his death in 1826 listed walnut tables, cupboards, four sets of bedroom furniture, a mirror, 11 chairs and other household furnishings that bespoke his success. The house is not furnished but instead exhibits detail Camden's role in the Revolution and the archaeological digs done on site. There is also a model of the Kershaw-Cornwallis House during British occupation. There is a replica of an early 19th century-blacksmith shed where craftsmen often demonstrate their skill. The McCaa House, built before 1825, was the office of Dr. John McCaa. It is scheduled for restoration.

At the top of Pine Tree Hill, you will see the reconstructed house of town founder Joseph Kershaw. After the British evacuation, Kershaw and his family returned and he died in the house in 1791. It stayed in the family until 1805, then saw a variety of uses:

orphan house, school and again a residence. Abandoned by the time of the Civil War, it was used as a Confederate warehouse and burned in 1865 during the Union occupation of Camden. Later archaelogical investigation revealed the foundation and, using two early paintings and an old photograph for reference, it was restored so that externally, it is an exact replica of Kershaw's 1780 Georgian-style mansion. The first floor is furnished with period pieces. One of the earliest known portraits of Andrew Jackson painted circa 1817 hangs in the reception room, a gift of the William Buckley family (they owned the 1854 Kamschatka house located in the historic district). The third floor, not open to the public, contains offices and a research library. Off the back porch is a formal garden typical of the 18th century. Several outbuildings, including the kitchen, were also revealed by archaeological digs, but these have not been reconstructed.

Archaeological investigation at the site has unearthed the town wall that surrounded Camden and the northeast and southeast redoubts. These have been partially reconstructed, as has the foundation of the powder magazine. George Washington, while making a presidential tour of the south, spent a night in Camden on May 25, 1791. He wrote in his diary that he inspected the remains of the "works and redoubts erected by the British."

After you have explored the 12 points of interest at the site, take the nature trail past small ponds and bogs to Pine Tree Creek. This creek supplied the water for Joseph Kershaw's mill and during high water was navigable to the Wateree River. It takes about 15 minutes to hike the trail.

There are guided tours of the 98-acre Historic Camden Revolutionary War Site from Tuesday through Saturday, and self-guided tours can be done daily. The site is open Monday through Saturday from 10:00 A.M. to 5:00 P.M.; on Sunday it opens at 1:00 P.M. Admission is charged for the guided tours only. A well-stocked gift shop with regional craft items is located in the Cunningham House. Throughout the year there are special events, living history and the early-November Revolutionary War Field Days Weekend, which includes daily battle skirmishes. Call (803) 432-9841 for a current schedule.

Be sure to drive through the **Camden Historic District**, which is listed on the National Register. There are 63 historic homes and sites that represent the various architectural styles of the antebellum south. There are also Victorian and winter cottages from the early 1900s. The town can also boast of its Robert Mills-designed courthouse. The architect wrote of this work: "An elegant court-house is now building here, which will be superior to the design of any in the state..." You can explore on your own by purchasing an audio tape or guide book and map available at the Kershaw County Chamber of Commerce at (800) 968-4037, or you can arrange a guided tour. Like Aiken (see selection), this is a community where horses are plentiful and riding a way of life, so much so that you will see street signs indicating, "Horses Forbidden on Sidewalks." The roads in many parts of the historic district are not paved in consideration of frequent horse traffic.

If you want to overnight in an historic property, stay at the **Greenleaf Inn**, 1310 Broad Street. The house was reputedly the Logtown store of Samuel Mathis, the first white male born in Camden. Later it was a girls' school. For a time it was the residence of Dr. G. R. C. Todd, a Confederate surgeon and the brother of Mary Todd Lincoln, the President's wife. It later was the home of Joshua Reynolds. Now it is the Greenleaf Inn; call for information about accommodations, (803) 425-1808.

Directions: From I-20 take Exit 98, Route 521/601 north to Camden. In 1.4 miles you will reach the entrance to the Historic Camden Revolutionary War site, which is on Route 521 at 222 Broad Street.

Kings Mountain National Military Park and Kings Mountain State Park

Overmountain Men Track Quarry

Five years after the American Revolution began, Lord Cornwallis turned his attention to the south, believing that these colonies were more loyal to the British crown. Initially, he was successful, capturing most of the south's Continental troops at Charleston in May 1780. Later in the month, he inflicted heavy losses on the Patriots in South Carolina at Waxhaws and, in August, at Camden. Most of South Carolina pledged loyalty to the British crown but the backcountry militia continued their resistance (see Historic Brattonsville selection).

Cornwallis appointed professional soldier Major Patrick Ferguson, a skilled marksman who entered the British army at age 15, as Inspector of Militia for South Carolina with orders to defeat the Patriots and recruit Loyalists. Ferguson fought a tough campaign, threatening to march into the mountains and "lay waste the country with fire and sword." His words garnered recruits—but for the Patriot force. Growing as it marched, the Overmountain men, with support from North and South Carolina militias, was 900 strong by the time they surrounded Ferguson's army at Kings Mountain on October 7, 1780.

The 60-foot-high rocky Kings Mountain was heavily wooded with a wide plateau at its summit. Ferguson had the high ground as the Patriot force formed a horseshoe at the base and began to climb the mountain. Although the Loyalists were able to fire down, the trees provided ample cover and the Patriots, as one soldier said, "took right up the side of the mountain and fought from tree to tree...to the summit." They withstood two bayonet charges and kept climbing. Ferguson was a highly visible mounted target, wearing a checkered hunting shirt with the silver whistle he used to maneuver his men clasped in his mouth. When he was shot and killed, his men raised a white flag, but the

Overmountain men from Tennessee, joined by the Carolina militias, turned the tide of the American Revolution at Kings Mountain. Authentically-costumed reenactors stage black powder shooting demonstrations during encampments.

SOUTH CAROLINA DEPARTMENT OF PARKS, RECREATION AND TOURISM

fighting did not end immediately. The excited Patriots continued to slay the disorganized Loyalist force. In all 225 Loyalists were killed, 163 wounded and 716 captured. On the Patriot side 28 men were killed and 62 wounded.

The men, exhausted from their hard march, slept alongside the wounded and dying. The Patriots were anxious to depart for home before Cornwallis sent a force in pursuit. Their haste prompted a lax burial with the dead buried in piles under logs and rocks. Some of the Patriots left, but a large force herded their prisoners to the Continental army post at Hillsborough, North Carolina. Reports tell of prisoners beaten and hacked to death with swords. There was also an impromptu trial by a committee of Patriot colonels, resulting in the hanging of nine prisoners.

The force that defeated Ferguson at Kings Mountain disbanded, but their victory revived Patriot spirits throughout the south. This battle is considered Cornwallis's, first misstep and it ultimately led to his surrender at Yorktown on October 19, 1781, just over a year later.

A free 18-minute film on this turning point in the American Revolution's southern campaign is shown at **Kings Mountain National Military Park** visitor center. Exhibits and maps provide additional details on the battle. A walking tour route has markers that provide details on where the Loyalists and Patriots were positioned. The National Park Service is also a partner in the **Overmountain Victory National Historic Trail**, which follows the route of the Overmountain men as they headed toward Kings Mountain. Cowpens is also a site along this route (see selection).

Adjacent to the national park in the foothills of the Appalachian Mountains is **Kings Mountain State Park**. Here you can get a glimpse of what the Overmountain and militia men were fighting for as you see an independent farmstead from the 1840s. The log and timber structures were moved here from elsewhere in the Piedmont region. A working farm once existed here, so the setting is entirely appropriate for the living history that is done by the park interpreter who lives at the farm and gives programs and demonstrations throughout the year. There are 14 points of interest around the farmstead. The Homeplace, built in rural York County reputedly by a returning Civil War veteran in the late 1860s, is the center of the farm's craft demonstrations. There is also a blacksmith and carpenter shop, sorghum mill and cooker, cotton gin, outbuildings and a vegetable and herb garden. In September, Pioneer Days feature muzzleloaders' competitions, crafts and pioneer games, country cooking and music.

The park offers a wide variety of recreational options. The three-mile Clarks Creek Nature Trail meanders through the hardwood forest to Kings Mountain National Military Park visitor center. For those who want to extend their hike, this trail becomes the 16-mile Kings Mountain Hiking Trail. There are also 20 miles of bridle trails, although its BYOH—bring your own horse. You can, however, rent pedal boats and enjoy the 10-acre Lake Crawford. There's also a swimming beach and bathhouse. The 65-acre Lake York has rental fishing boats and a fishing pier. Popular with fishermen, the catch is apt to include bass, bream, crappie and catfish. There is a 119-site camping area and two group camps with cabins, picnic areas with shelters, a playground and carpet golf. A log trading post sells groceries and other supplies, but it also houses a display of old farm tools and antiques.

Kings Mountain National Military Park is open 9:00 A.M. to 5:00 P.M. daily. Kings Mountain State Park is open daily April through September from 7:00 A.M. to 9:00 P.M. The rest of the year hours are 8:00 A.M. to 6:00 P.M.

Directions: From I-85 take Exit 2, Route 216 to the entrance to Kings Mountain National Military Park and, immediately following that, Kings Mountain State Park. From I-77 take Exit 77, Route 5 west to York. Head north out of York on Route 321 and make a left on Route 161. The parks are 14 miles northwest of York on Route 161.

Lancaster

Noted Native Sons

In **Lancaster**, even the casual visitor is soon acquainted with the town's illustrious citizens. Across the street from the county courthouse, muralist Ralph Waldrop has painted famous Lancastrians on a Dunlap Street building. The Wall of Fame includes: Andrew Jackson, seventh president of the U.S.; Charles Duke, astronaut; Nina Mae McKinney, actress and Broadway star; Elliott White Springs, textile industrialist whose family has provided numerous facilities in Lancaster County and Dr. J. Marion Sims, surgeon known as the "father of modern gynecology. "

The Lancaster County Courthouse, 1825-1828, was designed by Charlestonian Robert Mills, America's first native-born, professionally-trained architect. He is most noted for designing the Washington Monument, but he also did considerable work on the public buildings of South Carolina. The courthouse is constructed of approximately 300,000 bricks made on the site by slaves. During the Civil War, Sherman's soldiers destroyed most of the court records. They also stabled their horses nearby in the sanctuary of the 1862 Gothic-style Old Presbyterian

Church at 300 West Gay Street. The Union soldiers used the church's pews to hold grain and hay. Robert Mills also designed the Lancaster County Jail, 208 West Gay Street, which was used until 1979 and now serves as county offices. On the southwest corner of Catawba and West Gay streets, you'll see the renovated birthplace of Colonel Elliott White Springs, president of Springs Mills from 1931 to 1959. His house now serves as the town's city hall. Colonel Springs at one time had a private railway car that ran on the Lancaster-Chester Railroad and he listed exotic dancer Gypsy Rose Lee among the line's celebrity "vice-presidents."

East of Lancaster, off Taxahaw Road and Route 123, you will find **Forty Acre Rock**. This geological phenomena shows traces from the time when Native Americans ground corn in hollowed pits on the rock's surface. In the 1900s, promoters considered running an excursion train to this rock. At that time, the area still had traces of pre-Revolutionary earthen fortifications. The rock, which is only 14.7 acres, ranks as one of the largest and best developed flatrocks in the Piedmont. Growing on the rock are several plants on the endangered species list. Its size, history and plant life have contributed to the rock's designation as a national natural landmark. Forty Acre Rock is within the **Flat Creek Heritage Preserve**. This 1,425-acre preserve is the most diverse protected area within South Carolina's Piedmont region. The preserve includes granite flatrocks, a waterfall, cave, beaver pond, piedmont cove forest, piedmont flood plain, chestnut oak forest, upland pine/hardwood forest and other habitats. There are a number of trails through the preserve, which is open during daylight hours only.

The Lancaster area saw action during the Revolutionary War. In 1780, retreating troops under Colonel Abraham Buford were devastated by British troops commanded by Colonel Banastre Tarleton. The site on Route 9, west of its intersection with Rocky River Road, is now marked as **Buford's Massacre**. But the Patriots were avenged in August when Major William Richardson Davie surprised and annihilated a British force at Hanging Rock. Later that month, at the same spot, Colonel Hill, Colonel Irwin and Major Davie, all under the command of General Thomas Sumter, defeated the Prince of Wales' American Regiment and detachments of the 63rd and 71st Infantries under Major Carden. The Patriots lost 20 men and the British lost 130, including Tory sympathizers. The **Hanging Rock Battlefield**, on Route 521 south, has walking trails that let you cover the ground over which the battle raged.

You can pick up a walking tour map of Lancaster at the Chamber of Commerce, 604 North Main Street. The map has 19 points of interest along Gay and Main streets. You can also get a copy of *Points of Interest and Historical Markers* that covers the town and county.

Just outside Lancaster, you'll discover **The Wade-Beckham House**, one of the region's most delightful bed & breakfasts. It's a picture-perfect antebellum plantation house, situated on a hilltop surrounded by stately oaks. The oldest part of the house was built between 1802 and 1811. In 1915, the house was inherited by H. J. Beckham who doubled its size. It is now run by Beckham's granddaughter. The house contains antiques and artifacts associated with Wade Hampton. One of the plantation's out buildings serves as an antique store, open Monday through Saturday from 2:00 to 5:00 P.M. For information on accommodations call (803) 285-1105.

Directions: From I-20 take the Camden exit and head north on Route 601/521; continue to where Routes 601 and 521 diverge and bear left on Route 521 to Lancaster. For Flat Creek Heritage Preserve and Forty Acre Rock take Route 903 east out of Lancaster and when Route 601 converges with Route 903 continue on Route 601. Turn left on Nature Reserve Road; continue two miles and turn left on Conservancy Road, a dirt road. Proceed to the gate and take the trail from the parking area to Forty Acre Rock. For the Wade-Beckham House take Route 521 south out of Lancaster and bear right on Route 200. Look for the signs for the house on the left.

Landsford Canal State Natural Area

Spider Lilies, Rocky Shoals and Canal Connection

The river-based **Landsford Canal State Natural Area**, between Chester and Lancaster, has the state's best preserved remnants of a 19th-century river canal (South Carolina at one time had ten canals) with all the major structural features intact. Designed by Robert Mill, it was one of four canals built on the Catawba-Wateree rivers between 1820 and 1835. The canals allowed boats carrying staple crops from the Upcountry to coastal ports to bypass the river's rocky shoals.

The canal was built at Land's Ford, where the river is shallow and wider providing an advantageous crossing, or fording, point. In 1754, Thomas Land built a store and trading post at the crossing where settlers and Catawba Indians could exchange goods. The major trade item was fur. During the American Revolution, both British and colonial forces used the crossing. It was also used by both sides during the Civil War. Landsford Canal was built without benefit of power machinery. Workmen excavated the canal and cut and shaped the stones by hand. The first lock-keeper and bank ranger was John Carter. A bank ranger patrolled and maintained the canal banks.

Unlike some canals, no poles were used to power the slender, 60-foot long crafts (they were roughly the size of tractor trailers). The boats were towed by horse, mule, ox or were pulled by workers along the tow path. Today the tow path serves as a hiking trail that takes you past remnants of the canal—including lifting locks, culverts, guard locks, a basin and stone dam. The canal trail is three miles round trip and there is access to the trail from the beginning and the far end. There is a picnic area on the north side where the trail begins. Interpretive signs explain how the canal was built and operated. There are also remnants of a grist and saw mill built in 1810 by William Richardson Davie. When Union troops crossed at this ford in 1865, they burned Davie's home and mill. The location of the old river crossing, Lands Ford of Thomas Land's Crossing is near the remnants of the lifting locks about 1½ miles south of the picnic area. A lock-keeper's house from Great Falls, South Carolina was relocated at the park and now serves as a museum.

The park is also noted for its flora and fauna. The rocky shoals which necessitated the construction of the canal are home to one of the world's largest populations of rocky shoals spider lilies, Hymenocallis Coronaria. Peak blooming time is mid-May to mid-June. When they are in full bloom the phenomena has been described as looking like a white lace blanket thrown into the river. The park's trails offer a glimpse of the wildflowers and plants typical of the Piedmont region's pine-oak forests. The shoals also provide excellent fishing conditions for striped bass and bream. Bird watchers also frequent the park since it is on a major flight path and a wide variety of species can be observed. During one two-hour period, over 42 species of birds were observed.

The park is open Thursday through Monday from 9:00 A.M. to 6:00 P.M. There are picnic facilities, restrooms and a playground. A shelter and two-room 1790 settler's log cabin, moved to the park from elsewhere in the county, can be rented for group picnics and gatherings.

Directions: From I-77 take Exit 77, Route 21. Take Route 21 south for nearly 12 miles, turn left onto Landsford Road; the park will be two miles on your left.

Museum of York County

A One-Stop Safari to Africa

The **Museum of York County** really extends its scope! Its mission is to display the natural, cultural, historical and artistic heritage of York County and the surrounding upper Piedmont region of South Carolina, but it also exhibits a myriad of elements about the African continent. The African collection is so amazing, it is a misnomer to call this a county museum; it is closer to the Smithsonian than to most county museums.

In 1986, the Maurice H. Stans's Foundation purchased the 330 West African ethnographic objects in the Paul A. Clifford collection to enhance the Stans's collection, which already had an extensive array of life-size mounted African animals, representing more than 150 different subspecies. Collected by Stans and Clifford during the 1950s and 1960s, this is the world's largest collection of hoofed African animals on exhibition under one roof. Mounted is not the same as stuffed. When exhibitors mount an animal they build an armature on which the skin is stretched. Explanatory picture boards acquaint visitors with the methods used in mammal taxidermy, as well as how the diorama backdrops were created. The animals are depicted in their natural habitats of forest, grassland, desert and wetlands. There are also artistic and cultural artifacts from the African continent. These include ritual pieces, masks, jewelry, textiles, weapons and musical instruments.

Bears, wolves and mountain lions are exhibited in the Hall of Western Hemisphere. There is also a fascinating and educational exhibit featuring live regional snakes.

Contemporary art is not overlooked and the museum's galleries showcase regional artists. The museum serves as the repository for the Vernon Grant collection. This nationally-known artist and illustrator created the Kellogg Rice Krispies characters: "Snap, Crackle and Pop." Grant's promotional drawings were among the first to be directed toward children. For years his work appeared in a host of national magazines.

Vivid night skies are recreated in the museum's **Settlemyre Planetarium** where you can see programs ranging from the mysteries of the planets to extraterrestrial life. Planetarium shows are scheduled on the weekends; call ahead for current times and programs at (803) 329-2121.

The Museum of York County has more than 15 changing exhibits annually. They sponsor adult trips, summer camps, guest lecturers, films, art classes and planetarium shows. Among their most popular events are the Africa Alive! Festival and the Come See Me Art Show. The museum is open Monday through Saturday

10:00 A.M. to 5:00 P.M. and Sunday 1:00 to 5:00 P.M. It is closed on Christmas and Thanksgiving. Admission is charged. The museum store is filled with unique items including handmade jewelry and crafts, Catawba pottery and Vernon Grant items.

If time permits visitors are encouraged to explore the mile-long shaded nature trail through this southern outdoor habitat. Trees and plants in the hardwood forest are labeled and there are six specially planted garden areas. Picnic tables are set amid a grove of pines and oaks.

Directions: From I-77 north take Exit 82A and turn right on Cherry Road. At the first traffic light make a left onto Route 161 and then a right on Mt. Gallant Road. The museum is five miles on the left at 4621 Mt. Gallant Road in Rock Hill. From I-77 south, take Exit 82A and head west on Route 161; at the second light turn right onto Mt. Gallant Road and follow directions above.

Paramount's Carowinds

Winds of Whirl

Paramont's Carowinds is the most popular private family entertainment attraction in the Carolinas with more than 40 state-of-the-art rides and shows. The state line that runs through the 100-acre park is now enhanced by Paramount's Walk of Fame that encompasses 80 years of movie making history.

Many of the park's rides and subdivisions are inspired by Paramount movies. The 1994 release *Drop Zone* inspired the 174-foot Drop Zone Stunt Tower that gives riders the thrill of a high altitude free fall once experienced only by skydivers and stunt doubles. Riders are taken to the top of the tower at 16 feet per second, but they make the 100-foot free fall at 56 mph. Another movie, *Days of Thunder*, inspired the motion simulator theater. For more than 20 years visitors have enjoyed the giant, twin-racing Thunder Road, a classic wooden coaster and the untraditional Vortex, a stand-up looping roller coaster. There is also Animation Station, an interactive children's area featuring Hanna-Barbera characters, daily children's shows and a three-story climbing structure. In addition to the park's four splashing water rides there is the WaterWorks. The 12-acre water park has a 700,000-gallon wave pool, a lazy river, five water slides, a three-story water jungle gym and a $^{3}/_{4}$-acre area for young visitors, called SquirtWorks.

A perennial favorite landmark attraction at the park is the Skytower. Even those who don't care for park rides enjoy the gentle ride in its enclosed cabin to the 320-foot platform. From

Straddling the state line, Paramount's Carowinds has plenty of thrill rides, but none offers more white-knuckle excitement than the 174-foot Drop Zone Stunt Tower. Visitors can experience the thrill of a high altitude free fall.

here you'll have a bird's-eye view of the park and the rolling Carolina countryside. Equally accessible to all is the Carolina Sternwheeler, the three-deck river boat that navigates the lagoon in the center of the park. Young and old also enjoy the 1923 carousel with 68 exquisitely carved wooden horses.

The park is open weekends during the spring and fall and daily during the summer. For specific hours and admissions call (800) 888-4386, (704) 588-2600 or (803) 548-5300. To avoid crowds plan a weekday visit. There is a separate admission to the big-name concerts in the park's 13,000-seat Paladium Amphitheatre, but within the park there are a wide variety of shows included in the admission. Like all theme parks there are plenty of shops and eating venues.

Directions: On I-77 at the South Carolina/North Carolina border take Exit 90 and follow Carowinds Boulevard west to the park's main entrance. The park is located approximately 12 miles north of Rock Hill.

Ridgeway Walking Tour and
The South Carolina Railroad Museum

Railroad Impetus to Town Growth

Virginians settled in the central portion of South Carolina in the late 1700s, at the conclusion of the American Revolution. Another influx to this region occurred in the early 1800s when Charlestonians fled a particularly severe malaria outbreak. But the settlement known as New Town didn't really grow until the Charlotte and South Carolina Railway decided against a Camden route for their line, favoring instead the "ridge way." This brought new settlers, new businesses and a new name—**Ridgeway**.

You can pick up a walking tour map of Historic Ridgeway at the former town well and police station in the center of town on South Palmer Street (which is Route 21). There are 28 points of interest on the tour, including numerous private homes that are not open to the public. You may notice a striking similarity between the 1904 D.W. Ruff house (#1 on the tour) and the 1906 J. Spann Edmunds house (#7). When the Ruff house was built, a local architect was so impressed with its style, he copied the design when he built a house just down the street.

Another 1906 home is the Robert Charleton Thomas Victorian house (#2). Notice the distinctive tower and oversized porch. In the corner of the front yard near the street, you'll see a large, granite mounting block that was used by women to climb in and out of carriages. Queen Anne style is used for the 1895 Reid H. Brown one-story house (#5). One of the most striking homes in

Ridgeway is the 1910 Charles Wray house (#10) with its two-story columns and porches. Wray was killed with his wife and child in a tragic train accident, and local legend claims he can still be seen standing on the porch looking down the tracks for his family. One additional house that should not be missed is the 1856 Century house (#13). After burning Columbia, Union soldiers stopped at this house and demanded to see owner James Coleman, who was ill and bedridden. Coleman's wife met the Union officer in charge and sought his protection, thus saving the house.

A number of stops on the tour map are in the small business district. The Thomas Company Store dates back to 1880. A wood-stove still stands in the middle of the store. Six generations of Ruffs have been entrepreneurs in Ridgeway; there is the 1900 Ruff Furniture Store, the 1901 Ruff's Old Store and the 1947 Ruff's Gin House. The main drag boasts a first class dining establishment, the Wood's **Gold Creek Restaurant**; it's well worth a detour to dine here.

Not far from Ridgeway, a group of enthusiastic volunteers spend their leisure time restoring an extensive collection of old trains. These railroad buffs established **The South Carolina Railroad Museum** in 1973. A decade later the group received a donation of the old Rockton and Rion Railway, which they renamed the Rockton, Rion and Western Rail Road. After much work, two miles of the 11.5 mile line are operational. Rolling stock in varying states of repair sit on the tracks. Long range plans call for the restoration of these cars, the construction of a locomotive shop and educational excursions. Today you can take short rides on their restored train and chat with the volunteers.

Train rides are offered on the first and third Saturdays of the month from early May through late October. The excursions last 45 minutes and run rain or shine. Call for up-to-date schedule and fare information at (803) 776-9214 or (800) 968-5909.

Directions: From I-77 take Exit 34 and follow Route 34 Business into Ridgeway; turn left at the stop light. The first house on the left is the first stop on the tour map. (To obtain tour maps, call (803) 337-2213 or 635-4242.) For the South Carolina Railroad Museum take Route 34 west instead of east, head toward Winnsboro (from I-77 you will travel west 4.4 miles). Turn left onto Industrial Park Road and make a right into the museum parking area.

Rose Hill Plantation State Park, Juxa Plantation and The Inn at Merridun

Trio of Southern Plantations

Sprawling plantations were emblematic of the antebellum south. With the invention of the cotton gin in the 1790s, these agricultural strongholds expanded to thousands of acres. The plantations were often mini-communities with multiple buildings, sometimes even including a small church, but the crown jewel was the plantation house.

Rose Hill Plantation, the home of secessionist governor William Henry Gist is just such a showplace. It was built between 1828 and 1832 on land his father, Francis Fincher Gist, inherited. The mansion was named for the governor's rose garden, which was planted on three sides of the house. The governor personally raised more than 100 rose bushes in his garden. The brick house was designed in the Federal style. Later double porches were added in the front and back and the facade was stuccoed. This cotton plantation once covered more than 8,000 acres.

Gist's father, who was in politics, died while serving as a member of the state House of Representatives. Gist attended South Carolina College in Columbia, then read law and was admitted to the bar. He followed in his father's footsteps and was elected to the state House of Representatives in 1840, serving two terms before moving to the Senate where he served from 1844 to 1856. In 1858 he became governor. When his term expired he served as a delegate to the convention that decided South Carolina would secede from the Union. For the first year of the war, an executive council, upon which Gist served, replaced the state's legislative branch. Gist left public office when the council disbanded in 1862, spending the remainder of the war at Rose Hill.

Gist married Louisa Bowen the year he began work on his plantation house. She died after the birth of their second child, before the house was complete. The year Rose Hill was finished, 1832, Gist married Mary Rice. This was the year he also began his lucrative agricultural operations. During the Civil War, his son and namesake was killed. Gist took the amnesty oath and received a pardon from President Andrew Johnson in 1865. By 1870, the financial aftermath had taken its toll on Rose Hill, which had only a quarter of its original acreage. Gist died at Rose Hill on September 30, 1874. After the death of Mary Gist, the estate was divided among the many grandchildren. The house fell into disrepair, and parts were even used to store hay. Restoration work began in the 1940s and in December 1960 Rose

Hill became a 44-acre state park.

When you tour the Gist mansion you will see family furnishings, particularly in the bedrooms, and period pieces which were selected from estate inventories, particularly that of Mary Gist. In addition to the main house, the kitchen building is also open. There are several other dependencies including a slave house.

Rose Hill Plantation State Park is open Saturday from 11:00 A.M. until 4:00 P.M.; on Sunday it opens at NOON. The house is also open Monday, Thursday and Friday from 1:00 to 4:00 P.M. The grounds are open Thursday through Monday from 9:00 A.M. to 6:00 P.M. There are picnic facilities. As you explore the grounds notice the boxwood in the rose gardens. It is done in the style of an old English formal garden. The grounds have magnolia trees planted by William Henry Gist in 1835. The park also has a nature trail, picnic facilities and interpretative programs.

There are two plantations in the Union area (the town got its name from the old Union Church and not from the Federal Union) that accommodate overnight guests. **Juxa Plantation** was built in 1828 by the Gregory family on land granted to them by King George III in 1776. The family prospered by growing cotton and corn, but prosperity ended in 1844 after four years of drought. Today, the estate is owned by the Bresse family who

Travelers can overnight at Juxa Plantation, built in the early 1800s.

have restored the property and furnished the house with antiques, many of which are for sale. Juxa is also a bed & breakfast with three guest rooms.

Juxa Plantation and its surrounding 120 acres is open daily for tours. The estate is pet-friendly and also has facilities for horses. Many of the original outbuildings remain, such as the kitchen, well house and tool shed. There are restored gardens, a grape arbor and a gold fish pond as well as an antique & gift shop. There is also a tea room where groups can schedule brunch, lunch, tea or dinner. For more information or reservations, call (864) 427-8688.

The Inn at Merridun is an antebellum country inn, which boasts that it was one of the most beautiful colonnaded houses to survive General Sherman's destructive swath through the region. There are five distinctly different bedrooms. Overnight guests are served an evening dessert and a full gourmet breakfast. They are also welcome to explore the nine acres of wooded grounds and relax in the parlor and library. Merridun hosts Wednesday lunches from 11:30 A.M. to 1:00 P.M. and Sunday brunches at 1:30 P.M., call owners Jim and Peggy Waller at (864) 427-7052 for additional information and reservations. Tours are given by appointment only.

Directions: From I-85 take Business Loop 85 and then Exit 5 in Spartanburg and head southeast on Route 176 past Jonesville and Union. Rose Hill Plantation is eight miles south of Union off Route 176. Turn right on Sardis Road; the plantation is at 2677 Sardis Road. For Juxa Plantation, when Route 176 reaches Union take Route 215 south of town for five miles and Juxa is on the left on the corner of Route 215 and Wilson Road. For The Inn at Merridun from Route 176 in Union, take the fourth stop light and make a right on Rice Avenue. After 3/4 mile make a right on Hicks and bear right into the driveway of Merridun.

Springdale Race Course

Cups Here Literally Run Over—Over Fence, Field & Stream

Two of the most prestigious races on the National Steeplechase and Hunt Association calendar are run at **Springdale Race Course**: the Carolina Cup in late March and the Colonial Cup in November.

Steeplechasing got its start in Ireland in 1752. The first race was reportedly between Mr. O'Callahan and Mr. Edmont Blake who raced four and a half miles from Buttevant church to St. Mary's in Doneraile. The latter's tower was called St. Leger

Steeple. These early races used the church steeples as landmarks and participants vied to see who would first reach the steeple. By 1800, midnight steeplechases frequently followed parties, often with catastrophic results. It was in 1802 that Camden began holding steeplechase races—but at a far more reasonable hour.

Flat racing has always been dependent upon betting for its economic survival, but steeplechasing was as much sport as wager. In 1908, when betting was made illegal at the nation's racetracks, steeplechasing continued to be popular and saved sports racing. It developed a popular following that continued for decades. It was in the late 1920s that Springdale Race Course was developed. The course is two and three-quarters mile long and has 17 natural brush fences.

Camden's mild climate and near-perfect conditions made it an ideal training area. Battleship, the first American winner of England's prestigious Grand National, trained at Springdale. Four-time winner of the coveted Eclipse Award, Flatterer, also trained here. In 1983, Mrs. Marion duPont Scott willed the entire Springdale complex to South Carolina, along with a one million dollar endowment for its upkeep. In recent years, the course has not just been kept up, it has been substantially enhanced by the addition of towering grandstands with 250 boxes and an expanded infield. Onlookers now have a spectacular view of the 500-acre championship course.

Marion duPont Scott, who owned a race estate in Camden called Holly Hedge, was also responsible for establishing the **Colonial Cup** (it was part of the state's 300th birthday celebration). She bankrolled the first international Colonial Cup in 1970, offering a $100,000 purse. This was the highest purse in steeplechasing and made the race an immediate success. The Colonial Cup is dedicated to her. The Colonial Cup is also noted as the first hunt meet in the country to have off-track betting and the first to have a photo-finish camera.

The Colonial Cup is held in mid-November and it is an exciting spectacle to watch. The track gates open at 9:30 A.M. and during the morning activities on the field include terrier races and children's races and games. Tailgate parties are popular, but the crowd gathers for the running of the first race at 1:30 P.M.

The **Carolina Cup** is an older contest, dating back to 1930. It is one of the biggest events in the state—a sporting and social rite of spring. It's a fashion preview of the season without the runway, a time of elaborate tailgate parties and elegant buffets and a sporting event that draws 40,000 race enthusiasts. The victory cup was handcrafted in Ireland in 1704 making it one of the oldest trophies in the world. Gates open for this festive day at 9:00 A.M. and the first race is at 1:30 P.M.

Yo u 're welcome to stop at the track to watch the early morning thoroughbred workouts. There are usually horses out on the track until 10:00 A.M. Kershaw County also holds shows, polo matches and trials at several of the nearby equine facilities. The track is open daily for viewing and for special events. For additional information call (803) 432-6513. Even the big races are accessible to the general public; call for specific dates and track admission (it is very reasonable).

Directions: From I-20 take Exit 98, Route 521/601, north to Camden. Make a left on Knights Hill Road. Springdale Race Course is at 200 Knights Hill Road.

Winnsboro Historic District and Fairfield County Museum

Time Never Stops Here

Winnsboro, named after Revolutionary War hero Colonel Richard Winn and originally spelt "Wynnsborough," was founded in 1775. Five years later during the American Revolution, Lord Cornwallis occupied the town for three months. Local legend claims that it was Cornwallis who named the county. When observing the countryside, he commented, "What fair fields." In 1785, Winnsboro was chartered as a town and today it is, as it has been for almost all of its history, a county seat. There are more than 100 buildings that are over 100 years old.

A walking tour brochure of the **Winnsboro Historic District** and the surroundings that provides details on 51 points of interest can be obtained at the Fairfield Chamber of Commerce in the Town Clock at Congress and Washington streets. The **Town Clock Building**, a town landmark, was built in 1834 after the South Carolina General Assembly authorized Winnsboro to erect a market house, "no more than 30 feet in width," in the heart of the community. According to local lore, it took 50 wagons three weeks to haul the bricks from Charleston that were needed for construction. Although the tower was part of the original structure, the clock, made in Alsace, France, was not added until 1837.

The bell for the clock was also made in France and reputedly had a silvery tone. Vigorous ringing to warn of a fire in 1895 cracked the bell. Though it was repaired in Philadelphia, it had lost its tone (many felt that they had not gotten their original bell back). This is the longest continuously running town clock in the country.

Town clocks played an important role for many decades. They were the only means of alerting citizens to danger. They rang as an alarm for curfews, fires and other dangers and to herald announcements. They also proclaimed "butchering days" when fresh meat was available at the market. Legend claims that local dogs raced to the sound of the bell, creating easily discernible paths, because they associated it with scraps of meat.

Also on the town square is the Fairfield County Courthouse designed by Robert Mills in 1833. Mills was not responsible for the flying staircase entranceway that you see today; that was added by G. Thomas Harmon in 1939, who also added two rear wings. The courthouse has records dating back to the 1730s. They survived the Civil War because Sheriff Elijah Olliver put the county papers into bags and tied them around the waist of his wife and daughters to smuggle them out under the watchful eyes of the Northerners. These records are now in the Clerk of Courts Office.

Another government building of interest is the Winnsboro Post Office at Congress and College streets. A New Deal mural is painted above the postmaster's office door. Between 1937 and 1942, artists, mainly Northeasterners, painted murals and did sculptures for 15 rural South Carolina post offices and one courthouse. The one you'll see here was done by Auriel Bessemer in 1938 and is called *Southern Industrial Tapestry*. The Winnsboro walking tour also includes five churches, four church cemeteries and a Methodist parsonage.

Twenty-eight homes have either architectural and historical interest or both. Only one, now a museum, is open to the public. On East Moultrie Street, the Winn-Hannahan House, built after the Revolution, is one of the town's oldest homes. The first owner was John Winn, the brother of the town founder. Another home associated with the Winns is the Bratton House at Bratton and Zion streets. Richard Winn bought the property in 1777 and gave the house and land to his daughter Christina, who married Colonel William Bratton of York County. During the Civil War, Fairfield's leading general John Bratton lived here. When Union troops arrived in Winnsboro, they rode their horses through the hall and vandalized the house.

One of the town's most elegant mansions is the Boyleston House on South Congress Street. Built in 1853 on four acres by Robert B. Boyleston, it is noted for its classic look both inside and out. From 1906 to 1910, this was called the Colonial Inn, a hide away for hunters and Northerners escaping harsh winters.

On the southeast corner of East Washington and Zion streets is a home whose original one-story section was built around 1820 by Revolutionary War hero John Buchanan, who willed it to his niece Mary Ann Buchanan Carlisle. It is called the James H. Carlisle Birthplace because this educator, humanitarian and religious leader was born here in 1825. Carlisle attended the 1860

Secession Conference and was elected to the state legislature in 1864. Another home owned and occupied by John Buchanan is on Zion Street. It is called the Cornwallis House because it reputedly served as headquarters for Lord Cornwallis during his occupation of Winnsboro from October 1780 to January 1781.

John Buchanan was a friend of General Lafayette, and gave him the use of one of his slaves, Pompey Fortune. After the Revolutionary War, Buchanan gave his slave the area west of Park Street that is now the Fortune Springs Park. When Lafayette returned to America in 1825, Pompey Fortune traveled to Columbia to see him. Today, the park is a delightful area in which to stroll. There is a pond and beautiful old trees that provide welcome shade on hot summer days.

The Federal-style Cathcart-Ketchin house on Congress Street was built in 1830 by Richard Cathcart. From 1852 until the Civil War, the house was a girls school operated by artist George Ladd and his wife Catherine. Mrs. Ladd is said to have the saved the house from the Union torch by appealing to them to "please spare my girls." From the 1870s until 1911, it was the home of Priscilla Ketchin and her family. Now it serves as the **Fairfield County Museum**. The downstairs rooms are furnished as a house museum with a Victorian and Empire period parlor. Upstairs are exhibit areas with Native American artifacts, quilts, antique toys, pressed flowers, period attire and a collection of First Lady dolls. On the third floor is a military collection. The museum also has a genealogy room which is open on Wednesday. The museum is open at no charge Monday, Wednesday and Friday from 10:30 A.M. to 12:30 P.M. and from 1:30 to 4:30 P.M. It is also open at other times by appointment; call (803) 635-9811.

If you want to get a bite to eat stop at the **News & Herald Tavern** or **Hoot's**. For those interested in staying overnight in the heart of Winnsboro's Historic District try the **Songbird Manor Bed & Breakfast**, 116 North Zion Street. This lovely old house has a wrap-around porch and was constructed from pressed bricks brought from England as ship's ballast and carried by wagon from Charleston. This was the first house in town with indoor bathrooms. In fact, three of the five guest room baths still have their original tubs. For more information, call (803) 635-6963.

Fifteen miles east of Winnsboro is 238-acre **Lake Wateree State Park** on Desportes Island in Lake Wateree, one of the state's oldest and best fishing lakes. Frequent catches include black crappie, largemouth bass, striped bass, catfish and bluegill. There are no boat rentals but there is a concrete boat ramp. The park also has a tackle shop, 72-site camping area, playground, picnic facilities and a nature trail. The 1.5-mile Desportes Island

Nature Trail winds through flat, swampy terrain so hiking shoes are advisable. Also consider a liberal application of bug repellent. The trail provides plenty of opportunities to spot wildlife. The park is open daily year round. Daylight savings hours are 6:00 A.M. to 9:00 P.M.; at other times it closes at 6:00 P.M.

Directions: Traveling south on I-77 take Exit 48 to Route 200. After 11 miles it will intersect Business Route 321 in Winnsboro; turn left on Route 321 (which becomes Congress Street) and continue to the second traffic light. This will put you at the Town Clock and Court House in the center of town. If you are traveling north on I-77, take Exit 34 and turn left on Route 34. After nine miles you will intersect with Business Route 321 at the south end of Winnsboro. Bear right and follow Route 321 into the city where it will become Congress Street. At the third traffic light you will be at the Town Clock. A turn on the south side of the clock will lead you one block into the historic district on North Zion Street. For Lake Wateree State Park from I-77, take Exit 41 and turn on Route 41. Directional signs will point east to the lake. Follow Route 41 until it deadends into Route 101. Turn right on Route 101 and follow it across Taylor's Creek Bridge to the entrance to the state park on your left.

Regional Tourism Contacts For Olde English District (Area Code 803)

OLDE ENGLISH DISTRICT TOURISM COMMISSION
P.O. Box 1440 , 107 Main St.
Chester, SC 29706
385-6800, (800) 968-5909, fax: 581-8977

CHERAW VISITORS BUREAU
221 Market Street
Cheraw, SC 29520
537-8425

GREATER CHERAW CHAMBER OF COMMERCE
221 Market Street
Cheraw, SC 29520
537-7681

CHESTER COUNTY CHAMBER OF COMMERCE
P.O. Box 489
Chester, SC 29706
581-4142, fax: 581-2431

CHESTERFIELD CHAMBER OF COMMERCE
P.O. Box 230
Chesterfield, SC 29709
623-2343

GREATER CLOVER CHAMBER OF COMMERCE
P.O. Box 162
Clover, SC 29710
222-3312

FAIRFIELD COUNTY CHAMBER OF COMMERCE
Congress Street, P.O. Box 297
Winnsboro, SC 29180
635-4242

FORT MILL AREA CHAMBER OF COMMERCE
P.O. Box 1357
Fort Mill, SC 29715
547-5900

KERSHAW CHAMBER OF COMMERCE
P.O. Box 441
Kershaw, SC 29067

CAMDEN/KERSHAW COUNTY CHAMBER OF COMMERCE
724 S. Broad Street, P.O. Box 605
Camden, SC 29020
432-2525, (800) 968-4037

LAKE WYLIE CHAMBER OF COMMERCE
P.O. Box 5233, SC Route 49
Lake Wylie, SC 29710

LANCASTER COUNTY CHAMBER OF COMMERCE
604 Main Street, Drawer 430
Lancaster, SC 29721
283-4105

PAGELAND CHAMBER OF COMMERCE
P.O. Box 56
Pageland, SC 29728
672-6400

ROCK HILL AREA CHAMBER OF COMMERCE
115 Dave Lyle Blvd., P.O. Box 590
Rock Hill, SC 29731
324-7500

TEGA CAY CHAMBER OF COMMERCE
Four Tega Cay Drive
Tega Cay, SC 29715
548-2444

UNION COUNTY CHAMBER OF COMMERCE
P.O. Box 368
Union, SC 29379
(864) 427-9039

GREATER YORK CHAMBER OF COMMERCE
P.O. Box 97
York, SC 29745
684-2590

YORK COUNTY CONVENTION & VISITORS BUREAU
201 E. Main Street, P.O. Box 11377
Rock Hill, SC 29731
329-5200, (800) 866-5200, fax: 329-0145

Olde English District Calendar of Events (Area Code 803)

Late February
Africa Alive. A showcase of African heritage encompassing music, dance, storytelling, crafts and exhibits at the Museum of York County. Rock Hill, 329-2121.
Late March
Nations Bank Carolina Cup. Elaborate tailgating picnics enliven this annual steeplechase race at Springdale Race Course. Camden, 432-6513.
Mid-April
People's Craft Market. Approximately 75 Carolina and other regional crafters participate in this event. Rock Hill, 329-5645.
Cheraw Spring Festival. Living history, arts and crafts, a quilt show, road race, entertainment and food concessions are all part of this city-wide event. Cheraw, 537-8425.
Come-See-Me Festival. An international food fair, garden tours,

parade, concerts, fireworks, art exhibit and 80 coordinated events are part of this popular event. Rock Hill, 324-7500.

Mid-May

Carolina Legends Bluegrass Festival. Old-time country, bluegrass and gospel music are enjoyed at this event. There is also arts and crafts, children's activities and food. Lancaster, 285-7451.

Catawba Militia Revolutionary War Encampment. Military drills, musket and rifle demonstrations and an 18th-century encampment mark this event at Kings Mountain. Blacksburg, 936-7921.

Mid-July

Re-enactment of the Battle of Huck's Defeat. Living history depiction at Historic Brattonsville of the social and military events that occurred near the Bratton home in July 1780. McConnells, 684-2327.

Mid-August

Overmountain Victory Trail Encampment. Interpretive talks and weapons demonstrations bring to life the march made by the Overmountain Men at Kings Mountain, an event that turned the tide of the American Revolution. Blacksburg, 936-7921.

Late August

Summerfest. A classic car show, entertainment on four stages, crafts and food fair as well as other activities are all part of this event. York, 684-2590.

Early October

Jubilee Harvest of the Arts. Regional performers and national recording artists participate in this arts festival. Rock Hill, 328-2787.

Guilford Militia Encampment. An 18th-century encampment is brought to life with military drills and musket demonstrations at Kings Mountain National Military Park. Blacksburg, 936-7921.

Anniversary of the Battle of Kings Mountain. Re-enactment of the battle that turned the tide in the American Revolution. Blacksburg, 936-7921.

Mid-October

Red Hills Farm Day. Historic Brattonsville comes alive with history demonstrations, folk music, hands-on heritage farm activities such as butter-making, plowing and cotton ginning. McConnells, 684-2327.

Hillarity. An international food court, musical entertainment and children's activities are part of this special event. Chester, 581-2222.

Early November

Old Fashioned Christmas Craft Festival. More than 80 crafters sell handmade items. Rock Hill, 329-5645.

Colonial Cup: A day in the country with terrier trials, a market and the prestigious steeplechase race at Springdale Race Course that often determines the champion and winner of the NSA's Eclipse award. Camden, 432-6513.

The Festival of Lights. New Heritage USA has one-million lights in this holiday exhibit which includes a Macy's animated Nutcracker scene and a Nativity scene with live animals. Fort Mill, 547-8000.

Early December

Christmas Candlelight Tour. Bratton Plantation at Historic Brattonsville shows visitors an 18th- and 19th-century Christmas celebration. McConnells, 684-2327.

Christmas Candlelight Tour of Homes. Private homes and public buildings are decorated and open for tours. Camden, 432-9700.

Mid-December

Kershaw County Christmas Parade. Floats and bands celebrate the holiday season. Camden, 432-2525, 800-968-4037.

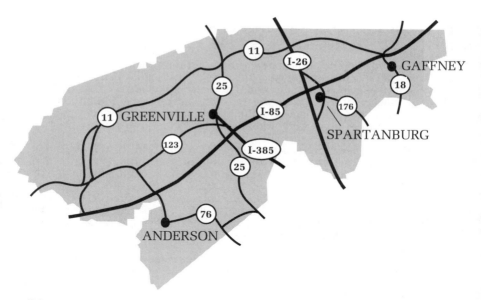

Discover Upcountry Carolina

Discover
═══ Upcountry Carolina ═══

Two discoveries await visitors in the Discover Upcountry Carolina region. The first is geographical, since many travelers are unaware that South Carolina has a mountainous area. The Blue Ridge Mountains end just west of Greenville and a series of state parks—Table Rock, Caesars Head and Jones Gap—provide access to waterfalls, glorious overlooks and a wide array of recreational options. You can explore the region on the Foothills Trail, which takes you into these parks and past some of the 25 waterfalls listed on a guide to the region's tumbling water. Keowee-Toxaway State Park reminds visitors of a time when all this land was Cherokee hunting grounds.

The second discovery is historical. More Revolutionary War battles were fought in South Carolina than in any other state. There were approximately 137 battles fought here and 90 of them were fought by South Carolina Patriots against South Carolina Tories. Nowhere was the Revolution more of a civil war than in the Upcountry. The Battle of Cowpens exemplifies this facet of the Revolutionary struggle and incidents at Walnut Grove Plantation reinforce the point.

Today this region in anything but insular; there is an enormous infusion of business, art and culture from around the world. The Greenville area has attracted international businesses that have enriched the community, as you will see at the Nippon Center Restaurant Yagoto and BMW Zentrum. Religious art and artifacts from around the world have been gathered at the Bob Jones University Art Collection, which is second only to the Vatican's collection in scope and depth. Regional, national and international art is also exhibited at the Greenville County Museum of Art and the Anderson County Arts Center, while the South Carolina Botanical Garden has added unique nature-based sculptures and artistic creations to the lovely gardens and arboretum on the Clemson University campus. The home of one of South Carolina's most distinguished national leaders, John C. Calhoun, is also on the Clemson campus.

Anderson County Arts Center
and Belton

Small Town Finds

Throughout the state, small communities are collecting their past, preserving their culture and strengthening their citizens' appreciation of the arts. Anderson County is making enormous strides on all three fronts with its **Anderson County Arts Center** and the museums in nearby Belton.

The arts center is housed in the imposing 1907 Andrew Carnegie Library, which remained operational until 1972. The library was purchased by the Pendleton District Historical and Recreational Commission and leased to the Anderson County Arts Council. Each year the arts center mounts eight to ten exhibits including two major shows of national and international work. To increase the appreciation and understanding of these exhibits, the center offers special workshops, gallery lectures and children's events. In the spring, the center has one of the largest juried shows in the state. Gallery exhibits change frequently; for a current calendar call (864) 224-8811. The gallery is open Monday through Friday from 9:30 A.M. to 5:30 P.M. and Sunday from 1:30 to 3:30 P.M.

The **Ruth Drake Museum** in Belton appeals more to local residents than to out-of-staters, as it has mementoes and articles from local residents including photographs, articles of clothes, old tools and school books. You have to smile at an exhibit that includes an "On Loan" sign above a gourd. This is a small collection exhibited in part of Belton's turn-of-the-century railroad depot. Museum hours are 2:00 to 4:00 P.M. Monday, Thursday and Sunday.

Also in the 1910 depot is the **South Carolina Tennis Hall of Fame**, which is of primary interest to winning players, their families, friends and tennis enthusiasts. Jim Russell, president of the South Carolina Tennis Association conceived the museum, established a support group and shepherded it into being in June 1984. Albums contain photographs and clippings on Hall of Fame members. There are trophies, rackets and other memorabilia from state champions. Each June, Belton is the site of the Wachovia Palmetto Championship and it is during this tournament that portraits of new inductees are unveiled. A key to this museum can be picked up at the Belton Library at the north end of the depot. On Sunday when the library is closed the museum is open from 2:00 to 4:00 P.M.

Also in Anderson County near the South Carolina/Georgia border is the 680-acre **Lake Hartwell State Park**. The park has 14 miles of shoreline along Lake Hartwell, which is a 56,000-acre reservoir. There are nature trails through the woods but it is the lake that draws most visitors. Fishing is excellent and the catch may include bream, catfish, crappie, largemouth bass, rainbow trout as well as other varieties. The park has a boat ramp and a tackle shop. There are 148 campsites for those who want to stay and try their luck another day. The park also has picnic areas and a playground.

Directions: From I-85 take Exit 19, Route 76 south to Anderson; once you reach the town, the road becomes Main Street. The Anderson Arts Center is at 405 North Main Street. For Belton take Route 76 ten miles east of Anderson. Belton's museums are at the Belton Depot, 101 Main Street. Lake Hartwell State Park is adjacent to the interchange of I-85, Exit 1, Route 11.

BMW Zentrum

Auto Ecstasy

While **BMW Zentrum** is not a guy thing—because what woman doesn't love beautifully designed luxury cars—it certainly is a spot that men need no convincing or cajoling to visit. Zentrum, which is the German word for center, is a crescent-shaped glass and steel state-of-the-art visitors center. Here, at BMW's only United States plant, visitors can interact with displays that entertain and educate the public regarding this prestigious company's long history of aircraft, motorcycle and automobile production.

There are examples of BMW's classic designs, plus unique prototypes and specially produced art cars. Roy Lichtenstein, who said that "art must be an element of everyday life," painted a BMW 320 with his easily recognized colorful images. Andy Warhol said about the car he painted, "I tried to portray speed pictorially; if a car is moving really quickly, all the lines and colors are blurred."

A "virtual factory tour" takes you inside the automobile manufacturing process. This innovative movie creates the illusion you are inside a car as it moves through the assembly points. From the first step at the body shop, when the car is welded together, you can see that there is not a lot of automation, instead there are a lot of skilled workers. It's interesting to note the extensive amount of hand work and visual inspection that is done for each car. Next, the car is painted and then 100 parts are added by hand. The doors that were removed so that the parts could be added, go back on the exact car from which they were taken.

The United States' only BMW plant has an innovative facility, the Zentrum, where visitors can discover how these upscale cars are made, see prototypes and specially produced art cars.

SOUTH CAROLINA DEPARTMENT OF PARKS, RECREATION AND TOURISM

At certain times of the year actual tours of the BMW factory will be offered. No one under 12 is permitted to tour the plant. For information on these tours call (888) TOURBMW.

Zentrum is open Tuesday thought Saturday from 9:30 A.M. to 5:30 P.M. On Thursday it stays open until 9:00 P.M. Admission is charged. The center has a European-style cafe and a gift shop.

Directions: From I-85 take Route 101 south. You will be able to see the BMW Zentrum from the interstate; it is located at 1400 Route 101 south.

Bob Jones University Art Collection

World Renowned Collection

Only the Vatican in Rome has a larger collection of religious art than the **Bob Jones University Art Collection**. Art connoisseurs from around the world have been impressed with this outstanding collection. Bob Jones, Sr. founded the Christian fundamentalist liberal arts university in 1927. When his son assumed responsibility for the school he felt that the college's emphasis on fine arts would be enhanced by a collection of religious paintings. Bob Jones, Jr. began amassing this staggering collection in 1951.

There are some visitors to Greenville who decide against a visit because they are under the impression that, as one reluctant individual stated *before* his visit, religious art is "static, repetitive and less interesting than a broader based collection." This could not be further from the truth. The museum's 30 rooms contain art treasures representing a wide spectrum of mediums and includes archeological artifacts, Old World attire, clerical vestments, Russian icons, European furniture and other items. Each visitor finds at least some part of the collection totally fascinating, and most find it all captivating.

European sacred art from the 13th through the 19th centuries is one of the primary thrusts of the collection. The settings vary. Three rooms are authentic wood-paneled Gothic chambers, others have gilded columns or brocaded wallpaper. On exhibit are works by such Old Masters as Rembrandt, Tintoretto, Titian, Sebastiano del Piombo, Cranach, Gerard David, Murillo, Rubens, Van Dyck, Veronese, Botticelli, Ribera, Honthorst and Dore. The Metropolitan Museum's associate curator of Italian paintings, Keith Christiansen, said, "Bob Jones has the best baroque art around." Paul Richard with *The Washington Post* wrote, "When it comes to baroque painting, Dutch, Spanish, and Italian, dating from the period 1590-1750, there really is no contest, Bob Jones wins hands down."

The noted Bowen Bible Lands Collection is also exhibited. Life-size mannequins showcase Biblical costumes. Others in the collection include dolls dressed as Moslems, Druse, Beduin, gypsy, Damascus peasants and more. There are 4,000-year-old vases from Egypt and Syria as well as canopic jars used during embalming. Another interesting item is an 80-foot-long Hebrew Torah scroll written on gazelle skin.

Some of the unique pieces in the Russian icon collection were presented to the Czar, or a member of his family, to commemorate a special occasion. These jewel encrusted icons are works of art. Nearby is a room of stained glass that glitters as brightly as the jewels. Throughout the museum there are pieces of European furniture—brocade sofas, ornately carved chairs, embellished tables and other items. Joseph Aronson, author of *The Encyclopedia of Furniture,* called this the finest collection in America. The museum is also noted for its array of vestments made for the Imperial Chapel in Vienna. These ornate robes were made in the 18th century of embroidered linen, silk and satin materials. The robes passed to Giesella Erdos, lady-in-waiting to Empress Maria Josephine, and were acquired for the Bob Jones University in the 1920s.

The collection can be viewed from Tuesday through Sunday 2:00 to 5:00 P.M. There is no charge, but donations are gratefully accepted. No one under six is permitted to tour the museum and children 6 to 12 must be accompanied by an adult. Modest attire is requested and no shorts are permitted. To fully appreciate the wealth of art exhibited, it is helpful to rent an audio tape. The galleries are closed Christmas week, New Years Day, July 4th and Commencement Day, which is always in May. For information, call (864) 242-5100.

While on campus stop at the **War Memorial Chapel** to see the seven huge paintings by Benjamin West. This is the world's largest collection of the 18th-century Pennsylvania artist. Local lore has it that West learned to paint with color from the Native Americans and took hairs from the family cat to make his brushes. In 1760, West traveled to Italy to study art, then moved to England where he worked until his death in 1820. He was "History Painter to the King" during George III's reign and helped establish the Royal Academy. The paintings at Bob Jones were originally done for a proposed chapel at Windsor Castle, but it was never built and the paintings were sold at auction and subsequently acquired by Bob Jones University.

In the university's **Mack Memorial Library**, rare Bibles are exhibited in the Jerusalem Chamber. This room is a reproduction of the room in London's Westminster Abbey where parts of the translation was done for the King James version of the Bible.

Finally, at the **Howell Memorial Science Building**, there are planetarium shows scheduled during the school year on Sundays at 3:00 P.M. The planetarium has a 30-foot dome and projectors which recreate the night sky. Call (864) 242-5100, ext. 4207 for a schedule of programs.

Directions: From I-85, take I-385. Then take Exit 40A to N. Pleasantburg Drive, Route 291. At the third traffic light, turn left. At the next traffic light turn left onto Wade Hampton Boulevard, Route 29. The main entrance to Bob Jones University is on your left at the next traffic light.

Cowpens National Battlefield

Contested Turf

The Carolinas, or lower south, became the major theater of conflict in the American Revolution during the last years of the war. With a virtual stalemate in the north, the British launched a second campaign to subdue the southern colonies. Savannah, Georgia was captured in late 1778, Charleston in May 1780 and most of South Carolina by the end of the year. But resistance was still encountered in the northwestern part of the state. A decisive victory by the Patriots at Kings Mountain (see selection) on October 7, 1780 provided a major impetus to the Continental Army's momentum.

The Overmountain Men from Tennessee and the Patriot militia from North and South Carolina disbanded after their victory at Kings Mountain. But many of the men returned to help Continental General Daniel Morgan defeat another British threat at Cowpens in January 1781. Morgan's force, outnumbered and outclassed, had been desperately trying to outmarch and escape from Colonel Banastre Tarleton's British Legion. Morgan had 970 soldiers, but only 290 were battle-experienced Continentals. He had a troop of light dragoons, and some of the militiamen from Maryland and Virginia were well-trained ex-Continentals. However, a large percentage of his troops were unseasoned militia. Tarleton commanded a detachment of 1,100 infantry and cavalry veterans. The British objective was to stop Morgan and his men, drive them across the border of North Carolina into the path of Cornwallis's army or drive them into Virginia.

When Morgan's scouts interrupted camp breakfast on January 16 with news that Tarleton was six miles south and approaching fast, the general had two choices. He could try to cross the Broad River and face almost certain massive desertions, or he could move his men to the advantageous flat, grassy pasturing ground at nearby Cowpens and make a stand. The terrain presented Morgan with some tactical assistance. With the river at his back, he knew his men couldn't retreat. The marsh on one side prevented a flanking maneuver by the British and the slight rise to the field gave his men an edge. Morgan was considered one of the best field tacticians of the Revolutionary conflict and this encounter tested his mettle. His plan matched the skills and weaknesses of his men with the advantages presented by the terrain. As his men prepared for the next morning's battle, Morgan explained his plans and assured them that he would "crack his whip over Benny (their nickname for Banestre Tarleton) in the morning."

Tarleton caught up with Morgan's force just before dawn on January 17th. He didn't even wait until first light before sending in the cavalry. He lost 15 men to Morgan's 120 sharpshooters positioned in the first of the three Patriot lines straddling the dirt road through the Cowpens. Tarleton immediately formed his men and launched an attack at the Militia line 400 yards in front of his position. The Militia, commanded by Colonel Andrew Pickens, fired two volleys into the British force and withdrew around the left of the Continental line. Commanding about 500 veterans from the Virginia, Maryland and Delaware Continentals was Lieutenant Colonel John Eager Howard. Leading the 120-man cavalry was Lieutenant Colonel William Washington, a distant relative of George Washington. Within an hour of close fighting the battle was over. It was a staggering defeat for Tarleton: 110 dead, over 200 wounded and 500 captured. Tarleton did escape and was with Cornwallis until the end. Morgan sustained only minimal losses: 12 killed and 60 wounded. This truly was the beginning of the end for the British Army. By October 19, 1781 Cornwallis surrendered his army at Yorktown. The major importance of this battle was that for the first time in the south, an American army stood in open battle formation on an open field and defeated an elite British force.

When you visit **Cowpens National Battlefield** start your tour at the visitor center where a fiber optic map outlines the action that took place here. The 22-minute laser-disc audio-visual program, *Daybreak at Cowpens*, presents the story through the eyes of a grandfather who tells his grandson what happened at Cowpens. Within the center you will see exhibits that include weapons, uniforms, military equipment, maps, portraits of leaders from both sides and paintings of the battlefield action.

There is a three-mile driving tour, with pull-off parking at significant spots along the loop. The first stop after the picnic grove, which is open 9:00 A.M. to 4:30 P.M., is the 1829 Robert Scruggs House, typical of the one-room cabins found in the Carolina Piedmont in the Revolutionary era. There are display boards on the grounds outside the cabin that provide additional historical details. The next parking area is the Thicketty

Mountain viewpoint. A short walk will take you to the site of the Washington and Tarleton clash. You can also pull in near the area where Morgan's men made their camp. A 45-minute walking tour starts behind the visitor center and takes you past the major action of the battle. Signs will indicate battlefield positions and combat events.

Cowpens National Battlefield is open daily 9:00 A.M. to 5:00 P.M. There is a small gift shop. There is a nominal charge for the multi-image laser disk presentation.

Directions: From I-85 take Exit 83 and head north on Route 110. Go to the intersection of Route 110 and Route 11. Turn right on Route 11; you will see the main entrance to the battlefield on your right. Heading south on I-85, take Exit 92 at Gaffney and follow the park signs on Route 11 west for ten miles to the park.

Devils Fork and
Keowee-Toxaway State Parks

Access the Natural World

In 1991, **Devils Fork State Park** was created just off the Cherokee Foothills Scenic Highway with the Blue Ridge Mountains as a backdrop and the 7,565-acre Lake Jocassee in the foreground. The name dates back to 1780. Its exact derivation is unclear but it may refer to the convergence of three creeks that formed Devils Fork Creek. When Duke Power Company undertook their power project, completed in 1973, they named two access areas Devils Fork and the name was eventually adopted for the state park.

Considered one of the most beautiful lakes in the state, it is the only one offering both trophy trout and small-mouth bass. Fishermen call Lake Jocassee "The Trophy Trout Lake of the Southeast." The state record brown trout weighing 17 lbs, 9.5 oz was caught in 1987 and the record for a rainbow trout from the lake is 11 lbs, 5 oz, caught in 1993. Winter and spring are best for trout fishing. You can hire guides at Hoyett's Grocery & Tackle Shop by calling (864) 944-9016.

Within the park there are two moderate hiking trails, a 3.5-mile trail leading from the picnic area and a 1.5-mile trail that begins behind the park headquarters. These trails give you a chance to see the park's abundant wildflowers that include bloodroot, trout lily, violets, Jack-in-the-pulpit and the rare Oconee bell, found here in profusion. Frequently-spotted wildlife include white-tailed deer, wild turkey and the more elusive raccoons and grey foxes. Bird fanciers enjoy the variety they spot hiking through Devils Fork, including a wide range of songbirds. Yo u ' re likely to see the brilliant scarlet tanager and many species of wood warblers. The peregrine falcon has been re-introduced into this area and may also be seen. Hoyett's store runs a shuttle service for hikers who want to link up with the **Foothills Trail** (see Table Rock Selection). This 80-plus-mile trail can be accessed at three points on the lake. The store also rents pontoons for those who want to explore the lake by boat. You can reach three major waterfalls from the lake and the store will provide maps indicating the falls locations. You can also arrange a four-hour guided pontoon sightseeing tour, by calling (864) 944-9016.

Devils Fork State Park has a bathhouse and lake swimming. There is also a boat ramp. Water skiing is a popular activity when the water warms in late June. Lake Jocassee has become a popular dive spot as it is one of the clearest lakes north of Florida. Many visitors choose to overnight in the park and there is a lakeside campground with 59 recreational vehicle sites and a 20-site lakeside tent camping area. Additional primitive camp-sites can be reached by boat. The park also rents 20 stylish mountain villas—not cabins, but villas with cathedral ceilings, stone fireplaces and magnificent views of the lake. These are on a first come/first served basis and reservations fill up as soon as the phone lines open, so call at the very beginning of the year (864) 944-2639.

Devils Fork State Park is open daily from late spring to mid-fall from 7:00 A.M. to 9:00 P.M. From late fall to mid-spring it is open Friday and Saturday at the same times; Sunday through Thursday it closes at 7:00 P.M. The park office is open daily year round from 9:00 A.M. to NOON and 1:00 to 5:00 P.M.

While in this area, at Salem take Route 130 north and cross the North Carolina border for **Whitewater Falls**, just over the state line on your left. The dramatic falls, with a 900-foot drop, descends over six cascades and two states (the lower portion is in South Carolina). Whitewater Falls is the highest series of falls in eastern United States.

At **Keowee-Toxaway State Park** rocky outcroppings provide spectacular views of the foothills of the Blue Ridge Mountains. Along the trails colorful rhododendron and mountain laurel add pastel hues to the greens of the forest. But this 1,000-acre park has another dimension. Along the trails there are four interpretative kiosks with cases filled with Native American artifacts and infor-mation boards that tell the story of the Upper Cherokee Indians, to whom this land once belonged. The name Keowee means "Place of the Mulberry" in the Cherokee dialect. Visitors sense the powerful presence of these indigenous people when they read the description written by naturalist William Bartram prior to the American Revolution, "The Cherokees are...by far the largest race of men I have seen; their complexion bright and somewhat of an olive cast, especially the adults and some of their young women nearly as fair and blooming as European women." Information boards focus on the Native America trade with the European settlers and conflicts that developed between the two groups, including the clash at Long Cane (see selection). There is also a small museum at the park, with Native American artifacts. Hours are 11:00 A.M. to NOON and 4:00 to 5:00 P.M. daily.

Keowee-Toxaway has ten recreational vehicle campsites and 14 tent sites as well as one large rental cabin with a porch overlooking Lake Keowee (there is also a private floating courtesy dock at the cabin). There are hiking trails, picnic facilities and a community building that is rented to groups. Park hours are daily April through September 9:00 A.M. to 9:00 P.M. From October through March the park closes at 6:00 P.M. Saturday through Thursday and at 8:00 P.M. on Friday. The office is open at the same time as the small museum.

Directions: From I-85 take Exit 21, Route 178 north to the Cherokee Foothills Scenic Highway, Route 11 and turn left. Devils Fork is four miles northeast of Salem on Route 25. Keowee-Toxaway State Park is on Route 11, before you reach the turn for Devils Fork.

Fort Hill: Home of John C. Calhoun & Thomas G. Clemson

At Home with History

In 1959, a Senate committee chaired by Senator John F. Kennedy chose John C. Calhoun as one of the five greatest Senators in American history. (The others were Henry Clay, Daniel Webster, Robert LaFollette and Robert Taft.) In 1825, when Calhoun purchased the 1,100-acre plantation that he named after a fort built on the property in 1776, he was serving the first of two terms as vice-president of the United States. He is one of only two (the other is George Clinton who served under Thomas Jefferson and James Madison) to hold this office under two different presidents—and the only one ever to voluntarily resign.

By this point in his political career, Calhoun had already served in the state legislature, the U.S. House of Representatives and as Secretary of War under President Monroe. Calhoun resigned as vice president so that he could champion the cause of States' Rights. He felt strongly that protective tariffs favored the industrial north at the expense of the agricultural south. In 1832, Calhoun resigned his office and took his elected seat in the U.S. Senate. After spirited debates in the Senate between Calhoun and Daniel Webster, Congress reduced the tariffs and

South Carolina repealed a nullification measure it had begun.

After being re-elected to the Senate for two more terms, he declined consideration for the presidency and retired to Fort Hill. But after the sudden death of Tyler's secretary of state, Calhoun was nominated and confirmed for the position without being consulted. Calhoun greatly increased the prestige of the country and its size. During his term of office, Texas became a state and the U.S. gained rights to Oregon and Washington territories. In 1845, Calhoun returned to the Senate where he served until his death in 1850. Gravely ill, his last speech was read for him by Senator Mason of Virginia on March 4, 1850—it was an impassioned plea to save the Union. On March 31st, Calhoun died.

Like Jefferson and Washington, throughout his public career Calhoun often longed to return to his beloved southern plantation. Fort Hill was a haven he sought as an escape from the political confrontations of the nation's capital. He found great comfort in being surrounded by his family. His wife was his second cousin, Floride Bonneau Colhoun (her father was a wealthy U.S. Senator) of Charleston and they had five sons and five daughters (although three of the girls died in infancy).

Fort Hill, called Clergy Hall when Calhoun purchased it, was built about 1803 by Dr. James McElhenny. At the time of purchase it was a much smaller house than you see today. Local stories claim Calhoun commented that every time he left town, his wife added another room. The expansion was not planned, the house just grew to its present 14 room size, with an equal number of fireplaces to warm the rooms.

When you tour this National Historic Landmark, you will see that 90% of the furnishings belonged to either the Calhouns or the Clemsons (John C. Calhoun's daughter Anna Maria Calhoun married Thomas Green Clemson. He founded Clemson University and willed Fort Hill to the people as a perpetual shrine to Calhoun). Some pieces have remained in the house since John C. Calhoun's residency. When rugs, drapes and wallpaper were replaced, material similar to the original was used. Anna Maria's wedding took place in the parlor. Here you'll see a wooden chair that belonged to George Washington and a Duncan Phyfe-style sofa that belonged to Samuel Washington, grandnephew of the first president. Thomas Clemson's sister married Samuel and obtained the chair from Mount Vernon before it passed out of family hands. (Legend claims that when the first silver dollar was being designed, Washington copied the pose of the eagles on this sofa.) Anna Maria's portrait hangs above the sofa. On either side of the sofa are small drum-head tables brought to America by Calhoun's grandparents when they emigrated from Scotland. The room has numerous other family pieces.

The state dining room reflects the hospitality for which the Calhouns were noted, both here and at their Washington, D.C. residence. The Duncan Phyfe African mahogany table with 12 matching chairs and original black horsehair upholstery reminds visitors of the banquets the Calhouns frequently hosted. You'll even see the original 88-piece flatware silver set, with the letter "C" engraved on each piece. The Constitution sideboard was given to Calhoun in honor of his impassioned speeches defending the U.S. Constitution by fellow Senator Henry Clay. The sideboard was made from mahogany paneling removed from the officers' quarters of Old Ironsides, the U.S. Frigate *Constitution*. The room has portraits of John C. Calhoun and his wife.

When the Marquis de Lafayette visited America in 1825, he was a guest of the Calhouns in their Washington home and spent the night in the huge mahogany bed in the master bedroom. The chintz spread was made by Calhoun's second daughter, Cornelia. The room has Calhoun's trunk and lapdesk and a large portrait of the statesman. Behind this room is the nursery with half-size furniture and a family baby bed. Another of Fort Hill's eight bedrooms is the Floride Calhoun Memorial Room honoring John C. Calhoun's great-granddaughter. The room has her four-poster bed, tables and chest of drawers. In the Thomas G. Clemson bedroom you'll see his seven-foot walnut bed. The bed and matching dresser were made in nearby Pendleton at the direction of Mrs. Calhoun. The bedspread and pillow cases are also original. Over the mantle is a self-portrait by Clemson; he is posed looking into a mirror. The family room has display cases with personal items belonging to various family members.

Joined to the west wing by a covered passageway is the kitchen, rebuilt in 1944 to duplicate the original. Here you will see a variety of heavy iron cooking vessels and other useful items. There are even some pieces that belonged to the Calhouns, such as the bread tray, pastry board, rolling pin, beaten biscuit mallet, clothes maul and coffee grinder. A boxwood path leads from the house to a second dependency that served as Calhoun's private office. Here he had his library and wrote most of his speeches and legislative proposals. There is a desk Calhoun used when he opened his Abbeville law office, after he graduated from Yale and studied law in Litchfield, Connecticut and in Charleston. In addition to his office chair, Calhoun's Senatorial chair now rests in this office. Calhoun's only hobby was collecting maps and a number of these can be seen in his office. Off the south portico is Cornellia's Garden, laid out by Calhoun for his daughter. She was crippled as a child but lived to adulthood and learned to walk with crutches and later with a cane.

After Calhoun's death in 1850, his widow continued living at

Fort Hill until 1854 when their son, Andrew, acquired Fort Hill. Mrs. Calhoun moved to "MiCasa" in nearby Pendleton. Andrew died in 1865 but his family remained at Fort Hill until 1872 when Mrs. Calhoun foreclosed on her daughter-in-law and gave the house to Anna Maria and her husband. Twelve years after acquiring Fort Hill, Thomas Clemson bequeathed it so a college could be founded. He died in 1888 before his dream was realized, but by 1890 the first buildings were being constructed and in 1893 the university began full-time operation. There were 4 buildings, 15 teachers and 446 students at what was first called Clemson Agricultural College.

Fort Hill is open at a nominal charge Monday through Saturday from 10:00 A.M. to 5:00 P.M. and Sunday from 2:00 to 5:00 P.M. On Saturday the house closes for lunch between NOON and 1:00 P.M.

Directions: From I-85 take Route 76 for 11 miles to the Clemson University Campus. From Route 76 make a left on Route 93 and another left on Williamson Road. You will see Fort Hill on your left at the intersection of Williamson Road and Fort Hill Street.

Greenville County Museum of Art

Roots in the South

Southern artists are by no means the only ones exhibited at the **Greenville County Museum of Art**, but they do make up the museum's acclaimed Southern Collection. From the colonial period to the present, art and sculpture related to the south are represented. Some of the artists are natives, others visitors and some chose to paint southern themes from afar. These works cover Native Americans, the American Revolution and the Civil War. The collection reveals the range of art vogues: history painting, portraiture, landscape, still life and genre scenes. There is at least one painting from every major movement in American art. The earliest work in the collection is *Man in Armor*, painted by Henriette de Beaulieu Dering Johnston, the first professional woman artist in the country. She arrived in Charleston in 1708 and painted to help support her family.

The permanent collection is well-represented with 20th-century American artists. Exhibited is work by Georgia O'Keefe, Jasper Johns, Andy Warhol, Hans Hofmann, Josef Albers and Gari Melchers (whose home and studio, Belmont, can be visited in Fredericksburg, Va). Augmenting these works are over 15 changing exhibits annually.

This museum has come a long way since its earliest days as a small regional gallery in the basement of City Hall. In 1958, with a move to the renovated Gassaway Mansion, the museum was officially organized. In 1974, it moved to its current home, a modernistic four-story structure with gallery space on each level, an art school, gift shop and theater. One young visitor, when writing about the museum in the comment book said, "Stairs were awesome. Could've been higher. Trampoline on the bottom would be really nice!" The museum does pay attention to the comment book, but there are no plans to add a trampoline.

The Greenville County Museum of Art is open at no charge Tuesday through Saturday from 10:00 A.M. to 5:00 P.M. On Sunday it opens at 1:00 P.M. It is closed on Monday and major holidays. For details on current programs and guest artist lectures, call (864) 271-7570. The museum has a gift shop with art books, jewelry, handmade crafts, toys and other unique items.

Greenville's downtown has been revitalized by its participation in the Federal Main Street improvement program. Since this is a city not a small town, where this distinctive upgrading is customarily done, there are more shops, galleries, restaurants, brew pubs and other establishments to enjoy along Main Street. Popular restaurants include Bistro Europa known for its Sunday Sinatra brunches; the Blue Ridge Brewing Company with its Copper Brewhouse; and Trio—A Brick Oven Cafe that makes scrumptious pizzas. The Coach Factory Cafe in the Peace Center is an upscale French and Continental restaurant. Visitors will need their will power, or their credit cards, at Lynn Strong's shop, 119 N. Main. This creative jewelry designer has filled her shop with unique items. Twenty-four dealers supply Antiques Associates at 633 S. Main Street. Another *must* stop is the Carpenter Brothers "Old-Time Soda Shop and Gift Store," 123 S. Main, where you can still enjoy an ice cream treat.

At 300 S. Main Street the **Peace Center for the Performing Arts** has a 2,000-seat concert hall and 400-seat theater. A Glimpse of Greenville, with a gift shop and information area in the West End Market (see selection), offers front and backstage tours of this center as well as other significant sites in town. You can also stop in the Greenville Convention and Visitors Bureau's Downtown Visitors Center at 206 S. Main Street to pick up a wide range of information on Greenville.

Directions: From I-85, take I-385 to downtown Greenville. The interstate becomes College Street after crossing Main Street. The museum is at the intersection of College Street and Academy Street, which is Route 123.

Greenville Zoo

Growing By Leaps and Bounds

Visualize the **Greenville Zoo** as a three-tiered operation: first there was the "old" zoo, then the "new" zoo and now expansion is underway to create Zoo2000. The zoo was organized in the late 1950s and, while animals were added over the years, the layout was what we now think of as old-fashioned, with confining cages offering only a minimal range of activities.

In 1985, the zoo closed for 18 months while major renovations took place, incorporating modern concepts of zoo designs using natural barriers rather than cages and providing more spacious accommodations for much of the collection. The zoo's 14-acre hilly wooded setting complemented the new exhibits which also incorporated plants, trees, rocks and other indigenous material. It is one of the most heavily planted zoos in the country.

Recognizing its upgraded status, since 1988 the Greenville Zoo has been accredited by the American Association of Zoological Parks and Aquariums. Only 170 zoos in the country have achieved this distinction. The zoo, which is owned and operated by the city, is also on the list of top 20 attractions in South Carolina.

There are more than 300 species of mammals, birds, reptiles, amphibians and fish. Elements of the collection are grouped by continent. There is a South American, Asian and African area. Periodically the zoo features exhibits of unusual animals such as water dragons, giant snakes, flying-fox bats, and a long-term loan of a rare white Bengal tiger. There is a reptile building, alligator exhibit and a new Discovery Center, where a full range of educational programs, lectures and activities are scheduled. The zoo works closely with area schools, reaching over 20,000 students annually.

Many of the children who took part in zoo programs, returned to celebrate the 25th birthday of Joy, the zoo's African elephant. Although most females wouldn't have agreed, as part of her party, Joy had a weigh-in and tipped the scales at 7,800 pounds. This didn't stop Joy from enjoying her birthday cake, a concoction made of four loaves of bread around pineapple cores and topped with peanut butter and hay 'icing' decorated with apples, lemons and berries. There were even carrot 'candles.'

The Greenville Zoo is open daily 10:00 A.M. to 4:30 P.M. It is closed on Thanksgiving, Christmas and New Year's Day. In October, there is a Boo in the Zoo celebration and in December, ZooLights. Admission is charged. There is a gift shop, food concessions and picnic tables in the zoo. For additional information call (864) 467-4300.

Outside of Greenville near Inman there is another collection of animals at **Hollywild Animal Park**. Here many of the animals are kept in small cages and enclosures while others roam large natural enclosures or expansive man-made islands. In order to see the animals within the large enclosure, you need to take a safari ride. The unusual aspect to this collection is that many of the animals on exhibit have been in movies or on television. A leopard Appaloosa was in *New Adventures of Pippi Longstocking*, a cougar was in *Last of the Mohicans* and an Asian elephant was in the Frisco Family Circus.

The park is open daily April through Labor Day from 9:00 A.M. to 6:00 P.M. From Labor Day to Halloween, it opens at the same time on weekends only. There is also a special Christmas Celebration which begins the Saturday before Thanksgiving with thousands of lights and herds of wild animals. Admission is charged; there is a nominal additional fee for the safari ride. The park has a gift shop and sells animal food to feed the animals. For additional information call (864) 472-2038.

Directions: For the Greenville Zoo, take I-85 to the Greenville area, then take I-385 into the city. Turn left on Church Street, then left on Washington Street. Turn left on McBee Street, then

At Hollywild Animal Park visitors can fondle genuine movie stars, although only four-footed ones. Many of the animals exhibited were featured in hit movies and television shows.

PHOTO BY TONY SMITH

right on Cleveland Park Drive. The zoo is at 150 Cleveland Park Drive. If you are going to Hollywild Animal Park take I-85 north from Greenville toward Spartanburg. Take Exit 56, Route 14. Turn left toward Greer and right on Route 29. The sign will be on the left in approximately six miles.

Hagood-Mauldin House and Pickens County Museum

Good Pickings in Pickens

A sense of the past, of the community and the family is extremely important throughout the south, and it is especially evident in the small towns of South Carolina. Those who appreciate the value of items and places with roots to the past, see that furnishings and art of earlier times is handed down so we can revisit those who lived decades earlier. Great efforts have been made to save homes as well. The **Hagood-Mauldin House**, for example, was moved from Old Pickens, 14 miles west of Pickens, in 1868.

The four-room house, with an exterior porch connecting the dining room with the kitchen dependency, was reputedly built around 1856 by attorney James E. Hagood, who was active in South Carolina politics. Hagood had been unable to serve in the Civil War because of his health, though he did bring wagons of supplies to the Confederate troops and aided the wounded. He was later able to hold public office, since those who had served in the Confederate army were forbidden to hold state or federal office.

When his daughter, Mrs. Frances Hagood Mauldin, inherited the house she made a number of additions. Mrs. Mauldin, wife of judge and state legislator T. J. Mauldin, was known as Miss Queen for her role as community social leader. A member of the Daughters of the American Revolution and president of the South Carolina Division of the United Daughters of the Confederacy, she always held a picnic on June 3 for the soldiers of the Confederacy.

In 1955, the house was purchased by Mrs. Irma Hendricks Morris, who restored the house and furnished it with her outstanding collection of fine furniture and art acquired through her antique business. She also obtained a number of outstanding pieces from the Oolenoy Valley Cabinetmakers, a local company that is highly regarded. In 1987, she gave the house and her collection to the Pickens County Historical Society. Hours are NOON to 4:00 P.M. on Saturday and 2:00 to 5:00 P.M. on Sundays and at other times by calling (864) 878-9459 for an appointment. A nominal admission is charged. Judge Maudlin's office is a detached dependency. There is an herb garden behind the house.

Another spot in town where the past is carefully preserved is the **Pickens County Museum** which, like the Phoenix, rose from the ashes of a disastrous fire in 1994. This gave the museum staff a chance to reorganize their exhibits and collections so that you can now view the history of the region through an amazing array of items. A 19th-century pioneer cabin has a wealth of details that weave a story without words—from the bearskin rug, to the iron kettle, long rifle and spinning wheel. Another area represents a typical early 20th century kitchen with a wide array of task specific kitchen aids such as the pea huller, apple peeler and corer, butter mold and cherry pitter. You can see a history of a people in the carefully collected items from their life. Items span the scope of the county's past: prehistoric, Native American, Revolutionary War, Civil War, textiles, railroad and natural history. Local heroes like John C. Calhoun, whose home, Fort Hill, is in nearby Clemson (see selection) and General Andrew Pickens, are remembered at this museum.

The museum is located in a restored 1903 "gaol" that is architecturally significant because of its crenelated turret. The building is on the National Register of Historic Places. You can see an old jail cell, leg irons, whipping straps and prisoners' garb. There is an executioner's noose used at the jail and a graphic photograph of the last execution in Pickens County, which took place in 1903. A Mr. Jones was hung for the crime of killing a deputy sheriff. Upstairs galleries house exhibits that are changed every two to three months. The museum, at the corner of Johnson and Pendleton streets, is open Tuesday through Friday from 8:30 A.M. to 5:00 P.M. and Saturday from NOON until 4:00 P.M.

North of Pickens on Route 178, you'll see the **Hagood Mill**, an early 1800s grist mill now in the final process of restoration. This 1825 mill is one of the few in the state that retains its original components. You can make arrangements at the Pickens County Museum to tour the mill. Also in the county south of Pickens in Liberty is the **Golden Creek Mill**, another 1800s mill. This picturesque gristmill is powered by a 14-foot overshot water wheel, one of the largest still in regular operation. Drop in visitors can picnic beside the mill. To tour the mill and its adjacent country store and museum call (864) 859-1958. For this mill, take Route 8 south from Pickens and turn right on Breaseale Road. Then make a left on Enon Church Road, which will take you to the mill.

In nearby Liberty, you can visit the **Schoolhouse Antiques and Museum**, the largest privately-owned antique collection in the southeast. You'll see rare antique cars and a wealth of household items, furniture, fine china, toys, dolls and merchandise from a general store, barber shop and dentist shop. It can take an hour and a half to explore the collection. Antique fanciers will be delighted to discover that this is also a store. It is open Wednesday through Saturday from 11:00 A.M. to 5:00 P.M.; on Sunday it opens at 1:00 P.M. (But it is a good idea to call ahead to make sure it is open at 864-843-6827.) Admission is charged.

Directions: From I-85 south of Greenville, take Exit 32, Route 8 northwest to Pickens. Or from Greenville's I-185, take Route 183 to Pickens. Route 8 will merge into Main Street in Pickens. Make a right turn on N. Lewis Street; the Hagood-Mauldin House is at 104 N. Lewis Street. For the Schoolhouse Antiques and Museum take Route 178 south from Pickens to Liberty; the museum is three miles southeast of Liberty at the corner of Route 135 and Flat Rock Road.

Historic Ashtabula House and Historic Pendleton

Family Roots

Names that echo through South Carolina history are linked to **Historic Ashtabula House**. It was built shortly after 1820 when Lewis Ladson Gibbes of Charleston purchased the land in Pendleton. Gibbes was descended from Colonial Governor Robert Gibbes and Dr. Henry Woodward, who was the first English settler in the colony. Woodward's arrival predated the first permanent colony in 1670. Reputedly he saved the Charles Towne Landing settlement by persuading the Native Americans, with whom he had become friends, to provide food for the starving settlers.

After studying at Eton in England and the Sorbonne in France, Lewis Ladson married Maria Henrietta Drayton. Her father was Charles Drayton of Drayton Hall (see selection) and her uncle was Arthur Middleton of Middleton Place (see selection), a signer of the Declaration of Independence. Maria Henrietta Gibbes died in 1826 and is believed to be the first person buried in St. Paul's Episcopal Churchyard; Lewis Ladson Gibbes was buried there after his death in November 1828.

In 1837, the Gibbes children sold Ashtabula, advertised as "the most beautiful farm in the up-country" to Dr. Ozey R. Broyles. The Native American word, Ashtabula, means fish in the river. A leader in the Pendleton Farmers' Society, Broyles invented a carriage safety harness. He and his wife Sarah Ann Taliaferro of Virginia had 10 children. In 1851, the Broyles sold Ashtabula to James T. Latta of York. The Lattas made the last structural changes to the house. In 1861 or 62, Robert Adger of Charleston bought the estate and his daughter Clarissa Adger Bowen and her children lived here; another daughter lived at the nearby Rivoli Plantation which Latta also purchased. Clarissa's sister-in-law was the wife of Governor Gist, called the Secession Governor, and her home was Rose Hill (see selection). After several other owners, the estate was purchased by the Mead Corporation for a tree farm. In 1961, the company gave the house and ten acres to the Foundation for Historic Restoration in Pendleton.

The house has been restored and furnished to look as it did in 1865. Some pieces date even earlier but it is understood that the first families to live at Ashtabula brought pieces with them from other properties. In the parlor you will see the Gibbes family Spode tea service. The Latta family added the two cast iron fireplaces in the parlor and in the family sitting room. Although there were no battles around Pendleton, Union soldiers returning home made several raids on the house and stole the family horses. The wedding silver was hidden behind the barn. One historical item is the contract O. A. Bowen drew up with his slaves in 1865; all but two stayed and they all made their mark on the contract. A doll collection is exhibited in an upstairs room. The four-room brick annex connected to the house by a brick passageway has also been furnished and the well house restored.

Ashtabula is open from April through October on Sundays from 2:00 to 6:00 P.M. You can call (864) 646-3782 to make arrangements to visit at other times. Admission is charged.

Save time to drive or walk around **Historic Pendleton**, a 207-year-old community on the National Register of Historic Places. Right up to the American Revolution, conflicts with Native Americans had kept many settlers from the fertile soil of the Upcountry, but at the conclusion of the war, they began arriving in earnest. By 1789, Pendleton County was established and in the following year so was the town of Pendleton. It remained a courthouse town until the end of 1826, as well as a mecca for wealthy Lowcountry families seeking summer relief from the coast. A map of the area has 42 sites of historic interest. The town is centered around a village green. Built on the site of the courthouse is Farmers' Society Hall, the ground floor is now the **Farmers' Hall Restaurant** noted for its fine dining at lunch and dinner; call (864) 646-7024 for reservations.

At the other end of the green is the 1860 Guard House and market house. The cannon on the green was used during Reconstruction when Pendleton men organized as Red Shirts (see Oakley Museum selection) to support the ultimately successful candidacy of Democrat Wade Hampton for governor. Near the green is Marshalsea, built as the district jail and now a private residence. It was named for a jail in London featured in a Charles Dickens novel. There are numerous shops and eateries on the square; many of the locals lunch at Ye Old Sandwich Shop.

The place to pick up brochures and maps of the region is the 1850 Hunter's Store at the corner of North Mechanic and East Queen streets. This is now the headquarters for the tri-county Pendleton

District Historical, Recreational and Tourism Commission. A series of shops now occupies what was once a warehouse for Hunter's Store. You might want to continue on E. Queen Street to see St. Paul's Episcopal Church. Begun in 1819, many historic individuals are buried in the churchyard including Mrs. John C. Calhoun, Confederate generals Barnard E. Bee and Clement H. Stevens and the first governor of Nebraska, Francis Burt. Also on the tour map are Woodburn (see selection) and Ashtabula.

If you want to stay overnight in this historic community, consider **Liberty Hall Inn**, with antique-filled rooms and festive dining; call (864) 646-7500 or (800) 643-7944 for details. Another bed & breakfast to consider is **One Ninety-Five East Main**, just off the village green; call (864) 646-5673 for more information.

Directions: From I-85 take Exit 19, Route 76 west. As you approach Pendleton bear right on Route 28. Make another right on E. Queen Street and turn left on Route 88. After three miles you will see the entrance to Ashtabula on your left.

Nippon Center and Restaurant Yagoto

Sensory Appeal

Relaxation exercises suggest that you begin by picturing a place where you feel a sense of peace and serenity and imagine yourself in it. In the Greenville area, it is not necessary to imagine a spot of great tranquility; you can visit the **Nippon Center** and experience in reality a serene place ideal for relaxation and contemplation. The Tsuzuki family, who have been a successful part of the Greenville business community for more than 30 years, gave this center to the city as a way of sharing their heritage.

The garden's designer brought an ancient style with him when he came from Japan to carry out this commission. The center is built in the Shoin Zukuri style, first used for residential architecture in the Muromachi period, 1336-1573. By the late 16th century, the style was used for guest halls and abbot's quarters in Japan's many Zen Buddhist temples. The style utilizes a series of rooms, each serving a separate function. Traditional elements at the Nippon Center include tatami mat floors, sliding screens, square posts, verandas and decorative doors. A variety of hardwoods were used, but not a single nail mars their beauty.

The building has a lovely exterior garden with small stones, boulders, stone lanterns and a graceful pedestrian bridge. But it is the interior rock gardens, visible from a number of rooms within the center, that are remarkable. It replicates Kyoto's Ryoan-ji, one of the world's oldest rock gardens. If you sit in the lounge and study the garden, the rock groupings in the gardens take on different forms, depending on who is gazing upon them. Some look like islands with smaller rocks appearing as waves crashing against their shore. Some see the larger rocks as boats, while still others who see the garden from another room imagine a rice field with mountains in the distance. From all the windows of the center one sees triangular patterns of rocks and the triangular pattern is repeated within. The dining room table tops, for example, form triangular shapes, and the ceiling of the banquet room repeats the pattern.

As you gaze around the Nippon Center you will see several exceptional pieces of fine Japanese art. Behind the bar, you'll see a silk screen that is well over 450 years old. This painting of seasons, a self-portrait of sorts, represents the cycles in the artist's life. In the lounge is a work painted entirely with 24K gold. Reputedly, each viewer sees something different in this work as it represents the hope for the future and that, of course, varies with each individual. It is considered lucky to make a wish as you look at this piece.

A different work of art is to be discovered in the Nippon Center's authentic tea room. The Japanese Embassy in Washington offers the only other spot in the country where you can visit a tea room like this. The tea ceremony, which is a symbolic ritual, dates back to the Shogun era. The tea room was a place of serenity—no weapons or armor were allowed within its confines and all the participants were considered equals. A low entranceway reminded participants to practice humility. No hierarchy existed during the ceremony that stresses removing all external distractions and achieving peace and serenity.

Dining at **Restaurant Yagoto** completes the experience. It offers a variety of traditional Japanese cuisine ranging from sushi to tempura and the classic Kaiseki dinner. There are dining rooms with traditional tatami mat floors or rooms with tables and chairs. Call for information and reservations at (864) 288-8471. Dining hours are Monday through Saturday from 6:00 to 9:30 P.M.

Directions: From I-85 take I-385 north toward Greenville and use the Roper Mountain Road exit. At the top of the exit ramp, turn left and go to Congaree Road, which will be the second traffic signal. Turn right on Congaree Road and proceed for about one mile. You will see the Nippon Center on the left at 500 Congaree Road.

Oconee State Park and
Oconee Station State Park

Foothills of the Blue Ridge

In the Cherokee language Oconee meant "water eyes of the hills," and there are certainly lakes, streams and waterfalls within the rugged foothills of **Oconee State Park**. This 1,165-acre park, developed in the 1930s with the help of the Civilian Conservation Corps, is one of the oldest in the state. Sprawling across a wooded plateau in the Blue Ridge foothills, the park has two scenic lakes popular with hikers, swimmers and fishermen. The park trails are linked with the 85-mile Foothills Trail that extends to Jones Gap State Park (see selection).

Within the park there is a three-mile Oconee Trail, marked in green, an easy hike that takes two to three hours. The Old Waterwheel Trail, marked in orange, only takes an hour, but it is a little more strenuous. The overshot waterwheel was the first water system in the park. It powered a piston pump supplying water to a wooden tank located at cabin #7. From the cabin, water was gravity fed to all areas of the park. A hydraulic ram located in the creek served as a back-up piston pump. The system was discontinued in the early 1950s with the advent of rural electricity. Another easy trail that takes about an hour is the Lake Trail (no markers). The Tamassee Knob Trail is a moderately strenuous two-hour hike (no colored markers). In cooperation with the U.S. Forest Service, the park has added the two-mile Hidden Falls Trail, which takes three to four hours and is moderately strenuous. It leads to a 60-foot falls that cascades to a lower rock formation, then widens dramatically. In the spring dogwoods, mountain laurel and rhododendron bloom on hillsides beside the trail.

Other recreational opportunities include year round fishing boat rentals and summertime canoe and pedal boat rentals. There are picnic facilities, a playground, archery range, ballfield and carpet golf in the summer. The park has 140 family campsites and 19 cabins; of these 13 are along one of the lakes. Call (864) 638-5353 to reserve a camp-site or cabin.

Oconee State Park is open daily year round from 7:00 A.M. to 9:00 P.M. The park office is open March through October from 7:00 A.M. to 9:00 P.M.; the rest of the year it closes at 7:00 P.M.

Don't confuse Oconee State Park with **Oconee Station State Park**; they are two separate entities. The latter is a 210-acre historic park in the foothills of the Appalachian Mountains. The property was acquired in the mid-1970s because of its historical significance. Oconee Station was decommissioned in 1799, the last blockhouse, or fort, in the state to have its soldiers removed.

The Oconee blockhouse was built around 1792 as part of a chain of protective fortified houses that provided sanctuary to settlers when warfare broke out with the indigenous population. Troops were stationed at the blockhouses to provide a bulwark between the settlers and the Native Americans. Several years after the troops left the blockhouse, in 1805, William Richards, a settler from Ireland, built a brick house 50 feet from the blockhouse. Richards operated a thriving trading post at Oconee Station. Both of these historic buildings survive and have been restored, although neither are furnished. They can be toured on weekends from 1:00 to 5:00 P.M. The park is closed in January and February. From March through December, park hours are 9:00 A.M. to 6:00 P.M., Thursday through Sunday. There is no visitors center, but there is an easy to moderate nature trail that extends from the park to the Station Cove Falls, a two-tier, 60-foot falls in the Sumter National Forest. In the spring, this hike provides a splendid opportunity to see a wide variety of wildflowers including trillium, hypatica, foam flowers and May apples.

Since both of these state parks are in the Walhalla area, another interesting stop is the **Walhalla State Fish Hatchery**, formerly a federal government facility but now under state jurisdiction. The huge brown, brook and rainbow trout you see in the outdoor pools aren't the ones that got away; these are the fish that were never stocked in local streams, lakes and rivers. Approximately one million trout a year are raised here, and you see them in all stages of development. A few specimens are retained at the hatchery and are the ones that seem to attract the concentrated attention of fishermen in the group.

The hatchery gets most of its eggs from brooding stock kept at the facility, hence the existence of these prime specimens. You can watch the artificial spawning of the fish in the long, narrow raceways periodically from October through January. To provide new brood material, the hatchery receives fertilized eggs from other facilities across the country. Large information signs explain the various steps in the breeding program. Visitors are welcome to look inside the hatchery building where the incubator and juvenile fish rearing area are located. Once the fish reach a size of between two and three inches they are transferred to the outside raceways. The hatchery is open at no charge 8:00 A.M. to 4:00 P.M. daily.

Adjacent to Walhalla State Fish Hatchery is the **Chattooga Picnic Area**, operated by the U.S. Forest Service. This lovely wooded area, through which a boulder-strewn stream rushes, is noted for several state champion trees. In this vicinity you will see the largest white pine tree in the state and the largest hemlock. A barrier-free fishing pier on the bank of the East Fork of the Chatooga River is accessible from the picnic parking lot. Large thickets of rhododendron and mountain laurel make this a delightful area in late spring. The picnic area is on the edge of the **Ellicott Rock Wilderness**. From the picnic area, you can take a 2.5-mile trail along the East Fork to the main Chattooga River. If you want to continue, the trail goes upstream to Ellicott's Rock, a distance of 1.7 miles; or you can go downstream to Burrell's Ford campground, a 2.1-mile hike.

Another interesting spot six miles northwest of Walhalla is **Stumphouse Tunnel Park**, one of three tunnels dug through the mountains in the area for a potential railroad project from

Charleston to Knoxville, Tennessee. By the late 1850s, the line reached Anderson, Pendleton and West Union, but Stumphouse Mountain proved an obstacle. Irish immigrants began working 12 hours a day, six days a week. They lived in a rough town called Tunnel Hill atop the mountain. One tunnel, 388 feet long, was finished (although rock slides have since sealed it), another had 200 of 616 feet dug. The real problem, however, was with the main Stumphouse Tunnel, at 5,863 feet, the longest of the three. Crews were digging at both ends of the tunnel and cut 1,600 feet into the mountain when funds ran out in 1859. The economic crisis in post Civil War South Carolina meant there was no money available to complete the project.

In the 1950s, Clemson University aged its blue cheese in the tunnel (see Uniquely Clemson in the South Carolina Botanical Garden selection). In 1970, the Pendleton District Historical, Recreation and Tourism Commission acquired the property under a lease agreement and established a park. Rock slides in 1994 prompted the commission to seal off the entrance to the tunnel for safety reasons. But there is a picnic area and a hiking trail that leads to nearby **Issaqueena Falls**, named for a legendary Indian maiden. The falls are a spectacular 100-foot drop. Both the falls and the tunnel are on the National Register of Historic Places.

In the area around Stumphouse Tunnel and Oconee State Park there are a number of whitewater outfitters who run rafting trips on the Chattooga River. These include the Nantahala Outdoor Center (800-232-7238), Wildwater, Ltd. (800-451-9972) and Southeastern Expeditions (800-868-7238).

Directions: From I-85 take Exit 1, Route 11 north. When it intersects with Route 28, bear left on Route 28, then make a right on Route 107. Oconee State Park is on your right, 12 miles northwest of Walhalla on Route 107. For Oconee Station State Park, do not turn off Route 11, but continue north on Route 11 until you see country road Route 95 on your left. Take that for four miles to the park. The Walhalla State Fish Hatchery is on Route 107 north of Walhalla approximately ten miles past Oconee State Park. For Stumphouse Tunnel Park take Route 28 out of Walhalla for five miles.

Poinsett Bridge, Campbell's Covered Bridge and Paris Mountain State Park

Out and About

A drive in the country, or Upcountry, around Greenville offers a number of picturesque stops. **Poinsett Bridge** is the oldest bridge in the state and while it was originally credited as being designed by Joel T. Poinsett, that is being re-evaluated. Poinsett was president of the South Carolina Board of Public Works in 1820 when the bridge was constructed under the direction of Abraham Blanding. Recent searches through the state Department of History and Archives indicate that the bridge may have been designed by Robert Mills. This theory is based on a drawing found in the archives at Tulane University. Certainly, the bridge's impressive stone work and pointed arches are extremely unique design features. The bridge was part of the first state road to connect Greenville and Asheville, North Carolina.

Southwest of Poinsett Bridge, you can discover the state's only surviving covered bridge. **Campbell's Covered Bridge** was built in 1909. This bridge near Gowensville is a popular spot with photographers.

Paris Mountain State Park is quite close to Greenville. Indeed its 1,275 acres were for a time owned by the city, before the state acquired the land in 1935. The park was developed by the Civilian Conservation Corps; they added support buildings and laid out the Lake Placid Nature Trail. There are eight marked points of interest along this trail: a pond teeming with aquatic insects and small fish, a metamorphic rock outcropping, the rhododendron and mountain laurel that bloom along the trail, a tree identification cove with 11 species, the Lake Placid Dam and several marked tree specimens.

There are other longer hiking trails within the park: the 4-mile Sulphur Springs Loop Trail, 2.3-mile Brissy Ridge Trail and 1.6-mile Fire Tower Bike Trail. Other park activities include camping, picnicking, swimming and fishing. There is a playground area near the picnic facilities and there are athletic fields.

An athletic field that should be mentioned is the seven-acre **Shoeless Joe Jackson Memorial Park** in Greenville. As a young boy Jackson began playing organized baseball on a textile mill team on West Avenue in the Brandon Mill community. The park has a playing field, with two dugouts, that looks as it did when Shoeless Joe played on it in the early 1900s. There are temporary bleachers now, but plans call for adding bleachers like the original ballpark with a pavilion roof. There is also hope of adding a small museum with tributes to Jackson and other major league players who got their start in the textile leagues.

Directions: For Poinsett Bridge from I-85, take I-385 around Greenville and pick up Route 25 north. Turn onto Old U.S. Highway 25 (the intersection is two miles northwest of Route 11). Travel 3.2 miles on Old Route 25 and turn right onto Callahan Mountain Road; continue for 2.2 miles and the bridge is on the left. The Poinsett Bridge is outside Tigerville. For Campbell's Covered Bridge, take Route 25 north and turn left on Route 414.

Continue through Tigerville and turn right on Pleasant Hill Road. Make another right on Campbell's Bridge Road and continue ¼ mile to the bridge. From I-385 take Route 253 north and the park entrance will be on your left. For Shoeless Joe Jackson Park, traveling north on I-85, take Route 25 north (Bypass/White Horse Road) and make a right on Old Easley Bridge Road, Route 124. The park is approximately 1.5 miles on the right.

Price House and the Regional Museum of Spartanburg County

Historical Pair

The house that Thomas Price built in 1795 became a "house of entertainment," but in colonial times that had no inappropriate connotations. His 2,000-acre plantation was on the stagecoach road halfway between the towns of Spartanburg and Cross Anchor. Price had a license to sell food and liquor and offer lodging.

Price, with his 28 slaves, farmed his large holding. He also operated a country store and served as the region's postmaster from 1811 to 1817. He was a wealthy man by the time he died in 1820. His wife Ann died a year later and, since there were no children, all their goods were sold. A 42-page pre-sale inventory, indicated that the Prices lived in considerable luxury for their time and location. An effort was made to match items on the inventory in furnishing the **Price House**.

Not only did the Prices have more luxury items than most of their contemporaries in the area, the style of their home was more typical of Maryland's Eastern Seaboard than South Carolina's Upcountry. Most of their neighbors were building with chink and logs, but the Prices built with bricks that were made in a kiln just across the road from the house. The bricks were laid in a Flemish Bond pattern, which is a length of brick alternating with a header, or the small side of the brick. The three-story house has a steep gambrel roof and inside end chimneys.

At a time when most Upcountry residents were still using pewter plates, the Prices had pieces similar to the blue feather edge Canton China you'll see in the dining room. The inventory also indicated they had wine rinsers like the ones on the table. A cherry sugar chest matches the inventory. Since sugar sold for ten dollars a pound, it was kept in a locked cabinet. Ann Price kept the key and used the sugar tongs to cut lumps from the cone. Even the paper wrapping around the cone was used, boiled to extract the indigo dye. The inlaid Chippendale-style sideboard is one of only five known pieces made by an unknown carpenter in an area of the Piedmont now called Wellford. Sitting atop this

366

piece is a hydrometer that measured the alcohol content or "proof" of spirits. The alcohol content was measured to calculate taxes and establish prices. A glass with low content would cost 50 cents, while a high alcohol content would cost $1.50. Each glass was individually measured before it was served.

The pine room, which is somewhat misleading since all the walls in all the rooms are made of pine, was used by the Prices as their sitting area, or living room. Here you'll see a 28-inch deep closet, another unusual feature at this time since closets were taxed as rooms. The Prices had a large library and a number of books they once owned again fill the shelves. There is also a copy of Thomas Price's store ledger. Representing Price's responsibilities as postmaster is a folded letter. As was typical for the day, the fold was sealed with hot wax and created a space for the name of the person who was to receive the letter since there were no envelopes. Postage was paid by the person who received the letter.

Upstairs is the master bedroom with a Charleston tester bed. There are closets on either side of the fireplace. A pocket watch was listed on the inventory and one hangs next to the mantle. At the time it was thought that watches kept better time if they were hung up. Although the Prices did not have children, they had many overnight guests. There is a child's bedroom with a bed close to the floor so a young sleeper would not be hurt falling out of bed. An 1825 sampler hangs on the hall wall. The guest bedroom has a trundle bed and a candle with a reflector to enhance the flickering light.

On the third floor is a ladies' bedroom for stagecoach passengers. The ticking on the hand made rope bed was filled with down in the winter and straw in the summer. It was common to sleep two or three persons in a bed. Another bedroom was for male travelers. A wooden device was used to tighten the ropes on the bed so that they could "sleep tight," otherwise the bed sagged and everyone rolled into the middle.

A back wing was added to the house in 1820. The front portion is interpreted as a travelers' dining room while the back is a plantation kitchen. In the dining room the cherry table is set with old pewter and redware. Dustless shelves keep dishes tilted so they will not pick up dust. There is a reproduction of an 1820s map of Spartanburg County that shows Price's post office. The out kitchen still has the original trammel (or pot hanger) in the chimney. Numerous cooking implements can be seen including a berry basket made in the style of the indigenous Native Americans. A nearby log cabin, moved to the Price House grounds, has a spinning wheel and weaving loom.

The Price House is open at a nominal charge on Saturdays from April through October, 11:00 A.M. to 5:00 P.M., and Sundays year round from 2:00 to 5:00 P.M.

Just a few blocks away is the **Regional Museum of**

Spartanburg County, a small museum with a collection of items relating to Spartanburg and its residents. Included is a small exhibit case filled with artifacts associated with the Battle of Cowpens. There is also a doll collection and old photographs of city properties and residents. Throughout the year, there are changing exhibits. The museum is open for a nominal fee Tuesday through Saturday from 10:00 A.M. to NOON and 3:00 to 5:00 P.M., and Sunday from 2:00 to 5:00 P.M.

Directions: From I-26, take Exit 28, Route 221 south for approximately a half mile. Make a left on Hobbysville Road and continue for 3.5 miles. Turn right on Price House Road for .8 mile to the entrance on the left. Return to Route 221 and continue to Spartanburg, where Route 221 becomes Church Street. For the Regional Museum of Spartanburg County turn right off Church Street onto Henry Street and make a right on Pine Street. Turn left on Otis Boulevard and the museum is at 501 Otis Boulevard.

Reedy River Falls Historic Park and West End

The Cradle of Greenville

At the conclusion of the French and Indian War, the Greenville area was part of land the British granted to the Native Americans. In 1777, a treaty was signed moving the Native population farther west. The original settlement of Greenville began one year earlier as a rustic trading post established by Richard Pearis along the banks of the Reedy River, an area now protected as the **Reedy River Falls Historic Park**.

A self-guided walking tour guide to the area and gardens along the river is available at most of the shops in the area. The walk begins alongside **Falls Cottage**, built in 1838 for George Dyer and his family. It served as their home and Dyer's shoemaking shop, though it's now Cottage Cuisine, a restaurant where you can enjoy lunch from Monday through Friday (864-370-9070). At the start of the brick path, you will see the first of the garden areas planned and developed by the Carolina Foothills Garden Club. You'll also see the first of the historic markers that provide details about this early settlement.

At the stone entranceway where Main Street and Camperdown Way intersect, you'll see two stones from grist mills that were built in the area. Shortly after he built his trading post, Pearis added a grist mill at the upper falls of the Reedy River. Other mills were built near his site as well as downstream. To the left of the falls overlook, you can see the remains of one of these mills—McBee's Mill. A historic marker near this location reveals how the addition of phosphates to the soil in the area made it possible to grow cotton, and signaled the growth of a major textile center in Greenville.

The walking trail continues to the lower falls of the Reedy River, where you will see the ruins of the Vardry Mill. Here the marker gives details about the development of mill villages. This is also the location of a picturesque picnic shelter. The last marker on your trail map is near a spring house built in 1934. This trail connects with a walking trail that leads to other Greenville parks: Cleveland Park, Rock Quarry Garden, Peace Center Gardens and the Greenville Zoo. There is no charge to stroll along the walking path at Historic Reedy River Falls Park.

The park is in the West End historic district, where old structures are being renovated to new uses. One of the most popular is the turn-of-the-century Cotton Alliance Warehouse that is now the **West End Market**, with a myriad of small shops, a fresh market and a restaurant. Many shops offer original arts and crafts, while others have an extensive array of antiques. B.J. Jones is one of the artists who has a studio here. His red-necked frogs are not only artistic collectibles, they are now the stars of a book, *Legend of the Redneck Frog*, written by Jones. The frogs are residents of his imaginary village of Sweetgum, which Jones says is located, "just south of your earliest childhood memory and six miles to one side of where your Grandpa said it was." Be sure and stop to see if Jones is in his studio. His work is delightful and he is a fascinating conversationalist. There is a deli, bakery and fresh food in the market. One of Greenville's favorite eateries, Occasionally Blues (864-242-6000) is located here. It is open Tuesday though Saturday for dinner and has nightly live local, regional and national entertainment. You can also enjoy southern cuisine while sitting on the deck overlooking Historic Reedy River Falls Park. West End Market is at the corner of S. Main Street and Augusta Street. West End Market is open Monday through Saturday. For store hours or tour information contact A Glimpse of Greenville at (864) 421-0042.

Just down the road at 315 Augusta Street, you'll find the **Little Stores of West End**, another collection of artists-in-residence creating jewelry, pottery, baskets, paintings and other unique items. Here, too, you'll find The Brick Street Cafe & Coffee House where you can relax and enjoy the music that is a backdrop to your shopping experience.

Directions: From I-85 take I-385 west toward downtown Greenville. Make a left on Main Street and continue through town until you cross the Reedy River. You will see the park on your left. Historic Reedy River Falls Park is in the West End at 600 S. Main Street and East Camperdown Way. You can pull into the parking area for Cottage Cuisine; there is ample parking to the right for the park. The same parking lot continues and connects to the West End Market.

South Carolina State Botanical Garden

Where Nature and Culture Meet

From a modest beginning in 1958, the public gardens at Clemson University have grown into the 270-acre **South Carolina State Botanical Garden**. Initially, a small corner of John C. Calhoun's 19th-century Fort Hill estate (see selection) was set aside to display a camellia collection. This was extended and, by 1973, the now 44 acres had become the Horticultural Gardens of Clemson University. Merging with the Forestry Arboretum and adding additional college land in 1987, a 208-acre Clemson University Botanical Gardens was established. In 1992, a referendum by the state legislature expanded its scope and it received its official title. The garden is an interdisciplinary center, an outdoor laboratory that promotes environmental and cultural conservation.

Camellias are still one of the flowering focal points and the collection is one of the finest in the south. The gardens are also noted for the native wildflowers and extensive daffodils along the wooded paths. A fern and bog garden has a wide array of native species along a creek bed in a lush valley. Annuals and perennials in a rainbow of colors adorn the Flower and Turf Display garden, while the Mediation Garden, with its pagoda overlooking a reflective pool, is the perfect spot to stop and rest. Throughout the garden there are special stations for the visually impaired and the Horticulture Therapy Garden, a small heavily planted area, has raised beds to accommodate wheelchairs.

The Pioneer Garden features the 1825 Ransom Hunt cabin, as well as other log cabins, a grist mill and a display of 19th-century farm implements. Also in the garden is the 1716 colonial **Hanover House**. Built by French Huguenots Paul and Mary Amy (Ravenel) de St. Julien in the Lowcountry, it was dismantled and reconstructed on the Clemson campus in 1941. It is restored and refurnished to reflect the lifestyle of South Carolina's rice, indigo and cotton planters. The adjacent grounds are planted with an Heirloom Vegetable Garden. This garden replicates a garden from colonial times when vegetables and herbs provided foodstuff, seasonings, medicine, cosmetics, dyes, as well as other needs.

Commissioned sculptors, with an eye on the natural surroundings, created works of art just for the site such as the rammed adobe and granite stone sculpture bridge at the headwaters of the duck pond. Another piece made of twisted vines creates a Moorish-style structure.

Visitors can learn how to turn their backyard into a nurturing environment at the Wildlife Habitat Garden and the Butterfly Garden; they'll also get gardening tips in the Vegetable Garden and the Compost Garden. Miles of trails lead past these specialty areas and into the surrounding woods where birdwatching is a popular activity.

The South Carolina Botanical Garden is open daily without charge from dawn to dusk. Hanover House hours are 10:00 A.M. to NOON and 1:00 to 5:00 P.M. on Saturday and 2:00 to 5:00 P.M. on Sunday. The house is closed on University holidays.

This Moorish-style creation is one of South Carolina Botanical Garden's nature-based artistic pieces. This 270-acre facility has numerous specialty gardens including a pioneer garden, a meditative garden and an historic vegetable garden.

Donations are suggested. For more information call the garden's office at (864) 656-3405.

While on the campus, you might want to stop by **Uniquely Clemson** in Newman Hall and treat yourself to ice cream or yogurt made at the dairy plant. It is also well known for its blue cheese, which Clemson began making in 1941. This Agricultural Products Sales Center is open Monday through Saturday from 9:00 A.M. to 9:00 P.M. and Sunday 1:00 to 9:00 P.M.

Directions: From I-85 take Route 76/28 for nine miles northwest to Clemson. The main entrance to the garden is on the eastern side of the Clemson University Campus off Perimeter Road; turn left off Route 76 and go .4 mile to the garden entrance.

Table Rock, Caesars Head and Jones Gap State Parks

Scenery and History

The Blue Ridge Mountains end northwest of Greenville and a series of state parks provide access to the mountain's scenic splendors. Striking rock formations, foaming waterfalls and a wide range of wildflowers, wildlife and state-record trees reward those who tackle the network of mountain trails.

Table Rock State Park, the oldest state park in the Blue Ridge, has trails to the 3,425-foot summit of Pinnacle Mountain (3.4 miles, roughly 2½ to 3 hours one way) and to the 3,157-foot summit of Table Rock (3.5 miles, roughly 2 to 3 hours one way). This trail system is designated a National Recreation Trail and links with the Foothills Trail, a more than 80-mile wilderness hiking trail from Jones Gap to Oconee State Park (see selection).

The Cherokees called the area around Table Rock State Park "Sah-ka-na-ga," the Great Blue Hills of God. Their legends claimed that the Great Spirit used the flat mountain top as a dining table, hence the name. Its striking appearance made it a visual landmark to Cherokee hunters, as it is for modern hikers.

Within the park's 3,083 acres there is a wide range of recreational opportunities. The 36-acre lake is used for swimming, fishing and boating. Canoes, pedal and fishing boats can be rented at the park. There are ten miles of trails within the park. The 100-site campground is augmented by 14 rustic cabins and a lodge with a restaurant built by the Civilian Conservation Corps. The many log and stone buildings constructed by the CCC led to the park's inclusion on the National Register of Historic Places. The park is open daily year round from 7:00 A.M. to 9:00 P.M. During Daylight Savings Time, it stays open until 10:00 P.M.

You have a view of Table Rock from the rocky promontories of nearby **Caesars Head State Park.** There are those who say the park received its name because one of the rocky outcroppings resembles the profile of Julius Caesar. Another local story is that a hunter named the mountain for his hunting dog who was killed chasing his prey down the rocky escarpment. If you want to decide for yourself whether the profile resembles the Roman emperor, take the short scenic trail from the bottom of Devil's Kitchen. This narrow rocky passageway is a geological phenomenon formed eons ago by intense pressure and heat.

In the late 1800s, a hotel stood near the steep precipice, but now the park has reverted to its natural state. In fact, the park and Jones Gap are part of the Mountain Bridge Wilderness Recreation Area, a 10,000-acre area with over 46 miles of hiking trails that connect the watersheds of Table Rock and Poinsett. Visitors get a spectacular view from the park's lookout tower, where they can peer down at the birds riding the currents in the valleys below. Raptors, such as hawks and falcons, are frequently sighted from mid-September into November during migratory flights. On a clear day the tower is also popular with photographers. The park is noted for its colorful wildflowers that bloom along the trail from spring through fall. Trailside camping is permitted with a permit, obtainable at the park office. The park is open daily 9:00 A.M. to 6:00 P.M. From Memorial Day through October it stays open until 9:00 P.M. There is a visitors center and gift shop where you can obtain trail maps and see exhibits on hawks that you are likely to observe.

One of the highest and most breathtaking waterfalls in the eastern United States, **Raven Cliff Falls** can be reached from a moderately strenuous 2.2 mile hiking trail that begins a few miles north of Caesars Head State Park headquarters on Route 276. It is quite a sight to see these falls plummet over 400 feet at what many consider South Carolina's most breathtaking waterfall. Also in the vicinity of Caesars Head is the not-to-be-missed **Eastatoee Falls**, locally known as Twin Falls, Reedy Cove Falls or Rock Falls (this is the waterfall pictured on the cover). Eastatoe is the Cherokee word for the brilliant green and yellow birds, now extinct, that became known as the Carolina parakeet. This falls with the multiple names tumbles 70 feet over a huge granite slab. The first of the two falls is the larger and the water spews in all directions as it crashes down to the granite base. If you are interested in waterfalls, be sure to get a copy of the brochure *Finding the Falls, A Guide to Twenty-Five of the Upstate's Outstanding Waterfalls*. The booklet with a map, description and directions to the falls is printed by *South Carolina Wildlife Magazine*. It is available for a nominal fee by calling (803) 737-3944 or by writing to the South Carolina Department of Natural Resources, P.O. Box 167, Columbia, SC 29202.

The last of this natural wilderness trilogy is the 3,346-acre **Jones Gap State Park**. The state's first scenic river, the Middle Saluda River, flows through the park and you can access the Foothills Hiking Trail from the park's trails. At the park's Environmental Education Center you will discover information on some of the more than 400 species of plants and trees found in the park, including state champions. Trout are exhibited in the restored remains of the old Cleveland Fish Hatchery.

Day-use hikers need to register at the park office where trail-side campers must obtain a permit. You also need a fishing permit to try your skill at trout fishing along the Middle Saluda River and its tributary, Cold Spring Branch. Artificial flies and lures are permitted.

This park obtained its name from a 5.5-mile road that Solomon Jones was alleged to have built across Caesars Head to Cedar Mountain, North Carolina. The Jones Gap Road, originally a toll road, was laid out visually without the use of surveying equipment. Begun in 1840, it took eight years to finish. It remained operational until 1910 and now serves as a hiking trail.

Directions: From I-85 take Exit 21, Route 178 north to Pickens. Table Rock State Park is 12 miles north of Pickens on Route 11 (turn right when you reach the intersection of Route 178 and 11). Route 11 is part of the **Cherokee Foothills Scenic Highway**. For Caesars Head State Park continue north on Route 11, then turn left on Route 276 for the park which is near the border with North Carolina. For Eastatoe Falls at the intersection of Route 11 and Route 178 take Route 178 north (toward Rosman) for 3.2 miles. Make a left at Bob's Place onto Cleo Champman Road and continue for 1.9 miles to Eastatoe Community Road. Turn right and go .9 mile to a dirt road you will see on the right. Follow road past houses to steel gate. Park and take the easy 5-to-10-minute walk to the falls. Law-abiding waterfallers are welcome despite the sign painted on the gate forbidding trespassers. Jones Gap State Park is north of Caesars Head State Park on Route 276.

Walnut Grove Plantation

History in a Nutshell

Walnut Grove Plantation gives a vivid and detailed look at life on a pre-Revolutionary plantation on the western frontier of South Carolina. The land, originally about 500 acres, although ultimately 3,000, was granted to Charles Moore by King George III in 1752. Moore began building a house atop a gentle slope a mile east of the Tyger River in 1763. The simple clapboard-over-log late-Georgian house, with a wide front porch and double-shouldered chimneys at each side, is typical of houses from the valleys of Virginia into the Piedmont Carolinas and on into the mountains of Georgia.

It is thought that because Charles Moore had been on the frontier since 1752, the house he built reflected earlier styles. But there are several unique features in this wilderness farmhouse. Unlike most contemporary houses the main front door did not open into a hall but into the great room, or parlor. There is a second large downstairs room that served as the master bedroom. The staircase was virtually hidden between the two rooms. Each room has a door opening onto the stair landing. Another departure for its time was the fulsome use of wood, a practice that was out of fashion in colonial interiors except for wainscoting and the fireplace wall. But at Walnut Grove, all the walls are covered in hand-planed boards.

When you tour you will see the original woodwork, except for the dining room mantel and the window moldings. Only one window molding survived, so it served as a model for exact replacements throughout the house. The mantel in the great room is Moore's adaptation of a late Queen Anne style, with the wood painted to simulate mahogany, a style called "deceit" and used on all the wainscoting in this room. Hanging above the mantel is Moore's double-barrel flint-lock musket which he had made for him in France. Most of the large pieces of furniture are unpretentious regionally-made items of simple design but excellent craftsmanship. The keeping room also contains a bookcase filled with approximately 150 volumes. Moore was at one time a schoolmaster and his library had one of the largest collections in this part of the colony. The oldest item in the house is the 1675 Bible box with the Moore family Bible.

The master bedroom has some intriguing architectural features; foremost is the chimney designed with panels above and below the mantel. There is a small closet in this chamber. It is the only one in the house because at this time, closets were taxed as separate rooms. The closet reveals the indigo color the room was once painted. There is a trundle bed, although when the children were older than six, they slept upstairs in the large open room. There is also a hooded-cradle for infants, as well as animal skin baby shoes. Mr. Moore's walking cane is in the bedroom; he used this to keep away wild animals. It is said that he called virtually all wild animals 'tygers.' There is a chest of drawers for the bed linen but there did not need to be much storage space for clothes. In those days, no one changed clothes frequently. There was usually a church outfit, although people typically attended only about once a month, since churches were frequently a distance away. There were seasonal clothes, an outfit for winter and a lighter weight outfit for summer. The upstairs doorway has an interesting lock, called an elbow lock, which could be opened by hitting it with an elbow if hands were not free.

At the rear of the first floor, there are the more simply designed dining room and changing room; both added about two years after the house was completed by enclosing the back porch. The dining room still has a fallen-leaf table and pewter that the Moores would have used for special occasions.

The stairs lead up to a large open dormitory-style room with a small fireplace. This room has the only original floor in the house. Charles and Mary Moore had ten children, and all lived to adulthood. This was highly unusual on the frontier where danger existed from disease and from the ever-present Native Americans. Up until 1776, it was necessary to carry arms in the fields around Walnut Grove to protect against Cherokees, whose hunting grounds this once was and who rejected the concept of individual ownership of land. Crops were sometimes lost because hostile braves made harvesting impossible.

The Moore's eldest daughter, Margaret Katherine, called Kate, was born in America in 1752. In 1767, she married Andrew Barry, who subsequently became a captain in the South Carolina militia. There are many legends about Kate; reputedly she was a Patriot scout and spy. An excellent horsewoman, she is credited with helping to assemble the local Patriots when the British were in the area and of warning her family of danger. Kate is supposed to have helped marshall the troops to fight with General Daniel Morgan at the Battle of Cowpens. A picture of Kate now hangs on the wall as you enter the bedroom.

Walnut Grove was the scene of a bloody incident when a former Patriot turned Tory, "Bloody Bill" Cunningham was marching with his men through the region and stopped at the Moore house. Captain Steadman, who was engaged to Violet Moore (another daughter), was lying sick in bed. Cunningham had him killed where he lay, and then shot two other soldiers who tried to escape by running from the Tories. All three are buried at Walnut Grove; their graves were the beginning of the family cemetery. There are still blood stains on the upstairs floor.

When Charles Moore died in 1805, he left Walnut Grove to his youngest son, Charles Moore, Jr. He had already given roughly 750 acres to his eldest son, General Thomas Moore, who served in the U.S. House of Representatives from 1801 to 1817, and to another son Dr. Andrew Barry Moore. Walnut Grove has continued as a working farm from its earliest days, although the crops and methods of farming changed over the years. The house and eight acres remained in the Moore family until 1961, when they were given to the Spartanburg County Historical Association by Charles Moore's great-great grandson, Thomas Moore Craig and his wife Lena Heath Jones Craig.

In addition to a tour of the house, there is a self-guided grounds tour that includes a number of outbuildings. Much of the vegetation that surrounds Walnut Grove dates to its earliest days. Huge oaks, walnuts and cedars have been growing for more than 200 years. There are also plantings done by the Moores—crepe myrtles and the boxwood surrounding the herb garden. The garden has been restored with the help of the Fannie Louise Holcombe Garden Club. The garden was not organized by color or size but instead grew culinary and medicinal plants. The plants you see today represent those typical of an 18th-century garden: lavender, lemon balm, tansy, basil, thyme, rosemary, sage, lovage, mint chives and many others. At the center of the garden is a dipping well.

To the right of the garden is Rocky Springs Academy, one of the first schools in the area. Charles Moore was the first in a long line of teachers. This plantation school would break for farm activities like barnraisings, harvesting, husking bees and others where even the children could help. Inside you see pine desks that seat two students and a reciting bench in front of the fireplace. The teacher's desk has an alphabet paddle as well as books and other educational aids. The room also contains a textile exhibit with a spinning wheel, weasel, carders and loom.

Also adjacent to the herb garden is the out kitchen, which actually housed Charles and Mary Moore and eight of their children while they built the big house. The one-room kitchen has a sleeping loft. The back has a wide porch, the site of many tasks such as pea shelling, berry hulling and butter churning. The porch has a variety of kitchen aids: a rabbit gum, bee houses, fish trap, flour bin and cupboard.

To the west of the main house are other buildings that served the plantation community. A well house has a dry cellar where crocks and jugs of dairy products were kept. A forge has an array of blacksmith tools. The forges kept the wagons rolling but also supplied kettles, skewers, toasters and other kitchen items. Salted and smoked meats were kept in the meat house, while the wheat house once stored grain. There is an 18th-century log barn in which you will see a Conestoga-style wagon built in Old Salem, North Carolina at the Moravian's Nissen Wagon Works. The grounds contain a reconstruction of Dr. Andrew Barry Moore's (son of Charles and Mary Moore) medical office. His actual office stood a mile away. He practiced in the county for 48 years. His medical records are displayed along with period implements. A short audio tape provides information from Moore's three journals.

There is a half-mile nature trail that begins at the Moore family cemetery and leads through the woods back to the main house. In the spring and fall when the wildflowers bloom within the forest, this is a walk of discovery. You may even spot a wild turkey or deer.

Walnut Grove is open April through October on Tuesday through Saturday from 11:00 A.M. to 5:00 P.M.; on Sunday it opens at 2:00 P.M. The last tour starts at 4:00 P.M. Admission is charged. There is a gift shop in the visitors center.

Directions: From I-26 take Exit 28, Route 221 north toward Spartanburg. Turn right on Stillhouse Road, Route 42/196 and continue for one mile; then make a right on Otis Shoals Road. Continue for another mile and turn right at Walnut Grove Plantation driveway.

Woodburn Plantation House and Pendleton District Agricultural Museum

Architecture, Agriculture and History

Family is highly significant in the south. An individual's family background is always introduced early in any conversation. Family links individuals to past generations and to the communities where they were born and raised. Charles Cotesworth Pinckney, owner of **Woodburn Plantation House**, was part of a family that contributed to the state and the nation. Charles's father, Thomas, was a general in the American Revolution and a governor of the state. Thomas Pinckney was U.S. Minister to England from 1792 to 1794. The uncle for whom Charles was named was also a Revolutionary general and a member of the U.S. Constitutional Convention of 1787. His brother, Thomas, who moved to the Pendleton area before Charles, was the first president of the Pendleton Farmers Society.

Charles, called Cotesworth, graduated from Harvard Law School in 1808, but preferred the life of a planter to the law. He championed the cause of religious education for African Americans. In 1833, Charles Cotesworth was elected lieutenant governor of South Carolina. It was just three years earlier that he had purchased the Woodburn estate and built a summer home. (Eventually, both Cotesworth and Thomas moved to Pendleton permanently.) Woodburn sat beside the country estate of Cotesworth's brother-in-law Ralph Elliot. In 1838, Phoebe and Cotesworth's daughter, Carolina, married Archibald Seabrook, son of Governor Whitemarsh B. Seabrook. Their grandson, Archibald Rutledge, was poet laureate of South Carolina from 1934 until his death on September 16, 1973.

Woodburn was designed by Thomas Pinckney, who also designed Altamont, his own home and St. Paul's Episcopal Church (where Charles Cotesworth is buried). Woodburn is a four-story house built on a knoll. To take advantage of

Upcountry breezes, the rooms had high ceilings and wide columned piazzas, on the first and second floors both in the front and back. Woodburn had a race track and the leading citizens of Pendleton would race their horses here on holidays. The estate was soon the social center of the community, many of whom were Charlestonians seeking summer relief from the coastal mosquitoes, malaria and heat.

Additions were made to Woodburn in 1852 when Dr. John Bailey Adger bought the property. It remained in his family for over 50 years. Numerous relatives refugeed (sought sanctuary) at Woodburn during the Civil War. A nephew, Major Augustine T. Smythe, who obtained the property in 1881, turned Woodburn into a stock farm with high bred horses and cattle. During the Depression, the U.S. Resettlement Administration claimed 300 farms in the area including Woodburn. In the early 1950s, a number of the historic farm properties, including Woodburn, were given to Clemson College who, in 1966 deeded the estate and 6.26 acres to the Foundation for Historic Restoration in Pendleton Area (now called the Pendleton Historic Foundation). The house is now on the National Register of Historic Places.

The house is furnished with family pieces and work created in the Pendleton area. There are portraits of many of Woodburn's owners dating back to Charles Cotesworth Pinckney and his father. Various personal items are displayed in glass cases. You'll see crochet work, fans, books, china and silver. Be sure to notice the dining room chairs, each has a distinct and different needlework design. The quilts, bedspreads and canopies are lovely pieces, a few more than 100 years old. Mannequins are outfitted in antique clothes and gowns; one ball dress from Paris is trimmed with genuine turquoise ornaments. A few items of interest were discovered in a rat's nest. These articles date from 1826 to 1834 and include a partially-chewed 1828 pamphlet on agriculture as well as a pair of shoes, bottle, portions of letters and other remnants.

Woodburn is open on Sunday from 2:00 to 6:00 P.M. from April through October and at other times by calling (803) 646-3655 for an appointment. There is a nominal admission.

On the right as you head up the driveway toward the house you will see the **Pendleton District Agricultural Museum** with its collection of pre-1925 farm tools and equipment. This collection was acquired by the Pendleton District Commission in cooperation with the Pendleton Farmers Society, one of the five oldest societies in the country. One of the significant pieces is a McCormick reaper; there is also a Gregg reaper, a Chattanooga reversible plow, an early cotton gin and other farm tools. Another section has kitchen devices and other home articles. There are also vehicles such as the fringed surrey. In the Stribling Room, there are antique tools from Walnut Hill Plantation. The museum is open by appointment Monday through

Friday from 9:00 A.M. to 4:30 P.M. by calling (864) 646-3782.

Directions: From I-85 take Exit 19, Route 76 west toward Pendleton. The entrance to Woodburn is right off Route 76, just a brief turn onto Route 279 then a right turn into the well-marked driveway.

World of Energy at Oconee Nuclear Station

Power to the People

South Carolina is one of seven states that generates more than half of its electricity from nuclear power. Duke Power's first nuclear power generating station was at Oconee. Construction began in 1967, and the first of **Oconee Nuclear Station**'s three units began operating in 1973.

At the Oconee Nuclear Station visitors can explore the **World of Energy**, which presents the story of how man harvests energy. The energy of the sun is stored in plants. As plants decompose over thousands of years they form coal, a primary source of energy. Even when explaining about the earliest forms of energy, the latest technology is used. This exciting center is state-of-the-art with moving lights, energy-producing models ranging from a gristmill's waterwheel to a simulation of the control room of a nuclear power plant. The self-guided walking tour through the World of Energy lets you set your own pace as you move through the exhibits. At one point you will enter a fission chamber to see how energy is made from an atom. There are hands-on exhibits and you can feel a seam of coal.

Young visitors gravitate toward the computer games that test energy IQ. The center also emphasizes Duke Power' s efforts to protect the natural beauty of the region. One exhibit details the elements of a backyard wildlife habitat, while another is a trout habitat.

The World of Energy is open at no charge Monday through Saturday 9:00 A.M. to 5:00 P.M.; on Sunday it opens at NOON. It is closed on major holidays. You can also call ahead and arrange to take an Oconee Nuclear Station tour; call (864) 885-4600 or (800) 777-1004. Tours are by reservation only, and participants must be 18 or older. There are picnic tables overlooking Lake Keowee and the scenic Keowee Valley. After an al fresco lunch, visitors can explore the half-mile nature trail.

Directions: From I-85 take Exit 19, Route 76 north to Clemson. Turn left on Route 123 and then make a right on Route 130, Rochester Highway. The World of Energy is at 7812 Rochester Highway in Seneca.

Discover Upcountry Carolina Regional Tourism Contacts (Area Code 864)

DISCOVER UPCOUNTRY CAROLINA ASSOCIATION
P.O. Box 3116
Greenville, SC 29602
233-2690, (800) 849-4766

PENDLETON DISTRICT HISTORICAL, RECREATIONAL AND TOURISM COMMISSION
125 East Queen Street, P.O. Box 565
Pendleton, SC 29670
646-3782, (800) 862-1795

ANDERSON AREA CHAMBER OF COMMERCE
P.O. Box 1568
Anderson, SC 29622
226-3454

CHEROKEE COUNTY CHAMBER OF COMMERCE
P.O. Box 1119
Gaffney, SC 29342
489-5721

CLEMSON CHAMBER OF COMMERCE
P.O. Box 1622
Clemson, SC 29633-1622
654-1200

GREATER EASLEY CHAMBER OF COMMERCE
P.O. Box 241
Easley, SC 29641
859-2693

FOUNTAIN INN CHAMBER OF COMMERCE
P.O. Box 568
Fountain Inn, SC 29644
862-2586

GREATER GREENVILLE CHAMBER OF COMMERCE
P.O. Box 10048
Greenville, SC 29603
242-1050, (800) 717-0023

GREATER GREENVILLE CONVENTION & VISITORS BUREAU
P.O. Box 10527
Greenville, SC 29603
233-0461

GREATER GREER CHAMBER OF COMMERCE
P.O. Box 507
Greer, SC 29652
877-3131

INMAN CHAMBER OF COMMERCE
P.O. Box 145
Inman, SC 29349
472-3654

LANDRUM CHAMBER OF COMMERCE
P.O. Box 62
Landrum, SC 29356
457-5315

GREATER LIBERTY CHAMBER OF COMMERCE
P.O. Box 123
Liberty, SC 29657
843-3021

MAULDIN AREA CHAMBER OF COMMERCE
P.O. Box 645
Mauldin, SC 29662
297-1323

GREATER PICKENS CHAMBER OF COMMERCE
P.O. Box 153
Pickens, SC 29671
878-3258

GREATER SENECA CHAMBER OF COMMERCE
P.O. Box 855
Seneca, SC 29679
882-2097

SIMPSONVILLE CHAMBER OF COMMERCE
P.O. Box 605
Simpsonville, SC 29681
963-3781

GREATER SPARTANBURG AREA CHAMBER OF COMMERCE
P.O. Box 1636
Spartanburg, SC 29304
594-5000

SPARTANBURG CONVENTION & VISITORS BUREAU
P.O. Box 1636
Spartanburg, SC 29304
594-5050, (800) 374-8326

GREATER WALHALLA CHAMBER OF COMMERCE
220 E. Main Street
Walhalla, SC 29691
638-2727

WESTMINSTER CHAMBER OF COMMERCE
P.O. Box 155
Westminster, SC 29693
647-5316

GREATER WOODRUFF CHAMBER OF COMMERCE
P.O. Box 636
Woodruff, SC 29388
476-8807

Discover Upcountry Carolina Calendar of Events (Area Code 864)

Mid-January

Battle of Cowpens Re-enactment. Living history encampments and tactical demonstrations bring back the Revolutionary Days. Chesnee, 461-2828.

Late March

Easter Eggstravaganza. Children enjoy hunting for eggs, lunch with Easter Bunny, pony rides and games. Greenville, 288-6470.

Early April

Historic Pendleton Spring Jubilee. Walking tours of historic district, arts & crafts, entertainment and bike rides enliven this event. Pendleton, 646-3782.

Mid-April

Birthday Celebration at Price House. Colonial demonstrations and crafts bring back the Price era. Spartanburg, 596-3501.

Early May

Spring Fling. Celebrate the arrival of spring with arts & crafts, entertainment and games. Spartanburg, 594-5075.

Late May

Freedom Weekend Aloft. Hot-air balloons, entertainment, amusement rides, crafts and a fireworks finale make this a popular event. Greenville, 232-3700.

Mid-September

Collector's Market on the Green. Antique market and pottery fair on Pendleton's historic village green. Pendleton, 646-3782.

Early October

Festifall. Colonial history comes alive at Walnut Grove Plantation with an encampment, crafts and a re-enactment. Roebuck, 596-3501.

Mid-October

Oktoberfest. German and American food, arts & crafts, rides, hot air balloon rides, dancing, sky diving and games highlight this annual event. Walhalla, 638-2727.

Back to Nature Festival. Walks, petting zoo, pony rides, music and crafts all celebrate wildlife and the outdoors. Greenville, 288-6470.

Early December

Holiday Fair. Over 600 artists and craftsmen demonstrate and sell their wares. Greenville, 233-2562.

Christmas Crafts Event. Hunter's Store features local artists and craftsmen at this annual event. Pendleton, 646-3782.

Index

ACKNOWLEDGMENTS

First I would like to thank my good friend and Society of American Travel Writers associate, Cheri Had, who made it possible for me to travel through South Carolina so productively and so enjoyably. Cheri knows the state—its charms, its secrets and its people.

I would also like to thank Jayne Scarborough and her delightful projects coordinator Katherine Morgan (now with the York County CVB) who made my trip through the Olde English District so informative and entertaining. Jim Westcott introduced me to the Lowcountry & Resort Islands and impressed me with his love of the region. I was enthralled by Kitty Green and her interpretation of the Gullah tradition. June Murff embued me with her fondness for Aiken and Susan Le Grand introduced me to the rest of Thoroughbred Country.

My third trip was an autumn visit to Old 96 District, where Barbara Ware and Vicki Loughner helped me explore the countryside. Anne Cox, Karen Rainer and Tim Todd introduced me to the scenic wonders, historical attractions and other points of interest in Discover Upcountry Carolina. Amy Blyth, another longtime SATW friend, and Victoria Bryant showed me the splendors of Historic Charleston. Mary Shriner revealed the secrets of the Santee Cooper Country.

My final journey through the state began with Nikki Ewing and Stephen Greene in the Grand Strand/Myrtle Beach Area. Fran Burr helped me explore Pee Dee Country. I spent the last day of my research trips with the friendly folks in Bishopville and enjoyed the company of the personable Allene McCoy.

About the Author

Jane Ockershausen, born in Richmond, bred in Maryland and now living in Pittsburgh, has been writing about the Eastern seaboard states for more than two decades. She recently spent more than a year traveling throughout South Carolina in order to write this, the 10th in her best-selling series of One-Day Trip Books for the Mid-Atlantic region.

Always centered on the ever-popular weekend travel market, she has been a correspondent for *The National Geographic Traveler*, and her byline has appeared in *The Washington Post*, *The Chicago Tribute*, *Mid-Atlantic Weekends Magazine* and elsewhere. She has addressed numerous statewide conferences on travel and journalism and lectured at the Smithsonian Institution in Washington.

She is a member of the Board of Directors of the Society of American Travel Writers, and the Society's president in 1999.